Trying to Get It Back
Indigenous Women, Education and Culture

Trying to Get It Back
Indigenous Women, Education and Culture

Edited by Gillian Weiss
with
Pearl McKenzie, Pauline Coulthard,
Charlene Tree, Bernie Sound,
Valerie Bourne and Brandi McLeod

Wilfrid Laurier University Press

[WLU]

We acknowledge the financial support of the Government of Canada through the Book Publishing Industry Development Program for our publishing activities. We acknowledge the financial support provided by the multiculturalism program of the Department of Canadian Heritage.

Canadian Cataloguing in Publication Data

Main entry under title:

Trying to get it back : indigenous women, education and culture

Includes bibliographical references and index.
ISBN 0-88920-378-4 (pbk.)

1. Women, Wailpi — Social conditions. 2. Women, Wailpi — Biography. 3. Sechelt women — Social conditions. 4. Sechelt women — Biography. I. McKenzie, Pearl, 1922-1997.
II. Weiss, Gillian M., 1948- .

DU125.W27T79 2000   305.48′89915   C99-931475-0

© 2000 Wilfrid Laurier University Press
      Waterloo, Ontario   N2L 3C5

Cover design by Leslie Macredie. Top front cover photograph: Australian outback with ancient mountains in the distance. Bottom front cover photograph: Skookumchuck Narrows, British Columbia, Canada.
All photographs courtesy of Gillian Weiss.

∞

Printed in Canada

This book is dedicated to the memory of Pearl McKenzie (1922-1997), who did so much to preserve Adnyamathanha culture and heritage, and to Brandi's daughters, Bianca and Bree, and Charlene's sons, Jadon, Kaleb and Marcus, who are the future.

CONTENTS

LIST OF ILLUSTRATIONS

PREFACE

This study developed from a larger project, "A Comparative Study of the Effects of Colonisation on the Art of Selected Groups of Australian and Canadian Aboriginal Peoples," undertaken by my husband, Tony Rogers, of the University of South Australia and Rita Irwin of the University of British Columbia. The Adnyamathanha and Sechelt Peoples were chosen as the major focus of the research for a number of reasons, including their traditional views on and practices of "art," the geographic position of their traditional lands at a distance from large urban sites, the relative lack of political and personal dissension within their ranks with regards to maintenance and revival of traditional practices and the interest of individuals in both groups in being part of an oral history project.

My involvement began with some of the initial interviewing of Adnyamathanha men and women in 1992, which included a session in which Pearl McKenzie talked with Tony Rogers. I was interested in some comments Pearl made about her early life in this interview, and as the topics of interviews were very open at this stage I decided to follow them up in a further taped discussion with Pearl later that same day. Shortly afterwards I met Pauline Coulthard, Pearl's daughter, who was acting as a coordinator for the project by identifying individuals who wished to be involved and arranging introductions to and meetings with members of the research team. We got to chatting about her own childhood and comparing it with that of Pauline's mother and daughters, and when I made a comment about the vast changes that had occurred in a number of aspects of the family members' lives since Pearl's childhood, this project was born.

Both Pearl and Pauline already had a history of working in various ways to preserve and revitalise their Adnyamathanha heritage, though not in such a personal way as I was suggesting, and were quietly enthusiastic. Pauline felt that her oldest daughter, Charlene Tree, would be happy to take part also, put the suggestion to her and arranged for me to meet her the next day. Charlene was a little hesitant at first, largely, I think, from shyness with a stranger and with doubts that she would have anything of importance to contribute, but after we had discussed the idea for a while she became enthusiastic and shortly after I began to record the narratives of all three.

The situation with Bernie, Valerie and Brandi was somewhat different. By the time my family and I visited Sechelt the Adnyamathanha interviews were complete, and I went with the express intention of seeking a similar group of Sechelt women whose lives might offer comparisons and/or contrasts. Valerie Bourne was employed in the Sechelt Band Office at the time, and was designated to liaise with Tony, Rita and myself. I told her what I had been doing with Pearl, Pauline and Charlene and asked if she could think of any Sechelt family with three generations of women who might be interested in talking to me. No one sprang to mind, she told me, but said she would think about it. The next day, she rather hesitatingly said that she had indeed thought about it and would like to be a part of it herself if that was possible. Her mother had been dead for some time, she explained, but her Aunt Bernie Sound, who had played a significant role in her life, particularly in her teenage years, was living in Sechelt, as was Valerie's daughter, Brandi McLeod. She had spoken with both, she added, and both were willing to take part. So the second family was identified.

The selection of the two families, then, was far from random. Indeed, once the Adnyamathanha and Sechelt Peoples had been identified as nations whose heritages and experiences were ideal for the initial project, and once permission to undertake the research had been gained from a group of key Adnyamathanha Elders and the Sechelt Band Council, the two families virtually self-selected for this project. Such willingness is essential. In this case it was not simply a matter of being interested in a project that might serve to record aspects of traditional skills and knowledge and/or interpret the historic experiences of their peoples, but required them to place aspects of their own personal experience into the public domain. This was a new experience for all the women but, having committed themselves, they undertook it with determination.

These women's stories, I believe, deserve to be brought to an audience beyond their own communities. The actions of indigenous peoples in regard to cultural reclamation, traditional practices and rights to traditional lands are all too frequently presented only in a way that represents them as inherently antagonistic to mainstream cultures in both Australia and Canada. These women, in talking about their lives, demonstrate that this need not be the case. Theirs is a way of compromise, of trial and error, of determined persistence and of hope. The fact that both families can see patterns in behaviour, in attitudes and in the changes that have occurred over the three generations strengthens their belief that they will achieve their goals of reclaiming their culture.

It is not uncommon in ethnographic studies to claim that friendships have developed over the course of a study. Such claims frequently sound rather trite so I hesitate to make them. But in a project such as this, which extended over a period of several years and in which a group of women revealed to me and to the world some quite personal, even intimate, aspects of their lives, certain relationships must develop. It might be argued that the unequal power relations between myself, as an academic, and these women, as representative of their people, make anything other than a good working relationship impossible. I don't believe this is necessarily true in any case, and it is certainly not true in this instance. This is partly because from the start I did not approach the women in the artificial, somewhat rarefied, but frequently too-common persona of "researcher," a person who comes in from outside with no feelings, no attachments, no life, to simply gather facts.

Because my husband, Tony, was also working with the Sechelt and Adnyamathanha Peoples, we generally made our visits to them as a family, accompanied by our two children, Molly and Ned. I have no doubt that the presence of the whole family made a mighty difference both in our acceptance within the two communities and in the nature and process of the relationships that I formed with the six women. Not only did we instantly have a broad topic for discussion but by bringing something of my world to them, putting a part of my personal life on display, the gap between us was lessened. I was a stranger, non-Aboriginal, a middle-class academic, but I was also a woman, a wife, a mother, and that gave us a commonality, a basis for comparisons, somewhere from which we could begin to know each other. And gradually we did.

My family and I have been invited into the homes and the lives of these two families, slowly at first, but now, I think, unreservedly. They have wanted us to meet the people who are important to them: for instance, an old friend of Bernie's who was visiting for a few days and Charlene's new boyfriend. Pearl, Pauline, Charlene and other family members have visited or stayed with us when they have been in Adelaide. During their visits they have met members of my family: my parents, my brother, sister, aunt and various friends. When a nephew of my husband was visiting from overseas and being shown the sights of the Flinders Ranges, nothing seemed more natural than to call in on Pearl and introduce him. On subsequent trips to Sechelt my family and I have stayed in Valerie's home. Our present relationships were not instant; like any relationship they grew, unevenly, in fits and starts. They will, I believe, continue to do so, though the project is finished.

Then there is the wider circle of relations and friends of these two families who have spontaneously invited us to family gatherings, or who have gone out of their way to help or please us, like Pauline's cousin, Joe McKenzie, who shot a kangaroo and invited us to his home to eat it cooked whole in the ashes because he had heard us say that we had not tried it that way before. Or Valerie's brother Randy who lent us his boat for a day-long trip up the inlet, and her husband, Ken, who skippered us. Anne Quinn, the Sechelt Band's cultural officer, offered advice and the use of office equipment and writes regularly to let us know how Band affairs and land claims are progressing. These people, and many others too numerous to name individually, have also come into our lives and we are grateful for their generously offered assistance, hospitality and friendship.

The major hurdle in our relationships, and one that I was very aware of from the start, stemmed from age difference. The fastest and easiest relationships came with Valerie and Pauline, women of my own age, with whom I have a lot in common despite our many differences. Feeling comfortable with the older and younger gener-

ations was harder work and took longer. Initially I approached Pearl
and Bernie with caution. I knew that in both their cultures respect
for Elders is important, but I was not at first quite sure of protocols
and did not want to give offence through ignorance. I was also
brought up to have respect for those older than myself and to treat
them somewhat differently from peers. So our meetings were
rather formal to begin with, only falling into ease and informality
after a while. The relationships with Charlene and Brandi were different again. They are young. I am old enough to be their mother.
We have less in common on which to base social chitchat. They are
involved in creating their lives; they have less experience and
somewhat less stake in the reflection that is of interest to Pearl and
Bernie and the debate and consideration that move Valerie and
Pauline. Nevertheless, we came to enjoy each other's company.

The changing relationships did give me some concern in terms
of balancing the subjective and the objective, but I think this need
not be a problem. The project was never envisaged as an objective
study and it rapidly became a collaboration. Collaborations work
better between people who understand and respect each other and
who see each other as individuals. Throughout, my worry was that
what had been said in interviews at the start when we did not know
each other well would be contradicted either directly or indirectly
in later interactions. To my great relief, this was not the case. Some
things have been said less guardedly or with greater emotion than
in the original interviews, but nothing of substance has been
changed from its first utterance.

Some circumstances have changed since the beginning of the
project. Sadly, Pearl McKenzie died in October 1997, a great loss to
her family, her people and her many friends. Traditionally the
Adnyamathanha and many other Australian Aboriginal groups did
not speak the name of a person after their death. This was a subject
that I discussed with Pearl on several occasions, and she made it
quite clear that she did not want this tradition to affect publication
of the work. Family members have also agreed that this should be
so.

Charlene broke her engagement and later began a new relationship which has produced three sons, Jadon, Kaleb and Marcus. She
and her partner Mark were married in September 1999. Brandi
married her boyfriend, Steve, and they are the parents of two
daughters, Bianca and Bree.

The preparation of any manuscript for publication always involves far more work than is envisaged at the start. I am indebted to Jean Barman, Bob Peterson, Craig Campbell, Rita Irwin, J. Donald Wilson and participants in departmental seminars in the Graduate Department of Education, University of Adelaide, for valuable discussion and criticism, and to the University of South Australia for a grant in conjunction with Tony Rogers that went some way towards covering research expenses. My thanks also to Tony, Molly and Ned. They did not just live through the experience with me – they were a part of it.

Orthographic Note

There are a number of different ways of writing both the Sechelt and the Adnyamathanha languages. I have used those that are preferred by the women with whom I have been working, namely, for the Adnyamathanha, the orthography developed in John McEntee and Pearl McKenzie, *Adnamatna-English Dictionary* (Adelaide: n.p., 1992), and for the Sechelt, that of Ronald C. Beaumont, *She Shashishalhem: The Sechelt Language* (Penticton, BC: Theytus Books, 1985). Both use a standard phonetic alphabet, but each includes a number of symbols that are not in the English language and that cannot be reproduced on a standard keyboard. These symbols differ for each orthography, and for the small number of Sechelt and Adnyamathanha words used in this text it seems unnecessarily confusing for the reader to have them included. I have, therefore, used the phonetic spelling of the two orthographies, but have not included the symbols. "Adnyamathanha" is not the spelling used in the McEntee/McKenzie orthography, but it is the most commonly used spelling of the word and is acceptable to Pearl McKenzie. All other Adnyamathanha words follow the orthography.

FOREWORD

After generations of European colonisation, indigenous groups around the world are working to regain and revitalise their traditional cultures—"trying to get it back."[1] For each group the task is different; for none is it easy. Canada and Australia are two nations in which the process is underway. In both, the dominant European-based society has been intent on its own power and hegemony since the days of first settlement. The traditional cultures, values and ways of life of the original inhabitants have been pushed aside, overwhelmed, in some areas almost completely eradicated. Sometimes this has been a consciously pursued policy; at other times it has been an unintended result of the gross imbalance of power between Aboriginal and colonist.[2] Regardless of intent, the outcome for the indigenous peoples of both countries has been very similar though the actual experience has often been quite different.

Brief sketches follow that introduce the worlds of three Adnyamathanha women from south-central Australia, Pearl McKenzie, her daughter Pauline Coulthard and Pauline's daughter Charlene Tree, and three Sechelt women from the Pacific Northwest of Canada, Bernie Sound, her niece Valerie Bourne and Valerie's

---

1 Discussion with Valerie Bourne, June 28, 1995.
2 The term "Aboriginal" is used throughout to denote indigenous peoples in both Canada and Australia and sometimes more generally around the world. For discussion of "naming" see 28-30 below.

1

daughter Brandi McLeod. They set the scene for the stories the women tell about their lives, their formal schooling, their informal learning about their culture and heritage and their aspirations for their children. Their memories, perceptions, beliefs and interpretations of aspects of their own lives particularly relate to their own childhoods but also to one another's childhoods, for Pearl McKenzie and Bernie Sound, the Elders of each family, have been involved in the raising of the younger generations. Charlene and Brandi, the youngest, have heard the stories that the two older generations of their family have told about their early lives and indeed about the lives of earlier generations. They have recalled the experience of their own childhoods and considered the possible experiences of children they will have in the future. Pauline and Valerie, as the representatives of the middle generation, can also look in both directions, to the past and to the future, as well as recalling and reliving their own experiences. Within each family the women exist in a myriad of relationships, either in past or present reality or in future possibility; each is mother, wife, daughter, granddaughter, sister. This interrelationship is reflected strongly in their narratives as they talk about their respective cultures, some of the ways they acquired their knowledges and the ways in which they strive to use, retain and preserve this heritage in their daily living and for their perceived futures. For each to separate herself out from the others of her family as an isolated entity is impossible. So we see in their stories, which form the major part of this book, a collective, intergenerational representation of two indigenous cultures, what belonging to them has meant for each of these women and what they want for themselves and their people in the future.

Setting the Scene

The Adnyamathanha People

The Flinders Ranges run north-south almost from the centre of South Australia until they reach the sea at Port Augusta. Although not high by the standards of most mountains (St Mary's Peak, the highest point, is 1165 metres), they tower above the flat and largely treeless surroundings. To the east and the west lie the vast dry salt pans of Lake Torrens and Lake Frome, and to the north the even larger basin of Lake Eyre beyond which the Simpson Desert stretches northwards to Queensland and the Northern Territory.

These lakebeds are the final destination of waters draining down almost a thousand kilometres from the north-east quarter of the continent. When full they are only a few inches deep and evaporation is rapid. Most of the time they are dry.

If you approach the Ranges from the south through Port Augusta, which sits on a narrow sea-level plain at the head of Spencer Gulf, you are faced with a smooth, rounded line of hills, bare except for sparse, short grass and salt bush. You wind upwards through the curves of Pichi Richi Pass, through the stately river gums that line all the (usually dry) creekbeds of the region, and then you are in Quorn, a sleepy town of 1300 that sits on a plain surrounded by low ranges. A thirty-minute drive across another flat saltbush plain, broken only by the ruined remains of early, unsuccessful European settlements, brings you to Kanyaka Creek, snaking with its complement of gums through a long, flat valley between two low ridges of hills. The valley gradually widens and suddenly you are in Hawker, population about 400. (See map 1.)

Only fifty kilometres north is Wilpena Pound, the circle of jagged mountains that has for thousands of years formed an important part of the mythology, or Dreaming, of the local Aboriginal peoples. More recently, in the last half century or so, it has become the focus for a thriving tourist trade.[3] Here the mountains, their rocks ranging from red to brown to purple and changing as the light changes from soft, gentle hues to harsh and fierce colours, are big and bold enough to pass for real mountains, though perhaps only just. Other parts of the Ranges are no more than hills, a result of millions of years of erosion. Between each spur are wide, flat valleys. It is along these valleys that the roadways mostly lie, heading straight into the distance until forced to deviate by another range. The roadways are all unsurfaced beyond Hawker, except for the main road to Leigh Creek at the northern end of the Ranges, the site of a huge open-cut coal mine. Beyond Leigh Creek the road

---

3 "Dreaming," or "the Dreamtime," are English terms used to describe the creative epoch of the Aboriginal peoples and the ceremonial that derives from it. It includes the ancestral gods or heroes who created the world and the ways in which they should be acknowledged and honoured, as well as the rules by which everyday life should be conducted. See Bill Edwards, "Living the Dreaming," in Colin Bourke, Eleanor Bourke and Bill Edwards, eds., *Aboriginal Australians* (St Lucia, Qld: Queensland University Press, 1994), passim.

Map 1. Adnyamathanha Lands

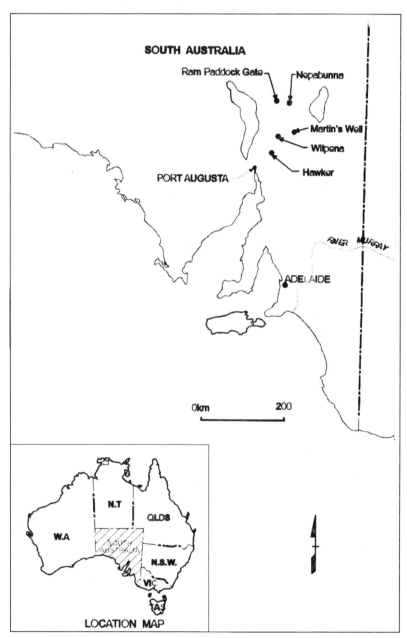

Source: University of Adelaide, Department of Geographical and Environmental Studies, Cartography Office.

reaches on to Marree, a railway depot on the line to Alice Springs before the line was rerouted, now almost a ghost town. Then the road becomes the Birdsville Track, a dry-weather-only route that stretches a further three hundred kilometres to the southern tip of Queensland, linking the handful of sheep and cattle stations that are the only permanent settlements in the area.[4]

The climate of the Flinders Ranges is semidesert; hot, dry summers with temperatures of forty degrees Celsius are common and dry, cold winters when the nighttime temperature can fall close to freezing. The rainfall is sparse, an average of twenty-five millimetres a year around Hawker, less to the north, east and west. Most usually the rain will fall in winter, but there can be flash floods in summer if rain clouds accompany a thunderstorm. Often, particularly in the north of the Ranges, rain may not fall for a year or more. When it does, the creeks that most of the time are dry, rocky beds become raging torrents of muddy brown water that disappear into the sandy earth as quickly as they appear. Then the land rapidly turns green, at least for a while, with grasses and flowers that can make the whole area look like a carefully tended park.

But mostly the land is dry and the vegetation with it, though this dry appearance should not be taken to indicate lack of life. The creekbeds are marked with fringes of river gums, whose roots grow deep into the soil to tap the underground moisture. In the course of several hundred years they can grow to a height of more than thirty metres. There are other areas that are thickly covered with native pines and other trees and bushes that rarely exceed three or four metres in height. But mostly the red earth is sparsely covered with tufty grasses or small shrubs and bushes whose colours range from browns and yellows to bluish or brownish greens. Vivid colours are found in the land itself and in some of the birds, but not in the plants, except after the rains when they rapidly produce flowers. At other times they seem to use all their energies for survival.

And everywhere there are rocks: from the huge cliff faces and boulders of the mountains themselves, to the smaller outcrops and rocks of the valleys lying where they have fallen from above or where they have been exposed by millennia of erosion, to the

---

4 "Station" is the name given to the huge sheep or cattle farms of the Australian interior, which are roughly equivalent though frequently much larger in area than the North American "ranch."

Plate 1. A flash flood can turn a dry creek bed into a torrent in minutes. And the rainfall has occurred kilometres away.

Plate 2. A dry creek bed may also be a roadway most of the time.

Plate 3. After a bush fire the new growth is lush and green—until next summer.

Plate 4. In places the ancient mountains have been weathered smooth.

smooth stones and pebbles of the creekbeds. It is a beautiful and breathtaking land, but the beauty is not of the sort that instantly or necessarily grabs the European eye or heart. It is a harsh beauty that both the eye and the mind have to learn to appreciate. Once they do, the heart is captured.

This is the land of the Adnyamathanha, whose name means literally "people of the rocks." The present-day Adnyamathanha are descended from four or five discrete groups who inhabited the lands at the time of white intrusion. They shared a common language though they spoke different dialects, and their cultures were similar.[5] It is no longer known whether the groups became one through a natural process of intermarriage or whether they were so weakened and reduced in numbers by the effects of early settlement that they drew together for survival.[6] Either way, until 150 years ago they lived in and with this land, understanding both its harshness and its bounty. Their spiritual and physical lives were tied to the land by the stories of their Dreaming, which explained how the land and its inhabitants had come to be and set out rules for the conduct of life.[7] They moved around their lands in small groups with the seasons, following the ever-repeating food cycles, knowing the whereabouts of the precious, permanent waterholes, building only temporary shelters as they needed them. Their physical possessions were few: hunting weapons for the men (spears, boomerangs, clubs), food-gathering implements for the women (wooden or bark bowls, string bags, digging sticks), kangaroo-skin blankets for winter warmth—nothing that could not easily be carried in their constant movement around their lands. Anything no longer useful was discarded and after an individual's death all his or her belongings were burnt. But if their physical culture was sparse and utilitarian, their social and spiritual culture was rich and comprehensive and revolved around the responsibilities of their complex relationships to each other and to their land. Periodically they

---

5 Christine Davis, Clifford Coulthard and Desmond Coulthard, comps., *The Flinders Ranges: An Aboriginal View* (Adelaide: Department of Environment and Planning, Aboriginal Heritage Branch, reprinted with amendments 1986), 1.

6 Peggy Brock, *Yura and Udnyu: A History of the Adnyamathanha of the North Flinders Ranges* (Adelaide: Wakefield Press, 1985), 13.

7 See Clifford Coulthard, Desmond Coulthard and Christine Wilton, *Mt Chambers: An Aboriginal View* (South Australia: Aboriginal and Historic Relics Unit, 1989), and Davis, Coulthard and Coulthard, comps., *The Flinders Ranges*.

would meet together with others of their people to perform their necessary ceremonies. Occasionally too they would meet with groups from other tribes who made the long journey south, sometimes from as far away as Queensland, to trade the high-quality ochre that lies in their land.[8]

Then came European intrusion, and with it great changes to the land and the people. Hawker today is a five-hour drive from Adelaide, the capital of the state of South Australia. When the first settlers arrived in 1836, near what was to become Adelaide, Hawker might have been a world away, but it was only a few years before the first white men were seen in the Flinders Ranges and only a few decades before their presence began to impact on the indigenous inhabitants.

South Australia was established as a planned colony of free settlers. Adelaide, its capital, was settled first, and the fertile lands immediately around it were rapidly developed. The local Aboriginal people in this area, the Kaurna, disappeared almost completely within twenty years. Purchase of lands further out was not allowed until it had been officially surveyed, but as soon as this was done settlers and their families moved out to take possession of suitable agricultural areas. Clearing the land for farming had an immediate effect on Aboriginal peoples by removing their traditional food supplies. Settlers, moreover, considered the presence of Aboriginal peoples as incompatible with agriculture. Little is known of what happened to Aboriginal groups who lived in what is now called the mid-north of the state, but few survived the intrusion of settlers into their lands.[9]

The impact of settlement on Aboriginal people in the drier lands even further inland was not as immediately devastating as urbanisation and agriculture were for those closer to Adelaide and in the mid-north. Very little of the Flinders Ranges, even the southern part, has sufficient rain for the cereal growing that, by the 1880s, had made South Australia the breadbasket of Australia. But sheep and cattle could survive in the drier lands, provided they had large enough areas over which to forage. Huge pastoral leases of Crown

---

8 Ochre is a clay soil that comes in a range of colours from white to yellows, browns, reds and purples. Mixed with water, fat or other media, it is used for body decoration and painting.

9 Brock, *Yura and Udnyu*, 10.

land allowed animals such space, and the natural environment was not destroyed straight away as with agriculture. Leases also permitted the free movement of Aboriginal people through the land in pursuit of their traditional activities. However, there were long-term effects for the original inhabitants as pastoralists controlled the water sources and stock ate many of the plants traditionally used as food by both Aboriginal people and the native animals they hunted.[10] The Aboriginal people in some pastoral areas were virtually wiped out over time; others survived with minimal impact on their traditional lifestyle; yet other groups adapted to the changed circumstances and survived. The Adnyamathanha of the Northern Flinders Ranges are one of the surviving groups.

The first Adnyamathanha contact with Europeans was in the 1840s when explorers pushed northwards, followed a decade later by the early pastoralists. The local conditions favoured sheep rather than cattle, and initially these were allowed to roam free tended by shepherds. Later the land was fenced, but each paddock, or division, was vast and the animals to a large extent still wandered freely. The Adnyamathanha, like some other Aboriginal groups, rapidly adjusted their hunting techniques to the new conditions and began to replace their native game with sheep and cattle.[11] Some violent clashes ensued between Aboriginals and settlers as well as the inevitable epidemics of diseases that European settlement brought to indigenous peoples around the world. By the 1860s the settlers were in full control, and two decades later those Adnyamathanha who survived had adapted to the pastoral economy.

According to Peggy Brock, who has written the most comprehensive history of the Adnyamathanha, they now "co-existed with the settlers, their values and their economy" though, as she notes, "at great loss to their health and the survival of individual members of their community" due to the poor nutritional quality of the government rations. These consisted mostly of flour, sugar and tea, and were given to the old and the sick, women and children and less frequently to men who could not get work to supplement the

---

10 Brock, *Yura and Udnyu*, 11. A pastoralist is a sheep or cattle farmer, the equivalent to the North American rancher. Much pastoral land in Australia is leased Crown land.

11 Henry Reynolds, *The Other Side of the Frontier: Aboriginal Resistance to the European Invasion of Australia* (Ringwood, Victoria: Penguin, 1982), 38-39.

increasingly sparse traditional food available.[12] "Co-existed" is, I think, an incorrect term, for it implies equality of both groups. The Adnyamathanha were certainly not equal; they lived as best they could in the small spaces, physical, social and psychological, that were still left to them. These spaces included a limited number of campsites now often near station homesteads and a mix of traditional and European customs, mores and roles. But the Adnyamathanha did not have a free choice of them; it was a matter of making the best of the situation. Some attempts were made to send children of "mixed race" to mission stations or residential schools, but the Adnyamathanha managed to avoid this action which had been so devastating for some other Aboriginal groups.[13] Station work was a major source of employment, though usually sporadic. Along with hunting dingoes and rabbits, for which they were paid by the scalp, and euros and kangaroos for their skins and occasional employment in local mines or at the Mt Serle Camel Depot, most families were able to survive even if they had to rely on government rations when the seasons were poor.[14] In times of drought they were

---

12 Brock, *Yura and Udnya*, 34.

13 The category of "mixed race" was a construct of the European intruders. The Adnyamathanha, like many other Aboriginal peoples, seem always to have accepted children of non-Adnyamathanha fathers as members of the group whether or not they approved of the circumstances of their conception (Brock, *Yura and Udnyu*, 35). For accounts of the institutionalisation of such children from other Aboriginal groups see, for instance, Tony Austin, "'Mainly a Question of Environment': The Kahlin Home for Aboriginal Children of Mixed Descent 1911-1927," *History of Education Review* 21, 1 (1992); for the Aboriginal perspective see Barbara Cummings, *Take This Child... from Kahlin Compound to the Retta Dixon Children's Home* (Canberra: Aboriginal Studies Press, 1990), and Sally Morgan, *My Place* (South Fremantle, Western Australia: Fremantle Arts Centre Press, 1987).

14 The dingo is a native dog which pastoralists believed caused great depredations to their flocks, particularly in respect to lambs. Rabbits were introduced by early settlers and soon ran wild across the country. They breed rapidly, have few natural enemies and can survive drought conditions by eating not only grass and leaves but roots and bark of bushes as well. This has caused great damage to the natural landscape and fauna as well as diminishing the food available for stock. In the nineteenth and early twentieth centuries the government paid a bounty for scalps of both rabbits and dingoes. Euros are a small species of kangaroo. Camels were imported from Pakistan in the nineteenth century to be used as pack animals in the desert areas. For a while the Mt Serle Station was used by the government as a breeding depot for them.

particularly vulnerable as they no longer had access to many water holes and, of course, native foods became scarce.[15]

By the end of the 1920s it was becoming increasingly difficult for the Adnyamathanha to move from camp to camp in the traditional manner. Many station owners were unwilling to have them camp on their properties and those who managed to find work on stations had their mobility restricted by their employment. Missionaries from the non-denominational United Aborigines Mission (UAM) had begun their work in the early 1920s at Ram Paddock Gate, a traditional Adnyamathanha campground, but the owners of Burr Well Station within whose boundaries it lay were increasingly unwilling to have the people stay there.[16] In 1930 Nepabunna settlement was established about thirty kilometres east of Ram Paddock Gate after prolonged negotiation by the missionaries with the owner of Balcanoona Station for some land.[17] This was not a traditional camping area as the ground was rather rocky, but wells blasted in the creek bed ensured a permanent water supply. The Adnyamathanha were not particularly happy with the location initially, but today it is very important to them.[18] The UAM continued to run the mission until 1973 when it was taken over by the government. Today the Adnyamathanha have freehold title over the land immediately surrounding Nepabunna through the Aboriginal Lands Trust, and the settlement is run by a committee of residents.[19]

Most of the approximately six hundred people who identify themselves as Adnyamathanha today do not live at Nepabunna. It is home to a handful of older people and frequently a temporary refuge for those who are unemployed, disillusioned or overwhelmed by the difficulties of being Aboriginal in late-twentieth-century Australia. Nevertheless, even for many who live else-

---

15 Brock, *Yura and Udnyu*, 39.

16 See Betty Ross, *Minerawuta: Ram Paddock Gate: An Historic Adnyamathanha Settlement in the Flinders Ranges, South Australia*, 2nd ed. (Adelaide: Aboriginal Heritage Branch, Department of Environment and Planning, 1989).

17 A. E. Gerard, *History of the United Aborigines Mission* (n.p.: United Aborigines Mission, n.d.), 21-22.

18 Cf. Diane Bell, *Ngarrindjeri Wurruwarrin: A World That Is, Was and Will Be* (North Melbourne, Victoria: Spinifex Press, 1998), 260-62.

19 Davis, Coulthard and Coulthard, comps., *The Flinders Ranges*, 1, gives the area of Nepabunna as about twenty-four square miles (approximately sixty square kilometres).

where, Nepabunna is a symbol of the Adnyamathanha relationship to their land. Brock maintains that "The retention of a 'home' has enabled the Adnyamathanha to retain a cultural and linguistic identity which they might have otherwise lost."[20] Many of the Adnyamathanha people wish to retain their traditional knowledge, skills and values side by side with mainstream Australian culture. The process of passing on knowledge from one generation to the next was not severed for the Adnyamathanha by residential schooling as it was for many indigenous people. Nevertheless, much has been lost and retrieval is difficult. The Adnyamathanha, like many Australian Aboriginal peoples who no longer live as a single, coherent group, do not have a strong group administrative structure. The Adnyamathanha do have the Flinders Ranges Heritage Committee, which is intended to make decisions of a general nature for the whole Adnyamathanha people mostly with respect to sacred sites and traditional lands that might be the subject of land claims. But it has no powers to implement decisions, and increasingly it is becoming factionalised along the lines of family and place of residence. As these divisions become deeper, the possibility of implementation of combined goals and actions becomes more difficult.

The Sechelt People

The traditional lands of the Sechelt Nation lie on the west coast of Canada, about forty kilometres north of the city of Vancouver (see Fig. 2) and half a world away from the Adnyamathanha. Their culture is different, as is their land. Where red and brown, rocks and desert, predominate in the Adnyamathanha lands, the Sechelt world is blue and green, water and forest. They too are surrounded by mountains, but the Coastal Range at whose feet they live is twice the height of the Flinders Ranges, reaching up two thousand metres at the coast. These mountains shelter pockets of snow even in summer and dwarf the mighty red cedar, spruce and hemlock trees that grow below them. One hundred kilometres further north, the mountains are yet another thousand metres taller and are snow covered all year round. Unlike the Flinders Ranges, they are not separated by wide valleys to make passage easy. Range after range huddles side by side, broken only by the swift torrent of streams rushing down from above. Only a

---

20 Brock, *Yura and Udnyu*, 13.

few logging roads penetrate these mountains and they go only as far as the accessible trees. Everything that goes in must stay or must turn around to come out. There are no through roads.

The town of Sechelt sits on a narrow isthmus only a couple of kilometres wide that joins the Sechelt Peninsula to the mainland. On its southern side is the Strait of Georgia, which separates Vancouver Island from the mainland of British Columbia. On a clear day you can see the city of Nanaimo on Vancouver Island, some thirty kilometres away. To the north is Sechelt Inlet, which connects to Jervis Inlet. Together they stretch and curve nearly eighty kilometres up into the mountains. The waters are deep and cold and the wind blowing down the inlet can make them dangerous. The tide can be dangerous too. When it moves through Skookumchuck Narrows at the head of Sechelt Inlet, it creates huge whirlpools with as much as a two-metre difference in the surface levels of the water. The whole of Jervis Inlet together with the coastline to the west as far as the end of the peninsula and for a shorter distance to the east was the traditional land of the Sechelt people. (See map 2.)

With a current population of about three thousand Native and non-Native people, the town of Sechelt is the largest settlement on the Sechelt Peninsula. A number of small resort villages cluster along the coast to the northwest, but while they are busy in summer their permanent population is small. A twenty-minute drive east on the mainland is Gibsons Landing, a somewhat larger town that looks across Howe Sound towards the city of Vancouver. It is close to here that the ferry, which is a vital part of the link to the city and the rest of Canada, offloads cars, trucks, buses and foot passengers after the forty-minute trip across the Sound from Horseshoe Bay just beyond the outskirts of the residential areas of West Vancouver. In real distance it is not far, but unless you have your own boat, the ferry or a seaplane are the only ways to get to the Sunshine Coast, the collective name for the strip coast from Gibsons up to Powell River, which is a further ferry ride beyond the top of the Sechelt Peninsula. Until the late 1950s, when the government established the BC Ferry Corporation, access to all these communities from the rest of the mainland was by the weekly boats of the Union Steamship Company, which served all the small communities from Vancouver north to the Alaska Panhandle.[21]

---

21 Jean Barman, *The West beyond the West: A History of British Columbia* (Toronto: University of Toronto Press, 1991), 291.

Map 2. Sechelt Lands

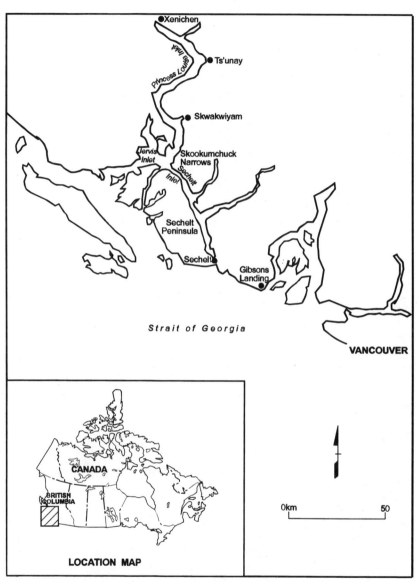

Source: University of Adelaide, Department of Geographical and Environmental Studies, Cartography Office.

Plate 5. Mountains loom over the Sechelt Healing Centre at Skakwiyam (Vancouver Bay), where Band members may retreat to heal the wounds of life.

Plate 6. Tide races through Skookumchuck Narrows, which provide the only outlet to the sea for the waters of several deep inlets.

Plate 7. Seaplanes and powerboats have replaced the canoe as the means of travel on the inlets. In the background is the newest section of Band housing at Sechelt village.

Plate 8. A graveyard guards the southern extremity of the Band lands at Sechelt. It is a monument to the early conversion of the Sechelt people to Christianity.

Because it faces west and lies to some extent in the rain shadow of Vancouver Island, this strip of coast boasts the longest hours of sunlight per annum in the province. But the name "Sunshine Coast" is deceptive, for this is also a land of rain and mists, and snow in winter. They water the thick forests of conifers and deciduous trees blanketing the mountains almost to the tops of their rocky peaks as well as the thick undergrowth of bushes, ferns and mosses. The rocky floor of these forests is covered with a dense carpet of decayed vegetable matter that provides a fertile bed for the next generation of plants and trees. Even in summer the atmosphere is damp and earthy. In winter it is cold and chill.

Here the Sechelt people lived off the rich bounty of both land and sea. From the former came deer, elk, bear and mountain goat for meat and skins, and fruits, nuts, berries and roots for food.[22] Perhaps most important of all were the cedar trees, which provided timber for making longhouses, boats, furniture and weapons, bark for weaving mats and clothing, even sails for boats, and roots for weaving baskets and making rope.[23] From the latter came the annual runs of salmon that, when preserved, provided food for a large part of the year, as well as other fish, seal and shellfish.

The present-day town of Sechelt was one of the traditional settlements of the four groups who comprised the Sechelt people, but not a major one. Xenichen at the head of Jervis Inlet and Ts'unay further to the south were more important villages, as was Skwakwiyam (Vancouver Bay); other smaller settlements were dotted along the shores of the Sechelt lands.[24] Today the Band has a

---

22 Charles Hill-Tout, *The Sechelt and the South-Eastern Tribes of Vancouver Island*, edited with an Introduction by Ralph Maud (Vancouver: Talonbooks, 1978), 104. Hill-Tout's anthropological studies of the Sechelt and other Coastal groups were carried out in 1902 and originally published shortly afterwards.

23 Hilary Stewart (*Cedar: Tree of Life to the Northwest Coast Indians* [Vancouver: Douglas & McIntyre, 1984]) describes in detail the many traditional uses for the tree; see also Hill-Tout, *The Sechelt*, 102-103.

24 Hill-Tout, *The Sechelt*, 95, and Lester Peterson, *The Story of the Sechelt Nation* (Madeira Park, BC: Harbour Publishing/Sechelt Indian Band, 1990), v. There is a discrepancy between these two authors as to the relative importance of the various permanent settlements of the Sechelt people. Both agree, however, that the present site of the village of Sechelt was traditionally a minor settlement.

campsite at Ts'unay where groups, particularly children, gather to learn more about their culture, and a residence at Skwakwiyam that is used as a healing centre. The Sechelt did not stay in one place all the time. They moved with the seasons, wintering in large groups in the warmer coastal areas and moving up the inlet in smaller groups in the summer. They were in contact, sometimes peaceful and sometimes warlike, with neighbouring Bands, and their large war canoes could take them up or down the coast or across the Strait of Georgia to Vancouver Island.

Most of the traditional sites contained permanent buildings: the longhouses that were found throughout the peoples of the coastal northwest.

> The dwellings of the old-time Sechelt were of the communal kind. They appear, however, not to have been so long generally as among some of the coast Salish, the nature of the ground at these villages not being so convenient for this purpose. In height they ranged from twenty-five to forty feet.... Usually each house was occupied only by persons connected by family ties.... The internal structure and arrangement differed some-what from that of the other tribes. For example, at the building of the house a permanent platform about two feet high and five or six feet broad was erected all round the interior walls. This served as seats or lounges for the occupants during the day, and during the night as beds.[25]

The Sechelt did not construct the totem poles that are commonly associated with the coastal tribes, but their homes and belongings were frequently decorated with carved and/or painted designs of an honorific rather than totemic nature.[26]

With their relatively settled and concentrated populations and with access to the multi-useful cedar, West Coast Indian Bands, the Sechelt amongst them, developed cultures in which the number and variety of physical objects and structures were very obvious. Their social and spiritual lives were also complex. They lived within "sophisticated social organisations based on the concept of inherited rank and on intricate patterns of sanctioned and prohibited

---

25 Hill-Tout, *The Sechelt*, 103-104.
26 Ibid., 102.
27 Barman, *The West beyond the West*, 13.

behaviour."[27] The Sechelt people were divided into three castes or classes, chiefs, nobles and "base folk." The chieftaincy was "practically hereditary, though theoretically within the grasp of any member of the tribe who could outdo the ruling chief in potlatching or feast-giving." The second group was "composed of heads of families of standing, and, generally, of the wealthy. The last were made up of the thriftless, the indolent and the slaves of the tribe." [28]

The long winters when the Sechelt could live off the foods caught, gathered and preserved during the bountiful summers were traditionally

> the period for exploring and celebrating the spiritual aspects of life. It was the time for winter dancing and for potlatching—the ritual in which Indians gave property away to establish their prestige and position. Much of the dancing and ceremony that frequently accompanied these rituals was designed to propitiate mythical figures ... [they] paid homage to spiritual and mythical beings who were then expected to work for man, to protect him and to help provide for his needs.[29]

In his 1902 visit to the Sechelt people, anthropologist Charles Hill-Tout recorded with a fairly typical nineteenth-century European paternalistic superiority that despite two generations of European contact and conversion to Christianity, much was still recalled of traditional spiritual beliefs and practices.

> That the forest, the air and the sea were full of mysteries to them is clear from their folktales; and their anthropomorphic conceptions of the animal and vegetable worlds coloured all their lives and thoughts, as among their neighbours. Even today, amongst the most advanced and intelligent of them, there is still a strong belief in the human or man-like side of animals, plants and other objects and forces.[30]

Contact between the peoples of the Pacific West Coast and Europeans began in the last quarter of the eighteenth century, as Spain, England and Russia began sending maritime expeditions both to explore the coast and to establish their rights to control it. Trade took place between the Europeans and the native inhabitants over a

---

28 Hill-Tout, *The Sechelt*, 99.
29 Robin Fisher, "Missions to the Indians of British Columbia," in W. Peter Ward and Robert A. J. McDonald, eds., *British Columbia: Historical readings* (Vancouver: Douglas & McIntyre, 1981), 115.
30 Hill-Tout, *The Sechelt*, 102.

period of years, with furs being exchanged for a variety of European goods; accounts from the period make clear that natives "used the control they possessed over the trade to their advantage."[31] But even this minimal contact had effects that modified, though it did not disrupt, traditional cultures. As early as 1790 there were reports of how, "except for ceremonial purposes, Indians of the chiefly class were abandoning their native garments of cedar bark and goats' wool for the ornamental European garments that the British and American traders brought to tempt their vanity."[32] This was the case with many other native artefacts, which were rapidly replaced by European-made goods though life itself was still lived in a traditional manner.

In the late 1850s the balance between trappers and traders was shattered when European intrusion began in earnest with the advent of a gold rush and the influx of thousands of prospective miners. The Sechelt people, whose lands did not hold the promise of gold, were spared the worst of the effects of European intrusion for a short while, but when it came the impact was devastating both physically and spiritually.

In 1860 two Roman Catholic missionaries, following in the wake of secular European intrusion into the province, arrived at Sechelt with the intent of offering Christianity as an antidote to both the effects of European disruption and the perceived shortcomings of the traditional spirituality and way of life. They were sent away by the Sechelt people. Two years later a smallpox epidemic decimated the indigenous population of the entire West Coast. It is not certain how many died in the initial smallpox epidemic or in subsequent outbreaks of influenza and other contagious diseases, but Captain George Vancouver had estimated the population of the Sechelt and Jervis Inlets at five thousand in 1792, while the federal census at the turn of the twentieth century estimated the local indigenous population at between 236 and 325.[33] By the 1920s it had dropped

---

31 Barman, *The West Beyond the West*, 29.

32 George Woodcock, *British Columbia, A History of the Province* (Vancouver: Douglas & McIntyre, 1990), 127.

33 Helen Dawe, *Helen Dawe's Sechelt* (Madeira Park, BC: Harbour Publishing, 1990), 127. The higher number, 325, was Charles Hill-Tout's 1902 estimation, though he notes the difficulty of census-taking amongst a people to whom such accounting is "entirely foreign" (*The Sechelt*, 94).

to about two hundred.[34] Possibly as a result of this disaster, the Sechelt Band changed its mind and in 1862 sent to New Westminster, where a permanent mission had been established, to ask for priestly attendance on their lands. Two brothers of the Congregation of Missionary Oblates of Mary Immaculate, the major Roman Catholic missionary order in British Columbia, were sent in response and within a decade the entire Band was converted to Catholicism. The architect of the conversion, Father—later Bishop—Durieu, planned not simply to introduce Christianity but to wipe out completely the traditional spiritual, moral and economic bases of the Sechelt people and replace them with those of "civilised" European society.[35]

The rapidity of conversion reflects the fact that the Band leadership and quite likely many individual members were already predisposed to make major changes in their lives as a result of the cultural disruption already caused by European settlement. The smallpox epidemic itself cannot be discounted as a factor in their change of heart. Some missionary settlements had been spared the devastation of the epidemic because the missionaries had supplies of vaccine that often gave them an undeserved reputation for spiritual power and miracle-making.[36] The Native peoples of the West Coast had rich and deep spiritual beliefs and elaborate ceremonials and, perhaps because of this rather than despite it, conversions up and down the coast were implemented more rapidly and with less effort than in many other places. Much of the traditional ritual was

---

34 Eileen McKibbin, "The Oblates of Mary Immaculate and the Sisters of the Child Jesus Mission and Residential School on the Reserve #2 of the Sechelt Indian Band, Sechelt BC," History 205 Paper, Special Collections, University of British Columbia Library, 1986, 6.

35 The Durieu "system" was later extended to the Squamish to the south and the Homalthko, Tlahoose and Sliammon to the north. For nearly a century it was considered by the Catholic Church and many European Canadians, Hill-Tout included, to be one of the most successful methods of converting and civilising Native Indian peoples, turning them into "devout and reverent converts ... cheerfully and generously sustaining the Mission in their midst" (Hill-Tout, *The Sechelt*, 94). Ralph Maud, 1978 editor of Hill-Tout's writings, points out that Edwin M. Lemert's 1954 publication, "The Life and Death of an Indian State," takes a different view, noting that the plan bore "unmistakable resemblances" to the Jesuit mission prototype in seventeenth-century Paraguay (Hill-Tout, *The Sechelt*, 94, footnote 2).

36 Woodcock, *British Columbia*, 132.

intended to propitiate mythical figures and for many the addition of the Christian God posed no difficulty; he could be added without making much change to their daily lives and customs.[37]

From the missionary point of view this was not at all acceptable. The priests objected strongly to traditional customs and ritual, in particular to the potlatch. Amongst other functions, potlatching served to expedite the circulation of goods throughout society, but missionaries condemned it for discouraging a work ethic and leading to a reliance on handouts; they saw it as "foolish, wasteful and demoralising."[38] It was largely as a result of their pressure that in 1884 the *Indian Act* was amended by the federal government to make potlatching illegal.

This was only one of the practices that missionaries tried to eradicate. In Sechelt as in some other missionary settlements the people were supervised in the building of a model village with a church as its centrepiece. Both homes and church were built in European style; there was not even a hint of the traditional building styles and techniques that had served the people so well for centuries past. Within Christianity too, there was no room for the shamans whose role was a combination of both priest and doctor. With their disappearance went not only traditional spiritual beliefs and practices, but also much of the traditional healing and medicinal knowledge.

Teaching their congregations was an important part of the missionary program: teaching them to abandon their own language and instead to speak, read and write in English; teaching them skills tied to European gender roles: cooking, cleaning and laundry work for girls, agriculture and husbandry skills for boys. To this end a large residential school, St Augustine's, was constructed in 1903 on what was then the Sechelt Reserve and opened the following year. It was planned, financed and erected by the people themselves with funds earned from logging and fishing, the two main occupations open to them.[39] Sisters of the Child Jesus came out from France to instruct in the school, so the first generation of students learned English with a French accent. The first school burned down in 1917 and was replaced by an even larger and more imposing brick

---

37 Fisher, "Missions," 115.
38 Ibid., 121.
39 Dawe, *Sechelt*, 127; see also Hill-Tout, *The Sechelt*, 93.

building which continued in use until the early 1970s, by which time all Sechelt students had been integrated into the local public schools.

The residential school had a profound effect on the Sechelt people for seventy years. Many older people have bitter memories of it, and currently it is the major scapegoat for the loss of traditional culture and lifestyle and the destruction of the Sechelt identity. Today many Band members, both old and young, wish to live in the culture of mainstream society, but they want also to regain the traditional culture, the knowledge, the values and the language, and to preserve them for future generations. In 1986 the Sechelt Band became one of the first Canadian Native Indian Bands to achieve self-government. This means, among other things, that the Sechelt people, through their elected Chief and Council, are excluded from the *Indian Act* and have sovereignty over themselves on their own lands. They also have control over the resources and services that are available to Band members.[40] Over the past decade the people, under the leadership of the elected Chief and Council, have been responsible for directing and conducting their daily lives. An important part of this direction has been working towards the goals of cultural preservation and renewal.

Writing Aboriginal Lives

There are a number of methodological considerations and problematics concerning these stories, the six women who own them and who have told them to me and the way in which they are presented. These issues can be grouped into three constellations, each of which in turn intersects with the other. The first concerns Aboriginality, the second involves the development of Aboriginal discourse and the third revolves around the ownership of the stories, the question of whose voice speaks them and the way in which they are presented.

40 For details see Union of BC Indian Chiefs, *The Sechelt Act and What It Means* (Vancouver: Union of BC Indian Chiefs, 1988), passim.

Aboriginality

Stephen Muecke has noted in the Australian context: "whatever 'Aboriginality' is, it has never been the same thing from one tribal group to another, from ancient times to the present, or even—according to some legal definitions—the same thing from one State of Australia to another."[41]

There are many Aboriginal peoples and Aboriginal cultures in Australia. They are all connected, some very closely, others less so, but they are not one homogeneous people either in terms of their traditional cultures or in terms of their contemporary experience, desires or aspirations. The same is true of the North American situation.

The precise parameters and content of Aboriginality will vary, depending on which group of indigenous people is being considered. It is very closely linked to both group and personal identity and experience, which include both historic and contemporary constructions of Aboriginal peoples as "other" in relation to the mainstream colonising society. It is frequently more easily identifiable by its effects than for itself.

The effects of Aboriginlity permeate the whole of the lives of Aboriginal people and many non-Aboriginal people too. They are contextual effects that appear in different guises in different situations. Sometimes they are clearly visible, sometimes they are just discernible, at other times they are invisible, but they are always there—a little like the smile of the Cheshire Cat in *Alice's Adventures in Wonderland*.[42] For these six women Aboriginality is a fact of life, a fact of which they are proud, although it often has had negative ramifications in terms of their lives and the way they lead them. What "Aboriginality" means most strongly to them is not some vast concept related to their indigenous status versus the rest of Western society. Nor is the meaning connected to the smaller but still huge concept of Australian or even Canadian Abo-

---

41 Stephen Muecke, *Textual Spaces: Aboriginality and Cultural Studies* (Kensington, NSW: New South Wales University Press, 1992), 19.

42 This may seem an odd simile to use in this context and I wondered why it had come to mind, but on further thought it seems that although it is a white, middle-class English text, it has in fact many similarities in form and construction to the traditional stories and mythologies of Australian and Canadian Aboriginal cultures.

riginal society versus mainstream Australian or Canadian society. Pearl McKenzie, Pauline Coulthard and Charlene Tree identify themselves as Adnyamathanha; Bernie Sound, Valerie Bourne and Brandi McLeod identify themselves as Sechelt. Aboriginality to them is first and foremost tied to their own specific cultural identity. Their loyalties and aspirations are towards the Adnyamathanha or Sechelt people and culture rather than to a concept of "Aboriginal" with broad, national parameters. This is not to say that they have no interest in other Aboriginal peoples within their respective countries or in other countries. There is a strong feeling of kinship and sympathy, but there is nevertheless a sense of separateness as well. My own observation is that there is a far stronger sense of solidarity with other Aboriginal peoples, stemming from the present and arising from a sense of shared difficulties and disadvantages in coping with the effects of the dominant society, than there is in relation to traditional cultural ties. During the course of the study these feelings of sympathy and shared experiences developed between the two groups of women vis-à-vis the mainstream societies of their respective countries. Because of their Aboriginality, they found they had much in common even though their cultures and frequently their specific experiences were different.

The huge variety in indigenous culture and experience, and therefore in the individual's experience and construction of Aboriginality, is not always reflected in the existing literature in either Australia or Canada outside of anthropological studies. This is partly because mainstream interest in Aboriginal studies and in writing Aboriginal people back into the histories of both countries is relatively new, and so the literature is not extensive in comparison with mainstream histories. Some recent Canadian histories have attempted to incorporate indigenous history into a mainstream history text. For instance, Margaret Conrad et al., *A History of the Canadian Peoples*, begins with a chapter that gives an overview of the major groups of indigenous peoples across the nation.[43] They are also included far more than used to be the case in subsequent chapters of the text. But it is a fact that it is the winners who write history, and this is still a history of European

---

43 Margaret Conrad, Alvin Finkel and Cornelius Jaenen, *History of the Canadian Peoples*, vol. 1: *Beginnings to 1876* (Mississauga, ON: Copp Clark Pitman, 1993).

Canada even though it gives a sympathetic coverage to the losers. Another approach is that of Jean Barman who, while she does not include separate coverage of all the British Columbia First Nations Bands in her recent history of the province, nevertheless integrates their experience where it intersects with that of mainstream society.[44] Paul Axelrod's overview of the history of schooling in Canada devotes one of its six chapters to the education of cultural groups other than the French and English and, working chronologically, begins the chapter with the experiences of Aboriginal Canadians.[45]

More common in Australia are studies of individual indigenous groups or specific historic situations.[46] These are intended to stand alone and to be specific in focus, although the well-informed reader may be able to make generalisations or comparisons with other groups or other situations. An alternative approach is to deal with vast geographic areas in which a multitude of groups are represented, as in Henry Reynolds's Australian study *The Other Side of the Frontier*.[47] This was a pathbreaking work in that it approached the history of white settlement in Australia from an Aboriginal point of view. But while it used examples from various parts of the country, the majority were from the east coast and from the early period of colonisation. There was no consideration of the experience of Aboriginal peoples of the central and northwest desert regions, for instance, who experienced white intrusion at a later period and in a different manner. Because the difference in the experience of individual groups at different time periods is not emphasised, the danger is that the experience in one situation may be taken to represent a non-existent general "Aboriginal" experience.[48]

---

44 Barman, *The West beyond the West*, passim.

45 Paul Axelrod, *The Promise of Schooling: Education in Canada, 1800-1914* (Toronto: University of Toronto Press, 1997), chap. 4.

46 For instance, Bruce Elder, *Blood on the Wattle: Massacres and Maltreatment of Australian Aborigines since 1788* (French's Forest, NSW: Child and Associates, 1988), and Barry Morris, *Domesticating Resistance: The Dhan-Gadi Aborigines and the Australian State* (Oxford: Berg Publishers, 1989).

47 Reynolds, *The Other Side of the Frontier*.

48 Bourke makes the point strongly, though briefly, that Australian Aboriginal culture contained much cultural diversity "within a common framework" (Eleanor Bourke, "Australia's First Peoples: Identity and Population," in Colin Bourke, Eleanor Bourke and Bill Edwards, eds., *Aboriginal Australians* [St Lucia, Qld: Queensland University Press, 1994], 36). The postcolonisation

The ways in which Aboriginal groups prefer to be named is another example of the diversity and at times the divisiveness of Aboriginality. Historically, terms such as "blacks," "blackfellas" and "aborigines" were used in the Australian context, but, with the growth of Aboriginal awareness and activism in the 1980s, the term "Aboriginal people" was preferred by many. Then the call was for a name that was itself Aboriginal. The word "Koori" came to be used on the east coast, and given the dominance of the east in most Australian affairs this was soon heard across the country, at least sporadically. Aboriginal residents of areas other than the east coast mostly prefer to use their own traditional names for themselves. The Kaurna, the original inhabitants of the Adelaide area, prefer "Nunga," the Kaurna word for their people. The Adnyamathanha who, relatively speaking, do not live all that far away from Adelaide, find this amusing, as "Nanga" (pronounced "nunga") means "Hello" in their language. They prefer "Yura," which is their word for an Adnyamathanha person but has, in modern times, come to be used for any Australian Aboriginal person. But if the situation is muddled at the group level in terms of preferred names, when one comes to deal with individuals there can be even more confusion. Some older Aboriginal people are still perfectly at ease using the old terms "blackfella" and "whitefella" and do so without any sense of embarrassment or offence. Some others, usually younger, find even "Aboriginal" highly offensive. In previous writings about the Adnyamathanha I have used their terms "Yura" and "Udnyu" (white), which were acceptable to all of them.[49] Charlene and Pauline use them consistently; Pearl uses them less often but is quite happy with them.

---

history of the Maori peoples of New Zealand shares many similarities with that of their indigenous counterparts in Canada and Australia. There are also a number of differences that are well illustrated by the recent publication by Judith Simon, ed., and a team of Maori researchers, *Nga Kura Maori: The Native Schools System, 1867-1969* (Auckland: Auckland University Press, 1998).

49 Gillian Weiss, "Three Generations of Women: Learning and Schooling amongst the Adnyamathanha, *Historical Studies in Education/Revue d'Histoire de l'Education/History of Education Review* (special issue) 23, 3 (October 1994): 171-99. "Udnyu" means corpse in the Adnyamathanha language and was applied to the first Europeans because of their pale colour.

This will not do, however, once I bring in the Sechelt people, for Adnyamathanha terms have no meaning for them. They refer to themselves as Sechelt People, but use no word from their own language to identify others. Bernie, Valerie and Brandi consistently referred to themselves as "Indian" or "Native Indian" when they did not use "Sechelt." Not once did any of them use the term "First Nations," which itself is problematical in parts of Canada.[50] As is the case in Australia, many Canadian Native Indian peoples prefer to refer to themselves by their own traditional names rather than by a generic term covering all.[51] "Aboriginal" or "indigenous" are being used more and more frequently in Canada, but I have also used the terms "Native" or "Native Indian" in the Canadian context as they are acceptable to the Sechelt women about whom I speak, even though the term "Native" is highly offensive to many Australian Aboriginal people.

There is difficulty too in referring to the non-Aboriginal populations of both Canada and Australia. I have used the terms "mainstream," "dominant" and, less frequently, "European," "non-Aboriginal" or "non-Native" and "white" to describe either or both the society and the individuals who, in the course of the past two centuries or more, have come to live in Canada and Australia. All these terms are problematic. "Non-Aboriginal" and "non-Native" may be politically correct and inoffensive to most people, but they set up indigenous peoples as irrevocably separate from all the rest of society. They also do not allow me to differentiate between one group of Aboriginal people and another. "European" may be more acceptable to some readers, but I find it awkward in some contexts and, moreover, it is inaccurate. The original colonists of both Canada and Australia were European, but it would be questionable to describe their descendants and the society of their descendants, two hundred years down the line, as European, even if these societies did not contain significant numbers of Asian and/or African peoples.[52]

---

50 During the five years of research for this book the term "First Nation" came increasingly to be used in Australia.

51 Julie Cruikshank, *Life Lived Like a Story: Life Stories of Three Yukon Native Elders* (Lincoln: University of Nebraska Press, 1990), 357.

52 Other attempts to find a suitable term include Australian historian Lyn Anne Riddett's use of "settler" (see "Finish, I Can't Talk Now: Aboriginal and Settler Women Construct Each Other," paper presented at the University of Saskatchewan, January 26, 1995). To my mind "settler" has the same shortcomings as "European." It is relevant in a historical sense but not in a contemporary situation.

On the other hand, the terms "European-Canadian" and "European-Australian" are unwieldy, particularly when the intention is to refer to both at the same time. "Mainstream," "dominant" and "white" also present difficulties because in both countries the population consists of many sub-groups who may or may not fall within the parameters of one of the terms. This, of course is the crux of the problem. To whom am I referring when I use these problematic terms? Do I mean everyone else in Australia or Canada except the Adnyamathanha or Sechelt Peoples? Or those who have/had direct or indirect contact with them? Or do I mean those sections of the community with the greatest control over the political direction of society at a given time? And indeed, exactly what time am I talking about? Each particular context may call for the use of a different term, and so I have tried to use the one that seems most appropriate in that context. The person who needs or desires to be politically correct faces a major decision in the right choice of word because there is no single correct term. I believe a modicum of sensitivity, a willingness to listen to the ways in which people talk about themselves and/or to discuss what names are most acceptable to a group, will remove most problems. If any term is offensive to anyone, I can only apologise.[53]

A further example of the diversity of attitude and approach of indigenous peoples is the question of who should be involved in rewriting the Aboriginal experience. Eleanor Bourke, the (Aboriginal) director of the Aboriginal Research Institute, University of South Australia, has called for white academics to back off for a period and allow Aboriginal people to write their own histories.[54] Writing by Aboriginal people is a means by which they can give voice to their own stories, take possession of their own past. But until quite recently, very few Australian Aboriginal people have been involved in writing about their individual or collective selves and experience. Aboriginal repossession of Aboriginal history and experience offers a number of exciting possibilities for the future regarding development of Aboriginal identity and the dissemination

---

53 Conrad, Finkel and Jaenen, discuss the problem of naming in *History of the Canadian Peoples*, xvii-xviii. They prefer the term "politically conscious" to "politically correct," and I interpret their meaning to be close to my suggested combination of sensitivity, and willingness to listen and negotiate.

54 Education Department Staff/Student Seminar, University of Adelaide, June 18, 1993.

of Aboriginal points of view. But I believe that there is a place for non-Aboriginal people in this project, just as there is a place for male writers in feminist and gender studies. "It takes two to either tango or tussle."[55] Or, as Gayatri Chakravorty Spivak has said, though admittedly in a somewhat different context, "it isn't necessarily bad being white, because to an extent it is what one *does* with the fact that one's white at this point that's more important."[56] Linda Alcoff has noted the current rejection of "speaking for others [as] arrogant, vain, unethical and politically illegitimate," but argues persuasively that backing off and refusing to do so, particularly when the "others" are in a position of powerlessness, may ultimately be more harmful.[57] She believes:

> We should strive to create wherever possible the conditions for dialogue and the practice of speaking with and to rather than speaking for others. If the dangers of speaking for others result from the possibility of misrepresentation, expanding one's own authority and privilege, and a generally imperialist speaking ritual, then speaking with and to can lessen these dangers.[58]

---

55 Kay Saunders and Raymond Evans, eds., *Gender Relations in Australia: Domination and Negotiation* (Sydney: Harcourt Brace Jovanovitch, 1992), xxi.

56 Gayatri Chakravorty Spivak, *The Post-Colonial Critic: Interviews, Strategies, and Dialogues* (New York: Routledge, 1990), 77 (italics in original). Spivak's work on the postcolonial situation of India and its peoples deals mostly with the situation of the subaltern classes in India and the educated individuals, like herself, who have dispersed across the Western world. See, for instance, Gayatri Chakravorty Spivak, *In Other Worlds: Essays in Cultural Politics* (New York: Routledge, 1988), and Ranajit Guha and Gayatri Chakravorty Spivak, eds., *Selected Subaltern Studies* (New York: Oxford University Press, 1988). Less well known is her consideration of the indigenous peoples of India, the "tribals." She does not use the words of real tribal women nor write their history, in the sense of relating actual incidents from the past; rather, she uses literature, stories about imagined tribal women, to "make visible the suggestion that the postcolonial negotiates with the structures of violence and violation that have produced her" (Gayatri Chakravorty Spivak, "Who claims Alterity?' in Barbara Kruger and Phil Mari, eds., *Remaking History* [Seattle: Bay Press, 1989], 281-82). See also Mahasweta Devi, *Imaginary Maps*, translated by Gayatri Spivak (New York: Routledge, 1995).

57 Linda Alcoff, "The Problem of Speaking for Others," *Cultural Critique* 20 (Winter 1991-92): 6. See also Cathryn McConaghy, "Fashion and Prescription in Representations of Indigenous Education," *Discourse* 15, 2 (December 1994): 81.

58 Ibid., 23. See also Riddett, "Finish, I Can't Talk Now" (n.p.)

At the present moment there are relatively few Aboriginal people who are both able and willing to "go it alone." A cooperative approach seems the best way, at least in the short term, to make sure that Aboriginal voices are heard. But such ventures must be firmly based on an understanding that Aboriginal people bring to the undertaking just as much, in many cases more, skills, knowledge, understanding and expertise as do non-Aboriginals.

At the other end of the spectrum from those who would have non-Aboriginal people excluded from the debate, the Warramirri people of Arnhem Land have allowed a white associate to assist them with publication of aspects of their culture that had until then been secret, in a move designed to assist intercultural understanding between themselves and mainstream Australian society.[59] Many, if not most, Aboriginal groups would be unwilling to go this far. There are no doubt all sorts of positions in between the two extremes. All are Aboriginal attitudes; there is no single Aboriginal point of view.

How does the fact of their Aboriginality affect these six women and affect the ways they and I together record and publish their stories? There are several considerations. The first is in relation to ownership of the data that they are allowing and assisting me to collect. Western academic tradition has tended to hold that once individuals have agreed to give information, whether it be factual data or more personal information, that information becomes the intellectual property of the researcher who is free, indeed must be free, to make whatever analysis and draw whatever conclusions he/she thinks appropriate. This is not the attitude of the Adnyamathanha and the Sechelt. Their stories, whether traditional or personal are theirs permanently as far as they are concerned. This sense of ownership arises from traditional beliefs but has a modern component as well. Muecke has noted that ownership of Australian Aboriginal stories or songs is certainly not a traditional practice:

> [I]n Aboriginal Australia, it is the case that *custodianship* displaces ownership of stories and songs toward a collective ownership—the idea being that individuals are temporarily in charge of various cultural things by virtue of being in a certain position in the society. They are

---

59 John Cawte, *The Universe of the Warramirri: Art, Medicine and Religion in Arnhem Land* (Kensington, NSW: New South Wales University Press, 1993).

not so much the creators of traditions but they are the holders of it and they repeat it.[60]

A custodian, in this sense, would certainly consider that he or she had the right to control the use of traditional stories or songs, particularly if the user were from a different culture. This sense of having the right to oversee, to control, has, I think, carried over to personal stories or life histories told in the present. It is, in other words, a traditional attitude to non-traditional information, for stories about every individual's day-to-day life would not have had the same place in traditional society as the Dreaming stories of the Adnyamathanha or the traditional myths of the Sechelt. The current emphasis on ownership of personal life stories arises in part from the bitter experience of having non-Aboriginal researchers come in and collect information and then use it in ways or for purposes that Aboriginal people have not thought acceptable—it is a form of self-protection.[61] These six women may choose to share their life stories with others, but they do not give up the ownership. And they have a lively interest in the uses to which their stories are put and the ways in which they might be presented to others. As a condition of sharing the information they wish to be involved in the preparation of the final product and to feel comfortable about its form, content and nature. It is their individual and collective selves that are being put on public view.

There is also a political facet to these women's desire to maintain control of their selves and their identities. Ever since European settlement, their peoples have been denied the right to

---

60 Muecke, *Textual Spaces*, 45 (italics in original).

61 James Axtell devotes the final chapter of *After Columbus: Essays in Ethnohistory of Colonial North America* (New York: Oxford University Press, 1988) to a discussion of "The Scholar's Obligations to Native Peoples." He quotes Francis Jennings, also a white historian as "reject[ing] as insidious the fallacy that a tribe holds exclusive proprietary rights to its history, with full control over access to information and ultimate disposition of, even proceeds from, the final product" (245-46). Axtell agrees with him and goes on to allow Aboriginal peoples only a limited role in the writing of their history. Basically he will accept any information they have to offer so long as he considers it appropriate, but maintains his right to retain full control of its use. It is the arrogance of the attitude rather than the resulting history (which may be quite acceptable) that upsets Aboriginal peoples. Cf. Bell, *Ngarrindjeri Wurruwarrin*, 21-23 and 366-71, for a totally different attitude to ownership of knowledge.

control and determine their lives. In the current political and social climate of both Canada and Australia they see possibilities for redressing this situation and are therefore determined to use whatever methods seem to offer the likelihood of success. Education of the whole community as well as of their own people is an approach that appeals to these particular women, but they wish to ensure that they have control of the "curriculum."[62] Recently, after a particularly long interview session, I asked Pauline Coulthard whether she got sick of being asked constantly by white people about her culture and her experience. Her answer was that, yes, she did get sick of it, but it was worthwhile if it served to advance Adnyamathanha goals of retrieving their cultural inheritance and acquiring greater power and recognition within Australian society.

Then there is the difficulty of what we might call intercultural incompatibility. Too often a dominant group automatically assumes that a second, less-powerful group can be understood, analysed and explained using the tools, parameters, constructs, etc., of the dominant group. Different cultures frequently have very different ways of looking at things, and if these differences are not recognised all kinds of confusions can arise. An allied research project with which I am involved began with the goal of looking at effects of colonisation on indigenous art, and quite an amount of work had gone forward before it became apparent that there was a problem with this in the Adnyamathanha context. Adnyamathanha people were quite able to discuss, in English, art and artefacts relating to their culture. It was only when interviewers began to ask questions about the relationship of art to other aspects of Adnyamathanha culture, questions specifically tied to language and its usage, that discussions came to an abrupt standstill. The Adnyamathanha have no words for art and the aesthetic concepts which are tied to it in Western culture, although participants were perfectly able to discuss them in English. We (both researchers and participants) were using a construct that is irrelevant to Adnyamathanha culture. It is

---

62 Georges Sioui (*For an Amerindian Autohistory: An Essay on the Foundations of a Social Ethic*, translated from the French by Sheila Fischman [Montreal: McGill-Queen's University Press, 1992], 30-38) points out that education of the Western world, in not just the history but also the beliefs and attitudes of Native peoples, has been on the Native Indian agenda for a long time, and the aim is not just to inform, to redress the imbalance, but to offer a workable alternative to Western culture and attitudes.

hard to keep a lookout for problems that may be invisible in this way, but if the results are to be valid the attempt must be made. Often the clues will come from indigenous people themselves rather than from accepted academic practice or knowledge. There may still be a difficulty, though, when the indigenous group is bi-cultural: equally comfortable and able to function in their own and the mainstream cultures. Even they may not easily recognise cultural incompatibilities or inconsistencies.

Developing Aboriginal Discourse

Aboriginal discourses have existed as long as there have been Aboriginal peoples. Traditionally they were oral discourses and until colonisation their validity was not questioned. But colonisers in Canada and Australia had no time for indigenous discourse; the discourses of their own societies were the ones they deemed important, and written discourses particularly so. In recent generations Aboriginal voices have increasingly been heard, but it is only recently that written Aboriginal discourse has begun to be accepted by the dominant societies. "Accepted" is the important word here. There is no question that these discourses have, do and will continue to exist. What is important is that they are accorded a place of respect and equality beside the dominant discourses. Also important is the fact that discourse is not static. It changes as the society that gives rise to it changes. Therefore, while traditional indigenous discourses may remain, more modern forms may also be developed.

Militant Australian Aboriginal novelist and literary theorist Mudrooroo Narogin has called for efforts to construct "new forms" of written literature as appropriate vehicles for a distinctive Aboriginal voice: forms that derive from Aboriginal culture itself.[63] He has little time for Aboriginal people who work with white collaborators in the writing of their life histories, seeing them as "surrender[ing] their Aboriginal discourse to ... the white recorder."[64] Oodgeroo Noonuccul (Kath Walker) and Kevin Gilbert, too, both strove to make the distinctive Aboriginal voice speak in literature: to allow it to stand defiantly and uncompromisingly alone, not bending or bowing to explain itself or its owners. This is the kind of writing

---

63 Mudrooroo Narogin, *Writing from the Fringe: A Study of Modern Aboriginal Literature* (Melbourne: Hyland House Publishing, 1990), 4.
64 Ibid., 147.

Narogin applauds. He has no time for the type of writing he sees as an example of "white dominance and either Aboriginal acceptance of, or a seeking to come to grips with, this dominance."[65]

But compromise can serve its own purposes too. In a discussion of five autobiographies by Australian Aboriginal men and women, Dianne Snow has noted that in each case "the individual life history retains its unique personal elements but more emphasis is placed on the wider colonising process and its implications for all Aboriginal people." Their writings therefore become "a vehicle for expressing concerns about the historical process of colonisation—including community and cultural fragmentation," which she argues is a consciously educative purpose.[66] She argues further that in pursuit of this educative process these Aboriginal autobiographies are directly attempting "to reclaim and rewrite a collective Aboriginal history, to preserve Aboriginal knowledge and to educate others about it."[67] Snow characterises this as attempting to "heal the ruptures to the individual and collective selves created by colonisation."[68] Narogin replies, "Can words of peace or thoughts of gratitude be expected from someone who has had their language stolen from them?"[69] His implicit answer is no, and he therefore wants Aboriginal people to tackle their own project alone. His stance is similar to that discussed earlier, which claims there is no place for whites in the writing of Aboriginal history. But I think it also assumes that there is a universality in Aboriginality that I have already argued does not exist. This is not to say, however, that contemporary Aboriginal discourse, or discourses given the multiplicity of Aboriginal voices, cannot be developed. They can be and they are.

Development of Aboriginal discourse is not limited to literature and autobiographic writing. It is relevant to any topic about which indigenous peoples might wish to write or speak. In an editorial in the *Canadian Journal of Native Education*, Carl Urion argues that

---

65 Ibid., 152-53.
66 Dianne Snow, "(Re)writing the Collective Self: Aboriginal Autobiography as Cultural History," paper presented at the Australia/New Zealand and Canadian History of Education Association Conference, University of Melbourne, December 9-12, 1993, 10, 11-14.
67 Ibid., 14.
68 Ibid., 15.
69 Narogin, *Writing from the Fringe*, 148.

the journal "acknowledges" and "reflects" traditional discourse about First Nations education, which he differentiates from academic discourse on Native education in a number of ways.[70] The former is based upon an assumption about

> the integrity of the person. It assumes a context in which there is unity and wholeness to be discovered or reaffirmed; people involved in the discourse may disagree in their statements, of course, but the discourse is one of discovering the properties of the unifying context and finding out how the discoursing individuals fit within the context and thus come to unity.[71]

He goes on to say that in a First Nations discourse the observer must be a part of the observation. "Statements are not disembodied, but are evaluated in terms of multiple contexts, and further evaluated according to where the statements originate." The moral authority of the person making the statement is of paramount importance because the relationship between a person of moral authority and another person is what creates the discourse.[72] Thus, in discussing an article based on interviews conducted in the Cree language with past scholars of residential schools he points out that the interviews themselves

> are a small part of First Nations discourse; they do not form simply a "data corpus" for academic exposition as ethnohistory. The validity of the generalisations in the article does not emanate from ethno-historical cross-validation, buttressed by archival sources. That kind of validity is elementary. The validity of the discourse is the moral authority of the interactants to the interviews, who know that the earth witnessed the things about which they spoke.[73]

This particular quotation struck a chord for me because it put a name to a phenomenon that I had been indirectly aware of in my interviews with the six women. They spoke about their past lives, some more consciously than others, with just such a moral authority; they knew "that the earth had witnessed the things about which they spoke." It therefore seemed essential to convey their

---

70 Carl Urion, "Changing Academic Discourse about Native Education: Using Two Pairs of Eyes," *Canadian Journal of Native Education* 18, 1 (1991): 6.
71 Ibid., 4-5.
72 Ibid., 5.
73 Ibid., 8.

meanings in their own words. This was not because Native discourses can only exist in Aboriginal languages. English is now the first language of many indigenous people in both Australia and North America, including the Adnyamathanha and the Sechelt Peoples. Native discourses can exist in any language: an indigenous language, Standard English spoken as "purely" as is possible, or English spoken with an accent and with grammatical structures and vocabulary that make it differ significantly from Standard English. The validity of the discourse stems, as Urion argues, from the underlying beliefs, attitudes and worldviews of the speakers, and from their moral authority. The problem in translating either from another language into English or in "tidying" up non-Standard English for a Standard English-speaking readership or in having a non-Aboriginal writer or editor is that the validity and authenticity of the Native discourse may be lost in the process. Krupat has pointed out that a recording of the natural speech and speech patterns of a Native speaker may be more important than producing a perfectly correct piece of text.

> the question ... is not whether language appears "good" according to some conventional model of textbook goodness but whether it *works* to good effect, whether it communicates to us, moves us, makes us see. Thus, we have held to our belief that Native American writers should speak *for* themselves while they speak *of* themselves, regardless of whether their speech seems polished and ironic in the (now old!) modernist manner (sometimes it may), or whether instead it seems to adhere to some very different manner that we ignore to our impoverishment.[74]

Likewise, it seemed to me to be best in this case to leave the women's words as much as possible as they were spoken. I will have more to say about this later.

Urion, having described First Nations discourse, went on to give some examples of articles that had appeared in the journal which did not

> claim a uniquely "Indian" facility for the understanding of their arguments, nor a uniquely "Indian" application. They include all of us—all of you—as audience. That is, they deny no-one's integrity; they hold no

---

74 Arnold Krupat, *I Tell You Now: American Indian Lives* (Lincoln: University of Nebraska Press, 1987), xiii-xiv (italics in original).

one culpable; they exclude no one from the discourse. They let us laugh a little. They recognise that learning is a transcendent experience, a kind of play. They reflect First Nations discourse.[75]

The attitude, and indeed worldview, represented in this quotation is, I think, one of the strongest arguments against the exclusionist attitude of those who share Narogin's view.

Jo-ann Archibald, a guest editor for the *Canadian Journal of Native Education*, also encouraged the development of Native discourse(s). In an issue of the journal with the theme "Giving Voice to Our Ancestors," white and First Nations researchers and authors, including Archibald herself, presented the words/teachings of Elders from quite different backgrounds and Bands. They used a variety of ways to present the Elders' teachings, but always aimed to do so "in ways that honour cultural protocols through respectful practices."[76] She noted that each of the speakers and authors had their own

> particular ways of hearing and re-presenting the Ancestors' voices. Their open but careful sharing of stories, research/learning processes, questions, ponderings, anxieties, excitement, and reflections contain an opening for the readers of these texts to join the circle, to join the conversations begun in this journal edition. Our conversations can become one with those who came before and with those yet to come. And this is *Giving Voice to Our Ancestors*.[77]

In a later edition she points out that respect, whether of Ancestors and traditional stories and practices, or "individual differences of opinion, experience, and knowledge" are crucial to the development of Native discourse. And this is not a problem only for white researchers to face. She reiterates one of the First Nations contributor's challenges in "trying to be respectful to his ancestral teachings and meeting the demands of Academe."[78]

Archibald's approach does not preclude the involvement of non-Aboriginals in the development of Native discourse(s), but rather welcomes their participation. This sort of collaboration appears

---

75 Urion, "Changing Academic Discourse," 7.

76 Jo-ann Archibald, "Giving Voice to Our Ancestors," *Canadian Journal of Native Education* 19, 2 (1992): 141.

77 Ibid., 143 (italics in original).

78 Jo-ann Archibald, "Researching with Mutual Respect," *Canadian Journal of Native Education* 20, 2 (1993): 192.

increasingly acceptable, at least to some First Nations individuals and communities in Canada. The very different styles and approaches of publications like Julie Cruikshank's *Life Lived Like a Story* and Freda Ahenakew and H. C. Wolfart's *Our Grandmothers' Lives*, to name just two, demonstrate the crucial requirements for successful collaboration.[79] They all hinge around the respect that Archibald emphasises: respect between interviewer and interviewee, respect for the language in which the women can best express themselves, respect for the stories themselves and for the traditional ways of telling them. With this as a central point, all sorts of other variations can be accommodated.[80] Cruikshank recorded her stories, as I have done, in English. Ahenakew recorded hers in Cree and then, with Wolfart, translated them into English, but the book contains the original Cree in both roman and syllabic orthography as well as the English translation. In their cases, as in mine, every effort was made to render the speaker into print as faithfully as possible.

Yet another approach to developing Native discourse can be found in George Sioui's *For an Amerindian Autohistory*. In this case it is not the language itself that is in question, for it was written in French and translated into English with no use of a First Nations language at all. The authenticity of its discourse in relation to Native peoples arises from the fact that it is written by a Native person in accordance with the values and worldview of his people, "because conventional history has been unable to produce a discourse that respects Amerindians and their perception of themselves and the world, one that would be appropriate to harmonising society."[81] Sioui styles his work "autohistory" because it approaches explanations of the past from the worldview of his people. Like Urion and Archibald, he does not preclude non-Native people from being a part of the project, provided they

---

79 Cruikshank, *Life Lived Like a Story*, and Freda Ahenakew and H. C. Wolfart, *Our Grandmothers' Lives: As Told in Their Own Words* (Saskatoon: Fifth House Publishers, 1992). Cf. Petronella Morel, ed., *Warlpiri Karnta Karnta-Kurlangu Yimi/Warlpiri Women's Voices: Aboriginal Women Speak Out about Their Lives and History/Stories* (Alice Springs, Northern Territory: IAD Press, 1995), for an Australian example.

80 Cf. Simon, *Nga Kura Maori*, in which the language is standard New Zealand English, but the Maori interviewees were schooled in English as were the Maori university research team. The book is no less an indigenous history for being written in English, for both its topic and its creation were uncompromisingly Maori.

81 Sioui, *For an Amerindian Autohistory*, 98.

take the time to develop a sufficient understanding of traditional values and social ethics to be able to do so accurately. His unique contribution is the fact that he uses the sources and methodologies of academic history (his data is culled from seventeenth- and eighteenth-century Euro-American sources) to show how, "through autohistory, a contemporary nation—the Wendat (Huron) nation of Lorette—has discovered ways to defend itself" from the Eurocentric worldview that has been threatening to overwhelm it since first contact.[82] The weakness of the work is that it fails to distinguish any difference between the experiences of specific First Nations groups. It confuses *a* Native discourse with *the* Native discourse.

Developing Native or Aboriginal discourse, then, is not a new project. It is an ongoing process. It can take multiple forms. Indeed it must, because there is a multiplicity of voices whose speech it must convey. Its essential characteristic must always be a grounding in the underlying worldview, moral authority, social ethic, as well as the voices, of indigenous peoples themselves.

Using the Stories

Reliability of the Data

How much faith can one place in the reliability of memory of past times, past feelings, beliefs and perceptions as data for a study of the past, particularly if one accepts that each individual remakes his or her past to some extent with each remembering?[83] The answer, I think, depends on who provides the data, the ways in which it is collected or recorded and what you want to do with it. If one is writing of and from a Western academic point of view, it may be that the criteria and the final product are very different from what they would be if one is writing of and from an Aboriginal point of view.

---

82 Ibid., xxiii.
83 Paul Thompson, *The Voice of the Past: Oral History* (Oxford: Oxford University Press, 1978), chap. 1; Margaret Peters, "Children's Culture and the State: South Australia 1890s-1930s" (unpublished Ph.D. dissertation, University of Adelaide, 1993), 29; Neil Sutherland, "When You Listen to the Winds of Childhood, How Much Can You Believe?' *Curriculum Inquiry* 22, 3 (1992): 235-56; Edward S. Casey, *Remembering: A Phenomenological Study* (Bloomington: Indiana University Press, 1987), 285; and Margaret Blackman, *During My Time: Florence Edenshaw Davidson, a Haida woman*, rev. ed. (Seattle: University of Washington Press, 1991), xi.

But the two are not necessarily incompatible. There is no doubt that Aboriginal culture and experience are appropriate topics for academic study. Difficulties may arise, however, when the discourse is Aboriginal rather than mainstream academic, for then the traditional base of the academic approach may appear to be questioned.

The Western academic tradition in history at least has always set great store by objectivity. The subjective might add colour, but considerable corroborating evidence was always demanded before any "serious" analysis could be made.[84] On top of this, traditional academic authors deliberately placed themselves between their subjects and the data in the interests of further ensuring the objectivity of the final product. In the past decade, both oral and feminist historians have done much to legitimise personal memories as a valuable source for the reconstruction of the past by identifying the necessity of balancing the subjective and the objective, both for interviewer and interviewee, and by emphasising the fact that what may be lost in the "faithful reconstruction of the past" may be gained through a deeper construction of social meaning.[85]

> When talking about their lives, people lie sometimes, forget a lot, exaggerate, become confused, and get things wrong. Yet they *are* revealing truths. These truths don't reveal the past "as it actually was," aspiring to a standard of objectivity. They give us instead the truths of our experiences.[86]

The plurality of truths embodied in life stories directs our attention to the importance of "attending to the conditions which create these narratives, the forms that guide them and the relationships

84 For instance, see Beth M. Robertson, *Oral History Handbook*, 2nd ed. (Adelaide: Oral History Association of Australia [South Australian Branch], 1983), 2, and D. Reimer, ed., *Voices: A Guide To Oral History* (Victoria: BCARS), 1988, 2 and 4.

85 Jean Barman, "'Oh No! It Would Not Be Proper to Discuss That with You': Reflections on Gender and the Experience of Childhood," *Curriculum Inquiry* 24, 2 (1994): 56-57. See also Thompson, *The Voice of the Past*, chaps. 2-3, for a useful discussion of the possibilities of oral history, and Sherna Berger Gluck and Daphne Patai, eds., *Women's Words: The Feminist Practice of Oral History* (New York: Routledge, 1991), 9, for some of the problems that have been addressed.

86 Personal Narratives Group, eds., *Interpreting Women's Lives: Feminist Theory and Personal Narrative* (Bloomington: Indiana University Press, 1989), 261 (italics in original).

that produce them," so that we can understand the meanings of the multiple truths.[87] This is usually not possible if objectivity is a goal, for in seeking a single truth we are deaf to the claims of parallel or alternate truths.

Having made these points, however, I must also say that I believe there is an important difference between the nature of the data gathered from white respondents by white researchers and the data that is obtained from Aboriginal people by those same researchers. In the former situation there is not the cultural gap between interviewer and interviewee that exists in the latter. Even where differences of attitude, values and experience may exist due to class, religious or other differences, there is still a vast pool of cultural commonality. In the latter case, while commonalities may exist they nevertheless stem from a profoundly different base.

Two differences that have been most obvious to me in my interviews with these six women are the influence of the oral nature of their culture and the strength of the collective or group ethos over that of the individual. Their stories differ significantly from those that might be gathered from a similar study in modern urban white society. They show a far greater consistency than one would expect to find with white respondents.[88] The women of each family independently, consistently and unasked, corroborate each other's narratives, not only in matters of fact but in areas related to values and attitudes as well. They report each other's experiences whether factual or attitudinal as they have been told them—not necessarily in the same words but with exceptional accuracy. Traditionally changes could not be allowed to be introduced at the whim of an

---

87 Ibid., 262.
88 Tony Rogers has expanded on the importance of the accuracy of transmission of traditional Australian Aboriginal cultures in "Art and Aboriginal Cultures," *Australian Journal of Art Education* 17, 2 (Autumn 1994): 14-15; cf. Muecke, *Textual Spaces*, 45-46. See also Paul Thompson ("Cultural Transmission between Generations within Families: A Life Story Approach," in *Memory and Multiculturalism*, Proceedings of the VIII International Oral History Conference, Siena-Lucca, February 25-28, 1993, 1145) for a brief discussion of similar clarity and accuracy in family memory in a very different culture. He uses an example from the western Scottish Isles when immigrants left for the United States in the early nineteenth century. Their descendants today tell the story of their departure as vividly as if they had observed it because the stories have been passed down so accurately. This is a Western, not an indigenous, culture, but its oral tradition is obviously still strong.

individual or the entire cultural base might be put at risk, but this
did not mean peoples could not adapt when necessary.[89] A stable
and secure conceptual universe can be remarkably flexible, and this
is evident in many indigenous peoples even when much traditional
knowledge has been lost. The oral tradition, as a part of that conceptual universe, can remain strong.

What these women are recounting are not traditional stories but
their own memories of their childhood and youth. I refer to their
narratives as "stories," for this is what they are insofar as they tell
the tales of the women's lives. But they are not the same as the
stories that formed a part of the traditional Sechelt or Adnyamathanha cultures. Stories in the traditional oral cultures served a number of functions. They were a way of preserving and passing on
knowledge and spiritual beliefs; they showed the people, both
directly and indirectly, how they should live their lives; and they
played a role in everyday social interaction as well as on ceremonial
occasions. The specific forms of storytelling as well as many of the
stories themselves have been lost to varying extents. The Sechelt
women are only now beginning to learn the content of some of their
traditional stories; they certainly do not know the traditional forms.
The Adnyamathanha women know and tell many of their stories
regularly, though not under the same conditions and probably not in
just the same way as their forebears. For both groups the fact that
storytelling was an important part of their traditional culture is an
important factor today, even though they live their lives within
mainstream culture as well as their own and are fully literate. Even
though they may no longer know the old stories or the traditional

---

89 This is particularly so in the case of the Adnyamathanha. One of the few surviving fully initiated men was adamant in an interview that in traditional society any change in the oral traditions would be frowned upon save in exceptional circumstances, and would then only be acceptable if the whole group
agreed. When asked what would happen if an individual made changes without
group approval he said simply, "They wouldn't." The idea of an individual, in
traditional society, insisting on change in the face of group disapproval, was
something he found very hard to understand, even though he could accept it
within both Aboriginal and mainstream contemporary societies (interview
with Les Wilton, November 21, 1992). Whether such strict controls existed in
traditional Sechelt society is not clear, but the custom, amongst West Coast
Bands, of specific families "owning" the right to perform particular songs and
ceremonial dances might strengthen the group responsibility for maintaining
the form unchanged.

forms of storytelling, there appears to be a stronger emphasis on spoken forms than in mainstream society. These women *believe* that the telling of stories is an important part of their heritage and they have come to place a similar importance on the telling of their own personal "stories." This creates a situation of multiplicity of truths that I mentioned earlier. One must be sensitive to the women's beliefs and understandings about stories and storytelling as well as listening to the tales themselves.

In one sense these life stories belong to them quite differently from the way that any of the traditional stories or other oral arte-facts of their culture might belong to them. The ownership is personal and the memories—or at least their significance in the present—are changed by new experiences, considerations or reflections. But this does not alter the importance of the relation-ship between the stories and their owners. To them the telling of a story has more weight than it might have for most people of European background for whom the written word carries far greater importance and significance. While their interpretation of the significance of their experience might change over time, the actual reporting of life experience appears more consistent than that of someone from mainstream society. That is, whenever they talked about a particular incident in their own or one anoth-er's lives, the same basic points were always included. It was not the case that certain points were included or omitted on particu-lar occasions to better suit a particular situation as is the case when I, for instance, recount an anecdote. With these women it was all the story each time or nothing.

The women also tend to report more from the point of view of the group than from a personal point of view, though this tendency is diluted to some extent with each of the three generations. To get Pearl McKenzie to talk about her own personal experience, particu-larly in her childhood, is difficult, for she still has problems separat-ing her own experience as an individual from that of the group with and for whom she lived. This tendency has ramifications that are still important in the present for, despite the development and growth of individual and personal opinions, the Adnyamathanha and the Sechelt Peoples still have collective goals and aspirations and the telling of tales, whether they be the traditional stories or per-sonal individual "stories," is seen as a way of pursuing these collec-tive goals.

A further factor in the consistency of their stories requires comment. Throughout the entire series of stories there is very little evidence of internal contradictions in the belief systems of each woman. However, I do not think this should be taken to indicate that they have no inconsistencies in their worldviews or their positioning of themselves. In fact, the careful reader will detect a number of small inconsistencies. The phenomenon can be partially explained by the fact that the stories, as I have already noted, deal only with some aspects of their lives. These stories were largely chosen by the women themselves and so many are aspects of their lives which they have already considered in greater or lesser depth; all of them, even the youngest, Charlene and Brandi, have been forced, by the fact that they are indigenous women trying to survive in mainstream cultures whilst maintaining a pride in their traditional heritage, to consider their situations, their beliefs and attitudes and their futures in ways that are rarely necessary for members of mainstream societies. Some of these areas have been painful or problematic in the past, but the difficulties have now been resolved; others remain painful and/or problematic, but are perceived by the women as areas in which change or resolution is possible.

Extrapolating from the Individual to the Group

What use can we make of the remembered past of six individual women? Do their own perceptions of their lives have a role to play in assisting others from their own culture(s) and from different cultures to understand and appreciate the broader history of their peoples? Can we make generalisations from the lives of six women from two families in two separate cultures to the numerous groups of Aboriginal peoples in both their countries, groups that are diverse geographically as well as culturally and whose members all have somewhat different individual experiences along with their commonalities? Or do their experiences have no significance beyond themselves? I believe that extrapolation to the wider experience of their own people and to other Aboriginal people is possible, but this process cannot be simply one of making generalisations.

If I could argue that each woman was representative, even in a tenuous way, of her generation and/or her culture, I might justify generalising about an "Aboriginal experience." But none of them is and so I cannot. However, as long as we see each of these women as an individual member rather than as a representative example of her respective generation and culture we can, I believe, extrapolate, make illuminative connections from one generation to another and from one culture to the other. There are certainly patterns that show through in both cultures and families that are significant both in terms of the effects of the imposition of mainstream culture and in the responses of the members of these two families to such imposition. While, as I have said, the families are not intended to be representative of their peoples, neither are they unique. Each woman remembers her life and experience as being similar to that of her peers. While all acknowledge their individuality, they remember their lives as lived amongst their peoples, sharing similar experiences, conditions and aspirations.

So these narratives are not intended to say anything about children as a group, about women as a group, about the Adnyamathanha or the Sechelt as a group, nor even about familial and intergenerational relationships in general. They are simply aspects of the lives of three generations of Adnyamathanha and Sechelt women as they see themselves, each other and the world they live in. Nevertheless, I believe that their stories contain truths and understandings and have significance beyond the boundaries of the lives they live.

A good example of how extrapolation can work is the way in which the women's own understanding of the similar results of colonisation, the similar points of stress in their communities and the similar fragmentation of their cultures developed as the project proceeded. To see such similar results in two different and separate cultures and to observe their effects through the eyes of the dominated cultures is particularly significant.

Assembling the Text

A final consideration is the way in which the data should be presented. Exactly how can it be most usefully conveyed to others? As biography? As autobiography? As history? And whose voice should speak the stories—mine or the women's? All three approaches have been used successfully though not extensively in the last twenty years, particularly to understand or to make understood the Aboriginal experience and women's experience.

The Western academic tradition in the writing of history has largely attempted to interpret and explain the individual only in reference to the whole group, whether that group encompasses an entire society and culture or a specific sub-group within it. This

seemed too impersonal for the very personal accounts the women
had given me of their lives. There has been an accepted place in
Western tradition for the examination of the individual, namely,
through biography and autobiography. But until recently it was
implicit in our understanding that this was a different kind of study
to that of history. For instance, the individual was examined in
these two genres precisely because he or she stood out, or felt he/
she stood out in some way from the group. Moreover, both biography and autobiography have literary as well as historic facets, and
frequently the literary component has been emphasised as much as
the historic.

In the past decade, feminist scholars have emphasised the relationship between biography and history, "approach[ing] women's
lives in ways that are different from those of traditional
biographers."[90] They have "called into question the masculinist
grounds on which biography has conventionally been defined and
accepted," so that now not only are biographies of women far more
numerous, but the women whose lives are now being examined
were not necessarily celebrities in their own times. The importance of ordinary women (or men) as a focus for examining and
understanding their times has been accepted. Barbara Tuchman has
called biography "the prism of history" which encompasses "the
universal in the particular." When the particular becomes female,
the universal can no longer be male."[91] The marginalised, the invisible, now have become central. This has significant implications for
writing the histories of any marginalised groups.

Through exploration of the subjectivities of the women whose
lives they are writing, feminist biographers have also recognised
the value of their own subjective experience.[92] Rather than denying

90 Sara Alpern, Joyce Antler, Elisabeth Israels Perry and Ingrid Winther Scobie,
   eds., *The Challenge of Feminist Biography: Writing the Lives of Modern American Women* (Chicago and Urbana: University of Illinios Press, 1992), 3.
91 Barbara Tuchman, "Biography as a Prism of History," in Marc Pachter, ed.,
   Telling Lives: The Biographer's Art (Philadelphia: University of Pennsylvania
   Press, 1981), 133-47, quoted in Alpern et al., eds., *The Challenge of Feminist
   Biography*, 6.
92 Some feminist theorists prefer to separate these two aspects of subjectivity
   under the headings of "affectedness" and reflexivity. See Mary M. Fonow and
   Judith A. Cook, eds., *Beyond Methodology: Feminist Scholarship as Lived
   Research* (Bloomington: Indiana University Press, 1991), 2-5, 9-11.

their own attachment to their subjects, many have found the process to be one of self-discovery, a way of working through intense personal, intellectual and professional growth, a recognition of the "connection between their [subjects'] lives and the personal, political or ideological issues of our own epoch."[93]

In comparison with the biography, the autobiography has the extra dimension of self-discovery as the writer selects and introspectively considers the significance of particular life experiences—an even stronger emphasis on the subjective. This aspect seemed crucial given the amount of input that the women had into interpretation and analysis of the information they provided about themselves. A biography, no matter how much it tried to explore the subjective, did not seem to go quite far enough.

The autobiographical account of indigenous lives has a long history if we include anthropological and ethnological studies that involve collaboration of a narrator and a recorder/editor. Recent work in the United States has identified a number of strands within the genre. Some scholars are at pains to distinguish between "authentic" Native autobiography identified as originating in an individual, personal desire to recount life history and that which is initiated by a white researcher.[94] Others highlight the collaboration process, stressing the "bicultural composite composition" with its attendant problems of one self being mediated by another from a different culture and in another language.[95] Hertha Dawn Wong has gone further to argue that contemporary Native autobiography is now being used by some writers to "resurrect and redefine tribal oral pasts in Western written forms, creatively adapting the two traditions."[96]

---

93 Alpern et al., *The Challenge of Feminist Biography*, 3.

94 For instance, see Gretchen Bataille and Kathleen Mullen Sands, *American Indian Women: Telling Their Lives* (Lincoln: University of Nebraska Press, 1984), and Anne E. Goldman, "Is That What She Said? The Politics of Collaborative Autobiography," *Cultural Critique* (Fall 1993): 177-204.

95 Refugio Savala, *The Autobiography of a Yaqui Poet*, edited with background and interpretations by Kathleen M. Sands (Tucson: University of Arizona Press, 1980), and Arnold Krupat, *For Those Who Come After* (Berkeley: University of California Press, 1985).

96 Hertha Dawn Wong, *Sending My Heart Back across the Years: Tradition and Innovation in Native American Autobiography* (New York: Oxford University Press, 1992), 10.

I am not sure just where in the spectrum this book fits. Perhaps all that really needs to be said is that, because the women were actively involved in its construction, it is autobiography and, because it spans three generations, it is history. And yet, where it does not fit firmly in the centre, it certainly touches the boundaries of a number of disciplines and a variety of theories as the preceding discussion has indicated. The women themselves are not acquainted with theory and feel no need of it as a tool for understanding the significance of their own lives. As a collaborator with them I have no right and, indeed, no inclination to attempt such analysis. However, the discussion indicates that there are many approaches that might be used by the reader to understand the significance of the women's experiences.

When we began the initial interviewing, there were two loosely formulated questions running in my head regarding the outcome. First, how should the stories be used and, second, what significance would they have both in terms of the history and experience of their individual owners and in terms of the history and experience of the peoples to whom the individuals belonged? Even at that stage one thing was clear to me: we would need to be very careful about the way in which the stories were used or the result would not be considered legitimate by either Aboriginal peoples or by academics. As the process of interviewing, transcribing, correcting, analysing, interpreting and writing unfolded, a further series of questions arose, all of which needed to be worked through before it was possible to proceed to the next step. Moreover, it was not just me who needed to do this. It became increasingly clear that the six women and I must work together to assemble the final product. Therefore we, I and each one of the women, or I and several of the women and, on one marvellous occasion, through the medium of video conferencing, I and five of the six women, met to discuss and analyse the significance of their stories as well as the significance of the experience of sharing them with me and with each other.

What follows—the bulk of the book—are the women's own words. But the way in which they were recorded and have been used requires some further explanation. The first recording with each woman followed a similar pattern. It was structured, though very loosely, on factual data and particular kinds of life experiences, including childhood, schooling and child-raising, which we had already discussed informally. Subsequent interviews, which took place following discussion of the first, were even less structured and allowed the women to both choose the aspects of their lives that they wished to talk about and to do so in their own time and their own way. Once each of the women had begun talking, I tried to stay in the background as much as possible, asking questions or making comments only when the respondent stopped speaking on a particular topic.

With the women of the two older generations particularly, this meant that the recordings are overwhelmingly their own narrations and their own reflections on the significance of their lives. My questions or comments were few. The two women of the youngest generation required more direct questioning and discussion in the course of their narrations, partly perhaps because of their greater distance from the oral traditions of their people but more probably because of their youth. They simply have not lived as long and have not had the time, nor perhaps the inclination, that their older relations have had for reflection on their lives and experiences, and so have less to say. The age difference between them and myself may also have had an effect.

In the telling of their lives all six women follow, to varying extents, patterns identified by scholars of autobiographical theory in life history and autobiographical reminiscences, both of indigenous women and women in general. That is, their ways of telling their lives differ greatly from male autobiographic tradition in both Western and indigenous cultures. Women's narratives tend to be discontinuous, reflecting the nature of their experience. Their tales circle back to repeat themes or to further embroider topics of importance to them.[97] But if they are fragmented in one sense they are also holistic in their emphasis on connections—in the case of indigenous women, connections to other people, to nature and to the land.[98] These three aspects are certainly visible in the stories of these six women.

But I am a part of the stories too, by necessity rather than choice. I appear at several levels. First, I influenced their

---

97 Estelle C. Jelinek, *Women's Autobiography: Essays in Criticism* (Bloomington: Indiana University Press, 1980), 17-19, and Wong, *Sending My Heart Back across the Years*, 7.

98 Cruikshank, *Life Lived Like a Story*, 3, and Bataille and Sands, *American Indian Women*, 3-4.

remembering by asking them to talk about themselves. The stories would not have been publicly told if they had not been asked for. If someone else had asked they would have had a slightly different focus. Nevertheless, I tried to minimise the effects of my presence wherever possible. Then, in order to transfer their words from hours of tapes to paper, I had to act as editor both of the content of their narratives and of the ways in which they were expressed. By this I mean that I could not just reproduce their narratives in toto; they are simply too long. So what follows has to be, to some extent at least, my interpretation of their words and their meanings. The changes I have made, though, are selections rather than alterations. In reproducing the text of the stories I have not included my questions or promptings because so often they had little significance to what followed—the response often took off on a completely different tack. Also, I have used a number of interviews, grouping parts of each together under particular "topics." In such a situation, inclusion of my questions would break up the flow of the text. Portions of the recordings have been omitted because they seemed peripheral or only marginally relevant to the main themes of the women's stories. Some repetition is important though, and parts of two or more sessions have sometimes been placed together because they deal with the same topic or repeat it. Some of the women came back to a topic three or four times in different sessions because it was important to them. Nevertheless, each life history has grown from the structure and patterns that its owner herself gave it as she talked. The interview from which each excerpt is taken is identified in brackets immediately after it finishes, for example, [2:13] where 2 identifies the second interview with that particular woman and 13 the page number of the transcript. Details of the interviews may be found in Appendix 1.

I have tried to carry out my task without imposing myself on the women's stories too much, but it is impossible not to enter the text in some way. I have tried to neutralise or overcome the intrusion of my presence by using their own words as much as possible, for the telling is as significant as the tale.[99] But still, much is lost in the transcription from tape to paper. The *sound* of the women's voices, the ways in which they speak, all add extra meaning to the words. I have tried to reflect this as faithfully as possible in the transcription

---

99 Muecke, *Textual Spaces*, 52-53.

by retaining hesitations, pauses and speech patterns as well as the words actually spoken, even if this makes the reading initially more difficult. The careful reader can see clearly the differences between the women's ways of talking. The Sechelt have a different way of expressing themselves to the Adnyamathanha; each generation speaks slightly differently to the other generations. Each individual woman speaks slightly differently at different times or when dealing with different subjects. The earliest interviews, before the women felt fully at ease with me or with the topics they were discussing, contain more hesitations, more stops and starts and more meaningless joining words. Topics that the women found harder to discuss or express are also indicated by changes in their patterns of speech. Therefore it seemed crucial to include them.

Muecke has noted the dilemma a non-Aboriginal editor faces in trying to choose between "a written text which is more like performed speech—narratives as they are told" and an ethnographic text which, while it may produce a lot of information about traditional society, "has nothing in common with the Aboriginal modes of verbal performance."[100] I am not quite certain where between the two the following text would fall. I am not attempting to reproduce faithfully a traditional "verbal performance," but rather to render the women's narratives into written text without consciously or unconsciously translating them into "correct" English as tends to happen when any speech, Aboriginal or not, is written down. Muecke is not alone in his preference for doing away with all standard punctuation and instead using "breath groups" to punctuate the narrative, each breath group being started on a new line with dashes or a blank line indicating longer pauses or changes of topic. This is an accepted convention. But Cruikshank points out that as a written style it is "better suited to poetry and to traditional narrative than to discussions of experience."[101] I have used fairly standard punctuation with the addition of several indicators to distinguish pauses of different length. Thus the period (.) and the comma (,) are used as in standard English. For a brief pause of about a second a dash is used (–), for a pause of two seconds two dashes (––) and for a pause of three to five seconds a series of four to six dots is used (......). A pause longer than five seconds is indicated by the

---

100 Ibid., 42.
101 Cruikshank, *Life Lived Like a Story*, 18.

bracketed words [long pause] or even [very long pause]. Paragraphs are not used at all.

All six women have read what has been written and made comments and changes where they considered it necessary. The result is something that we have agreed upon and discussed singly and as a group. But it is certainly not a form that comes direct and unaltered from the traditions or practices of either the Adnyamathanha or the Sechelt People. Neither is it "traditional" history or any other traditional discipline in the Western academic field. None of us is completely happy with it as it stands, but we believe that we have successfully dealt with the challenge of finding one out of many possible ways of using the data so that it is acceptable and useful to both indigenous peoples and academe.

PEARL McKENZIE

Pearl McKenzie was born sometime in June 1922 at Burr Well Station, the daughter of Henry and May Wilton.

I was born at, er, Burr Well Station, or what used to be Burr Well. Then it turned, er, a different name then, Depot Springs Station, but it isn't no more – any ...... stations or any there now. But main station they've got at Patsy Springs. It's on main road to Arkaroola. Ah, then, I was born at Burr Well and, er in the year 1922, and er, apart from there and we used to roam around, you know ...... But, er, I do remember that I grew up at Ram Paddock Gate. That's just past, um, er ...... Patsy Springs. You'll see a ruins there, what Aborigine used to built out of, you know, stone and mud and water. And there used to be a soak, just what we used to drink, and er, that soak is still there. And er, at one stage they put a windmill there, when we all moved that way – to Nepabunna in later years, they put a windmill but they already taken that down now, but you still can see the water just from the road on the surface. And, er, I grew up there. [3:1]

She was the second of nine children, three boys and six girls.

Well, er, I'm their second child. I had another older brother and, um, ... five from there – I had two more brothers. Well, two was ...... Well, one actually was born, I was married and gone. In 1940 ...... 45, I think, and I never even saw him. He got this cold and er, Mum and Dad sort of brought him. There was no doctor. Well, doctor used to go up from here. And when he met them half way at Puttapa Siding there, you know, they was bringing him down to er, Beltana. That's where used to be only nursing place. So, but he died before they even met the doctor on the road. Yeah. [3:4]

The children were all born in the traditional manner in a creek bed.

... out in the open. Yeah, the creek down some way. And er, I remember Mum having another baby, ... at Ram Paddock, and out from the house in the creek. Only the womenfolks would be there, and even the father wasn't allowed to look at the baby until it's a week old. ... Until the mother goes back you know. ... And, er, 'cause father used to go and see them. My Dad used to go and, er, take water and that, you know, but, er, you had a woman was looking after her at that, you know, and keeping her company. It was not far from the house. Yeah, it'd be as far as from here to the corner I suppose, like our building was. Mightn't be as far as that. And tell him, because she come in here on account of the rain, and Dad not supposed to see the baby. But, ah, one of the younger sisters showed it to him. Was pleased about the baby sister. Yeah. [1:27]

Yeah, even the youngest – was born in '45 – he was born. And funny thing, in those days father never used to see the child. And they were two or three days old, might have been a week old. But nowadays the father he's even seeing it being born, but you know, that wasn't allowed. Only the womenfolks. ... Well, like the father used to go and carry wood. They used to ...... have an open camp break or something like that you know, and carry some, you know, get some wood and water for the womenfolks. And there used to be a lot of women there, you know, taking care of the baby and er, until they old enough to bring back into the camp before the father sees it. So that wasn't allowed, for father to see the baby until he's .... I don't know, I can't tell you for what reason. [3:4,5]

But young children of both sexes were allowed.

Oh yes, any children used to be always there. But nowadays now father – which I don't really agree on that. You know, nowadays father's right there seeing the baby born. But my husband didn't come to see. They were all born in this hospital, five of them. So I wouldn't have ...... I don't think I'd like him coming and seeing the babies born. [3:5]

Traditional ways of childbirth were still important to many Adnya-mathanha women at this time for skills at childbirth were an integral part of their female culture.[1]

Really, our rule would never really ah – . [long pause] What do I say? That the women never had a ...... like secret rules what the mens had. The only things that they really knew about is er, child bearing. That's all the women sacred part was – in our day. But now nothing ever concern – . Up that way [gestures to the north] I think they sort of have their own rule, dancing and that, but uh, we never had that. Early days they could have, but we never was passed on that, you know. [2:4]

For many Adnyamathanha women, even years later, there was little alternative to traditional childbirth if they were far from white medical assistance. At Nepabunna there was a sufficiently large population for the traditional midwifery skills to be passed on. But all Pearl's five children, from the first in 1947, would be born at the Hawker hospital because there were no Adnyamathanha women to assist her where she and her husband were living.

... my older one, he was born in 1947 and I came down from Wer-taloona ...... to have him here. And we moved down when Ivan was er, about er, four months old. We moved down to Martin's Well and that's where my husband worked in there. Because er, Pauline came along and I just came in here for Pauline to be born. I lost

---

1 Birth practices could be, but were not necessarily, similar amongst sep-arated peoples. See Bell, *Ngarrindjeri Wurruwarrin*, 258-59.

another one between Pauline and then my youngest boy, Clive. So there was all five of them was born here. ... Because there wasn't many womens around ...... see. Before, the women had to know how to deliver. Like now, I wouldn't know how to deliver a baby because they was all delivered by the ...... nurses, yeah. [3:4,5]

Pearl had great respect for and confidence in the traditional midwives, but nevertheless she chose to make the long journey to Hawker for all the births rather than an even longer trip to Nepabunna.

My mother was a really good midwife, you know, and some others, you know. But I rather came down here I thought. [3:6]

As Pearl grew up her life continued to be very close in many ways to a traditional one, despite the increasing influence of Udnyu ways. Housing, for instance, was a mixture of the traditional shelter and a basic Udnyu cottage made from castoffs.

It was only made out of tin shanty, and the outside part was clean and we had a bush – ah, broom. You know, we used to go out miles to get those, and then carry them back, you know, and tie the bushes together and then make a broom and then we used to clean up. And even we used to use that inside. We never had a decent broom to sweep up inside. [1:26]

The tin came from kerosene cans usually, though occasionally larger sheets of galvanised iron could be obtained.

Kerosene tin. Something like that [indicates size] and it was open, square, you know. ... Cut them, yeah, and the two ends and um, on the sides, and flatten them out. That's what they used to use for roofing. And, er, Dad used to – . Once I think he got it from the missionary, I think. They had about twelve sheets of galvanised. That's all for one room, but the outside wall was what you called, um pug house, you know, timbers. And they'd fill, er, the holes with a piece of rag and this mud. And, er, the rest of the two room was, er, just kerosene tins. [1:27]

This was at Nepabunna, but the housing at Ram Paddock Gate had been much the same.

Oh, we had a similar. Like made out of stone and mud, you know – two room. And the bags, those wheat bags. And he used to get a flour – . Out of those big – flour bags, you know and, er, cut those in strips and make a sort of "widla," they used to always call it like, and put it up as a tent. [1:27]

The missionary church was constructed in a similar manner.

Yes, well, first of all we had a brush shed the menfolks built, you know. No top to it, just the side walls, you know. And we done our bit of education there, you know. ... Yes, they used it for school. No chair or anything, you know, just wheat bags cut out and we used to sit on the ground like that, you know. Even we used to go to church and sit on a wheat bag, you know, as a mat. [3:6,7]

While the family never moved outside of their traditional lands, within them they moved around frequently, depending on jobs that her father could get and where other relations were living.

We was, you know, going around from station to station. My Dad used to do a bit of anything, or a few crutching and so forth.[2] We all landed back at Ram Paddock Gate, and that's why we – . I don't remember going there but I remember growing up there. ... Then we moved on to Nepabunna. We was there a long time. [1:21]

And I always says our fathers' generation they was more clever in doing things than the ones that are around now, had a good education. And they just learnt by working it out on the station. And they used to do anything. Fix up buggies, you know, and put in new spokes to the wheels and do all sorts. And if, and if, you know, a wheel used to have a tyre round, it was iron tyre. Well, if they want to cut it they'll burn it, you see, until it's red hot and cut it off with some chisel. And burn them again and weld them together. No welding machine, just hammer it down together. So as I say they used to be very .... No education .... I mean more or less in my father's generation, but older ...... Their father used to be really good horsemens you know. Could break in horses, and things like that, and do – . If they were given a contract to do, they'd finish it, you know. Because that's what I'd like to put down too one day. Like there's a boundary fence between Nepabunna and Angipena run. You know, it is called Boundary Gate. And an old chap, one of the Coulthards, name of Ted Coulthard, you know. And hardly any jobs around but he had all the Adnyamathanha people there working for him, and he was really .... You know, way back in the old days, and he had everyone working from Mt Serle ...... and they done the fencing at Boundary Gate right across to Mt Lyndhurst Corner.

---

2 Crutching is the removal of soiled wool from around a sheep's tail to prevent the animal becoming fly-blown.

That was in 1924, and I couldn't remember that time. But after that I think we must have all moved back to Ram Paddock and just where I grew up then from that time onwards. [3:7]

Food gathering occupied Pearl and the other young girls for quite long periods.

So most of the time we used to just roam around, you know, setting rabbit traps or picking wild peaches, wild pears and that, you know. [1:21]

Well. [pause] You know, we used to be told, ... you know, to respect the elders and, er, not to go out late, which we really didn't want to do that. So we was kept under, you know, close. And we was scared, not like just nowadays. You know girls, they go anywhere, the younger ones you know, roaming the street, but we never used to do that. We were sort of scared, you know, and we used to always ...... be with Mother and Father, yeah. And if there was a group of girls, we used to go out say, getting wild pears or food and stuff, you know. Or a broomstick too, – come back and clean that. Womens had that rule outside. Clean the place up. But it's always in groups. [2:5]

Boys largely worked and played separately.

No, never with boys – they were separate. Yeah, boys go their way and – only the boys. But we used to mix up a bit. And my brother, you know, used to take us out looking for donkeys and that, and he was only the one. So not with any others. Oh might be cousin, but very close cousin. ... Oh, yeah. So not the other moiety, you know.[3] [2:5]

Pearl did not remember food gathering as being a job that was required of her; it was simply a part of life. And even if it was expected, the enjoyment that it generated is the strongest part of the memory, and that pleasure remained with her.

---

3 Adnyamathanha society was composed of two moieties, "Matari" and "Arraru," which were passed down through the mother. Marriage could only take place between persons of opposite moiety. There were a number of restrictions about interaction between persons of opposite moiety and also obligations between those of the same moiety. See Colin Bourke and Bill Edwards ("Family and Kin," in Colin Bourke, Eleanor Bourke and Bill Edwards, eds., *Aboriginal Australia* [St Lucia, Qld: University of Queensland Press, 1994], passim) for a clear overview of the structure of Aboriginal relationships.

Yeah, it was more fun you know. I know we'd love to go out and ......
to hunt for bush tucker.[4] I still loves it today, ... I still love to eat
those wild tuckers you know. ... we used to take it home. Oh yeah
.... We never used to eat it out in the paddock. We had to get it
and take it home. ... For the whole family, yeah. ... well, we wanted
to do it. We had to take some back home you see. ... Oh, I suppose I
might have been ...... thirteen might be, or fourteen, fifteen, like
that. ... I would have been about seven, I suppose, when we used to
be out at Ram Paddock. Because we used to, 'cause it was the
Depression time. No wild bush tuckers were around. We used to go
where we could dig up this root from wild pears and really ...... you
know. Because all your bush and leaves would be dropping off. Can't
get any bush tucker. Yeah. [1:24] ... you cook that in the ashes. And
sometimes you can eat it raw. But if you eat it raw too much you get a
headache. The main thing is to live on that.[5] [4:1]

The girls also helped with other domestic tasks.

Oh, we used to do a lot of those. Like we used to go out and, ah,
get wood, get water. And sometime we used to all go, all family
you know. And Dad would be cutting up a mulga tree or something like that. And one things we used to do, climb up the – . You
been up Nepabunna Gorge? Along the side of the hill there's a
really hard wood, you know, dead, finish. We used to take them
down on to the creek bed and Dad'd be down there, you know,
with an axe, and chop some up in little bits. And, er, what we used
to do – it was me and Aunty Gertie and her sister and my two sisters – we'd be climbing and tipping these dry woods down and
Dad'd be at the bottom. And even Aunty Gertie's mother, she was
old, but yet she used to carry firewood back, you know. What we
used to do, like a piece of sugar bag, you know, the same thing.
Well, cut him out like square, then tie ...... cross it, like that, and
put the woods there and pull it up like that and put on our back
[demonstrates]. ...Yeah, chuck it over the shoulder. But sometime
we used to just put a knot like this [demonstrates] and just carry
it on the shoulder. ...Yeah, even little children used to help. So we

---

4 "Bush tucker" is a general term, used throughout Australia for food that may
be caught or gathered in the wild. In other words, traditional Aboriginal food.
5 The Depression years coincided with a series of poor seasons in the Adnyamathanha lands so there was less than normal bush tucker to supplement the
increasingly hard to obtain non-traditional food.

used to, apart from that, we used to get water – from the creek, you know. [1:25]

Work and pleasure were frequently very closely tied together.

... they used to have two buckets. You know, two, on each side of the windlass we used to put them. One'd go down and one bucket will come up with water. And there used to be a landing trough if we wanted to water our donkeys. And they watered the donkeys. One bucket would be down, you see. When you put the other one down, the other comes up. Oh, it was really fun. [3:7]

Ceremonial activities also combined enjoyment with their more serious cultural and spiritual elements. In Pearl's childhood they were still an important part of Adnyamathanha life.

They used to have ah, ceremonies there. And er, I always tell anyone this story. And er, they used to have ah, sort of two ceremonies. The first one is when they put the boys through in the first stage and they call this "vadnapa" you know, the first stage, initiation. And the second one, er, is "wilaru," and wilaru really goes right back, er. It (vadnapa) really started from ...... er, Wilpena Pound, and it's in history but they kept that going, you see, and they used to always say it started from there, from Wilpena. And vadnapa, you know, it was really fun for everyone. It more or less er, like a sports day for us girls too, doing little odd jobs and you know. The part that we used to take part used to be a big camp. Everyone used to move out from the main camp to a certain area around, you know. Stay there all day, ... and a night and, er till next morning when they ...... finished and we all moved back to our usual camp. That's the first stage. [3:1]

Boys would be young teenagers when vadnapa took place. Wilaru would follow a couple of years after.

Oh in their teenages I suppose, yeah. That's the first lesson. And the second lesson is very ...... More or less w ...... We used to take part in bits and pieces but, ah mens, all the mens, go out into the gully and er, stayed there all day and all night till next morning – they come in. All the mothers sort of paint up. You know, they only wearing a skirt and they paint themselves black and cocky feather on their forehead ...... was stuck on. ...... And they dig a little hole where the fire is, and we used to take part in, you know, going around in between the mother. The two mothers sitting here and the father'd be here. [indicates] Just a little .... That's the plum bush, Pauline was talking about. The leaves that they used to sort of put down there and it really hot coal, but used to love to ...... breathe the steam, you know. And when the boys, newly man, come in and they sort of kneeled down to take a sniff of that, and they each got a mate there to hold him up. And then, and that'd be finished and he's out in the bush now for a couple of weeks until ...... after a while he comes in again, you know, with his father (who had been with him while he was out in the bush) and, er, really painted up (with red, black and white stripes and spots). We used to call it like, "wilaru mulka," all really done up flash you know. Still wearing a cocky feather. And then anyhow they .... And he got everything. You know, what he's supposed to taught and how to behave and all that sort of thing. And that'd be finished and he'll go out for work – it's finished. [3:1,2][6]

Yeah, and of course missionaries came there but didn't really stopped us from ah, doing our ceremonies. They used to put a lot of boys through at Nepabunna. The last five went through in 19 .... 40 .... 8, 49. The last mulkalpu (young man before initiation) dance. No wilaru, but my husband was that last wilaru man that went through in 1939. And, you know, sort of we still carried that on until 1949. It was completely ...... The two bosses closed it because they know the people was, you know, ... going more on the ...... European ways. And the two bosses were ...... One was my father – he was the second leader – and er, my father-in-law, old Fred McKenzie. [3:3]

---

6 As she listened to me rereading this to her, Pearl said, "Oh, but I didn't include much detail about what we actually did. There was so much." Some of the extra detail I add here:

During the night of the "vadnapa" ceremony, firesticks would be thrown up into the air to make a display like rockets. Pearl remembers the excitement of this very clearly. In the "wilaru" ceremony, when the initiates returned to the main camp, the women of the opposite moiety would dab red ochre onto their elbows, knees, forehead and back to give them strength. The women were also involved in cooking the feast that took place several days to a week after the ceremony. Women of both moieties did this, but those of the same moiety as the initiate had to provide more food. But much of the "wilaru" ceremony, even parts that took place in the main camp, women were not allowed to see. For instance, when the initiates returned to the main camp they were accompanied by three men, the kingfisher man, the man who put the shell around the boys' necks (a sign of their initiation) and a man who carried a long pole with brush on top. A dance followed, but the women had to go and hide themselves so as not to observe.

The ongoing group activities were learning situations. Like her peers, Pearl would watch until she was ready to try for herself. Some skills, like weaving rugs from strips of kangaroo hide, she never felt the need to try for herself, though she is sure she could do it if she wished.

Ahh. Know, know how to make it, but ah, my mother made it. But I think, you know, that I can make but didn't have much trouble – no, didn't get around to doing it. Yeah, every time I'd er, skin a roo (kangaroo) and, you know, when they used to peg it out, well, I used to cut up the strips and that, but I never got around doing anything, yeah. ... Just peg them up, out on the ground. ... Until they dry, yeah, and ah, when you take them up you cut some into squares and ah, make a sort of pattern. You scrape them with a knife first until you take er, the top er, layer of skin. Then when it peels off easy, then its, then its skin itself will be soft where you can make little squares, you know, pattern. ... Oh yeah. ... Just keep on, you know – making a pattern of it then, you know, after you've laid – pegged a layer of the skin – and keep folding it. And then – and usually the pattern of squares – . You know, keep scraping it with the pocket knife. You'd fold the skin like this [demonstrates] and a pocket knife, you know, and you'd just make it. ... That's what you – got to make it soft, otherwise it's – . If you don't do that around the skin it ...... will be hard to – . ... Yeah. And you put them together then, you know, and make a big rug of it.... nowadays we use [pause] those big threads, you know. But in the earlier days they used to use sinew to sew it on. ... Kangaroo tail, yeah. ... Oh, like used to – they used a special bone from the – . What do you call this? [pause] Narrow – you know narrow part. Well, you scrape that out and make a sharp point of it, and that's what they used to use for needle, you know. Poke it through like this [demonstrates] and when you sew them together, well, the hole's already made on both skins, and just, you know, thread it with them then. Yeah. [1:1-3]

Other skills, like carving emu eggs, she utilised years after.

... I just, you know, thought that up myself. But I saw a chap doing it years ago when I was a kid, you know. ... At Nepabunna. We used to play around and this old chap, he used to sit around, you know, doing emu egg. And he used to put er, a bucking horse or a eagle or something like that, yeah. But ah, I never ...... take to it then until ...... in '40 ...... '46, I think, when I – when we was out at Frome.[7]

---

7 Frome Downs Station.

'Cause I had nothing to do, no children. 'Cause my husband used to go out track riding all day and I thought I'd do something, so I made these emu egg – you know, carved it out. But the toughest part is to take the top layer off, you know, with a pocket knife. ... Yeah, dark green. You've got to make a pattern on top on both sides, and er, scrape that with a pocket knife until you, you know, take it all off, then keep on doing it until you come to a really fine layer of light green. Then sort of put a drawing there then, you know, whatever – kangaroo or an emu.[8] That's about all I used to always do, kangaroo or an emu – that was my sort of favourites. And then people always say, "Why put an emu," you know, "on that drawing?" And I said, "Well, that the egg belonged to the emu." [laughs] So why not, if it's going to be, you know, be there? [1:5,6]

Domestic skills were learned by watching too.

Well, we used to always be around her (Mum) when she used to ...... Especially when she's um, patching up old jeans or anything like that. I remember at Ram Paddock to do ...... We never had no material, you know, dress material. What they used to do, cut off a ...... in those days they used to be called dungarees – now it's all jeans. And sew them as a skirt and put a top to it, you know. That was really good. [3:12]

Pearl used the same method to pass her skills on to her daughter, Pauline, and granddaughters.

Ah, I think she just picked it up. To see what I'm doing, same as I did. But they all can cook. Pauline really, you know, make anything, and so's the two daughters (Pauline's first two daughters, Charlene and Kerri). But with me I just all hand makers. You know, sometimes I use a cup. If I want to mix a scone or anything I don't use a proper measure. I just use my hand or something like that. And even Pauline, er Charlene, always loved me doing this apricot pudding. Oh, she loved that. She's starting to make it now and she reckons mine's are still good. I guess ...... You know, my own measurement because I saw Mum, or my sister-in-law doing it. No

---

8 The final product is a picture with the detail in white surrounded by a background of light green, sometimes several shades of this, depending on how much is removed in different places, set on the dark background of the outer shell. The inside white layer is paper thin and requires very careful working or else the knife will pierce it and make a hole, ruining the whole work.

measuring of cup or anything you know. Mix it by hand, hand measure. Or sometime I'd use a cup. It turns out just as good. So, ... I don't think I had a really hard trouble with learning Pauline to cook. I think when you're interesting enough you pick it up yourself. Yeah, that's how I feel. Yeah, but sewing she don't like – sewing. But when my mother used to sew we used to be always there. And even the washing. When she used to wash, you know. And we used to wash by hand and we used to use a copper. Like an open bucket. Used to boil whatever we need to be boiled. And no powders, only soap. And we used to chuck in this ...... boil this piece of soaps and that – cut up some soap – let it boil, you know. And we used to do that. And many a times if Mum had been washing, I used to go down with my sisters you know and I used to do a lot of washing – two or three tub full – and boil them in a bucket. We used to sit down with Mum, you know. Patch a trouser or anything like that. We used to love watching her sew. [3:12]

Yura and the Udnyu ways were combined in the family's lifestyle, though the older ways seemed always to dominate. Discipline of children was traditionally the responsibility of the maternal uncle, the mother's brother, but Pearl's mother took authority too and used it, though her father rarely did. "He was a wee bit softie," she recalls.

... you've been, you know, naughty with your swear or something like that, you know. Wouldn't do anything for your mother or something like that, the uncle's always the one that disciplined the children. Even girls too ... . But they had authority. Anytime you couldn't argue with your parent if they around and you'll get a clip under the earhole. You know the uncle's the one that had control. [3:3]

Yeah. Yeah, he was the one that sort of ...... disciplined the sister's children. Yeah, he's got the right. Yeah, when talking to, like nieces and nephews – he's got the right. And like – another step down. Like, ah, he'd be a great uncle then. Well, he'd got the right to discipline those too, yeah. [2:2,3]

Pearl remembers her parents with affection, as much for their relationship with each other as for their relationship with her.

I had beautiful parents ... . I never see a couple like that nowadays. Yes, they was really good mother and father. ... Yes, they were close, doing everything. I tell everybody this. What they want to do, they both do it. Yes, when all working out, cleaning up, getting water, they'd both do it. [2:6]

... other parents ... used to have arguments, my Mum and Dad never used to have them. They could have argument when I'm not there, but as far as I can remember they never fought against each other while we were around. ... But that's why I always says, my parents never ever had an argument. Yes, well, that's why I think I had good parents, yes. [2:24-25]

Her own parents had had their marriage arranged for them in more or less the traditional manner.

And they more or less had that when Mum was grown up. Before her mother died [pause] she told them, my other grandmother, "When this," you know, "girl grows up, she got to marry, that – Dad." So she knew that and Dad knew that they was marked. ... Yes, when they was quite young. In fact they just could grow up never to learn about any other boys and girls and when the time was right, you know, their uncles asked and if they want to marry, then just married them. [2:5,6]

Even this was a change from the original process of choosing marriage partners, which took place as soon as the girl was born.

They usually picks them when the girls are born, and say, ask the boy, "Are you willing to call this girl, you know – girlfriend?" They say, "Yes," and um, sometime, some would say, "No," and they'd leave it at that. But from that day on, then we used to know. Oh, we used to call, like a husband. You know, not to mean to, you know, go around you know, having sex with them. No, nothing like that at all. What it really means to become like man and wife, that man could go and sit down, or she could sit down with that man, you know --. [4:14]

In other words, the boy and girl, knowing that they would one day be married, had the opportunity to see much more of each other and to develop an intimacy that was not allowed with any other of their peers of the opposite sex.

Yeah, and then not only getting married, but they can still have, for the boyfriend, but you can have – girls could have boy, and boys could have girl with you, but when you don't call them like that, boyfriends, you're not allowed to. If you happen to er, fall in love with that man that you didn't call boyfriend, well, that means "pulling a star." "Vudli uru-matu," that's what er, it means, pulling a star down. But er, when they was asked when they was quite small. ... When the child, girl, is born, and the girl's got to be younger than the man. The man's got to be always older. ... I don't know why. So he can set the rules down, I suppose. [4:14,15]

In 1929 when Pearl was about seven, missionaries came to Ram Paddock Gate where a large group of Adnyamathanha were camped. She remembers them kindly for the physical help they gave to her people.

Well, I give em, I thank them, because when, they come it was the middle of the Depression. I mean we would have perhaps died out of starvation. Well, Mrs White (wife of the owner of Burr Well Station) is the one that sort of kept us going. Well, there were few (walking) sticks, and Dad and them used to (make a) boomerang, a shield or something like that and take it down to White's at Burr Well and she'd exchange it for ration. So that's how it sort of kept us going. It was only through that station. ... Yeah, and oh, we used to go out and get, er, wild pear root, you know, digging that up and eating. And they're waiting for, they used to go down with a horse buggy and they're taking those (carved walking) sticks and selling them, or exchange it for ration. And we was working around, digging up these roots, yes. But, you know, really feeling that I wasn't really .... You know .... Dying or starvation or something like that, you know. ... Yeah. I think she might have been the one that sort of reported to the government we need a missionary up there, you see, to feed the people. Like all the people was round the day you could get a bit of ration at Angipena. You know the elder ones would. The younger ones never used to get it see. And a few odd jobs, they used call up on the station you know, but the hard times, everything was .... Work was hard to get. A bit of crutching and something like that.

Some Adnyamathanha, particularly those in the generation after Pearl, have little good to say of the missionaries. They accuse them of making too many rules, breaking families up, refusing to let people visit Nepabunna and preventing children from speaking their language. This seems very much dependent on who the missionaries were. Those who arrived when Pearl was a girl seem to have had a different attitude and therefore a different approach to those who came after.

Nah, I don't think .... I don't. I don't agree with that, yeah. Yeah, I thank the missionaries coming out there and er, ... And there are a lot of ways I can look at things. [2:7,8]

As a child, Pearl attended the missionary church with her family. Her parents had had brief contact with a missionary in their own childhood and from him they had learned some hymns.

I used to love singing. Still do, but the voice is not there now. ...
And er, funny thing, when we used to learn chorus, or hymns, without the book. We used to memorise them – some of the old hymns
that I can sing, without a book. ... There was a missionary came
long time ago when Mum and Dad was, you know, young – quite
small. ... a fellow name of Cramer. He's the one that sort of taught
them Christianity ... And er, hymns and that Mum and Dad used to
sing to us. [4:4]

*Singing, both hymns and traditional songs, was something the whole
family enjoyed.*

Oh they had lots of them (traditional songs) but I couldn't pick it
up. I tried, but I couldn't .... sing that .... it's very hard .... My
mother and father was, my Dad was a good singer .... any songs
there they used to sing, you know. ... When we was at Nepabunna
too, Mum and Dad used to – you know, laying in bed or we'd sit
around and they'd sing us a song, you know. ... Some of the songs
are really good. Dad tried to — . Well, we tried to learn, but I, I
couldn't. [4:5]

*Pearl is a committed and active Christian. She was baptised into the
United Church some nine years ago, although her belief has been
growing throughout her life.*

... when I got married I always er, have a Bible in – in my bed, you
know. Most of the time my husband used to go out (working), I'd be
reading it. Yeah, from the beginning, the Bible ... And er, I got lost
in a bit of the way there somewhere, because we start to move
around. But when you staying right, you know, one place, nothing
else to do .... you do nothing else but reading. Although I — wasn't
much of a reader, I only went to .... grade two. But I know, I picked
it up myself .... which is good – I wish I had a better education –
nowadays. [4:7]

*While Pearl and John were living out on stations, church attendance
was not possible. Even when they moved into Hawker later on, Pearl
did not attend regularly, but with her children grown and off her hands
she made the decision.*

I thought, "Oh, this no good," you know, "I'll just .... accept the
Lord you know, dedicate my life to the Lord and follow the church,"
which I did – get back to the Lord. ... Then er, after that there was
......, you know. I used to be regular church attendance and that. And
they made me a Counsellor, and now I'm an Elder, so I mightn't be

for long now. Well, next Sunday will tell. We're going to have a meeting. Yeah, I'm telling them, not that I don't like it, but it's the, the sickness and that, you know. [4:9]

Pearl had been diabetic for years and had just recently been diagnosed with liver cancer.

Sometime I goes around, go to Adelaide, you know, and I miss out on the meetings and that. The sickness really put me back a lot. So when I did step back to the Lord and [pause] – – . And he (her husband John) change his mind too – he come along to the church. ... And then, you know, I praised the Lord for that. [4:10]

Increasingly with age she saw strong connections between Christianity and traditional Adnyamathanha beliefs.

I think ...... that our, – our Dreaming time and the Christianity is very much the same, yeah. 'Cause I tell this to ministers in my church group now. One thing about our spiritual belief. All belief we got from the spirit in the olden days and that is (what) Christianity is now today, yeah. Your, – help they used to get (from) witch doctors and that (was) through the spiritual, you know, and they had a name for heaven. So it really ties in with our culture, the Christianity. But never the way they taught us when the missionary came. But our way lead to heaven and we already knew. 'Cause in our old way we've got, in Aboriginal name he (the way to heaven) is, "Wikurutana." "Wikuru" is "narrow," you know. And they're all good people you know. They go there. But ones that's really bad on – , you know, cruel and doesn't ...... worship um, the Lord, you know, in the right manner, they stays here. ... On earth here, yeah. But the good ones, they go. ... Our heaven is "kindara."[9]

And in our culture we knew there was God because we had a name for God in our culture. You know, he's "Undakarra," our God. And we knew the teaching that we really had. ... And from three days we was told ...... you know, when the person dies, after three days he rises. And er, you know they'd bury him, bury the body, and at this plum bush comes in again, be placed on the body and whatever rug he's been – the person's been wrapped up – after three days you'll see that he's er, out from the grave. It'll be a little hole – that's where the spirit rises. And from, and westerly side there'll be cold

---

9 Literally, "a place where spirits go."

southerly wind, north south breeze'll be blowing with a little show-er of rain. It'll be bitter cold and you'll see a little cloud floating. Well, that's the person – the spirit's baptising him and taking him home. That was our belief. And, you know, we had a spiritual belief. And all the doctoring they had, a witch doctor, it was through the spirit and not from anywhere else. But, you know, it was really belief that we had. That's our Christianity. [3:6]

But beyond their religious teaching Pearl saw the missionaries as hav-ing little effect on the people's lives at that time.

Oh nothing particular different. Because er, all they taught us about was the Lord, you know, Jesus, but we already knew about that.

However, the combined effect of the missionaries and the rest of main-stream culture have had a profound effect, over the course of Pearl's lifetime, on the younger members of the group.

Now, like we are now, younger generation don't believe in any of those, either white Christianity or our way of Christianity. But ours and – the Christian, European ways – similar to ours. So they've lost everything now. They don't believe in anything, which is sad. It's what I always tells people around here – even I tell the minister – and they can see that we are sort of a spiritual people. [3:6]

Not only did the missionaries support the Adnyamathanha with food throughout the Depression, but they were also a source of extra money for those like Pearl's father who were desperate to maintain their self-respect by earning for themselves. They acted as agents for craft work.

Well, er, useful ...... sell it too you know. Well, Mr Eaton (the mis-sionary) – he isn't there now – '38, '37, that's all Dad used to do. Well, sometime he'd go out get odd jobs crutching now and again, but in '37, '38 he never done anything, only boomerang, walking stick and shield, well, the missionaries was buying that. Umm, I don't know how much .... He used to sell it for – five shilling a boomerang I think, that's all. ... And sometime he'd get exchange for ration, extra ration. 'Cause we was on government ration, so whatever extra Dad wanted then, you know jam, potato or some-thing like that, he would make some sticks. A lot of these artefacts went over to, – Eaton used to send it over England. ... Yeah. And one boomerang's still in museum there (in Adelaide). ... When I saw it at the museum a few years back, and I said to the museum, "I wouldn't mind, you know, buying this back." "No," he said, "I think it would be better for you to leave it here." I still like to have that boomerang back. And I should have remembered one other thing, a shield, yeah. ... Well, it kept us going – ration you know. And those days was very cheap living, you know. ... The missionaries used to give him order and he used to go out, and walk out mind you, and out in the paddock he'd be cutting mulga trees and, um, take the rough part away and shave them and bring it home with a sugar bag then, about a dozen at a time. And he'd be working at home then, you know, rasping them and putting the sandpaper and all that then. [2:18,19]

Pearl attended the missionary school, but this was only held sporadically.

We had a bit of schooling, but I never had that much education because missionaries used to have us in school about a week – it might be fortnight. Then we'd be off school for, oh, couple of months perhaps, and I only went to grade 2. [1:21]

Her parents were evidently quite happy with this arrangement, as was Pearl herself.

That's right, yeah. ...... I didn't find any fault in it at all and neither did my mother I think. [3:11]

Her mother and the other women also had quite a lot of contact with the missionaries, but the men seem to have had less. Whether this was intentional or coincidental is not clear. The men were away from the camp more often, hunting or working, and they had their own secret knowledge and spiritual lives. On the other hand, they were practical people and not likely to reject the physical benefits that the missionaries were offering, particularly when the religious teaching was acceptable.

Yeah, that's right. Although my mother's generation doesn't even read or write you know. But yet they used to have women's meeting, you know. Go along and have a singsong and all these sort of things. And they used to teach them a bit of handcraft and that you know – a bit of sewing. 'Cause my mother used to be a good sewer like. [3:11]

The missionaries introduced more than just formal learning. Udnyu games like rounders and cricket were also taught. Pearl also remembered the fun of skipping and playing Camel and Duckstone, but no specifically Yura games.[10]

---

10 Cf. Claudia Haagen, *Bush Toys: Aboriginal Children at Play* (Canberra: Aboriginal Studies Press for the Australian Institute of Aboriginal and Torres Strait Islander Studies, 1994).

Yeah. [pause] Yeah, I don't know where they really come from – might have been from European. You know our main game was .... I don't know .... You know, like playing .... It might sound stupid – Camel – that was our main – . You know, we'd draw a big circle and ...... we'll make a mark and one person would stand there. One group of people got to try to get across the other side. ... Yeah, the other side of the circle. If the one in the middle touch you, well, you were a camel too then. Something like that. Yes, you've got to be a camel and they were too. And until they get old ...... they played that game over and over. That's the game that we used to always love playing. Mixed – we used to play with the boy and girls. ... I would have been about six or seven I suppose – or seven I think, when the missionary came. We used to play that. And another game is a Duckstone, we used to play. ... Oh, similar, but er, – this might come from the European, but I don't know how they got it. But they used to make a square, ... mark on the ground, and then cross like that same as the camel. And they'd put a little stump there and put a stone on top, and the person who was standing there, from this end, each one have a rock and they'll try and hit that little stone off the block. That um, stone would go and they'd just, one got to go and try and to pick up this stone. It goes on and on. If this one can put this – boy can put this rock back – and touch that, well, you're out. You've got to stand there with him then. It goes on and on, you know. And sometime if he [unclear] stone would be still in there and then we just cornered – the duck couldn't get out. Sometimes I might sneak out. [laughs] Oh, that was a really good game, you know. Yeah, until they catch everyone, and that's finished and they'll start all over again, yeah. ... Oh yeah, that used to be, used to be our main –– until the missionary came – . Well, in those days they used to call it rounders, but it's baseball, isn't it? ... Yeah, and taught us and we used to be mad ...... , and the boys used to play cricket, yeah. [2:23,24]

And the boys made a, a swing. That piece of wire still hanging there – I think I showed you that, yesterday. But in the ti-tree there, the boys made a nest and we always climbed down, set in, a bit like a bird's. Yeah. ...Cubby, yes, yeah, ... And the boys used to go on the hill with their motor tyres, and then .... they used to roll that down the hill. And they used to, you know, come down and – . Just like a ......, hitting rocks and that, you know. ... bouncing along and making noise, you know. [4:1,2]

Together, the traditional activities and the introduced Udnyu games filled Pearl's life. She remembers her childhood as happy, despite the hard times of the Depression.

I reckon it was very good. [pause] We never find it boring, not like nowadays children say, "Oh, I'm bored here," but we never used to. [2:24]

When she was nineteen, Pearl was married to John McKenzie. As with many aspects of her life, the courtship was a mixture of old and new. She and John chose each other, although the marriage was clearly acceptable to both their families and the ceremony was, in fact, conducted by them.

Yeah. It wasn't a big flash wedding. It was a fire-stick wedding. [3:21]

The fire-stick wedding was the traditional marriage ceremony. It was Pearl and John's choosing of each other that was not traditional, but then neither of them had been promised to a partner at birth in the traditional way.

Well, ah, [pause] we just picked ourselves, you know. ... You know, just picked ourselves, and we got married and an uncle had to put the fire stick. He was the minister. Not close uncle but er, next uncle, like um, Mum's first cousins. It got to be Arraru (someone of the same moiety as Pearl) see, and that was er, Big Les's uncle, own uncle. And er, my two uncles weren't there, like Mum's brothers, but the others were there and he's the one that sort of – , you know, Les Coulthard? Well, his father was the minister for me. He placed the fire stick and give us a lecture. We've got to be good, you know, and I've got to do whatever ...... I can for my husband. You know, if we have a argument, all that they bring up, you know. You've got to have argument in your own place and .... And then the same for him. He's got to treat me good, you know, and do everything for me, and that's all. [3:21]

The fire stick was simply a burning stick from the campfire.

They just want two couples (Pearl used this term consistently to mean "a couple") sit down. They place it in the front, in the front of you and they say, "This is a fire stick," but they'll say it in the language, and "You two are married now. So you two got to be good and kind to each other," you know. And er, "You've got to do work for your husband, and your husband's got to do –" You know, he's got to sort of provide you with um, food and that, you know, and all that they'll put in. And that's all. ... And, er, one thing we was really strict in those days, I'll tell you that. You know ...... to see boys and girls now, you know, going around. As soon as they leave school they hand in hand in love, and .... And some of them just take off and make double bed, but we weren't allowed to – we didn't want to. We just strict. Want to, we obeyed, you know, not to go to bed until we given to. [3:22]

There was no build up to the fire-stick wedding—it occurred when the elders thought the time was right.

Oh, he (John) just asked me. They told him. They asked him if he want to get married, and he come and told me, and I agreed. So uncles never asked me, my mother never told me. He told me himself – "They going to marry us tonight. Be all right?" "Yes," I said. ... Like that. [laughs] ... Oh yeah. So why not, you know? 'Cause I wanted to go with him out in the bush. ... Yeah. ...... and then you know, it used to be really, I suppose er – . See when it's Christmas time and he goes away, it's really, you know, sad and lonely and he used to go away sad I suppose. Well, you know what love is. As the saying is, love is a funny thing. [3:23]

The missionaries seemed to accept fire-stick weddings without any problems.

All right – they accepted it. ...... And there was another getting married afterwards. We never told our missionary, Mr Eaton. But we never had any paper to sign. Mr Eaton said we could have if we wanted to, you know, but what's the good of it. Our Aboriginal ways are enough. So he accepted it and it was the correct method. ... I was satisfied, the Aboriginal way, and it still is. [3:24]

Pearl saw the old ways as helping to support marriage.

Well, er, I think they couldn't leave one another too.[11] And, er, 'cause we, I had Aboriginal ...... culture way in married. I was married by fire stick, and I don't care when I might sound poor. I wasn't married in church but I kept that marriage. I had a hard time – with

---

11 In a later interview Pearl mentioned that it was possible to terminate a marriage, but that it happened very rarely amongst the older generations. The process was the reverse of the marriage. The same uncle who had placed the fire stick had to remove it and throw it away and then the couple was no longer married.

my husband, but I still had that. And Les (her brother in Adnyamathanha kinship, cousin in Udnyu kinship), he was married by fire stick. [2:25]

The limited education that the missionaries introduced began to affect Pearl's life choices in early adulthood. Soon after her first child was born, Pearl and John moved to Martin's Well Station where he became head stockman. There were no other Yuras on the property, so Pearl did not have the support of extended family in everyday living or in raising her children that she had experienced as a child. In most respects this did not seem to cause problems except when it came to formal schooling. Because of the isolation, the children had to do their lessons through correspondence and School of the Air.[12] And Pearl, of course, had to help them.

Yeah. I wish I had more education than I had now. ... Yeah. So. I mean teaching them correspondence might have ...... learned me a little bit, you know. [pause] But it was too hard. And the worst trouble was .... Because sometime they used to sneak out on me, you know. Rather to go out in the paddock cleaning troughs with their father, "We'll do it when we come home. We'll do our work." Come back. They wouldn't do it and it was, you know, piled up. Yeah. [1:29,30]

While only the eldest two children were getting their schooling in this manner, Pearl managed, but as more came along and Ivan, the eldest surviving boy, moved into higher grades, the task became too much. Pearl believed that a good standard of education would be important for her children's futures and the only way to achieve this was to move to where they could attend a regular school. Ivan, Pauline and Clive, the three surviving children, all completed year ten at Hawker Area School.

I felt that I wanted my kids to know more than I did. Because I just could read and write, and the bit that I knew – and I have my three on correspondence. So it was getting hard when my fifth child was on, coming. And that's how I came in here, moved in here. For Ivan

---

12 School of the Air was begun by the South Australian Education Department for children living in isolated areas. Two-way radio enabled the teacher and students to speak directly to each other and provided social contact as well as specific teaching assistance for the students and the adults who oversaw their work. School of the Air was frequently used in conjunction with the correspondence courses provided by the Department.

and Pauline to get well education. And this youngest one now, Clive, he went right through, you know, from grade one upward. To three years high school he done. [3:9]

Moving in from Martin's Well meant changes for every member of the family, including John.

... in '67 – no '64 when Clive was only eighteen months old I suppose. That's where he had his second birthday. 'Cause I had him (Ivan) up at Beltana, going to school there. 'Cause my husband used to go there and work a bit and he used to – . He give up, er working on the station and get, done roo shooting. When we came in here (Hawker) he got a job on the highway. Yeah, with the bitumen gang, until he retired. [1:28]

Discrimination was something that Pearl says she never felt actively directed against herself, but she could not fail to be aware of the second-class status of Aboriginal people generally. And as a woman, her status was often below that of the men.

And those days, when they used to work on the station, menfolks used to either eat at the wood heap or in a laundry – they used to feed them. And at Wertaloona there was heaps of them, menfolks ...... there. They used to have a separate table for ...... black boys and a separate for white boys. And yet going out in the camp they used to all do the same sort of work, you know. And, yeah, when we start to .... 1952 we moved down to Martin's Well. Wirrealpa was a little bit better than Wertaloona. [3:8]

And at Martin's Well, when I got there, I was treated like a queen. Not to lift any water bucket or chop any woods. My husband had to have time off to do that before he go for work. So the manager was there, old Harry Ross, he was really strict and very .... You know treat womens very kindly.

Ross, in fact, must have been very different to most station managers. When the MacKenzies moved to Martin's Wells, they were provided with a newly built home with running water, probably better than the housing of many white workers on other stations. It was certainly far superior to the memories Pearl's cousin Molly has of station housing at that time. Molly remembers living in tin and galvanised iron humpies and having to go a long distance for water. The McKenzies' house is still standing and lived in, a neat, fibro building with a galvanised iron roof and a deep verandah across the front. And in the front garden is the pine tree that Ivan planted from a cone he collected at Pt Augusta—now forty feet high. Pearl showed me the house with obvious pride, even after all the years living in Hawker. When they moved to Hawker, the Mckenzies were well received. They have clearly always been respected in the community as individuals. They obtained their "exemption," that is, they were permitted to buy and consume alcohol and to enjoy various other "privileges." The exemption card made them "honorary whites," but in order to get it they had to give up some of their Aboriginality. They were not now allowed to visit family on reserves without express permission from the missionaries.

Yeah. So when I came into Hawker I find it really different. I was er, you know, I was welcomed as a human being, although my husband, we had this exemption too.[13] Had to go – you know, leave the ...... Mustn't go back to the Aboriginal camps or anything. If you want a drink well, you've got to have it sent you (from the hotel). So I mean my husband he applied for it. So ...... and I used to have a little drop of beer when he working on the station. He used to get a couple of bottles after work and I used to always take a glass – top bit and that's all. But when I got exempted I didn't even like the smell of it. I don't know why. It might have been just through Christianity, I don't know. That could be the turning point for me you know. Not that ..... . I didn't mind beer. Now I hate the smell of it. That's why I can't stand it, even the smoke (of cigarettes). [3:9]

Pearl was pleased with the schooling that the children received at Hawker. She was also glad to be relieved of the burden of supervision and gratefully passed this on to the teachers, whom she expected to get on with the job.

Oh yeah. You know, I didn't mind if they was getting told off for not doing anything. Not once I went up to the teacher and said to him, "Anyway, you're not treating my child, you know ...... good." A lot of mothers used to, but I never did that because I reckon it was the teacher's place to discipline them. They were out of my hands, you know. If that teacher's reckon they were doing wrong and they

---

13 *The South Australian Aborigines Amendment Act 1939* defined "Aboriginal" as including all people of Aboriginal descent. It also introduced the exemption certificate which made possible "the exemption from the provisions of the Act, Aborigines, who, by reason of their character, standard of intelligence, and development are considered to be capable of living in the general community without supervision." Cited in Bourke, "Australia's First Peoples," 38.

were told, that's their business, not mine. I never took side from my children. [3:10]

Pearl had seen many changes in her lifetime, and in recalling earlier days she was aware that she now saw some things differently from when she was younger. Her reconciliation of Christianity and traditional Dreaming is one example. What had not changed was her desire to pass on her traditional culture as well as what she saw as good in Udnyu culture to her children. From the time that her children were born she was concerned that they would have the benefits of both. This included physical care as well as the educational concern that we have already seen.

I had a really concern for my children to have the best. You know I didn't want them to go hungry or anything you know. They'd go to bed without a feed, which sort of annoyed me. I used to always have something ready for them in case ...... in the night they'll wake up and getting hungry. I used to always have something prepared for them, you know, and most of them .... Not most of them, all of them were raised on a breast, yeah. But this youngest one, Clive, he was a bit greedy I think, and he used to have bottle. And er, but he was a good child. You know, if he went to sleep and wake up, like after seven or, you know. But he used to have feed. I used to make sure I could give him something to eat and he'll go straight back to sleep. But with Ivan and Pauline, if they slept late in afternoon, they'll sort of keep me awake for a while. I keep telling them that. [laughs] They don't like it. But with Clive, you know, it made no difference. If he wakes up eight o'clock he'll just get up and might be hungry. I'll feed him and he'll go back to sleep. But these other two want to sit up and play. And therefore, when you trying to sit up and trying to talk to them and all this sort of things, yeah. [3:10]

Pearl was concerned to protect the moiety system, which is not always observed when younger Adnyamathanha choose marriage partners.

Like I'm Arraru and all my children's Arraru, grandchildren's Arraru. It stays in the mother's side. But father is Matari. No, we couldn't marry Arraru, and Matari couldn't marry Matari. ... my mother's brother's children, you know, we could marry, you know ——— . [pause] What that's called, the opposite moiety. A cousin on that side, Mum's brother's children, but we couldn't marry our father's sister's children because that'll come under us, same moiety. But the other moiety would be Matari, see, so we could marry. Yes. [pause] It's going to be lost, but we try to, you know, keep that. There's two things I am really concerned about, is my moiety, kinship, and the language. That's what I don't like to lose, you know. [1:17,18]

The moiety system is now being extended to include non-Adnyamathanha spouses.

And some ...... get married in different tribes, or a white person, well, we've got to sort of put them in our culture, yeah. ... Fit them in, yeah. So if you was er, married to that woman, well, whatever that woman you married, the moiety, well, you've got to attend the different moiety then, yeah and we class you in that group yeah. A lot of white blokes are married, and um, so we've got to class them in either moieties then. So that it fits in. [2:3]

And that's really strong today. Well, I hope .... But some childrens now have a mixed marriage, you know, and they don't be careful where they get married into. ... It's been happening but er, we're not really happy about it, but what can we do? You know, us older ones, like me and Aunty Gertie, well, we still feels it, but we still in our old culture. [3:15]

Pearl wanted to write down a clear genealogy along with all the Adnyamathanha kinship terms so that the younger people will not only know their relationship to each other, but what the words are to describe them.[14]

I've got some of it written down, but they don't seem to help me write it down clearly you know. And then ...... you know, for them to put it down and perhaps they could make a book of it. I don't really need .... I just want to leave for the people, the younger generation. Yeah. That's what I've done again with the genealogy, for people to know which moiety they belong to. And now I'm really working at. I want to just write out a family. [3:14]

---

14 Kinship was a very important social tie in traditional society—every one was placed quite clearly in relation to everyone else and each relationship had a special term, depending not only on the relationship itself, but also on who was describing it. For instance, a mother talking about her daughter and son-in-law would use a different word to describe them than would another unrelated person, so that the listener would instantly know how each was related to the other. Pearl had already done some work on a genealogy with her kinswoman Christine Davis (nee Wilton) (see Christine Davis, with Pearl McKenzie, *Adnyamathanha Genealogy* [Adelaide: Aboriginal Heritage Branch, South Australian Department of Environment and Planning, 1985]).

Pearl was also concerned to preserve her language. Very few of the younger generation can speak it fluently, although many understand it and can converse by using English words interspersed with the Adnyamathanha. She worked for years with a local station owner and linguist, John McEntee, and together they published a fairly comprehensive Adnyamathanha-English Dictionary.

It's the same as this man McEntee made a .... What do you call it? This book? Aah! That big book there. You know, with the language. ... You know, I didn't really want, like doing it for the money sake.

The main difference that she saw between the way she grew up and the way children grow up today is in the lack of time to learn and absorb traditional ways.

[pause] First of all they'll be missing out on their own culture, ... you know. And, er, I know Charlene in particular, she said even for the language, why go and try to learn the other language? You know, why not learn our own? You know. Well, the same with doing things. I reckon they should learn more doing their own culture, you know, like there is so much to do. ...... Like – boomerangs and stuff like that, and certain dishes, like to use ...... And also as I mentioned early on, that er, – what do you call it? Rug making, out of skins. And they'd be, you know, something they learn from their own culture. They don't know a thing about it. And there are some more other things perhaps that I mightn't know, that the other person might know how to do them. Yeah, the only thing I really missed out on is weaving stuff, you know. They used to .... People used to get a fur, or a hair, you know, and they'd spin it. But I was thinking it was a bit late, then. But I made enquiries there into [pause] how to make that. There's no one round here to do it now I don't think. [2:12]

No, I think it would be best for all children, no use just doing it –– . Because why not? A white kid can learn Adnyamathanha as well. Other ways the Aborigine kids, you know, they teach them whatever white people does. It's only fair to share some of the Adnyamathanha things back to white kids. ... Yeah, you know, be fair. Because we're all in one now. [2:20]

Pearl had specific ideas about what should be taught.

I don't know, whatever they take to I suppose. It might be the language, or ...... I reckon that is the main one, is the language, yes.

...Well, living like .... On the food part, that's what I always say to them. 'Cause there are some white kids, when they go out bush, you know, then they don't know what to eat if they're stranded. But if there's a bush tucker there, they could survive on it. But, ah, where the Aboriginal kid, they know what to eat and what not to eat, yeah. [2:20]

However, the demands and speed of Udnyu culture serve to push traditional practices and therefore traditional culture into the background, where, she feared, it might be lost.

Well, it might sound stupid I suppose. You know, they don't take much time in doing things, sitting down. And what I'd like to sit down and do with them – you know, give them the story and for them to write it down for me – but they can't seem to do that for me you see. "Oh, tomorrow we might do it." They'll you know, keep putting it off. And I keep telling them that tomorrow might be too late. [3:12,13]

PAULINE COULTHARD

As we have heard, Pauline was born in Hawker, in very different circumstances to those of her mother. She was the middle child of the five children and the only girl.

Ahhh, I've got two brothers. I did have four, but two died. One, er, my eldest brother died when he was nine. He had, er, I think, cancer or something in the stomach, yeah. We came in from the station. I was only very little then – I can just about remember him. But I mean back in those days, I mean, medical staff, you know, doctors didn't really know too much um, about cancer. They give him an operation here instead of sending him straight to Adelaide. Then they ended up sending him down because they couldn't really do much for him, and they give him another operation and he was too weak to take the anaesthetic. Mmmm, so ... I mean Mum still sort of gets very upset about that, you know, when she talks about it. Then I had another little brother who's, a bit younger than me, and he died when the whooping cough stuff was going around, so he had bronchial pneumonia and stuff. He was only three weeks old when he passed away. [1:14,15]

I'm the, the middle one I guess. Um, I've got two older brothers and two younger ones. ... Er, my eldest brother that died, he ...... he must be at least ...... four years older than me. And my elder, like my elder brother now that's living, he's, he'd be two years older. ... Then, then my, er, youngest brother er, is, er ...... I'm eight years older. That's the baby one that's alive now. [2:1,2]

The year was 1954 and her life, and that of her siblings, was markedly different from the start to that of Pearl's. She is, however, very aware of what her parents' early lives were like.

Ah, Mum was born up in ...... Burr Well Station. That's about, oh, [pause] fifty k's (kilometres) east of Copley. My Dad was born on Wertaloona Station, ... which is sort of over the – near Balcanoona (Station). And then Dad – I mean, they've sort of um, sort of grew up around Nepabunna area ...... until they were married. That's when they moved out to the stations. Dad sort of worked, sort of on the eastern side of the ranges, sort of, you know. [1:3]

As we have heard from Pearl, the lives of most Adnyamathanha were still traditional in many ways, but the effects of white settlement had produced many significant changes, so that the two cultures were already mixed for her people.

A bit of both I guess. I mean, when they were in Nepabunna they had sort of what they called the kerosene .... And they made like little shacks out of kerosene tins, and her (Pearl's) father sort of, you know, put that together and ...... sort of .... They sort of lived in a house, even at Ram Paddock, before the, the missionaries, ummm, and before Nepabunna they all lived at Ram Paddock, and that's when they moved into Nepabunna, which was something to do with the pastoralists wanting that area for ...... cattle or something. ... Yeah, she (Pearl), has sort of told us a lot. You know, her childhood days and how they used to um, ... collect food and stuff. Because, you know, a lot of the times, you know, food was, wasn't really, there wasn't much around, you know, because then they was on what, what they called the government rations and stuff. But now she can really, sort of, she sits back. You know, even for the cooking and stuff. I mean, you know, she used to say it was, how it was really difficult, sort of cooking on an open fire on a hot summer's day. And of course I mean we sort of say now, "It's hot," you know, and we're living in a house that's got air conditioning, and, and ...... she says, – well, she sort of ...... whether she can cope with the heat, but at the same time she often says, you know, "How did I manage before without it?" you know. Yeah. [1:3,4]

Pauline did not grow up in the company of extended family in a traditional community. With her father John working at Martin's Well Station, visits with family and the wider Adnyamathanha community were short and sporadic. Nevertheless, Pauline's sense of family is very strong and she regrets that even today she does not always immediately recognise many of her cousins and nieces and nephews, though she knows who they are and where they live.

One thing – it wasn't really frustrating, but like when I grew up out there and I didn't have much contact with, sort of, other ...... kids apart from, you know, School of the Air and Carrieton rodeo stuff, but the thing I used to find, like, was a lot of my, you know, my other cousins that I didn't really get to see until I, sort of, actually moved in here – then I was actually, and even when Nepabunna, I mean, nobody was allowed, unless you lived in Nepabunna, my parents had to have a permit to get back in there and see their own, own relatives, you know. Because that was, you know, the missionaries wouldn't allow you in there unless you had a permit. Then after sort of moving in here, I mean even now, because I've lived up in Hawker, I mean, I never saw my cousins and I didn't see their kids. I mean they'd know me but I didn't know them and I used to find that very frustrating. I didn't really get to know, you know. Unless it was just my immediate family. I didn't get to know the rest of them – a lot of my other cousins. I mean you knew of them but didn't know what they looked like, you know. The only way that you might sort of know who they were is because they might look like, you know, one of your aunties or uncles, and you take a wild guess, you know. And that used to be, that's what I used to find very frustrating sometimes. You know, I'd go to Port Augusta even after, you know, my girls were born. You'd go down there and some of the kids that were my own age group, I mean, you know, and they'd have kids, I didn't really know them. They knew me but I didn't know them, and that was very hard sometimes. [2:20]

However, one traditional aspect of Adnyamathanha life remained strong and was to have a profound influence on Pauline's life—the tradition of learning through practical experience. Amongst Pauline's earliest memories are accompanying and helping her father as he went about his work. The helping, as in traditional society, led naturally to learning.

Well, I guess, er, I certainly remember a lot of station life. I mean, you know, when we was living out at Martin's Well, we was actually doing a lot of .... Actually working with, with, you know, with Dad, I mean, you know, as kids. Um, it was really, really, um, you know, I enjoyed it even before I was sort of going to school. It was still, sort of like, like real life experience stuff with him – rather than sort of doing school work as well, you know. ... Yeah, we used to go fixing the fences, I mean, and doing shooting. Um, even at times when he wasn't actually working on the station he did a bit of part time work like shooting roos and stuff, and we, like me and my elder brother, used to actually take part in that. I mean, I used to do the spotlighting, and although I was really small – I couldn't reach over the top of the hood of the car – he used to put tyres up for me to, so I could actually see. And, you know, we'd go out till two to three in the morning doing that sort of stuff. Then, um, even the middle of winter when it was really cold. I used to remember sort of sleeping with roos, you know, when he used to gut them. Sort of, 'cause they were still nice and warm until he got the last one and there wasn't any ...... then he used to decide to, you know, wake up and ...... have a warm by the fire, then we'd go off and, you know, ... shoot a few more. [2:2]

Because her father worked away from the house, she was away from her mother more than may have been the case in traditional society, and while, as we have seen, Pearl passed on to Pauline her own house-keeping skills, particularly cooking, Pauline seemed always to prefer the outdoor activities with her father.

... even on weekends when Dad still wasn't working, we – like, you know, wasn't actually doing any station work – we used to still sort of go out to the family barbecues and – and, er, picnics out ...... around sort of on the property, you know. So we didn't really have much time to stay home and do any sort of housework or anything like that. It was still always on the go all the time. [1:3]

This was no doubt in part because she had two brothers. But also she remembers her father as not making any distinction between what she and her brothers could do and the level of skill they could attain.

Yep. And I guess, I mean, you know, I just find sort of in mine, there was more pressure put on me because I was a girl, from my Mum, and when my Dad, it was, he saw me no different to the boys. It was sort of, you know. If he knew that, I mean, when he was doing anything – I mean whether it was gutting roos or fencing or fixing the wingle or whatever – if I could help him, I mean, you know, I'd help him. He wouldn't sort of say, "No you can't do that because you're a girl." I mean, if he wanted to have a grease monkey for doing the engine on the car, I mean, I was always there by his side. But, um .... I think it was just old-fashioned sort of belief. I mean "girls can't do things as good as boys," and I don't believe that, you know. I often used to grow up thinking – and even my Dad used to always say – well, you know, "If you can't do it, at least have a go at it," you know, no matter what it was. And you don't have to be a boy to go out riding motorbikes. I mean I used to sort of live on motorbikes, you know, stuff like that. But, um, more mothers seem to think, you know, girls should be staying home doing this and doing all the, the girlie things. But I guess because I grew up with all boys in the family too, I mean, I had no choice but to compete. [2:14,15]

She always enjoyed competing with her brothers and had no trouble doing so successfully.

Oh yes, yes. My brothers didn't seem to think so but .... [laughs] I remember one time we were out mustering and my brother didn't really want me to go out bike riding, so he used to drain my petrol (gas) out of my petrol tank of the bike. So that way I wouldn't go out mustering you see. But little did he know that Dad had another stash of petrol elsewhere and he used to always give me petrol you see [laughs]..... Even now I can see all those years paid off. I can sort of skin a roo better than my eldest brother, and he knows it too [laughs]. [2:14-16]

Helping her father was not all "work" and would have allowed for many of the traditional "play" activities enjoyed by previous genera-tions of Adnyamathanha children—in the sense of practising and per-fecting skills and the general social interaction and relaxation that interspersed traditional life. She and her brothers also had some Udnyu toys. She remembers trucks and motorbikes but no dolls—she wasn't interested in them. Mostly games were played without toys, reenacting daily activities.

I mean, even as kids we used to still sort of pretend doing the things that we actually did. Like, you know, I remember sort of, even the games and stuff we used to play, it was still sort of, we were out pretending we were shooting or mustering, you know.

They were the sorts of games we played. ... I never really had much toys. I mean, I wasn't into dolls or anything like that. I mean, if I did have a toy it was sort of trucks and motorbikes. But, you know, no sort of really special – I didn't have a toybox or anything. Like I said, it was either out, sort of digging wells with channels and stuff like that, you know. [2:3]

She also remembers playing marbles with quandong seeds[1] and chasies (tag) with the friends and cousins she would meet at the Carrieton Rodeo.[2]

And that was actually, not actually just to see the rodeo. It was just a time – where everyone used to actually meet too, you know, all the other people – relatives and stuff and .... Well, sometimes we'd come in for, you know, have a sort of camp somewhere – you know, might be a big camp – sort of close by. Either it was here (Hawker) or close to Carrieton. Otherwise, you know, we used to actually go down there and ...... I don't think I'd ever really see the rodeo even. It was just a time of, you know, playing with other kids. ... Uuumm, I can remember playing chasies, you know, between cars and stuff like that. I mean not travelling cars, but parked cars, and I know it used to annoy a lot of people, and they couldn't actually see the rodeo you know with screaming kids running through. But – and, er, that's, that's, yeah, about all the games that we used to play, just practically chasing and hide-and-seek – and, um and hot dogs. That's the only time we used to see hot dogs, you know. We never ever got them out there (in the bush). [2:6,7]

But while many aspects of Adnyamathanha tradition continued in Pauline's life, Udnyu influence began much more strongly and at an earlier age than it had for her mother. In the absence of a maternal uncle, for instance, discipline became the daily responsibility of her parents.

... like the Adnyamathanha way, it was always the uncle that was responsible for disciplining the children. ... Not the father. ... No, it

---

1 The quandong (*Santalum acuminatum*) is a native tree that grows to a height of about three metres in isolated groups of generally less than a dozen in spots throughout the Flinders Ranges. The sweet/tart fruit, known also as native peach, was traditional Adnyamathanha food. The seed, about the size of a marble, is about half the volume of the whole fruit. Like much other bush tucker, the quandong is enjoying a growing popularity amongst non-Aboriginal Australians.

2 Carrieton is about fifty-five kilometres southeast of Hawker.

was always the uncle. ... And I guess that's where you're sort of in a, you people saying, "Oh, extended families." Well, you know Aboriginal people living in houses, and they've got so many people staying with them, you know, that's where the extended family stuff comes in. Everyone sort of looks out for each other. ... All that didn't sort of happen too much when I was growing up. I mean, because I was really isolated too, I guess. I only had my parents around. But a lot of the time I think that was sort of going when they had their ceremonies – like when we had our ceremonies and stuff. [1:14]

Within the family it was Pearl who took major responsibility for discipline and general care of the children.

I guess traditionally before, what I gather, it would have been the mother because the father was always out and about and doing things. I could be wrong. [pause] But I know with us, like when I was growing up, it was always Mum that did the smacking and it was always Mum that did the bossing around and stuff, because Dad wasn't sort of at home most of the day. I mean, you go out, sort of mustering and stuff, and come home late. So, you know, the time we, sort of, had any times together was, you know, camping and stuff on weekends, and nine out of ten he used to stick up for us anyway. You know, you'd do something wrong and ... . [1:14]

Family life and family celebrations were important to the McKenzies, but again the experience of the children was far removed from that of their parents. No traditional ceremonies remained. Those that were celebrated were Udnyu. Pauline remembers birthdays as being important for the children although the celebrations were simple. A cake and a few presents made them special.

... we used to have like, just for birthdays, we just sort of —— . I mean, no matter where we were, I mean, I could always remember we'd still have a birthday cake, you know – and even before we sort of moved into Hawker. I mean we, yeah, we used to have, um, like, just for birthdays, we just sort of, I mean no matter where we were, I mean, I could always remember we'd still have a birthday cake, you know – and even before we, sort of moved into Hawker. And my eldest brother's birthday used to always, sort of fall on the Carrieton rodeo, er, weekend and Mum used to always make us a cake and we used to always have this little birthday party in the back seat of the car at the rodeo, you know, with candles blowing

everywhere. And that used to be always very special, you know. ...
No, I mean .... I mean when you were a kid in those days any sort
of cake was always very special, you know. Because we didn't
really, although we used to eat cake and stuff out there, but ...... we
always used to like the cakes made with emu eggs because it used
to always really make it nice and yellow and you didn't need any
food colouring in it. ... We got presents. I mean it wasn't sort of anything fancy, but I would be really – just sort of appreciate just even a
packet of lollies (candy) or a block of chocolate, you know. I don't
think I –– . You know, not like kids now. I mean they get all sorts,
you know. [2:5,6]

*This was something that was for the children only though, for John
and Pearl did not celebrate their own birthdays.*

Really a kid's, I mean, I can't even remember. I've only just been
finding out since, like now, when my Mum and Dad's birthdays are.
I mean, they've never really, I didn't know when their birthdays
were when I was a kid. But now, I mean, I ...... wouldn't say that
they're not really too sure about when their birthday – but they
never really had the exact date. I mean they've always put it down
to like they can remember, you know, when such and such happened. You know to a happening type thing. And they'd sort of work
out the year, you know, when that sort of was and that's how they
sort of find out. It's not like myself. I know exactly what year I was
born in and the date – you know, and the month, mmmm. [2:6]

Christmas was a special family time too.

I can remember Christmas – but not really Easter. We didn't have
Easter eggs or anything like that. But certainly Christmas, and the
thing that I could remember about Christmas is the fruits. I mean,
it was the only time of the year that we could, you know, get things
like apricots and cherries ... [2:6]

*The Carrieton rodeo was important too because it was a time to meet
up with friends and relations. Until she was ten this was the only time
she saw people apart from her immediate family.*

And that was actually, not actually just to see the rodeo. It was just
a time where everyone used to actually meet too, you know, all the
other people ... sometimes it used to take us a while to actually get
out of the car. But other times if you sort of ..... if you felt comfortable and like, there was other kids that you knew, that was fine,
you'd go for a bit of a walk. But other times, you know, we were

quite happy to actually sit in the car too as well and just, you know, look at people as they go past. But, yeah, I mean, you know, that was the only times I could remember. Other times, you know, we were quite happy to be sitting around and not actually listening to parents talk ..... . [2:6,7]

The School of the Air Christmas party at Port Augusta each year was also a special event, though, as with all large gatherings, it was something of a trial to Pauline. She was a shy child and mixing with large groups of strangers was not easy.

... as a child, I mean, I was very shy too and that made a lot of -- . I mean, not sort of difficult but, you know sometimes you just -- . You know, with seeing so many people around you didn't feel comfortable, sort of, actually. ... I think it was because, you know, like where we lived out there, I mean apart from my other cousins, I mean, you know, I didn't really have much contact with other kids. And, er, it was fine when you were talking on a radio because nobody can see you. But, you know, when you're actually .... Even like School of the Air we used to go down to Port Augusta once a year for our Christmas parties and, you know, that was really um, ... frightening from time to time seeing so many people around, you know. [2:7,8]

There was also the added embarrassment of being aware that she was a Yura in a crowd of Udnyus. She remembers being very uncomfortable when her mother would speak to her in Adnyamathanha when Udnyus were around, even though the family normally used both languages in daily conversation.

... I guess sometime I used to be a bit embarrassed. Like when Mum used to be talking to me in our language, you know, like if we were down there at School of the Air, or maybe down, you know, in the main street of Port Augusta. She'd be, you know, trying to talk to us in Adnyamathanha and we didn't want to listen. We'd sort of say, you know, "Not here. Wait till we're out there," you know. [2:8]

Her parents seemed to have few misgivings about acknowledging their culture or their Aboriginality in public. They wanted their children to be at home in both cultures. But while Pearl might accede to her children's requests to speak English in public, John was less amenable.

Yeah, I guess .... I mean that's what they wanted to do. I mean that's what they were trying to do I think. Um ...... Because I mean, you know, I know my Dad, I mean, he wasn't really embarrassed of talking about, you know, Aboriginal stuff, you know, whether there was, you know, anyone else around. I mean, you know, it was either you learn it now or you don't learn it at all sort of thing, you know. [2:11]

At home the family spoke both English and Adnyamathanha in about equal proportions, but Pauline still feels today that she is not as fluent in the language as she could be, certainly not as fluent as her mother. Two factors are probably important here. First, the level of language used around the home by parents and children is usually fairly simple. One may be fluent at this level but have difficulty in carrying on a conversation at a higher level. This leads to the second factor: the problem of using the language across two cultures. Adnyamathanha just does not have words for many Udnyu concepts or objects, so even a fluent speaker must include English words in Adnyamathanha speech.

Just swapped backwards and forwards. But even now, I mean, you know, it's sort of – you might say a sentence in Adnyamathanha, but you still have to put in a couple of English – it's sort of all mixed up now. I mean, I can't really have a conversation – just, you know, speak Adnyamathanha – unless you put in English as well, you know. Sort of half and half, sort of still. ... Yeah, both I think. I think it's both. I mean, you know, there's still a hell of a lot of words I'm still not really sure of and the easiest way is to actually fit it in with English, you know. Or then there is some, some things, like um, ... some words that we haven't really got a name in Adnyamathanha so you've got to put it in English. [2:8]

At about age five she joined her older brothers in their correspondence and School of the Air lessons. Pearl's attitude to schooling was quite clear to her children.

... she felt it was very important, you know, for us to .... Because she never really had any schooling herself. I mean apart from sort of, you know, doing a bit of Sunday school and a little bit of schooling, like when they was on Nepabunna. So she really wanted, you know, for us to, us kids to have a bit more education than what she did. [2:4]

It was Pearl after all who had to supervise their lessons and give what assistance she could to three lively children who would generally rather be outside playing or helping their father. Despite the fact that schooling and the rest of life were not separate in the way they are for a child who actually attends a school, there was nevertheless a very real separation.

It may have existed as much in Pauline's mind and attitudes as in reality.

Yeah, we actually, sort of, had a set time on the radio each morning to speak to our teacher and to other kids in the area. Um, then we used to sort of send in our worksheets. We used to have sort of little worksheets – colouring in and addition, you know, maths – what they used to call them, sums, or whatever, then. And we used to send them in weekly. ... Well, I didn't really care much I guess. I mean nine out of ten I used, you know, we used to sort of skip lessons – and be quite happy to go out doing things with Dad. Cleaning troughs and ...... whatever, you know – making the stuff he was doing around on the property ...... to Mum's disgust. I mean she, 'cause, you know, there was times where we'd sort of tell Dad that we'd finished our lessons, which we didn't, and Mum'd be looking for us and we'd be gone with him, you know, so. [2:4]

John's attitude to schooling was different. He clearly valued the practical learning that came, in the traditional way, from being actively involved in daily life. But that is not to say he placed no value on formal Udnyu schooling. The decision to move to Hawker for the sake of the children's schooling was a mutual one and meant a change of work for him. The fact that he taught himself to read and write indicates that he could see the necessity, or at least the desirability, of a basic education.

I think he wanted us to actually, you know, go to school and stuff. But, you know, like I say, I mean he never went to school at all himself. But sort of in the later years, I mean, the things that, I mean he sort of, he taught himself how to read and write himself. He was sort of looking on labels of jam tins and sauce bottles and stuff, so that was their schooling. [1:5]

Once the family left Martin's Wells, schooling began to play a much larger role in Pauline's life.

Yeah, we went to Beltana for a little while, then we came, then we came back here. So then back out to Erudina but that was only, er not Erudina, Martin's Well. Then that was only for holidays and then, then we finally moved in here. I'm not too sure if it was '64 or '67. Sometime in the sixties we moved into Hawker. [2:9]

From then on they remained in the town, although the links with the land further out were still strong and they returned frequently for visits. Erudina was one of the places that Pauline took my family and me to visit, and to stay, in the course of the research for this book. Arrangements were made for a cousin to come along to shoot a kangaroo so that it could be cooked in the traditional way in the ashes. It was the one place, out of many, that Pauline and her family chose to use to introduce us to further aspects of their lives and culture; it is clearly a very special place for them.

... we've been in Hawker ever since. We go out to John McEntee's property (Erudina), and that's about another twenty k's further on from Martin's Well, just sort of for weekends or, you know, holidays. ..... And that's lovely, yep. [1:3]

The experience of schooling at the tiny Beltana School probably served as a good introduction to public schooling after the isolation of School of the Air at Martin's Well.

That was one classroom. It went up to Year 7 and it was Grade 1 ...... one teacher. Grade 1 to 7 were all in one class. ... I reckon half a dozen or so, eight, Yura kids, and I think about twenty-five white kids. ... I mean we were all sort of, you know, each individual grades had their own um, like lessons. Like the teacher sort of started us off. We sort of knew what we had to do, you know. And he'd sort of ..... go around sort of, just helping the – well, he sort of interacted more with students on that, one-to-one -- . [pause] Because the grades were all sort of mixed and he had no choice I think .... he was a really good teacher. Sort of spent a lot of time with the kids as well, you know, at the playground, you know, playing with the kids and stuff, which was good. ... mainly like cricket and that, sort of, baseball – baseball, not baseball .... softball, that was a very popular game up there. You know, a lot of kids sort of had um -- . Well, we only had, had a swing and one of those rockers, yeah. ... I remember the rocker, we had an accident there one day at Beltana. I don't know how it was done. Some of the boys were a little bit more .... played a little more rougher than what the girls did, you know. The boys put us in one end and the boys would be in the other, and it tipped over one day. Luckily no one got hurt, but they sort of cut themselves – fell out. ... (Dad) was still working out at Martin's Well. Because we only went there because Mum was, er, in hospital having Clive. So we went up there and stayed with my grandparents. It was great. We went back. Dad used to come up there every weekend, or practically every other weekend. ... Probably for, I don't know, a couple of months, two, maybe three months.

I don't really remember too much, how long. Because as soon as Mum sort of came out, she came up and stayed with us there for a little while. 'Cause, you know, we was doing School of the Air and she found it was a little bit difficult then, you know, the baby and stuff, to have to spend time with us. That's the reason we moved into Hawker. [3:2,3]

All the rest of Pauline's schooling was done at Hawker Area School. It was a typical country school, combining primary and secondary grades and pulling in children from the surrounding countryside as well as from the town.

I went up to Year, er Year 10. It was third year (of secondary schooling) then and that's only what they offered here at that – time. [2:9]

This was a very different experience from School of the Air with her mother supervising and only her brothers for company.

Yeah, it was, it was, you know, a hell of a lot different really. I mean because we had, you know, that one-to-one on it with a teacher from time to time if we were sort of having – you know, you always had the teacher with you which we didn't really have out there, you know. ... Uuumm, oh, must have been at least a hundred and fifty (children at the school). And the school was bigger then than what it is now. [3:9]

When I came into Hawker –– I started school at the start of the year in Grade 3, and um ...... just going back on, on the school, I don't really remember too much about like the set subjects that we had. ...... But we used to um .... have um ..... I mean like at the time when I was at school, it was er, it's a lot different to what it is now, because, you know, we used to always sit up, um .... sort of the teacher talking to us and sort of teaching that, sort of whatever subjects that we're doing. It's a lot different to what it is now um, ... because there is a lot more interaction with the kids now than what you, what's before. I mean going to school it was just you weren't allowed to talk, you weren't allowed to do any group activities. ... when I first started it was, it was er, Year 3 and 4 together, and er, sometimes we had –– what's the word. We had a couple of kids that were a lot older than ..... than like we were, but because they weren't really doing – you know, weren't really sort of up to standard I guess. I mean, you know, one boy I think I had, he was ...... thirteen. He wasn't really –. He was a bit slow, I guess, in learning. But we did have a couple of kids that were sort of, you know, the odd ages that were in our class. ... The numbers weren't really very, um – there wasn't many Aboriginal kids when I first started. Um. ..... But it wasn't until sort of late, later in the sixties that, um –. It was when Neuroodla Siding was here that a lot of our, well, the Aboriginal kids – there was a lot more then –– started, because you know the parents were sort of working out here at the Siding, railway work-ers. ... Yeah, they didn't have a school. They all came in on the bus run. And when that finished, I'm not too sure. It was sort of late in the eighties I think when Neuroodla Siding closed. We lost a lot of our, you know, the Aboriginal kids. The bus run, and, you know, we would have lost about twenty kids. [3:1]

Pauline did not like school any more than she had done at Martin's Wells, but being with other children had its compensations

Not really ...... no. [laughs] Oh, there were certain things I liked about school I guess. I mean, you know, sort of ...... actually sort of mixing with other kids. I mean I enjoyed that. ... Uuumm ...... yeah, I guess, I mean, you know, there's certain subjects I couldn't really like – I didn't really like – at school. Umm ...... I used to remember I used to really hate sewing. We used to have sewing classes. Oh I don't know, even now, I mean I hate sewing. ... it was once a week. I mean we didn't have a um ...... sewing teacher sort of on. She used to coming visiting from Quorn once a week and we used to sort of do some practical stuff and some theory and things like that. But I just didn't ...... didn't have the patience for sewing. I used to love cooking when we used to have cooking classes, home ec., but not sewing. I remember it took me twelve months to make, make a, one of those shift dresses. You know, just the straight .... I mean I was forever hiding my sewing at home, or losing it or forgot it, or you know. I think it took me a whole year to actually just do a bit of stitching. Goodness, I just didn't like sewing. ... Uuumm ...... I'm just trying to think what sort of subjects we did do at school. I liked science. That was a whole lot of fun you know, when you used to actually .... Doing experiments and stuff at school, that was good. Umm. What else did I do? [long pause] Didn't really like maths much. I found that a little bit difficult. I mean, you know, things like additions and multiplications and all that stuff, that was fine, but when you had to sort of work out, you know, the area of this and the area of that, I mean, I just couldn't cope with it. Even now I mean, look at the stuff that the kids are doing at school now, I wouldn't know how to do, you know. [2:9,10]

Attendance at Hawker School had other compensations too.

Yeah, well, when we ..... milk, the cartons of milk allowance that we used to have daily.[3] That stands out very clear in my mind. We used to actually look forward to having that milk, because you know, we never could get fresh milk like that often at home. It was a bit of change from powdered milk. But sometimes when you would get the milk, it was sour like I was saying earlier on too. But that didn't put us off really. [3:3]

Overt discrimination has never been a problem at Hawker as far as Pauline is concerned.

I think, yeah, I think Hawker's just a place where people are just people, you know. They don't actually see you any different ...... to er, anyone else, you know, down the street. So – and I guess that's, you know, once you grow up in an area like that, you know, it's really hard to sort of come into, I mean you read about it, you know, the stuff that's happening, and it's hard to believe sometimes. But I even find with being prejudism or racist, you know, there's, our people are just as bad as, you know, white people as well. I reckon, you know, there is as much racist or prejudice amongst our mob as well. [1:5]

However, she was aware of a problem as a child that she could not at that stage put into words. Even now it is not easy for her to express, but it concerned the absolute lack of any acknowledgment of Yura culture in her schooling combined with condescension on the part of some Udnyus. She felt she and other Yuras were treated differently from Udnyu children by the all-Udnyu staff at the school. Teachers were not interested in Aboriginal children sharing their culture or experience with the rest of the class. The ideal was for them to be, except for skin colour, just like Udnyus.

Yep. Uumm. [long pause] I guess in a way, I mean, although there wasn't .... You know, I didn't grow up with any sort of racial prejudism or anything like ...... that, but sometimes you'd just get that feeling in the way they used to speak to you. I mean I'm sure they wouldn't, you know .... They wouldn't speak to a little white child the same. It was sort of .... You know, sort of the pat, pat on the head and that sort of stuff. ... Yeah, sort of, you know, and we just couldn't ..... . At the time, you know, you sort of felt that, you know

---

3 In the 1950s and 1960s the Education Department provided free milk daily to all primary school children.

.... It was hard to really explain, you know – um, what am I, what I'm trying to say. ...... I mean you used to get a lot of teachers saying that there weren't any .... You know, like, like this school was trying to sort of, you know, stamp on any prejudism or anything like that, but at the same time, I mean, they used to say that there wasn't any difference in the kids. But at the same time there was a difference, you know. I mean, they didn't really want to know that, you know, they had Aboriginal kids in there. But they were not actually sort of .... I'm getting all confused here. Um ...... so they were saying that there isn't any difference, but there is a difference, you know, and I just felt that there was times that they would actually, didn't want us to be sort of sharing, you know, the stuff that we knew and make us feel proud to be what we were, rather than sort of, you know – I mean the stuff that the kids are doing in school now, is, um, I wished I did it when I was at school. I mean things like Aboriginal Studies, you know, and it's really making a hell of a lot of difference with our kids at school now. and, um – but I was really embarrassed, you know, at times, when they'd be sort of looking at – we might have did a history class and Captain Cook or something, and – and er, they often used to say – oh, you know, talk about our, you know, these Aboriginal people, they were savages and stuff like that. And I used to feel really terrible about that, you know. ... No, there was nothing of that sort of sharing – talking about that, you know. And um .... And I'm sure if there was I'd probably, I reckon I'd feel really embarrassed about it. I think it was just that sort of inner feeling that, you know .... Yeah, it was hard sort of, you know, like there was my growing up in that Aboriginality bit and at the same time I was sort of trying to grow up in, in the white society as well. It was really difficult at times, you know, but you didn't really say much about it. [2:10,11]

This may explain her interest and involvement in the education of both Yura and Udnyu children today. Pauline is now the Aboriginal Education Worker at Hawker Area School.

An Education Worker mainly looks at sort of helping, setting up programs for Aboriginal students in the school and sort of looking after .... Also working side by side with the teacher if there is Ab. Studies going in the school – Aboriginal Studies. Setting up programs. Plus it sort of does, um, a lot of other odd jobs we have to do. Sort of setting up – if students need sort of extra help with their homework and whatever, we sort of get in touch with DEET in Port

Augusta and they sort of set up sort of homework centres and extra tutorial for them.[4] [1:1]

Despite the wide-ranging parameters of the job, Pauline finds that the majority of her work is focused in two areas.

I guess with classroom support, working on a one to one with students if they're needing extra help with maths or English or whatever. And also paying visits. Part of my job is also visiting the parents, finding out if there is any problems as well. [1:1]

She works predominantly with primary students, although she is there for secondary students as well. The school extends to Year 12 now, although the final year must be done basically by correspondence with only minimal supervision by teachers. Pauline works

... Mainly with the primary, although I'm for the secondary students as well. ...Yeah. The only help that they need, if they sort of need help with – you know, at the beginning of the year with their forms and stuff. [1:1]

She is quite well established in the job.

I think it must be nearly six years now. [1:1]

She has considerable experience in the education field, having worked in schools and preschools most of her adult life. But her first job on leaving school was nursing at the local hospital.

Yeah, I did nursing I reckon for .... nearly twelve months. ... Well, because there was a job going there at the time. You know, at the time I applied for the job and I got it. And um .... I fell pregnant with Charlene. Then I worked right until I was eight months pregnant, then I left and I went back again after –– she was only – a few months old – back for another twelve months I think it was. And um, then I just didn't ––. Then I just finally left one day, just didn't sort of, you know, enjoy it any more. ..... But I sort of did, you know, like odds and ends, like doing ––. Mainly taking temperatures and stuff, and sort of looking after the patients there, giving injections. And it was really frightening, because when you're on night duty, you know – like you were the only staff member on at night duty – and that was very frightening, you know. Because, although the

---

4 The Department of Employment, Education and Training (DEET), a new "super" department of the South Australian government, which includes what used to be the Education Department of South Australia.

sister was on call that lived in the quarters right next to the hospital. I was really, you know, packing it if, you know, if a bad accident case came in, I wouldn't have been able to, you know – because I wasn't trained properly. I mean it was sort of on the job training, more or less. ... And it was really hard, sort of, you know. I remember we had a lady come in having a baby, and I sort of panicked you know. I mean by the time I got to ring the sister up, practically the baby was hanging out sort of thing, you know. That all was very frightening, but you sort of learnt by that. ...... Yeah, then the hours really got to me, like, you know, especially when you're on the night duty. You couldn't, couldn't sleep, I couldn't sleep during the day. So, you know, I found it very hard to sleep. When you couldn't have your sleep during the day – you had to work really. So that's another reason I didn't, I didn't really enjoy it any more. [3:4,5]

She continued to work while her parents helped with looking after Charlene.

I went fruit picking for a little while. ... to Renmark, because we all sort of heard there was these – they were looking for fruit pickers – and, you know, they were paying hundreds of dollars. That wasn't so. It was really hard work, you know. You worked from sun-up till sun-down and not really getting paid, you know, as much as what we thought. I went there with an aunty of mine, Aunty Clara – Coulthard – she was living here at the time. We went down there and I think we spent three months fruit picking down there. .... And that's .... Yeah, and after that ah, the job came up here again – they wanted me back, the hospital, so I went back here for another few months at the hospital. And um, then I just left. The next job I had was the kindergarten. .... Started doing that. Oh, there was a lot of Aboriginal people. Like all of us were in, in like teacher's aides at kindy. Then they decided to do this um ...... like train, train us as teachers, and they put this course through ..... um, externally we were able to, you know, study early childhood through, I think it was Hartley College at the time. And um, that sort of meant we went down like, when we first started – sort of go down for a week every semester. So we were coming back when they started up a, a group in Port Augusta. We actually could be there – like, us students all together. I found that very hard. [3:6]

... I mean I didn't finish that course because the whole idea was actually – when people were doing that course, like to become

teachers. And I think at the time when I first started there, ...
must have had about twenty-five Aboriginal aides that actually sort
of went down and enrolled in that course. But a lot of them actually
within that course, they actually split. Like either, either sort of it
was an early childhood teacher, or a lot of them just went for their
childcare certificates -- they would just be childcare workers. But
where .... and um ..... and there was actually a lot of ..... people actually chose just to do childcare because it wasn't as long. Because I
found it very hard. You know, like being isolated. I'd be trying to
study and having two girls at the time, and it was very difficult.
Then I'd come to Port Augusta to be in with the group, and that was
hard, you know. [3:9]

While she was working at the kindergarten, Pauline had two more
daughters.

Then I had Kerri in between. Charlene would have been what? [long
pause] I can't remember. [long pause] No, that's right, Kerri --. Yeah,
Charlene would have been er – she went for, for the -- . At first,
when I first started at the kindy, she was um .... four at the time,
and she only went to kindergarten I reckon for a few months before
she started school. Yes, she would have been about four and a half,
and Kerri was something, about two years old then. And um. [long
pause] Yeah, because Kerri used to come to come to work with me
all the time since I started at kindy. It was like, it was at the old
RSL Hall, down here, up from the pub.[5] That's where the kindergarten first started, there. [3:7]

Working, studying and mothering made for a hard and heavy load. It
was the study that lost out in the end.

Mm. ..... Because I found even this -- . I mean all the kids would
stay with Mum from time to time, but most times I used to take
them. Like when I was to go and study at Port, take them with me.
You know, that's when, some of the times I couldn't find a babysit-
ter and couldn't go, sort of study -- . And with the Colleges changing over,[6] I mean, you know, I did that for seven years and I only got

---

5 Returned Servicemen's League, equivalent to the Canadian Legion.
6 When Hartley College of Advanced Education, which had originally been the
   privately owned and run Kindergarten Teachers' College, amalgamated with
   the government-run Murray Park Teachers' College in the mid-1970s, many
   students, especially those studying part time, were disadvantaged. Pauline's
   cohort lost credit for nearly a year's full-time study.

as far as second year. And plus doing it part time, I was .... you know, sort of work, and you'd have time to do your part-time studies. I found that very difficult. [pause] 'Cause at the time, you know, that's what we were doing. We were all part-time students, and I think, you know, if you're not full time, then you have to work at the kindy and do your part-time studies, well, that was, that was very tough as well. ... There was five, um, five people actually succeeded in finishing the course. There, there's been a lot more now that the course is all set together. You know, they can finish it in three years now. You know, you can either go and do it on campus or – . Because there's a lot of support too for Aboriginal people to do that. Yeah, at the time when I started, there's five people that came through and finished the course. [2:9]

Yeah, actually one of the – one of the ladies that actually finished the course – actually came up here as a kindergarten teacher, because her husband was working out at Neuroodla. She was here teaching I think for about two or three years. Once the Siding sort of finished, she ended up there with the kindergarten. But they haven't got an Aboriginal person in the kindy up here now. [pause] They haven't even got, I don't think ── . Like people that have actually .... like teaching at the kindy are not trained teachers anyway. They're sort of mainly volunteer parents and ── . ... They have play group as well where parents go along, but I think that's on different days. [long pause] I think they might only have one .... one Aboriginal boy that goes to it at the moment. It was really good while I was working there. Like sometimes the parents would have .... although there weren't all that many Aboriginal kids at the kindy. If they weren't at kindy I'd – you know, one of my jobs was to actually go and find out, you know, what their problem was, or if they had any, or ── . Sometimes, you know, the parents had just gone away or something. [3:8-10]

The kindergarten was small, with a staff of just the teacher and Pauline, the aide. It was run by the Kindergarten Union of South Australia,[7] which at that time was actively extending its services,

_____

7 The Kindergarten Union of South Australia was established in 1905 as a charitable body to provide educational and philanthropic services to poor families in Adelaide. In the early 1970s it became a statutory body and in the early 1980s it was taken over by the government. It is now subsumed within the Children's Services Office, a section of the DEET.

whenever possible, to country centres. It was also beginning to give particular consideration to the Aboriginal community, parents, students and prospective teachers.

When they started it up, yeah. They had about twelve (Aboriginal students). And you had to have so many kids before you got an aide or something, and at the time, you know, they made it that – you know, they need an Aboriginal aide to help with the policy or something or other. And when that job came up I applied for that, and [pause] then I was there for, I think, about seven years at the kindergarten. ... I just applied because I was interested, because I enjoyed sort of working with kids, at the time. Um, still do I guess. [laughs] And after –– yeah, when the job came up I applied for it, and um, it was more or less – I mean, you know, it was just an ad in the paper and I didn't have to write anything at the time. I just went down and saw a lady down there and ––. ... it was Barbara Webb at the time. Um, she came um ...... yeah, and I just went down there and within a couple of days ––. Well, she made, made a couple of phone calls, and I was, been working there for about seven years. Right until Carmie was a baby I think I was still working there. Carmella was ...... about two or three years old. She went to kindy – she didn't like kindy very much though. .... Got really annoyed. ... She just didn't like mixing with kids, or sharing. She just thought that because I was there, you know, she was allowed to have everything to herself, and I found that a bit difficult. [3:6,7]

Educational bureaucracies, like the Education Department and the Kindergarten Union, had, at this time, only just begun to consider the special needs of Aboriginal communities. Pauline's presence as an aide and the work that she did with Aboriginal parents was about the extent of the innovation. The educational program had no particular Aboriginal content.

No, not as much, not that I can remember. Um. [pause] I'm not too sure when NADOC started and they used to have, um ...... National Aborigines Week.[8] There might have been, but not as much, not as much as they're getting now. ... that was the initial idea, to actually have an Aboriginal person there, because sometimes that was the

---

8 The National Aborigines Day Organisation Committee was one of the first official Aboriginal groups in the 1970s to begin working for white recognition and acceptance of the Aboriginal community.

problem. Like, you know, Aboriginal kids did not go to kindy. They would just go more or less straight — . [pause] Like as soon as they were five or whatever, or six, go straight to school, and I think the schools actually found that, you know, the Aboriginal kids weren't as – um, what do I say? ..... I mean they didn't have that background, sort of build up I guess for them to go to school. The teachers found it very hard to actually — . If a child hasn't been to kindy, I mean, whether it was black or white, you know, if they didn't go to kindergarten then they always had to start from scratch. It's really hard to sort of, you know — . Because they were actually, when they started school, they were actually doing kindergarten stuff. And I found, you know, with even the kids with their interaction, they didn't really — . [pause] Kids, they learnt to share – I mean at kindergarten they learnt to share, you know, their paints or whatever – and that sort of got them to the stage where really they were ready to start school. ..... That's another reason that they wanted Aboriginal people in the kindergarten, so they could encourage Aboriginal families to send their kids to kindy. [3:9]

Aides, unlike teachers, were not paid during the long summer holiday, so to make extra money Pauline did station work at Erudina Station.

And even when I was at the kindergarten, like Christmas holidays, I used to go out working, out at John's place, John McEntee. And John wasn't a manager at the time. He was just like a worker and he had a manager on the place. And 'cause my father used to go out, sort of every Christmas holidays, and one day I went out there and the manager said, you know, he needed someone just sort of over Christmas, to just do like this mustering and stuff and do some shed work. I said, oh well, I was interested, you know, so he actually put me on. I used to go out there, you know – out there for three years, in a row. [pause] Sometimes, you know, that was — the heat — . ... I remember the time, you know, we were out there one Christmas .... out for six weeks .... and it was that hot, you know, everything was dying. Like the birds and stuff were dying in the tanks and you'd get, um, roos in the dip and, you know, we'd go and dip the sheep – got kangaroos in there dying. Because they were so hot they was just coming in close to the shed looking for a bit of shade and shelter and — . But we were forever cleaning tanks out. Even the cockies was going to have a drink – they'd just drop dead in the tanks.[9] [3:7]

---

9 "Cockies," short for cockatoo, is used to describe almost any wild parrot.

The children came with her and for them it was a holiday.

A bit of both I guess. I mean there were times, you know, where I'd question myself, "What the hell am I doing out here?" but at the same I just enjoyed being out there, you know. .... But um, of course, it was the place where, you know .... like a holiday for the kids as well, because they'd enjoy coming out there and cleaning the troughs, and you know. It was really funny one day we went out cleaning the troughs, me and my father and ── . [pause] Every time we cleaned the trough the girls used to jump in there and have a swim when the troughs were filling up. And it was really funny – I saw Kerri, I still remember that, because Kerri would have been only what? About three, four, then. And then she'd sit in the trough waiting for the lambs to go and have a drink, then she'd grab the lambs by their legs, or by their heads, and ──. [pause] It was funny. It was always just the way the lamb was kicking and she was hanging on to it you know – arms sort of splashing around the water. Mm, I used to enjoy that, you know, being out there. They used to sort of come out with us if Dad's going out in the Daihatsu. 'Cause mainly I used to go out on motorbikes. Then they used to want to come but sometimes it was no good, especially there – I used to be terrified of snakes, going out. I didn't want them to be bitten. I mean, if I, you know. It's bad enough if I'm out there, out in the scrub, you know, because I could be panicked if I did run over a snake – drop the bike, on a bend or something, you know. But no, it was hard work, especially ── . But sometimes when you're working in the heat, you didn't notice the heat. You was always working up a sweat and you got a bit of a breeze, you know, you said, "Oh it's cool ── all the time." [pause] Used to do that during the Christmas holidays. And then I sort of stopped doing it. I mean, you know, especially when I had Carmie, because she was very sick as well as a baby. She spent three months at the Royal Adelaide Hospital, so I couldn't really go out as much. [long pause] What did I do after that? [3:7,8]

It was then that Pauline began her job in the Hawker School.

Yeah. [long pause] Then I started my job up at the school as a AW, education worker, which I'm still doing. I'm on leave at the moment. [pause] And I guess that job is more or less similar, but it's more sort of focused on Aboriginal Studies. Like, you know, each school has to have an AW since Aboriginal Studies came in the schools. And, um, one of our jobs is not actually to teach Aboriginal Studies, but you work close, very closely with the teacher, you know, setting up programs and ── . And our duty statement is that long, I mean sometimes I just wonder how the hell we have got time to do it, you know. I mean I have to sort of work in, like a one-to-one support for Aboriginal kids in the classroom, and plus, you know, working in closely, very closely with the teacher, and doing Ab. Studies, and ── . And one of the things also is to liaise with the parents, [pause] a sort of a stepping stone, I guess, for the parents to go through you – then we get that information back to the school. [pause] That can be very nerve-racking, you know, and you're expected to do all these things. [3:10,11]

The content of the Aboriginal Studies course is general rather than specific to Adnyamathanha culture. It examines three Aboriginal groups that broadly represent the range of Aboriginal cultures and lifestyles in South Australia. The Pitjantjatjara live in the vast, flat desert in the northwest of the state, while the Ngarrindjeri people live along the River Murray and the southern coast.[10]

Yeah, it's general. I mean, I think in the courses it's got mainly three groups, like Adnyamathanha, Ngarrindjeri and Pitjantjatjara, and that really gives the whole range of information to the teachers and, and the um, students. Because it gets the message across that not all Aboriginal groups are the same, you know, and the areas are different. I mean then they find out the food source is different and, you know, a lot of the beliefs. And then like the language is differ-ent, which I think in the past a lot of people thought, you know, all Aboriginals speak the same language and, and ate the same sort of things, you know. But they find out. I mean kids are really ── . They find when, when they do the Ngarrindjeri people, they find

---

10 See *The Pitjantjatjara in Change* (Adelaide: Educational Technology Centre, Education Department of South Australia, 1981); George Woolmer, *Traditional Ngarinyeri People: Aboriginal People of the Murray Mouth Region* (Adelaide: Aboriginal Education Section, Aboriginal Education Resource Centre, Educa-tion Department of South Australia, 1986); and *The Adnyamathanha People. Aboriginal People of the Flinders Ranges: An Aboriginal Studies Course for Sec-ondary Students* (Adelaide: Education Department of South Australia, 1992) for older curriculum material, and *Aboriginal Education: Aboriginal Perspectives across the Curriculum* (Adelaide: Department for Employment, Training and Youth Affairs and South Australian Department for Education and Children's Services, Aboriginal Education Unit, 1996) for a more recent approach.

out they eat fish, and we don't get fish up this way, you know. Try to keep, sort of, the kids really — . They get really into it, you know. But, yes, it's mainly, you know, those three courses. It's not compulsory, but I think only in — . I think it's in the Year 12 um, Aboriginal — like the kids have to do a course. ... For SACE, yeah.[11] But at the moment, I mean, in the primary levels — . We found it very hard to get, get it started up here, because the teachers weren't really confident in teaching it. But I mean, we sort of really had to push it, sort of, and you had to push it because — . [pause] And I think the reason that, you know, a lot of teachers felt uncomfortable with teaching it, is because they didn't know too much about it themselves. It's really good, like you have support from the district officers in Port Augusta where, you know, they come up and do a – like a PD training, you know.[12] For the staff itself and um — . But eventually now, I think, apart, [pause] apart from, um —. [pause] Well, nearly all, all the teachers are teaching it down here now in our classrooms now, which is good. [3:11]

Parents are pleased with the program too.

Yeah, and I think it was, it was the parents that kept on pushing it, you know. We wanted Aboriginal Studies. Not only the Aboriginal parents, but some of the white parents as well wanted their kids to learn like, you know. Because I mean they'd do things like, um — . ..... Like language for instance. I mean some of the kids learn German and, er — what's the other one? German and French but, you know, some of us thought, "Well," you know, "why not learn the local language as well?'; I mean it's going to have more .... I mean I can't see a lot of the kids going overseas to .... you know. You know, because I – and I found out too with ..... in summer when I first started there, a lot of kids just ...... they'd learnt the swear words, you know, and I wasn't happy about that. I thought, you know, it's time that we did, started Adnyamathanha language classes here. [3:12]

The classes are run in six-week blocks.

---

11 The South Australian Certificate of Education, which is awarded on the results of a public exammination at the end of Year 12.

12 Professional Development. DEET administers and services the education system both directly from Adelaide and through regional branches. Port Augusta is the regional branch for the Hawker area.

That's, that I mean is not now, but it was only ...... to actually sort of get —— we found it hard to get funding. I mean you had to pay for like people like Mum to come in to actually —— . I mean I used to just donate my time for it, you know, especially to get it going. It only went for six weeks at a time. That's, that's, you know, how long that we could more or less fit it in. And that was at night, that was only offered to you. It was offered to anyone really, and one year we had about twenty-four people doing Adnyamathanha language class. ... They were mainly adults. ...We only had a couple of kids in. But now, I mean, we've sort of been doing a lot of that stuff, I've done on Language Master for kids at school, so they actually know —— the old Language Master? Sounds and the Language Master cards. ... And it's getting better I think, you know. Most kids, you know, feel proud too that they are and, you know, learn. Sometimes you know they get to learn a bit more about themselves or about their, you know – the group that they belong to. [3:12]

The major difficulty is finding people with Adnyamathanha language skills to work with the teachers.

That's what I've been sort of trying to do – a lot of stuff with Mum, you know. Even the dictionary that um, she put out, we actually put a lot of um —— . [pause] One of the teachers actually put this, like a dictionary, together. ... we've always been pushing that. And I've sort of got Mum and Aunty Bessie to actually put —— like come along as speakers and, you know, we more or less just picked out stuff from the dictionary that Mum put together. And um, and a lot of it was just mainly greeting words, you know, that we just introduced each week. Eventually we just got everyone going around sort of saying, you know, "Hello" and you know. Um. ...... And then just giving them their, like Aboriginal kinship names.[13] That was one of the things, and

---

13 Traditionally, Adnyamathanha infants were named according to their sex and their order of birth, i.e., there was a name for a first child, if it were a girl and another name if it were a boy, a name for the second child if a girl and second child if a boy, etc. The names go up to tenth son and daughter. Thus there were only twenty personal names in Adnyamathanha culture. If a couple had more than ten sons or daughters, they would begin again from the first name. Babies who were miscarried prior to full term, who were stillborn or who died at birth were named so that the complete reproductive history of a couple was apparent from the names of surviving children. Pauline, as the third child and female is named Unakana. These names are rarely used any more, although all of Pearl's family know their names. Some surviving Elders are, however, still known by their kinship names or by pet versions of them.

they'd have to say it, you know. You know, "Hello – how you going?" and sort of, you know, "My name is so-and-so," you know, but do it all in Adnyamathanha, and that was good. One thing I found, I mean, it should be really an ongoing thing –– for six weeks –– by the time the end of the six weeks, they were only just being able to grasp that. ... And, you know, you're back from scratch one again, you know, instead of having it continuous. And I think each, er ––. There is no really set courses on Adnyamathanha. ... I mean, you know, Pitjantjatjara's got a set course. You just go there and pick it up and do it, you know. [3:13]

Because one thing I found was doing ––. Like even when we do Ab. Studies I go in for the classroom support –– you know, whenever a teacher's teaching Ab. Studies I go in as support teacher, and a lot of the times it was, you know, pronouncing words, which, you know, they found it very hard to grasp. But I found the younger kids were a lot better than the older kids. You know, they weren't afraid to say the words and make a mistake, but the older – like when they got into the high school, year eights and nines – they were a lot more –– embarrassed at this, you know. If they make a mistake in pronouncing a word, they'd never say it again. [3:14]

Pauline has quite strong views about what children should learn and how the teaching process should be constituted. One day as we drove past the Hawker School she commented to me that schools were like prisons. I found this interesting because even though she says she did not much like some aspects of her own schooldays, she gives no impression, when talking, of having felt imprisoned herself.

I think it's just developed as I've grown older and working at the school and stuff like that. I know I shouldn't say it – but you can't learn everything just sitting in classrooms, you know. I think you're better off out and about and actually doing and seeing things. And that's why I always, even sort of with Aboriginal Studies, you know, for kids now, I mean, to get any meaning out of anything it's best if they actually go and visit some sites or ––. [1:12]

Sometimes I find, like in the schools and stuff, you're telling kids Dreaming stories and it makes no sense to them, and I feel that sometimes you have to take the kids out actually to the sites. That makes more sense. I mean they can see like the magpie and the crow story, for instance, you know, where you see where the ground is black, you know, where the fire was and stuff. When kids visually see that, I mean, they can sort of .... It makes more sense, you know. Rather than saying, "Oh yes, I don't really believe that," you know, "it's only a fairy tale." But when they can actually go on to sites and sort of see this, you know, where it all happened, it makes more sense, and they'll remember it a lot more too. [1:10,11]

Pauline feels strongly that Udnyu children should learn something of Yura culture too. She sees this as important for actually retaining Adnyamathanha culture as well as in passing it on. However, she has an increasing conviction that the simple inclusion of Aboriginal Studies in the normal school curriculum is not the answer. The traditional Yura way of learning by doing is essential too.

Well, this (making boomerangs) was sort of something that was passed on, you know. Like they might have saw their parents doing it, and their parents before them, sort of thing. So I guess a lot of it was actually people seeing – and that was very important, you know. If they were able to sort of see ...... see what, you know, and I think that's, that's a lot of things that are missing now, you know with kids. ...... They don't actually sort of get the experience – real-life sort of experience stuff like that, you know. ... I mean they only see the boomerang the way it's made, but they don't actually see the process how it was made, you know. That's what we sort of focus on doing. Like our NADOC celebrations in the schools, we try to get, you know, people in so that kids can actually watch. [1:17]

NADOC Week in the schools has more recently been changed to Cultural Awareness Week, but regardless of its name Pauline sees the idea behind it as valuable for both Yura and Udnyu children.

I think they should (be encouraged), you know, ... and that's what we try during our cultural week. Just, you know, get the kids to actually watch and make one of their own. I mean not using, actually using the real wood, but making it either out of cardboard and stuff, you know, just so they get a bit of an idea. Because kids find it very difficult to sort of understand. How can you make a curved boomerang after it was just a straight tree, you know? How can you get that shape? But once they actually, you know, see how it's done, – it makes it a little bit more easy to understand. ... I think it should be for all, all kids really. [1:18]

She sees the value of this sort of activity not just in the fact that children learn about Adnyamathanha culture, but because it is a practical experience; if not identical to the traditional method of teaching, it is at least similar in its emphasis on learning by doing.

Ah yes, yep. Because it's something different I mean, you know, they're experiencing. [1:18]

This was something that she values highly from her own childhood.

Yeah, well, that's the way I sort of feel that I grew up I guess. I mean, you know, even like the stuff that we were doing, I mean it was still .... Like now, I mean, instead of reading a book how to sort of go and put a hinge on a gate, I mean we actually saw that happening and it was sort of a real-life experience at the same time it was work for Dad, you know. But we actually was able to see that and take part in that. I mean he was sort of earning the money for it but at the same time, I mean, if we was around I mean he'd get us to do that sort of stuff for him, you know. ...... Even like, you know, the roo shooting and stuff like that. I mean although I really enjoyed it, at the same time it was earning him money to keep us going, sort of thing, you know, but we took part in whatever he was doing or working and stuff. [2:12]

But often today, there is no time for sitting and listening that is so important for traditional learning. Udnyu culture intrudes everywhere.

... in the past the kids used to always sit down and listen to the stories, but now we've got too much interference. I mean, you know, we've got things like video and TV and stuff, and you can't really sort of sit down and talk to somebody, or tell stories if they're watching the video. I mean, you'll get told off, get out of the room. [laughs] [1:9,10] ... I think they're very much into white culture. [1:12]

The situation in respect to traditional craft work is even more problematic than that of storytelling. Traditional artefacts are no longer made for everyday use, so children have no chance to see them being made unless this is consciously arranged for them.

... my grandfather, I mean, he used to make walking sticks and boomerangs and stuff, and he used to trade that for food, so you know. ... Er, some of the, some of the station owners and stuff, you know. Whenever he used to do a bit of work for them, and sometimes you know work wasn't really available, he used to sit down and do some woodwork, and a lot of those old people, you know, used to do that, sort of sit down and – .... Do it, sort of, in the traditional way and sort of make, sort of, big – boomerangs – the big size, you know, not the miniatures that they make now. [1:17]

... but I find too now, I mean, you get people doing it, they don't really put as much effort into it as, you know, like the older people used to. I guess you know time is the biggest factor too. You sort of have to, sort of do a lot, and if there is demand, you know. [1:20]

Pauline sees this as a threat to the survival of the crafts, both those that are purely traditional, like boomerangs, and those that have developed since white contact, like carved emu eggs.

Well, I'd really like to see young people who are getting more involved, because I mean — . [pause] Yes, even like ..... carving (emu eggs). I mean that's a very hard thing to do, you know. I mean I've tried it. But I guess, you know, we should be encouraged to try and sort of do that sort of thing, because I mean that's going to be lost. ... because I mean you need a sharp sort of knife and stuff to do that. I mean, all the pocket knives and stuff were readily available when Mum was growing up, but I'm sure they weren't so, going back, you know. ... And I mean, you know, trying to do it with a stone would be really, really difficult, because it's so really sort of fragile, you know, and delicate that – you know the shell. [1:20]

Likewise with the language.

Because, I mean, it's a really hard, especially the language is very, very hard to sort of, you know, ... put, put things down, and it's hard to explain. Just I guess, you know, to ... if there was more stuff orally, and for people to listen to, I guess it might make it a lot more easier, because a lot of people can't really read the stuff, you know. So I guess if there was more tapes and stuff made available. [1:6]

Although there is no Adnyamathanha language program within the Hawker School, the role of the AEW is to work through the language when necessary.

Yes, I guess if we had a child starting for the very first time and didn't really understand English – you know, English would be, you know, the second language – we'd certainly be looking at sort of ways to, um, get the language across. Not only sort of, you know, Adnyamathanha – speaking to them in Adnyamathanha – but also, trying to set up programs to help them with their English, you know. So probably uh, make up little booklets and stuff like that. ...

We'd sort of, you know probably, if they didn't sort of understand hello and stuff like that, we'd say "Nanga?" ("How are you?") but that's only in Adnyamathanha and uh, you sort of get into other languages where "nanga" means something different, so you've got to be really careful, you know whether they're .... You have to make sure that they're actually .... Find out what group that they're from, because that can be a bit of a problem too. You know, sometimes you might have ...... sort of people, like Pitjantjatjara, or ...... students with other sort of language backgrounds. And so you have to more or less sort of, you know, try to find a resource person to come in to help them. [1:7,8]

Dealing with students from other tribal groups can be a problem, but all is not easy with the Adnyamathanha either. Only a handful of surviving Elders, including Pearl, can speak the language fluently.

Uncle Les, Gertie. Um, there's about two or three old people from Copley. So only about ten. That's sort of, you know, really fluently. Then you get sort of younger generations coming in. And I can actually sort of – I mean sometimes I even make mistakes when I'm pronouncing words. And I, I know that I'm sort of making mistakes, but you get a lot of people that, you know, who haven't sort of an ear for listening to, you know, the way to pronounce words. And sometimes you feel like saying, "Well," you know, "that's not the right way to speak that." ... And that's another thing I find very hard to sort of .... Like, sometimes Mum might come out with a word that I haven't even heard before and, you know, you might question her you know – "Gee that's a new one. I've never heard that." And she'll say, "Well, it means, you know, this," and I mean, it might mean sort of the things that – I mean we might talk about something sort of all the time, and we've got a word for it. It's a common word, but I mean, a lot of the rarer words is gradually disappearing, you know. And the only time that she actually talks about it, when she's with people her own generation. People like Uncle Les and oh, Aunty Gertie ...... Johnson from Nepabunna. I mean that's the only time that, you know, I often hear new words coming out, because I guess they're the same generation, you know. Well, they sort of grew up with those words. So you probably feel that by telling us we wouldn't understand, you know. [1:28,29]

Pauline is also particularly interested in traditional ways of using plants for both food and medicine. She has learned much from her

mother, but feels she still has more to find out. This is not just a matter
of personal interest, but essential, she believes, in order that this
knowledge be preserved for future generations.

I'd really like to see a lot of the, I'm really into the foods – food side
of it, you know. I'd really if, if, you know, the Cultural Centre does
...... get going, I'd really like to see a lot of the foods. ... [pause]
Ummmm, ah, sort of, you know like now, I mean, like to have a
native nursery type thing – going. You know, bush foods like, you
know, the wild pear and stuff, and they're, they're quite easy to
grow. But that's what I'd like to actually see, you know, sort of. And
people can actually make something. You might tell people about,
you know, "Oh this is the plum bush and it's good for sores, you
know. Use the bark and stuff." But they really don't know, you
know, what a plum bush looks like. They probably think it's a
domesticated plum, you know, but not really knowing that, you
know. They've probably seen a plum bush out in the bush but not
really knowing what it was. So it's sort of educating people a bit
more on that sense, I mean. And we still use that ointment, the,
um, plum bush ointment. ... Before we used to sort of, what my parents used to always tell me, that you sort of get the bark off the
tree and you burn it – you just throw it in the coals or on the fire –
and it's got a real red glow to it. Then you just take it out and you
sort of crush it up into a powder form, and now we mix it with olive
oil but they used to use emu fat before. And that's really good for
sores and burns. ... [pause] Oh we've got that Shrubby Rice Flower.
... That's a medicinal plant as well, and it sort of grows into a real
sort of little shady shrub. Not very, it doesn't grow very big. And
they used to peel it, 'cause when you sort of break the stem off it,
it's got a real stringy ...... sort of a stringy bark to it. You can just
peel of the bark, ... and what they used to do before, they used to
pluck, like, you know, peel a lot of the bark and plait it and wear it
around your neck for colds. It used to be good for, like if you had
umm, sort of nasal, throats – sore throats and stuff – and I think
they said it was good for asthma. So, you know, that used to clear
up all the congestion and stuff. ... this year that I've taken off, well,
I'm planning to do that Adnyamathanha cook book. ... That's what
I've taken the time off, 'cause I just find it, ... I've sort of taken a
lot of notes, sort of, over the years, like from, you know, certain
uncles and stuff who have passed on now, but I didn't do anything
with it. I've still got it all in note form, you know, because person-

ally it's just that I'm interested in all the plants ...... and if I can, sort of, you know, I'm taking Mum out there (to Erudina) and what we actually do. Like, whatever foods need cooking, sort of cook them traditionally, you know. And, um, also I want to have a section on medicinal plants as well, because I think that's really important for, you know. Because once they pass on I don't think that, you know, we'd be able to – . ... I don't know whether you've seen Mum's little booklet, it's a plant and bird book, but it's only just got, um, ... just the names like they've got, the Europe, European names. They've got the Adnyamathanha name. They've got the scientific name sort of. But, um, ... but I find, you know, if you're actually reading it and there's no picture, you can't really identify the tree unless you know it, you know. ... You've got to do it when the foods are in season. ...... So, but I guess I'll start with a lot of the basic stuff, you know, like things like the wild pears that's readily available. ... I don't know, yeah, I don't even know why they're called the pear, but I think they call them bush bananas too. ... Oh yeah, when they're really young they're nice. And we used to pickle them when we lived on the station, and they were like – like especially the small ones – they were just the size of an olive, and they were quite nice. But once they get a bit older they get a little bit ― . You know, a bit bitter in taste. ... There's one plant I'm still not really too sure on. Because when I did the seasonal program up in Balcanoona a couple of years ago, during the holidays – had like a bush trail walk and I was still on the ...... Mum showed me that plant so many times and I'm still not positive to tell people, "Look, this is OK to eat." Because, I mean, there is a confusion, yeah. Because, you know, the other plant is, is identical – got the same sort of flower and the same sort of fruit – and it's poisonous. ... Oh, Mum knows. I mean, you know, she just have to go by the sm, smell of the leaf. A lot of the plants, I mean, even if she can't see it properly, she'll have a smell. She's got a really good sense of smell and she can tell, you know, she'll give you a name over the plant while you're smelling it. ... So ...... I mean I can't tell the difference even just looking at them, you know, but she can just go by the smell, mmmmm. [1:29]

Although Pearl is a committed Christian, it is traditional beliefs that are of greater significance to Pauline.

Yeah, I mean I don't – I mean, I don't knock, you know, Christianity. Well, I mean I guess I, I have got a lot beliefs like in the Adnyamathanha way, you know, that sort of spiritual stuff and that was ― and that's one of the things that actually comes out in Ab. Studies courses anyway, you know, we're always looking for the three aspects in it – Dreaming stories for instance. ... Our three aspects are like, the spiritual world, and er, then the environment, um, and the rules for living, and I guess that's, that's the way Aboriginal, Aboriginal kids, like Adnyamathanha kids learnt, um ..... like when you got all that respect and stuff coming out, you know. I mean that's normal anyway. That was one of the main sort of, you know, things that comes out in a Dreaming story. Sometimes you might get, er, the whole three in a, in a one Dreaming story, or you might just get the one, you know. But it's really good, you can compare when teaching Ab. Studies with the kids. You can actually ask them, you know, "Well, what sort of messages did you get out of that story?" you know. Like if you heard the magpie and the crow story, one of the main thing that comes, is, you know, because the eagle was the magpie and the crow's uncle, and the way they teased him and mocked him, I mean, you don't do that sort of thing, you know. And even nowadays it's, kids can compare it to their everyday life at home as well, you know. How you're supposed to have respect for the Elders. You don't laugh and, you know, mimic people or stuff like that. Then it tells you a little bit about the environment. You know, like the magpie and the crow story, for instance, if you're actually on, on, on the ground, you can actually see the area when the cave was and the area's really black. So you can actually come to terms with, you know, "Yes, there must have been a fire here when the magpie, er, the eagle, hurt the magpie and the crow when he lit the fire." And in, and not –– yeah, and sometimes you know, and the spiritual stuff does come out in the story. And I guess I sort of believe a lot more of that, you know, in our context. It's hard to explain it. [long pause] I mean ––. ... you know, like when you're ...... when they used to gather food and stuff, you never take every-thing from just the one plant. Like the wild pears and stuff, you always sort of leave a few there so you'll know that you'll always sort of get, you know, food. Um. [pause] And I guess that's the way the Aboriginal people did things. They didn't ...... when they were out hunting and gathering food, they made sure that they didn't take everything from the one area, because they knew that if they did that, you know, there won't be anything for next season, or whatever. Yeah. ... Yeah. And I would guess, I mean, you know, like I said, we never did Ab. Studies before, but we already knew that –

things about respect, I guess, in school – you learned that from your parents anyway, but you know. But I find that sometimes ── . [pause] I mean when like Mum sort of really ── . When she talks about her childhood and stuff, because I guess they didn't have so much influence like we – like what I did. Like, you know, TV and stuff came in and, you know, stuff like that, and sometimes I find it very hard to ...... like the stories and stuff, I mean, that I've been told, I find it very hard to, most of them, remember. And I guess since I've been going, doing, you know, working at the school here, I've learnt a lot more. It was good learning, you know, stuff for me as well because you're doing it every day, you know, with the kids and stuff, so you sort of, sort of remember – "Oh yeah, I remember part of that story," but didn't remember all of it. Because now I know when Mum, even now, when she's telling me about some of, you know, the Adnyamathanha ways, and I just find it very hard to ...... I mean I might just switch off. You know, I'm still thinking about work or, you know, something that's going to happen next week. But, you know, back in, like when Mum was growing up it was different too I guess, because they didn't have those other things that interfered in their life like we have now. Or the phone rings, or something like that, you know – someone knocks on the door. And, but before it was ...... they were able to sort of, you know ...... they listened a lot too I think. With this younger generation there's a lot more questions being asked. Sometimes you haven't got the answers, you know. [3:14,15]

Pauline did not actively attempt to pass on traditional spiritual beliefs to her daughters when they were younger. But, particularly in Charlene's case, she knew that much was being passed on by her father.

Not so much me, but I think with Charlene, because when I was working and she was sort of, you know, growing up, she spent a lot of time with her grandparents, and she sort of um ── . And my father, her grandfather, used to always tell her lots of stories and stuff, you know, and I guess she sort of got interested because ...... even now she says, you know, she sort of still wants to remember because, you know, she still misses her grandfather and remembering these stories, it's her way of sort of, you know, still keeping his memories alive too, I think. ... Not Kerri. No, not those two. I mean Kerri was from time to time, but Carmie really never spent any time with him, apart from ── . Because I was more or less with Carmie I think, more than Charlene and Kerri really. But Kerri was sort of really young too. I mean she wasn't really interested in those things. But Charlene's always been the one that's very interested. I mean she's really, like I said, spent a lot of time with her grandfather, and even camping and stuff. Kerri wasn't really a camper. She'd prefer not to go camping because she'd rather, you know ── . [pause] She'd always be scared, Kerri, that somebody was going to grab her if she was in her sleeping bag – bag or swag or ── . So she'd just stay home. [3:15,16]

There are a number of younger Adnyamathanha who are interested in their cultural heritage and who are trying in various ways to regain it.

Just a small group I think. I mean like Terry's been organising these cultural weekends up at Oraparinna, and they've been sort of really successful. ... Terry Coulthard. He's um ...... he's a teacher in Port Augusta. He's actually one of the persons that finished that kindergarten course – he's teaching at Flinders View (School). But, I mean he's ...... he's sort of a um ...... cousin I suppose with my husband – my husband's cousin. ... yeah, well, Mark (Mackenzie, another cousin, of Pearl's generation) did come up here when Terry organised a cultural weekend and he did some dancing up there. ... Yeah, because it's all of the younger that are, like – you know, Charlene or Kerri's age – have actually gone up there, and they've learnt a lot, you know. And um ..... and I was only just being told the last one they had up there – one of my cousins, Noeline Ryan, Mum's niece – she sort of said, you know, of all the young kids that she sees in Port Augusta all the time, since that weekend in Oraparinna, it brings people closer together. Like, you know now that ── . You know, "Now that," Noeline says, "you know, I walk down the street and those kids will come up and say, 'How you going Aunty Noeline?'," you know, but in the past that didn't happen. So I guess it's bringing, you know, like especially the younger ones, to know who you are well, you know. It's not only sort of learning. It's like getting to know your own people as well. [2:17]

Pauline's own lifestyle is probably more Udnyu than Yura in many respects, at least in its everyday visible forms. She has clear aspirations for her own daughters.

... I've been really putting a lot of emphasis on the need to stay at school and finish their education, you know. Because without ─── . Even now, without your Year 12 Certificate or whatever, it's really hard out there to get a job. [2:17]

Charlene has finished her education and moved away from home, but this is immediately relevant to Kerri, her middle daughter, who is finishing off her secondary education.

Yeah, she, um, she's actually going for it this year, because she didn't do well in one subject. She didn't really sort of, um, sort of pass. So she's actually got to go and actually, you know, get her Year 12 Certificate. [2:17]

Well, that's another reason I think she's gone back, because she didn't really know what she wanted to do. Uh, she has talked about nursing – she wants to get into nursing – and I think she'd be really suited for that because just the way she does things for Mum. You know, she sort of .... I mean when she does it. She certainly isn't doing very much lately, but just the way she handles, sort of, older people. And, um, 'cause she did work experience up here. Just her whole sort of attitude towards older people, and she really had the skills for that you know, and I think she'd, you know, be really good. But now there's talk about park management – she wants to get into, I think, Salisbury or, – she's sent away for the information and stuff. But then again next year it could be something else. And she's really sort of musical too. She'd really wants to, sort of, get somewhere where she can actually do um, get into, sort of, music. She's really got a good ear for music. I mean she can hear a song and she knows, just by listening to it, she can pick up the chords and stuff and just play it on her guitar. I think she just needs extra, sort of, you know, tutorial stuff and that. [2:19]

Carmella, the youngest, is still in primary school.

Well, when she was sort of .... Up until about last year I reckon, she, she hated school. I mean if she could get out of it she wouldn't go. But I think because she's sort of, she's very shy from time to time. Like at school, although she understands most of the work, but, to actually ask a teacher in front of your classmates, like if she's not too sure, she'll feel really sort of ...... um, ... what's the word for it? ...... Oh, she's going to think that if she asks the teacher, you know, that they're going to think that she's dumb. She's sort of felt like – she didn't have the confidence in herself. And it was always like, when she used to bring her homework home, she'd be sitting there and, you know, and I'd check her work and I'd double check her work and she'd say that that's still not right. You know, I said, "Well how do you know?" "Well I know it's not going to be right." She still didn't feel confidence in herself. But, you know, I said, "Well too bad, you haven't got the right answers for everything." I said, "Even, even if, you know, the main thing is ...." What I was trying to actually get her to do, just have a go, no matter whether it's right or wrong, you know, and that's the only way you're going to learn. But Carmella, everything had to be perfect, otherwise she wouldn't hand in the work. And she'd feel then, like, if she was asking a lot of questions, it was kids are going to think she's dumb. But now, since um, – then we set up this um, home tutoring stuff with a um, a registered teacher who'd actually come in and do some tutoring after school. And just after sort of, a few months of that she's not frightened to tackle any problem now, you know. And she's even got the attitude, "Well if it's not right, well at least I had a go," you know, and I'm, I'm really pleased with that for her. And she's not really too frightened to ask any, any questions now. ... . She was too proud I think to actually go and ask for help. I mean even though she would get it all wrong and she'd feel really bad about getting it wrong, but she just didn't want to ask for help. So. [2:17,18]

The fact that Kerri went away to Port Augusta for some of her schooling was an advantage, in Pauline's opinion. She feels that this has given Kerri greater confidence than if she had done all of her schooling in Hawker.

Kerri's – she's actually, she's, um, I think because in the last two years she went down to Port Augusta and went to the Catholic school down there for two years, and I think that's set her a lot of um, pace I guess. Because there were so many more kids there and there was more competition and, you know, she actually sort of kept up to the work although it was, you know, for hours she'd be sitting home doing school work, but I think it's paid off even now. I mean sort of she's done all that down there, and now she's got sort of --- . [2:20]

Like most mothers, Pauline, has some misgivings about her daughters growing up.

It's actually frightening really. Um, 'cause I reckon when I was a kid it just took me forever. Well I just thought, you know, it was just forever that .... You know even Christmas, I mean, used to take years I thought, you know, to come. But now when you get rid of one, you know, the other, you know, Christmas is already on your doorstep, you know, and it's just happening too fast. And the kids are now, I mean they're just growing up too fast. Whether we're living in a faster pace I don't know. ... But just to look back, I mean, you know, with my kids. I mean one minute they're babies and now they're – you know, they're engaged and .... And Carmella, I mean, you know I can just remember she's just been born yesterday – now probably if she passes she'll be in high school next year. It just makes you wonder where has the years gone. ...... Yeah, it's frightening. [laughs] [2:19]

She maintains that she has no difficulty accepting the two older daughters as adults, although Charlene disagrees with this and feels that her mother still treats her in some ways as though she is a child. This is probably a fairly universal problem of generations; it is certainly present between the three generations of women of this family. Pauline is unsure about when she herself felt adult and was accepted as an adult by her parents and the community in general.

[long pause] Oh, I guess when I had my first daughter, Charlene. [laughs] I guess when I left school, that's when I felt that, you know. I was sixteen. [2:14]

It certainly did not occur before this when she was in her final years of school.

No. no, not really. I mean my Mum didn't let me feel that way. I mean it was still, you know .... I mean she still doesn't. [laughs] ... I mean it's always wanting to know where you're going and what time you'll be back and you know. It was that sort of .... [2:14]

And yet she realises that for her parents' generation, as in traditional society, adulthood came much earlier.

Because even, I mean, yeah, I mean, just going back, I mean not so much in my, like when I was – in my generation – but just going back to my parents, I mean, some of them were working, out working on stations when they were twelve, thirteen you know. So as long as they're able to actually get out there and work, I mean you know, they were able to sort of and they were classed not actually as kids but as adults then. So, you know, sort of going back into their generation, I mean, although, I mean, now I think twelve year old, that's still a baby. Out sort of in the workforce, you know – well you're not able to anyway. You still have to be at school because, until you're fifteen, you know. But, um ...... I guess the older the generation, I mean, they were sort of out in the workforce a lot younger. [2:13]

A common source of dissension between generations is a difference in aspirations or standards. In the case of Pearl and Pauline there is certainly some difference of opinion regarding sex roles. As we have seen John always encouraged Pauline to "have a go" at anything she felt she wanted to do. From Pearl there was always more pressure to be domestic.

She used to try to. She used to try to, yeah. ... I tried to (ignore her). A few times I used to succeed, other times I wasn't so lucky. But, yeah, I used to try and .... I mean I can even see her doing it with my girls now, you know. It's just the way that, you know, and I don't really, I'd prefer it, I mean, you know, if they are able to go out, well why not, you know. So I sort of grew up with that equal opportunity .... [2:15]

And between Pauline and her daughters there are also differences.

I really thought I had a good childhood. I really enjoyed it. I mean, although it was a little bit more ...... er, harder, no not harder, but ...... I mean now, when I was a kid we didn't have air conditioning or anything like that, um, didn't have, and we had a fridge but, like, if we were out fencing or whatever we didn't. Apart from a water bag that was it, you know, and we used to really appreciate just an icy cold drink of water, you know. That's what used to make me mad. Now that, you know, you've got fridges and things and the girls will drink it dry and they won't even bother to fill it up, you know. That used to make me really ...... cross. Or they won't walk down the street to get a packet of milk because it's too hot. But then again, you grow up a little bit tougher I guess. [2:21]

But she realises that she has the advantage of being brought up in a family in which Yura ways were still strong and in which there was a clear link with the traditional culture and the preceding generations. It is this sort of link that she believes her generation must preserve for the future.

Yep. But only thing, I mean, now that I look back on like when I was a kid, and I often think, you know, when I was a child growing up, just looking back on it, all our older people you know. There was a lot of them around. Like, you know, my grandmother and grandfather and all my uncles and aunties. And sometimes you wish that, you know, the stuff that I'm doing now, I wished that I was more interested in it when I was a child and actually sort of, you know, helped ...... um. I just felt that I just didn't listen. Now that I'm, I'm really sorry, you know, and all our older people are passing on and that's one of the things I want to actually do, this book with Mum. Because, you know, once people like her and her generation's gone, I don't feel comfortable in sort of actually you know, passing on that much information to my kids. And the frightening thing is, is when my kids have kids, I mean, where's it going to be? I mean they probably won't know nothing unless we start really, you know, doing a lot of documenting of the stuff now. Because, I mean, although my three girls, now they can understand the language, but they won't speak it very often, you know. There isn't a need – or they feel there isn't a need, you know. But maybe in years to come, I mean .... You know, they probably won't be able to pass any of that on to their kids, and their kids, or whatever. So that's what I feel. You know, now it's come to the stage where ...... you know, we're starting to be interested in it too late I guess. I don't know. [2:19,20]

CHARLENE TREE

Charlene is the oldest of Pauline's three daughters. She was born in the Hawker hospital on September 9, 1972. Her next sister, Kerri, is two years younger and the youngest is Carmella, born when Charlene was nine. Charlene has lived in Hawker all her life so far, though she does not anticipate remaining there forever. Outwardly her life has had the structure and format of a Udnyu with formal schooling playing a major role. Indeed, her formal education has been more comprehensive than that of many Udnyus. She began by attending the local kindergarten, where Pauline was a teacher, then went right through to year eleven at Hawker High School, doing the last year by correspondence. Initially she thought she would like to be a lawyer, but changed her mind.

Umm, I went up to year eleven here (at Hawker Area School). I didn't go right up to matric, but matric's not – it's not that good because it's all by correspondence. Yeah, so I was going to go to school in Adelaide but then, like I'm a horse lover, so I went down and I studied horses for a while, done a pre-vocational veterinary

125

course in horses. ... Yeah, that was quite good. And then, um, I had a traineeship at the shop in retail and sales, but that wasn't what I really wanted. I done more like, doing dishes and cooking hamburgers when I really – I wanted to learn how to run the place, not how to clean it. [1:1]

Then she came down to Adelaide to do a business course at Adelaide TAFE,[1] *with the intention of establishing, with a group of her relatives, an Adnyamathanha Cultural Centre in Hawker.*

... so – so I decided to go Adelaide and I did two courses in business planning and business management. And now that I've completed those courses we've put a business plan together to set up a cultural centre. We hope it will go ahead pretty soon. [1:1]

See, we want to have a permanent cultural display in the centre and it'll be something like artefacts and food and stuff – like bush foods and bush medicines and stuff like that in the centre – and like, create more employment for Adnyamathanha people around Hawker, and it's for the general public. [1:2]

The preparation for this is an excellent example of the way in which the two cultures, Yura and Udnyu, are mixed and combined in Charlene's life and in the lives of many of her people. It was clear to them that in order to set up a going concern, and in order to attract the government funding they needed, they would have to present their plans in Udnyu form. But the way in which they went about gaining their expertise was very much Yura. They did it together as a group enterprise. If the outcome is successful it will benefit them as individuals, but the whole group, the Adnyamathanha people, will benefit too.

Um, there's eight of us. ... I'm the youngest. Um, a lot of, the others are my uncles. Like there's Darcy Coulthard, Brenton, Clive, Joe and a few other guys as well – a few cousins. ... eight of us – started off doing the course. But, um, all of us completed the first course but only three of us completed the second course. Like the second part of the course, that was the management, like doing all the bookkeeping and stuff like that, and the guys couldn't – it's not that they couldn't handle it, it's just that a lot of them haven't been to school for over twenty years and they found it really difficult, so they, yeah, so a lot of them pulled out. [1:2]

---

1 A College of Technical and Further Education.

This was a project that Pearl and John, her Nanna and Poppa, had long wanted to get off the ground, but did not quite know how to organise. Charlene sees the approach that she and her uncles and cousins took as being a practical and rational one and, moreover, one that is likely to be successful.

Well, we first had lots of ideas the middle of last year, and now that we've completed the courses and know a bit more about running a, running a business, and we've done our business plans and done all the groundwork, or most of it, and we've submitted our plans to ATSIC,[2] so we're just more or less just waiting now. [1:2]

The fact that it was something that both her grandparents wanted is clearly important to her. It will serve to preserve and pass on the Adnyamathanha culture that they passed on to her, and this is important to her both as a sign of love and respect for them as well as for the benefit of the children she may one day have.

'Cause like our culture is a dying culture and as each um, Elder dies, a lot of our culture dies with that person. I guess like, because for the past twenty years both my grandparents, like Pearl and John, and my great grandmother, May Wilton, they worked with the linguist John McEntee on our language, recording our language, ... and I guess it's their determination and dedication that sort of gives me the get up and go, makes me sit up and think, you know, "Well, if they can do it to preserve our culture, why can't I do something like that?" [1:3,4]

Despite the fact that she grew up in the town, her earliest memories are of going into the bush with her grandfather and helping him with jobs. She found him a lot of fun and learned all sorts of things from him, Yura and Udnyu, as had her mother before her. Being the first grandchild was probably an advantage for her. She would have several years of her grandparents' exclusive attention before her first sister was born. Her cousins, children of her mother's older brother, are all considerably younger than her as well. The relationships with her grandparents, but particularly with John, have clearly been very significant in her life.

[laughs] Umm. Well I guess it's 'cause like when I was growing up, like my own parents were working and I didn't – . ... Um, they, they

---

2 The Aboriginal and Torres Strait Islander Commission, a federal government body that oversees Aboriginal affairs.

were working most of the time and I didn't really get to see them that often and I spent most of my time with my grandparents and they more or less raised me when I was younger. ... And, um, 'cause my Mum, Mum was a nurse and she had, she was doing shift work and stuff so she couldn't really look after me. ... And um, so I spent a lot of time, I spent most of my childhood with them and ever since, you know, even when I was a baby they used to, I think when I was about a month old they first took me out camping and then ever since then I just went out with them all the time. And like my grandfather, John MacKenzie, he was my idol and my hero. Like he taught me how to shoot and how to prepare bush foods, and different types of bush tucker and stuff, and I just really enjoyed the bush. I loved being out bush and I loved learning from him. See, he wasn't just ...... I mean, he was more like a best friend I guess than a grandfather. He, he was a lot of fun and um, it was just through him, 'cause like, he made learning fun. ... Well, like ...... I mean, there's this ...... I guess it's a delicacy, I guess. It's called alka walka – that's a blood pudding – and when he used to make that, he used to make me hold the, the bag, the stomach bag with all the bits in it.[3] [laughs] And, like he used to just – you know, just tell jokes and just, just make it fun. Keep me laughing, and it was good. Do silly things and make you laugh and stuff. [1:3]

Oh, ... like we used to go out, I wouldn't say almost every weekend, but probably every other weekend. Whenever we could – whenever we could get out we would go. Sometimes like, during the week. If we didn't go out camping then Poppa and I'd go out shooting during the week. Or when I was younger I used to go out spotlighting with him. But like, on school holidays and stuff we used to have, – when we used to get like, the three-month break over Christmas we used to be out on the station with Pop. Just go out there. [2:3]

She remembers Pearl and Pauline staying back at camp doing the cooking and other chores, but she was not interested in these and pre- ferred to be with Poppa instead. Childhood was a happy time for her.

Yeah, definitely, yeah. I think I always had the best of everything. Um, I think I was a lot luckier than some kids because I was, um,

---

3 Alka walka is made from the stomach of the kangaroo, turned inside out and stuffed with the kidneys, liver, caul fat, navel fat and blood. It is cooked whole under coals and ashes in a fire pit.

able to learn like, two cultures at once and had a lot of fun doing it. There was never a dull moment. Um, everything was always exciting and good, and I loved going out bush. And, um, ... I don't know, like a lot of the kids I was friends with, they were like, they were from stations and stuff and they never really appreciated the bush I guess, because they lived out there all the time. But, I mean, I lived here and whenever I'd go out I used to have, – it was good. [2:3]

John taught Charlene to shoot, as he had Pauline, and she was about ten when she shot her first kangaroo. Prior to this she watched, in the traditional manner. When she was at home she remembers playing "boys'" games – she always felt happier doing "boys'" things. Like her mother, she was a tomboy and this was not discouraged by John. In fact, although her siblings were girls, she recalls mostly playing with boys throughout her childhood. For a couple of years, when she was between five and seven, she had a foster brother. He was a couple of years older than her and she remembers playing with him quite a lot. She didn't have many toys at all that she remembers, though Pauline recalls a large orange teddy when she was a toddler. Mostly it was cars and active outdoor pursuits like swimming, horse and motorbike riding and the regular bush camping with Poppa. She sees herself as being much like her mother in terms of her love of the bush and preference for "boys'" pursuits. But she sees herself as having a greater freedom than her mother in that she could choose whether she would wear girls' or boys' clothing and play girls' or boys' games. She sees Pauline as not having been given this choice by Pearl.

Charlene sees herself bringing up any children that she may have in much the same way as she was, although she is adamant that any daughter of hers can grow her hair long whenever she likes and will not have to wait until she is old enough to look after it herself as she did. Like her mother and grandmother, Charlene has a strong sense of the importance of passing down knowledge and culture from generation to generation. I get the sense, talking to all three women, that they have a strong feeling about the importance of handing down culture from one generation to the other, but particularly through the female line. Charlene sees herself as having both Yura and Udnyu culture to hand on, but the Yura is of particular importance because its very survival is under threat. She feels an obligation to pass on all that Poppa taught her to her own children in the future. "He taught me for a reason," she says. On the other hand, she realises that there were many things that he could not tell her because they were "men's things," so

*she sees her major obligation as passing on her knowledge through the
female line. "I'd have to have a daughter."*

*Special family times stand out in her memory. The children's birth-
days were always celebrated. Pauline would make a rocket cake – two
layers, iced and decorated with smarties or such and with a single
large candle in the middle. There were presents: Poppa always gave her
bags of various sorts; Pauline also gave practical items like clothes
rather than toys. These celebrations were for all the family, and relations would come over for a barbecue. Christmas was another time
that the family spent together. Aunts, uncles and cousins would come
up from Port Augusta. Each nuclear group would have separate
lunches, then all get together for tea in the evening. Easter was not celebrated at home. Charlene remembers Eastertime at kindergarten
because she got prickles in her feet searching for eggs, but not any celebration at home other than eating hot cross buns and each girl having
a single Easter egg.*

*Charlene enjoyed school, though it was no competition for bush life
with Poppa.*

Yes, I did like school. I wouldn't say that I hated it because, like, I
enjoyed learning. But, I mean, if I had a choice between school and
staying out bush with my grandfather, I know where I'd be and it
wouldn't be in school [laughs]. [2:3]

*She had no difficulty with the work and was always a reasonable stu-
dent, at least until her mid-teen years.*

Um, yeah, I did fairly well. Like I wasn't, I don't know, um. [pause] I
mean I did OK at school but, like, when I turned about, um, ...
when I was about fifteen or sixteen that's when I became like,
really rebellious and um, like, I started to go down in my school
work a bit. I mean, I wasn't a stupid student. I mean, I had brains
but I just didn't use them. [2:3]

*There is some discrepancy between the way she reads her mother's atti-
tude to schooling and the way Pauline expresses it. Charlene does not
feel that her getting a good education was a major priority for Pauline.*

No, well, she wasn't really ––. I don't think – looking back now, – I
don't think she was really interested in our schoolwork. Because,
like, the only time I can remember her ever, like ––. She didn't
really encourage us. She'd just tell us off whenever we used to get
behind or whatever and give us a bit of a push. But I guess, I don't
know. No, I can't remember.... . [2:4]

Charlene had an independent spirit and knew what she wanted in a way that did not always sit well with her mother's ideas and desires. For instance, Charlene wanted to do her last years of schooling in a regular classroom situation rather than working by correspondence, but Pauline was unwilling to let her move so far from home.

Because when I went through that rebellious stage she um, well she wanted me to do well, and I did, but then, you know, she wanted me to go on and do matric (matriculation). And, um I wanted to at one stage but, like, at the end of year ten I wanted to go away and go to a school in Adelaide or Port Augusta because year eleven and twelve is not good at Hawker. Like, it's all by correspondence and I think it puts a lot more pressure on you. You just fell too far behind when you have to do it by correspondence. And she didn't want to send me away and I wanted to go away so that I could do better. ... But you know, she didn't want to send me away and I wanted to go. And I thought, "Well, I'll just leave," so I left school, but I don't regret it – I don't regret leaving. [2:4]

Likewise, Pauline was not happy about Charlene's plans for a student exchange in France.

... Like when I was in year ten I applied for an exchange to go to France, like, because I was studying French at the time, and I got accepted but Mum wouldn't let me go. You know, "What if the plane crashed?" or "What if you got hijacked?" or "Oh, my God," and she just wouldn't let me go. And I thought, "Oh well, I can't go unless she gives me her permission I guess," and she didn't want me to go, so I stayed. [2:5]

Charlene still thinks that this was an unreasonable attitude and is sure she would not feel that way about any children she might have.

Yeah I think it is. I mean, you can ...... I mean, there's just as much chance of you dying staying home than what there is forty or fifty thousand feet up in the air or whatever. You know, there's no difference if you die on a plane or getting hit by a car. I mean, I don't know. It's really stupid to think like that I reckon, because I mean it was a good opportunity. It would have been a good, really a good experience. I mean like I've got my culture, like Adnyamathanha culture, and European culture and going over somewhere else to learn about a different culture would have been an excellent experience I reckon. [2:5]

She admits that "Mum's really stubborn," but nevertheless feels somewhat resentful that she was not able to persuade her.

... Yeah I did (feel resentful) in a way, yeah. Because like, she's always held me back in doing things that I wanted to do. Like when I wanted to go on that exchange she wouldn't let me go, and then it was I wanted to go away to school and she didn't want to let go – "No, you stay here. I'll organise that next week." You know, "Organise it now. I want to go away at the end of the year." "Oh yes I'll do that a bit later on," but she just didn't want us to go. Like even when my younger sister, Kerri, she wanted to go away for school and Mum said, "Yes, well I'll organise it next week," and we knew for a fact that she'd never get it organised because she didn't want Kerri to go away. And we got to the stage where Kerri just rang up the school herself and eventually that gave Mum a bit of a poke and she filled out all these forms and Kerri went to school at Caritas (College) in Port Augusta. Had a private school down there, so she went down there. [2:5]

Her feelings are so like those that Pauline has about Pearl. Probably this feeling of always being a mother to your daughter, regardless of age, and, conversely, of always being a daughter to your mother, are universal and cannot be escaped. In fact all three generations get on very well most of the time.

I think she was ...... [pause]. I don't know, she just doesn't like letting go, even now. Like I'll be moving out soon but she doesn't want to let go. She's always ...... I don't know, she's ...... [2:5]

Although Charlene's experience of school is recent, she regrets that there was little Yura content in the courses.

There was this one time when a few of us wanted to learn, like the Adnyamathanha language, and we were currently taking French and German lessons and, you know, that's when I first started to get ––. About two years after I started taking French, I thought, "Well, why should I speak another language when I can't speak my own?" So a few of the other Aboriginal students in the school and myself we got together and said, "Well, we want to be taught our own language." And we approached several of the teachers and the Principal, but they just wouldn't be in it. [1:12]

No reason was given for the decision.

No, they just, they just wouldn't allow it. They didn't tell us, they, they first said that there wasn't anybody to teach it, and um, and that was really stupid, like, because my Mum can teach it and my grandmother, and plus John McEntee, the linguist, he would, he would have been willing to come in and teach. But nobody, the teachers wouldn't allow it. We had French and German – they were our choices. [1:12]

However, Charlene has her own ideas about the school's lack of enthusiasm.

Yeah, I could think of one reason why they might have said no, is because if we did start learning our own language, we could communicate with each other in, in school and the teachers might not be able to understand us. They might have been afraid of all the students talking about them, or something, I don't know. [laughs] ... Oh yeah. It would have, it would have been good. I mean we spent – like it took eleven years learning white man's culture and all about Captain Cook and how to speak the language properly, and how to write English properly, and then I wasn't allowed to learn my own. That was pretty sad. [1:12]

Yeah, well I can understand it a lot more than what I can speak it. I mean I'm learning slowly. Like my Mum, she's still learning so it's pretty, I mean, it's not that difficult to pick up but I guess for a while I didn't – I didn't want to learn. It was like, it was just too hard. It was like, I mean, there was English then there was my language at home and plus, you know, I was studying French at school and it was just too confusing and too difficult, so I thought, "I don't want to learn it." But now I sort of – I do, yes. It's a bit, I mean it's not too late, but, you know, I left it for too long. I should have started a lot earlier. [1:6,7]

Charlene would like to see the opportunity to learn Adnyamathanha open to all the students at the school.

I mean, – not only like, I wanted like, just the Aboriginal students to learn it, but the white kids at the school as well. I mean, I felt it would have been good for them too. I mean if they can, if we have to learn their way of life and how to speak and whatever – it would have been good if they could learn our way. [1:12]

Aboriginal children, not all of them Adnyamathanha, made up a sizable proportion of the school population when she was a student.

Well when I was going to school there would have been about at least thirty, thirty-five. [1:11]

Um, probably [long pause] thirty percent of the kids at school were Aboriginal. [2:1]

And some of her Udnyu friends already had some familiarity with the language.

Yeah. A lot of my – . I've got a few friends that speak it. Like they don't, they can't speak fluently, but they know a few words here and there – like to say, "hello," "goodbye," "how are you going?" and stuff like that. [1:13]

Apart from the Adnyamathanha language, Charlene would like to see bush lore and skills and Dreaming stories taught in the schools.

I'd probably go in and teach, like, I'm really interested in Aboriginal plants, different sorts of plants, like medicines and stuff, and bush tucker. I guess that's because I spent time with my grandfather and like he showed me, you know, different plants and stuff that were used for ––. I guess Mum's influenced me too, because she's pretty well interested in that ... I guess plants. [pause] The Dreaming stories I reckon. Teach them how the Dreaming stories connect us with the land and that. [1:18]

Her people's and her own personal connection with the land is of great importance to Charlene, both in terms of her own life and happiness as well as in terms of retaining and passing on Adnyamathanha culture to future generations.

No, it's sort of like ...... it (the Dreaming) connects us to the land and, yeah. Yeah, it connects us to the land. Like, I mean, a lot of people say – you know, you get a lot of people that cry out for land rights, "We want more land," and stuff – but my grandfather always used to tell me, you know, that they can cry for as much land as they want, the land doesn't belong to the black, it doesn't belong to the white. We belong to the land, you know. And, well – . [1:10]

Ummmmm, I guess I'm more interested in like medicinal plants and foods and bush tucker mainly, and a lot of the Dreaming stories – I find them really interesting. ... I guess it's just the way, like, how they connect. How the dream stories connect with like um, particular parts of the Flinders Ranges, and how Wilpena Pound was formed. Like we believe that, that, that two giant serpents formed the Wilpena Pound, and stories like that, they just fascinate me. [2:4]

For this reason she, like many of the Adnyamathanha, is adamant that their stories must be preserved and passed on.

[pause] Yeah, I think it's 'cause, like, you get a Dreaming story, and when that story's passed on to a younger generation, it has to be

exact. Has to be exactly the same as what it was –. Like, say, if my father told me – like Nanna's father. Nanna told say her story about how the Wilpena Pound was formed. Well that would have to be exact so when she passed it down to her children they know exactly how it was formed and not, I mean, if she decided to be creative and change that, nobody'd really –. Oh, nobody from our Aboriginal group would really know how the Wilpena Pound was formed. [1:9]

And this must be done correctly and accurately.

Well there was one case where we had a lady who came up and she recorded a lot of the Dreaming stories, and she put out a book, and – a lot of the stories were inaccurate, and I think it angered a lot of the um, Elders because, um because, like, when they all go and their children goes, I mean like my kids, if I have children one day and they go –. You know, they might get really interested in, like in their culture, their Aboriginal background, and if they go back and read through this book and all the stories will be inaccurate, they wouldn't really know how – . ... Oh she wrote them down very well, but she decided to be creative and change them to make them sound – better. So it's really silly. ... some of them were really twisted around. They don't make much sense. Like um, a lot of the stories have got – a lot of our Dreaming stories tied, like, us to the land and, like, how things were formed, and, like, how you should respect your Elders and your uncles and stuff. You know, there's a lot of Dreaming stories like that, and she's twisted them all around and they just – it's like picking up a little fairy tale book, you know, like Cinderella and you're reading through a book like that and everything's new. ... it doesn't mean anything. It's just – a story. [1:9,10]

To make changes not only threatens the culture, but, indirectly, demonstrates a lack of respect for Adnyamathanha culture and Adnyamathanha people. Respect for Elders is a central aspect of the culture that is still maintained, though perhaps in a different form than in the past, and this is still very important to Charlene. She wishes to maintain this as well as maintaining the traditional knowledge.

Well I guess –. [pause] I don't know. Umm. [pause] I guess I sort of do follow it. Like, say some dream stories that tell you, like, you can't eat this otherwise you'll turn into something, and you can't do this because it's not right and this will happen to you. I guess it's sort of like superstition, I guess, and I guess I do – in some things –

I do follow it. ... Yes, that's true, yeah, but we still um, like in Adnyamathanha way, like, I'm sitting down talking with you now. I mean there's a lot of things, like I can't even, I mean, not that I would swear in front of you, but if I did, like just. Like something like – . [laughs] ... Yeah, yeah, because it's not – . It's disrespectful, you know. You can't swear in mixed company or whatever, and you can't be mean and nasty to your uncles or whatever you do. Be nice and stuff. [1:5]

Like Pearl and Pauline, Charlene sees Hawker as a town remarkably lacking in prejudice towards Aboriginal people, at least in an active way. She has never felt any active feelings directed against her personally in Hawker, though as we have seen there were the indirect attitudes at school regarding the lack of importance of Yura culture and content that both she and her mother felt.

Well, for as long as I can remember, like, like I've lived in this town most of my life. For as long as I can remember there's, I mean in this community there's no blacks and there's no white – we're just one race, which is good. We're just people and I like it like that. I mean, I don't think it's fair to class people out 'cause of their colour or disabilities or whatever. That's not really fair. It's not like that here. I mean you get the odd, like you get new people that move to town and they might have had hassles elsewhere with Aboriginal people or whatever, but in Hawker we're pretty down to earth and just normal people and the colour of our skin doesn't mean anything. [1:20,21]

No, like, I mixed and played with everybody and anybody. Like, as long as I can remember in Hawker, um, there hasn't been blacks – or whites – we're just one race. They don't single us out because of our colour or our race or anything. I mean they don't care. Um, yeah, we're just one race in Hawker and it's good like that. There's no prejudice, no anything, not like when Nanna first shifted here. [2:1]

But even this prejudice she identifies more as institutional rather than personal.

Yeah, um. I mean I can't ...... I wouldn't like to say whether they were, like, people prejudiced against Nanna and Poppa when they first shifted here, but I know like her and Poppa had to fill out um, like an exemption card to become exempt. Um, they had to cease to be an Aboriginal to be able to go down to the pub and, you know, stuff like that. So that was the only lousy thing that I could remember about them. But other than that it's been pretty good living here. It's only people that have shifted here recently, like in the last two or three years that, like have come from towns where there's always feuds between Aboriginal and the non-Aboriginal people. They're a bit wary of us and, you know, can be a bit rude at times, but other than that the locals have been pretty good. We've been pretty good to them, so. [2:1]

Charlene's friends were both Yura and Udnyu, and she recalls no particular differences in their ways of life.

Not really, 'cause um, like one of my best friends was um, a girl that used to live up the road here and, like, um, they were white, and like, her father and my grandfather, um, they used to be like the best of mates and they used to go out shooting a fair bit. And her and I'd get together and we'd go out with them, so um [coughs]. Excuse me. No, they didn't play any different games. Like a lot um, of the people I used to hang around, a lot of the guys, a lot of them were like um, non-Aboriginal and we used to play like um, the same games I used to play with all my cousins. Marbles – it wasn't any different. [2:2]

But she has experienced active prejudice elsewhere.

Well, yeah, I did, like when I was, I was doing a traineeship here down at one of the – at the bakery – and um, I had to go to block over in Whyalla, to school for a week in Whyalla, and a lot of the kids there – like they were from Port Augusta, Whyalla or Ceduna,[4] and, and like I was the only Aboriginal person in my group – and I copped a bit of flak, you know. Yeah, you know I, well, smart little comments from some of the other students, like "Blacks. My car got broken into and my windscreen got smashed. Black fellas must have done it." I ignored it for a while but then I couldn't ignore it any longer. [1:20,21]

She was somewhat surprised because, while she knew such behaviour was not uncommon in many places, she didn't see it as something that happened amongst people who knew each other personally and who interacted well in other respects.

---

4 These are three South Australian country towns that have relatively large Aboriginal populations and frequent racial disharmony.

Yeah. Well I sort of, sort of half expected it, I guess, because even though I live here, you know what, sort of, other towns are like towards Aboriginal people, you know. I mean I didn't expect it to happen there, I mean, because I'm not that dark. I'm not as dark as what my sisters are. I didn't expect it. ... it was a bit of a surprise. I mean I sort of expected it from several people, but I mean I didn't think I'd get it from anybody in my class. ... Yeah, and like most of them, you know, thought that I was white because I was so light. [1:21]

Her solution may not have been ideal for removing prejudice, but it worked for her.

I thumped him.

Did it work?

Yep. [laughs] [1:21]

To a much greater degree than her grandmother and more too than her mother, Charlene has a sense of her own individuality and the importance of shaping her own life. This is no doubt a personal characteristic to some extent, but the changing combinations, over the three generations, of Yura and Udnyu culture, life and learning have also had an effect. Unlike many Aboriginal people, she still has at least a part of her culture. Her grandparents and her mother have passed on to her not only what remains of the culture but the belief that she has the ability to retain and regain the power that is inherent in it. She understands that much is gone and that the loss has been a recent one.

[long pause] I think it'd be .... Like a lot of the artwork, like the paintings out at um, Arkaroo Rock and say, I mean, Yourambilla Caves.[5] Nobody really knows what they mean, well not this generation, not my generation, not Mum's. But, you know, some people in Nanna's generation did, but a lot of them are gone and, you know, Nanna wouldn't know because like she's a woman and she's not allowed to know. .... Yeah if, you know, somebody like Mum, or like

---

5 Arkaroo Rock and Yourambilla Caves are two easily accessible sites of Adnyamathanha rock paintings and carvings, visited by large numbers of tourists. They have been made at various times in the past, the earliest perhaps thousands of years ago, the most recent perhaps only hundreds of years ago. However, contemporary Adnyamathanha no longer know their meaning or purpose, although some of the Elders, including Pearl, believe they were done by spirit beings in the dreamtime.

one of my uncles, or anybody talking out there, to those sites and asking, you know, "What does this mean?" You know, "What does that painting mean? What do those circles mean?" Because nobody knows. I mean a lot of people take guesses but none of it's correct, which is really sad. ... I think it was because like [pause] I think at the beginning of Nanna's generation they weren't – that's sort of, like, when like they stopped really living traditional ways. They didn't really, but like they had to go and work for the white man and stuff like that. And, like, my grandfather was, he worked from station to station all the time, and like the tr, the Aboriginal group was sort of like split up because everybody was out working on different stations and stuff and they didn't really have, so they sort of neglected their artwork. Um, and it's not that they, I guess they, it's not because they didn't take any interest in it any more, it's just because they couldn't 'cause they were out working. I mean, they didn't work for money, they just worked for rations to support the family. So they, I guess it's because of that. [1:19]

She is sad about this loss, but not, like many Aboriginal people, angry. Perhaps this is because she grew up with grandparents, and then a mother, whom she could see actively preserving what they could of their heritage at the same time as they accommodated Udnyu ways to their own needs and desires.

I'm not really angry, just sad. ... I think, lot of people just feel sad, I guess, because a lot of, well most of the problem, most of it, you know, there's certain parts of the culture that have just gone and they can't get it back, and that's pretty, I think that's pretty sad. I mean, that's nothing to be angry about because we've got nobody to blame but ourselves, you know. I mean we could have recorded it if we wanted to, but we didn't, you know, and it's been lost, you know. And, but I think it's like .... You get a lot of, you know, the country Aboriginals up around here, and I think they'd feel that way, but you get a lot of the urbanised Aboriginals jump up and down saying, "We're angry, we're angry. This should have been done. You should have done this." But they've got a big chip on their shoulder. ... I don't know. I guess they sort of feel, I mean this might not be correct, but this is how I think. I reckon they feel like they're ripped off and like the government owes them everything. You know, they owe them more money, they owe them land, they owe them this because, you know, they've lost this in their culture and, you know, they can't live traditional ways. I mean if they all went back now and wanted to live traditional ways now, none of them would survive. They wouldn't. Nanna wouldn't go back there now. Even if she could, she wouldn't go back, because it was just too hard. [1:19,20]

All three women value their traditional heritage, but their emphasis and priorities are slightly different. For Pearl the important thing is to simply make sure that the knowledge that she and other Elders have is passed on to younger people before it is irretrievably lost. For Pauline the priority is the collection of the knowledge. Charlene wants to ensure that what is collected will be safeguarded for the future in a way that will make its survival less dependent on the passage from one individual to another. After that she has things she wants to do for herself.

So I guess I want to stay here long enough just to see that (the cultural centre) set up and up and running, and then hand it down to one of my little sisters or some of the younger ones in Hawker that want to stay in Hawker, or some of the older ones that, you know, want to stay – that have decided they want to stay here and they want to run it. And once I know that they will run it effectively and it won't fall through or whatever, then I'll leave. [1:22]

BERNIE SOUND

Bernie was born on the Sechelt Reserve to Lena (nee Jeffrey) and Clarence Joe.

I was born right here at Sechelt, in ...... 1932, um February the 9th, um right behind, our big church that we lost – it was a great big – it was a loss for the whole of Sechelt. It was a great big, er, church that our whole people had built. And um, right – and used the money right out of their pockets. Nobody built it for them or gave them the money. And um, there was a hall, er, connected to a house behind that church and that is where I was born. ... Um, my grandparents were living, were living there. Um, Basil Joe, Mary, um, and we were living with them I guess at the time, my parents were. I'm the second of the oldest, so. I had an older brother there – William. He's passed away now. And I'm one of twelve children. ... Yeah, and I'm the oldest of the girls. ... My Dad was out hunting at the time I was born. Like about 2 o'clock I guess in the morning, two – three. And um, he was coming home and he seen the light on and "Oh, oh, something is happening." He got in, my grandmother told him, "It's a girl, a baby girl." [1:1]

Bernie's family were not all from Sechelt.

My grandmother actually was from the Fraser River. Her family was over there – she was married over there before, um, she lost her husband. I don't know how my grandfather met her from here, but she had a family over there that's why we have relatives over there at um, what they call that place? ...... Um. ...... Katsee? Reserve anyway. We have relatives over there. ...... uuum, then my – on my father's side, my grandmother came from here but her husband, my grandfather, was an English – there was three brothers that came – I don't really know that story. Three brothers that came from, I don't know where – they all married Native women. This one married over here, the other two landed at Edgmont I think. I remember him. He was tall had white hair – he had a moustache, but he married my grandmother here. [1:9]

There was twelve of us in my family so – I'm the second oldest. My older brother was William, then myself, and then Gilbert and then Gladys, and then there was Junior which was Clarence Joe Junior. And, um, okay. Gee this is difficult 'cause there was twelve. Junior, Iris, um, Carl, um, Terry, Howie, Shelly and then there was – we lost one, Albena – she was just a little baby. Now I missed one. Who did I miss now? There's William, myself, Gilbert ...... and what did I say, Gladys, did I mention Gladys? ... Gladys then Junior, I thought I had them fixed – I must have – um. I should be writing this down. Okay – I think I've got them all. Junior, Clarence Joe Junior, ... um, OK, oh Carl, um, Terry, Howie, oh, Hubie is the one. Hubie is the one that I missed. And um, like we were all healthy and strong when we were born – except for my youngest baby sister. [3:1]

Bernie was slightly annoyed that she had trouble recalling all of her siblings.

I mean like, now I don't remember but at that time I knew. I even knew what year they were born, I knew how old they were and I knew who -- but now I sort of forget. Um, I would remember every year, um every month whose birthday is, was or how old they were. But now I've lost it all. [1:5]

Large families were common in those days, but often several children in a family would die. Eleven surviving children from twelve births was good.

She – my youngest sister passed away at three years old. She had um, what do they call this now – when we have um, oh, what was that? Cancer I guess. What do they call that when they get that in their bones? ... Leukaemia. Um, um she was three. Three years old. ... Gosh, I can't remember what year it was when she passed away. And um, they had a hospital in Sardis, in Chilliwack, I don't know if you ever heard of that hospital at that time it was called Coqualeetza, ...[1] [1:3]

... so she was the first one that we lost amongst the twelve. [3:1]

Bernie's paternal grandmother assisted her mother at the birth.

She was the um, midwife of a lot of the people around here. We had no doctor I guess at the time and um, she was the um, midwife to a lot of – . ... Her name was Mary-Ann, Mary-Ann Joe. And her, um – I don't know if that would be a nickname or –– um, everyone called her Mommie. You know, I guess as in mother, I guess. And um, she was quite um, liked around the, reserve I guess, they called it – it's called Band lands now. But um, she brought into the world a lot of children around here. There was also another lady that I remember um, I can't remember her name now. Um, but she was another one. I knew two of them. I don't know if there was any more – but they were midwives – you know? [1:1]

Because of the lack of a doctor, or even a nurse and medical facilities, this was the normal practice for Sechelt women on the Reserve; they had no alternative. It continued to be the case until well into the next generation of Bernie's family.

Um, let me see. I have to go by the children um, ... I guess right into the 1940s ...... or maybe –– yeah into the 1940s – early 1940s. Then I think we finally got a doctor over here. We still had no hospital. Our hospital was at Pender Harbour, you know where Pender

---

1 Coqualeetza was for the treatment of long-term Native patients from the southern half of mainland British Columbia. Many of them were suffering from tuberculosis and as we shall see several others of Bernie's family, as well as she herself, spent time there. Although not all that far away as the crow flies, even today with modern ferries and highways it is two hours travel from Sechelt. In Bernie's childhood the possibility of visiting patients regularly was small.

Harbour is? And that was a long drive. It wasn't paved, it was a dirt road. I think in the late forties or something like that there was still, you know – they didn't ban, (midwives) like today I think they are you know, they don't allow them to any more, like you know. But um, – . [2:1]

Bernie's grandmother, Mommie, served a broader role in the Sechelt community than just midwife for she still retained much of the traditional healing knowledge.

So um, where was I, oh, about um, my grandmother. Oh yeah, being a midwife – and also not only that, she took care of a lot of people that took sick. Like you know just sick, like with the flu or whatever, even earaches you know. We – of course, we had our own medicines that they used. I remember me getting earaches and she would chew some tobacco, and I don't know what else she would put in there, some kind of oil or something and warm, like warm and stick in it my ear to keep it warm I guess. And leave it in there for a while. From swimming – I used to get earaches. ... Um, it helped – you know, but I, of course I kept getting earaches. She'd say don't swim today, of course I would go in, the same night the ear would ache again and so –– . And um, wounds they used to use frog leaves, stuff like that when there was a sore or something. Um, she helped a lot of people. When they were sick she would go to their homes, you know and look after them. [1:3]

And they used um, bear um, grease or oil, for, for even, to rub in their hair, their scalp and that. They said that was good for, all the things that were good for you. Of course our Indian medicines – I think I mentioned in our last session, I used to go up with my grandmother to – um, – these cherry bark, I can't remember. Barbie bark we used to call it. It was a medicine. ... But they, of course, they had an Indian word for it I can't remember, and er, there was lots in them days, but you hardly see any now, you know. We used that too, they drank it like a tea. They'd have it on the end of the stove and you'd have um, ah, I don't know how much they drank, but they gave us like a teaspoon, or not a teaspoon, a tablespoon, maybe once a day or twice a day or something. Supposed to keep you system cleaned out, or whatever. That was one. Another thing they used was frog leaves for, if you had a cut or sore or something. Or boil, a boil, lots of boils in them days and they'd put that, you know, clean it all – oh I think they would soften it up, put it in hot water and soften it up, peel the vine (vein) in the back of it, roll it up, soften it up and put it on – your – whatever, a boil, especially this, and it would take out all the stuff out of the boil, you know, just suck it out. ...... And, ... and that they used. There was another thing they used for warts. I can't remember the name of that. It's like a berry, they're little white things that grow on the bushes. [2:23]

Mommie's acceptance within the local community developed through a combination of her personality, her practical experience and her knowledge of traditional medicine.

Well, her having a big family I guess and knowing that she looked after them and brought her own family into this world, I guess they knew about her so they would call her, you know. Knowing that she was good. And mind you she was a very kind lady, very motherly, everyone loved her, right. [1:3,4]

Bernie had much practical experience of her grandmother's care in the course of her childhood. She contracted tuberculosis at age ten, and after a year in hospital she returned to Sechelt to her grandmother's care. Sechelt grandparents frequently played, and frequently still play, a considerable role in the bringing up of their grandchildren, but Mary-Anne and Basil Joe took on extra responsibility for Bernie because of her convalescence and because her own mother was so busy with the younger children.

I had tuberculosis when I was ten and I missed a year and a half of school. I spent a year and a half there. There was a lot of tuberculosis at that time, but um – . ... I think I was the first one, then my mother, later on after all her children were born and she –– . And then another – two, two brothers in – within a few years. ... There was also another hospital across there at Nanaimo (on Vancouver Island) where a couple – two or three of the people went over there. But um, I don't know – that went on for a few years. Now nothing, there's no tuberculosis now. [1:3]

But at that time tuberculosis was not at all uncommon amongst Native people and the Sechelt Nation was no exception.

Um, I think this, I can't remember the year but I was ten, I think ten ...... years old. I was in the school. I didn't know that I had tuberculosis. Like, I felt kind of healthy. Course you don't know – it wasn't that dark of a shadow on my lungs, and um, I got the word. I had to go to the hospital. "Oh, what for?" – you know. I didn't know how long I was going to be there, like months and then you know, my parents, used to come and visit me. And um, there was four of us. Um, from the school. We lost one girl. She had tuberculosis so bad that – I didn't know – I used to go and visit her in the hospital. And um, in the hospital there I met a few friends, –– from different places. One from Port Alberni. I heard she passed away later on. And then another one I met was um, ... my late brother's wife. [2:1]

Bernie was one of the lucky ones. She recovered from tuberculosis with no ill effects, although for a few years after her family was careful not to let her exert herself too much for fear of a relapse.

... my grandmother practically raised me as I was getting older, my mother was having more children and um, after, especially after coming out of the hospital, they were sort of, sort of nursing me you know back to health and I was not to do – lift heavy things, and this and that so –– and we used to travel up the Inlet, up um, Jervis Inlet so they took me up there one summer and we would take walks you know. They said, "A lot of exercise," you know, so we'd go up and pick berries. She looked after me, you know? [1:4]

Simply surviving was hard work in those days. The number of houses on the reserve was limited so families had to crowd in together.

... and it was very difficult for us too in them years when there was hardly any homes. Like we were all crowded into one house, you know. And especially in my day we were like twelve in my family and we had to crowd in – with my grandparents. I guess they were pretty big houses. Then finally, I don't know, at what age I was. My Dad finally got his own home. And um, and then my brother, Valerie's Dad finally got his home. [2:2]

As the eldest girl, Bernie would have been expected to do much more than she did if it had not been for her illness. Her grandmother provided an example by her own constant work.

She was a small little woman by the way, very tiny. And she worked hard. She used to have a garden in the back and she would be there with her boots and I don't know where she –– mind you, our people were very strong in them days. Not like today. We don't have their strength, you know. A lot of people talk about that, you know. She was small and worked hard. Chopped wood, even saw wood. We used to be – we had wood stoves. And we worked, even I myself growing up I, I – . ... Yeah, because see with my – well this came

after – I think I got healthy, my mother needed a lot of help with raising children, so after I was well enough as I was growing older, then,
then I helped my mother quite a bit. In them days too we – like I said
we travelled up the Inlet quite often. Like every summer maybe. My
Dad used to fish up there and log up there. Logging during the day,
fishing at night. And um, we had no um, um, like washer, dryer –
things – stuff like that. We lived like in a shack. And um, we had to
wash our clothes by hand, rinse in cold water. We'd heat our water
on the stove for washing. And there was a little river, something
close by, like say about a five-minute walk, you know. We had to pack
our water there so I had to be pretty strong in my day when I was
younger, you know. I did a lot of work like my grandmother did. And
helping my mother raising my younger brothers and sisters too. And
that was – and then later on my grandmother would take me away
again you know just to give me a break or, you know? [1:4]

*Other families would travel up Jervis Inlet in those days too. It was still
a strong remnant of the seasonal travels that the Sechelt people had
been making for generations around their traditional lands, following
the food supply.*

... them were my happy days up there. Up the Inlet. This is where
my grandmother came in. Not only with me – with, with the other
children too, as well. All the families were up there at that time.
Not only our family there was other families around. They had, you
know, shacks, houses, some had better houses you know, around
the Bay there. And they were logging there. The women would go
out fishing. I would go out with my grandmother um, she'd have a
line you know and I'd be rowing the boat for her – to catch a fish,
salmon. All the children would be swimming, but she'd say, "Come
on we're going fishing," you know? And um, if not that, we'd be
going out picking berries, and then another time um, a day they
used to, what did they call it, these trees, Barbie bark, they used as
a medicine, we'd go up there and she'd pick out some trees for me;
slit it down the middle and we'd peel it off the tree and then we'd
dry it. You know, just leave it on a rack or something, – out, you
know – it's a nice summer – dry it and then we'd crush it up. And
then put it in sacks and then they used to bring it down to Pender
Harbour and sell it. They used that Barbie bark for – . ... I don't
know. Cherry or Cherry bark. I don't know what they used it for.
But we used to sell it down at the store at um, Pender Harbour.
We'd come down by boat, you know, once a week, got a few sacks,

very cheap. But later on I heard that the price went up. ... They shipped it to Vancouver. I don't know what they used it for. Well, they knew it was a medicine, but I can't remember the um, what it was called what they got from that bark. I can't remember. ...... But anyway, um, we did that and then um, what else did my ── . Like I said I learned a lot of things from my grandmother eh? Um, helping her – I was always helping her. You know, everything that she asked me to do I would do. [1:5]

I used to love travelling up there (the Inlet) and the boats were slow, eh? Took all day to get up there ── and um, our, my grandfather would tell stories on the way going up about the mountains where they used to hunt. They used to hunt um, these um, mountain goats too at that time. They ate mountain goats at that time. I don't know if I ever did as a kid – I don't think so. They called me the fussy one. I didn't eat too, I didn't – I wasn't too fussy for wild game. You know. But they cooked like deer meat, I ate that, you know they ── they were all good cooks, you know. But clams I still don't eat. ... No, I don't like it. Um, like crabs I just started eating as I got older. But um, food in them days was quite different you know. Crabs, clams, whatever. Um, like we lived off the land eh? They got their flour, stuff you know, from the store here, in sacks you know, boxes of apples, mind you they had fruit trees up there too, eh? Apples, cherries, whatever. My grandmother did her own garden. She had potatoes, potato garden. We used to have wild rabbits come into the gardens for the lettuce. And um, so we had our like, vegetables, and just deer meat, fish ── . [1:15,16]

In winter, much of the food supply was that which had been grown or collected and prepared in the warmer weather.

In winter they, they um, like um, oh, I don't know, well she, like I said, my grandmother had potatoes but like we got our potatoes from the store. Like we had too, like rations too eh, you know in them days. And we got, I guess they had ...... um, I don't know how they ──. Oh carrots and stuff like that, you know, they stored. We lived off mainly potatoes, we were potato eaters, you know? And um, once in a while we'd have vegetables, you know, carrots mainly. ... Dried berries yeah, berries, fish. ...... And um, and even um, herring eggs. You know, the herring that used to spawn up the inlet and they used to put um, cedar branches – they'd sink the cedar branches down and the herring would spawn on it and then when they take it out they would put it on a rack too, you know, outside. I don't know what they made the racks out of though. And they'd just set the branches on there – dry it in the sun and then you'd peel it off and then they'd put them in sacks and put them up – they had racks too in these old houses, you know and just sit them up there. And um, in the winter they'd just soak it you know, and um, the smoked fish, they really had to dry the fish for it to keep, you know. And they'd also soak that too and even meat – they dried meat too. And then later on in years as I grew older my Dad used to get these um, barrels and salt the fish and the meat. ... Um, um. And the herring eggs too. And there was so many different way I just can't remember right now all the different things we used to. Like when I lay at home a lot of things come back to me you know when you think about it. [1:16]

Formal schooling played a big part in Bernie's life. The nuns and priests ran a residential school in Sechelt for Native children. Many were brought long distances from their homes to attend. Of those who attended this and other similar schools across North America, and indeed in other countries where similar situations occurred, many have very bitter memories. Bernie does not, however.

Oh, the school, okay, um, like I said umm, I can't remember when I first went. Six, I guess, seven maybe. They all must have been when they were six, I think. I sort of um, enjoyed the school. A lot of people would talk, condemning, "I hate the school." And while I didn't like the school really, I mean, I had a lot of happy days in school. And um, like the same things, we had chores to do and ...... of course, there is the religion. Everyone knows that. They talk about this, and not only here – different –– the first thing you do in the morning you get up out of your bed, you're on your knees, you go to Mass and from there you would go for breakfast. After breakfast we were doing chores. And then school –– . School, class they still put religion in there. Like, we laugh about it today you know, when we talk about it. I think I always got A's in religion. [laughs] And like, math was my hardest in school right? Mind you I was in the kitchen a lot of times too when they always had like, two or three girls in the kitchen during the day. And I would miss, um, there were nuns, there were nuns, and one sister, sort of um – they didn't um, um, how would you say it, like take one girl you know, treat one – give them special attention like, to one person. But this one sister did to me, you know. It was always "Bernadette" not

Bernie in school, it was "Bernadette." Um, "Maybe you should come in um, during um, like recess hour and I'll get you caught up on your math." I think I went maybe just once or twice you know. She took a little interest. Mind you, the others, you know, they were strict, they don't pay attention to you, or they just go by the rules. And there were things happening in this school that weren't right. How they, they disciplined, they used straps and –– they never did to me because my father was coming up to school quite often. And he was um, getting to be known. He, my father was starting to get into power then like um –– the old Chiefs and that were starting to look at him as a leader. You know what I mean, as a leader. And um, a lot of things –– well these things happened in their day too, you know. But um, there were things happening in the school where children were getting strapped and this and that –– even sickness you know, they, they, some kids were getting sick. [1:13,14]

The food, or lack of it, at the school is one thing that stands out in Bernie's memory.

Yeah, um. The food, ... wasn't that good. We were always hungry, you know. And some of us were lucky that had our parents living over here. Um, they, like I said before, they had a lot of fruit trees here plums, pears, apples, you know. And they always made like, Indian bread and sometimes, you know, our mothers would come up during the week and bring us some Indian bread and some apples and stuff like that, we were, but we all shared it. Kids that came from other Bands, you know, there was some that came from Powell River, North Vancouver, and other places I can't remember. It wasn't only for Sechelt, the school, and um, I'm coming to the food. We – as I grew older we had to take turns cooking. You know? But mind you, they had cows, horses, chickens –– I don't know what they did with the eggs. I think they sold it you know, the eggs, 'cause we only tasted eggs like, once a year which was Easter or something like that. And corn flakes, maybe. But we always had like, mush in the morning and maybe one slice of toast. And um, kids were always hungry you know? [1:17]

If parents brought extra food up to the school for their children the nuns would take it and dole it out in small quantities.

Um, um. What, what, they put it away for you. And like we got it and I'd keep so much out and share it with my friends, you know. But if they brought us a whole bunch, you know, and they give you only one apple a day or something like that, or oranges. And then later on in years they even had their little store, you know, where they sold little candy and that. Penny-candies, things like that. And um, like I said later on in years we started cooking, we started, like what we learned from our parents how to do Indian bread, and we used to make our Indian bread, you know and the meat ––. Oh, they also raised pigs and that which they [unclear] would have oh, them big pans, they'd bake the, chop up the meat and that, like big chunks, you know like stew of something, gravy, potatoes and maybe carrots. They grew their own, they had their own gardens up there too. In the school, carrots um, and stuff like onions and things like that, eh? [1:17]

In line with the gender roles of the time, and also as a part of vocational training for their adult life, it was the boys who worked in the garden while girls assisted with the cooking and cleaning.

... The boys worked in the garden. And um, ... and then we'd, we had to serve the staff also too, you know. Um, I think that was one of the biggest complaints they had in the school, was the food, you know? I remember we'd talk about it, like today when we had our Indian Agent come over for a visit, you know. We'd, we had to dine with him, you know. He'd come just to see what they were feeding us, if we were fed well enough or if they were, you know? And they would give us half a grapefruit, you know, with our meal just to make it look good, I guess, you know. And um, try to make our meals a little better just to show that we were eating good, I guess. And like I said we had our chores. One thing I didn't like was the laundry part of it. In the winter we had to hang clothes outside and our hands would be freezing. You know hanging clothes outside, like, you know, especially the bedding sheets and stuff like that. You'd hang them out – mind you they had a big dryer in that laundry room, you know, for some of the clothes. But I hated that part when I used to have to go out and do that, it was like, in the winter, cold. And um, a lot of chores, you know. And um, mind you, my Dad, like after I was sick there for a while they still used – he'd go up and tell them, the principal and say, "Now I don't want her working too hard," you know. Because there was reports from, maybe, well, one in my time, one girl passed away when we all went to the hospital – I was telling you. ... So, ... mind you, like when I was growing up, getting older they, the people started, we came up like, you know, like I said, in my Dad's time when they started, him and a, another man from Powell River, um, they started um, looking into the school, what was happening in the school and they started um, they, the nuns and the priests started thinking, "Well we better look out for these two men, they are always checking up with what's going on in the school." Things, I think were starting to change then, you know. They weren't so mean, nor weren't so –– we were always complaining we were hungry, things like that. Not myself. But other children, I've seen them. ... When I left I think it was still going on a bit but not as bad as before. [1:17,18]

... we all had different chores to do. Like, um, every week, like um, one week I'd be maybe doing the classroom. Another – then the next week I would do the hallway that had a hardwood floor and they would have to polish it. I found that one to be fun too 'cause we'd put someone on a cloth and pull them back and forth. ... Like um, old woollen sweaters or something you know and we would have fun just doing that. And um, one, and then another week I'd be doing the chapel. Which I loved doing – just polish and polish you know. The only one I didn't like doing was the kitchen work. Or, and the laundry. Because we had to go outside and um, in the winter time and hang clothes up and it was cold, and um, let's see. Recreation time we played outside and like I said before we had um, baseball, little baseball games or we'd just lay around outside perhaps if you had a book. They had um, some, a row of trees, they were hazelnut trees or something like that. And when it was getting warmer we'd just find a shady spot there and be there with a book or comic books or something like that if we didn't want to get into the –– . And we had swings and whatnot. And plus basketball outside. Things like that were our recreation. And um, oh, er, speaking about laundry too they had another building way over from the school where we had to do ironing. That's another job I didn't like doing. [laughs] There was one time I was doing kitchen work and we had to peel potatoes I think it was. And then the bell rings when it's time for class, eh? 'Cause this is after lunch, eh, we go right into the, I forgot, the pantry or whatever they called it. Course they had the big machines to do the potatoes and it takes off most of the peels but then you have to you know, um, clean it up a little more you know. So I'm there taking my time you know, and one nun comes in – she was – she was one of the better nuns um – I can't remember her name but –– . Anyway she comes and I was always called Bernadette in school. Today they – my Aunty Mary called me Bernie after I left school but the nuns you know,

"Bernadette." "Bernadette um, you'd better hurry up for school. Pretty soon classes will begin, the bell is going to ring pretty soon." And I'd say, "Oh Sister I have all day," I said to her. You know if it was any other nun she would like, get mad me talking to her like that, you know. But this nun – she never forgot it after you know. My mistake that time, I guess she let me get away with it that day. And then um, other times –– It seems like I had done a lot of kitchen duties because I always missed – I don't know if I mentioned it – um Math, um, we had tests for math and I was always in the kitchen. So I had to get tutoring. ... Well there was always like two that had to stay, I think, a week at a time in there, we'd miss classes because you're there like preparing dinner, for what, – there was 100 kids, I think there was. So there was always somebody to try and do .... I don't know. I can't remember, but there was always somebody there during class and that so you'd miss like, one week. Not all the time. Maybe one week and then you'd change – switch jobs you know. Oh, what else can I say? Course we were separated in our dining room. We had a dining room, the boys sat on one side, and the girls on one side. Course we had a nun in there you know, and um, we had to serve the, the meals you know. Just as they were coming in you know. Instead of like, you know, they had – you put them at the end of the table, the dinner, whatever it was, pots and they would serve themselves. Each table, you know. But in them days food wasn't very good, you know. We didn't get very much. A lot of children were hungry. That I remember. That I – I felt sorry for a lot of children. I for one was lucky because I had my family living close by here, where they used to bring me food. Bread, homemade bread and stuff like that you know. But like I said, I think I mentioned that I would share with other children that were –– you know, so ––. That's, that's the only thing that I really didn't like about the schooling. Course other children had more problems than I did. Where they got into trouble and they would get whipped or whatever, like that. I didn't. Because I think my Dad was a threat to the school. So I had, my days weren't that bad in school. Even though listening to a lot of people talking about residential, you should hear some of the people talk about it. It's awful. But like I said my days weren't that bad in school. So ––. [3:7,8]

The school, although it kept students until they were sixteen, only offered tuition up to grade eight. Few students got the chance to go further than this even if they wanted and were able to.

When I turned sixteen that was it. I'm out, you know. And at that time too they, some of them made it through, a couple of um, my cousin for one – they – when she, after grade eight they sent her to the white school and another two or three – I can't remember. To do their grade nine and I don't know how far they went from there. It was just up to grade eight here in the school. ... I didn't even reach eight. Like I said, I missed a year and a half of school. Mind you they were doing, coming into our – when I was in the hospital I wasn't even allowed to get out of bed, you know, but that um, I guess a whole year I was – so they would have somebody come in and, you know, a teacher. And after that they put us into another building where we were able to get up and have a little class there, but I was already falling way behind, you know. Then when I came out they (her parents) kept me out for another like part of the school, you know, they were afraid to send me back. Until I was healthy, more healthy and stronger, you know. ... My Dad went up – yeah they – I think they realised then, you know, that they were – um, my Dad was talking to them, "She's not very strong," you know, so I guess I would say I got special privileges in school, you know, where other children didn't. ... I remember there was a couple, maybe two or three girls, I don't know, that used to wet their bed, you know. And I used to feel sorry for them, the way the nuns treated them, you know. They had, they slept on straw mattresses where they had to take it out everyday and bring it out and air it out or whatever and um, I remember one time the nun came in because she was fed up with this one girl, made her get up and made her put her panty on her head and you know things like that, that I remember. Course there was lots more happening before that but I didn't see, you know. And I pity that girl you, know. And another time I seen a couple of girls get the strap just for looking over on the boys' side. You know they were so strict, you couldn't look at your own brother on the other side. You weren't allowed to talk to them or if you did you'd be punished, strap or whatever, you know. That's how strict it was, you know. And they played outside, even if they caught you looking on the other side they would –– it was awful. [1:19]

But Christmas provided at least a change in routine for a while, even for those who did not go home.

Um, we would have um, a little Christmas tree thing for the kids before some of us went home. Course there were a lot of kids that were left at the school, that came from different areas.[2] Say like North Vancouver, and some from up in Powell River and I don't know where else, Nanaimo – different places. Their parents didn't come and pick them up so they were left in school. But um, for us we had our parents right down here, so we were home for the, Christmas, I guess maybe just for the Christmas weekend. Not too many days, I guess two maybe three days. But we would have – at first we would have um, our little Christmas tree at the school where they gave us a little gift and some goodies. Some oranges you know, the Japanese oranges (mandarins), and some apples, some peanuts – whatever. And then, um, I don't know whether it was the same evening or the next day that we would go home. And um, well that was the Christmas tree thing. Oh, we'd have concerts. That's a big thing that I was missing. We had concerts. Which was real – I really enjoyed, you know – I really enjoyed that. Um, different plays you know – The principal we had at that time was really – was really something, you know, the way he always set up things in the concert. The boys even had a little band, you know, like with their instruments. We even had little roller skates things, you know, doing our thing on the, what do you call, the stage – the stage. ... And we had plays like Cinderella and whatnot. I remember once, one Christmas, I – there was a few kids that were brave enough to run home – like just run – we weren't allowed to, to leave the school grounds at all eh? But there was a few that would run home and pick some goodies – whatever – they were a little scared but – I was always a fraidy cat eh? But this one evening before the concert I knew my parents came in from Vancouver and I knew they were buying me some nice shoes for the concert, eh? So I had to have them. And I waited and waited and they weren't bringing it up so I took the chance and I ran all the way down there just to pick up the shoes. And this is like a three-storey building. Like I leapt through the fire escape and came down and then I went back. But I wasn't missed because there was such a commotion going on preparing for the concert at that time. ... I just had to have my new shoes. And they had two sessions of the concert, I don't,

---

2 In Canada, the Christmas holidays come at the end of the first term of the three-term school year, so, unlike in Australia, the break is only a couple of weeks. The residential school seems to have had an even shorter break than the public schools.

you know, this was in them days. They had one just for our Band, for the Reserve, and then they would have another one for the white people. Two nights, two separate nights. Maybe because it was kind of small. It was all classroom area and there was a stage up at one end of – like two classrooms where they opened up doors in the middle there. So that was Christmas in the school. And then we'd just go home after than and spend Christmas with our parents for a couple of days. Wasn't much happening then on the Reserve in them days. Until after school, when I left school um, then they started having Christmas like, what they call a Christmas tree in our hall there where they had all the kids. They'd buy presents for the kids. Or the parents could bring a present to the hall. They had a Santa – you know, from the Reserve. He was a very good Santa, you know, my Dad would help them prepare, you know. Before he went he'd write him out something what he's going to say you know when he's coming in the hall. Which was really funny eh? The kids would be all waiting in the hall and he'd have a bell, coming you know, and then the kids would be all excited eh? And then he'd come – he was really good. This was Johnny Joe, his name was. Well he changed his name to Dixon. But he was really good. And he'd tell stories as he was walking in. "Oh, I broke down, such and such, when I was coming in from the North Pole." Things like that you know? And he was really, really good. Lots of fun. You know, the kids had fun. And that kept on for years after. The Santa and the gifts and um – . [3:3,4]

As with nearly all residential schools for Aboriginal peoples, the children's own language was forbidden.

That's another thing. When we um, went to school we were not allowed to um, speak our language. [1:19]

For some children, whose people still used their own language predominantly and had less use for English, the first days at school must have been terrible, although, unlike some residential schools where Native language was forbidden absolutely, the Sechelt school allowed non-English speakers to use their own language until they had learned some English.

In school we weren't allowed but um, kids from up Sliamon, that's Powell River, they were allowed to – when they first got into school because they couldn't speak English and um, so they were allowed until they learned how to speak English. I don't know why. I remember that. Like, everyone says "No, we weren't allowed," and they said, but I remember them using their language because a lot of them couldn't speak English. For years after they still – their children, I was surprised when we didn't, we couldn't speak our language but they could speak theirs quite well. Like the girl my age, I have a friend up there, she – she knew her language pretty well when we were in school. Course she couldn't speak 'cause she – she spoke English quite well, eh. So that was the language part. [1:20]

The Sechelt people had already begun to put their language into the background and used English for everyday use so, for their children, school was not so much of a culture shock.

Um, I understood and I spoke a little bit but not um, you know, um, and maybe when I come to think of it now, our grandmother, my grandmother and my parents didn't ask us to answer them back in our language, maybe because of the school, you know, didn't want us to really, because when she goes back to school then she'll be, so we always answered in English, you know. ... But they spoke to us in our language. Mm hm, quite a bit, you know, like I said I was practically raised with my grandmother who spoke to us in our language. [1:20]

But I didn't answer back in the language, you know. Um, when we tried they would laugh at us, you know, because we weren't saying it right or, but um, um, we knew what they were talking about. [2:17]

But listening to a language is obviously not enough. Today Bernie has forgotten much of what she could once understand, and speaking the language is not easy for her.

Um, not all of it, you know. We, we sort of lost, then from years and between, like, when we come to our sessions now a lot of words come out, "Oh, yeah, I remember that word, I used to hear it." Like we don't – we never practised it since, like maybe since my parents passed away. Sort of just died off. [1:20]

The discipline the family still exerted over the young, children and teenagers, is something that Bernie remembers clearly. In fact it was not only family that held young people in line but neighbours and friends too.

Course in them days we were very disciplined, eh, not like today. Um. ... like coming from the school, like we were still in school, we would spend the summers up there and then we would come back to the school and, and um, religious, religion had a lot to do with it too. Um, ... I think um, well we were getting disciplined from both, like from the school and from our parents. ... Like when I was becoming a teenager and we were, we weren't going up the Inlet so much then, um, we still were doing our chores, listening to my mother. Before we went out, you know, to go for a walk, there wasn't too much to do. We would have to do our chores, wash dishes, whatever we had to do, laundry. And then we would come out and go for a walk, come around, you know, the church – there was three of us I remember. And there was this other lady that I was talking about that was a midwife, well actually she was a relative to my other grandmother. Two grandmothers from my Dad's side. This woman I'm talking about, this woman was from my, it was my Dad's mother. But this other one I want to mention her name was Mary-Ann also, but she was Jefferies. And she lived just on the other street down here and her sister-in-law lived over here, up the hill here. The school used to be here and we'd be passing by and they'd be talking to each other or hollering at us in our Native language – "Look at them – what are they doing – I wonder if they did their chores at home?" You know, and sort of saying, you know – just walking normal, you know, we're getting to be bad girls, we're out, just, you know. See, like, not only our parents at home were disciplining us, but my other grandmother would get to the house and, "I seen her walking around over there, did she do – ?" you know, and more or less scolding my mother to see if she was, you know, taking good care of me. You know, it – there was, everybody was involved. ... Yeah. And um, then if somebody did something wrong they would go and let the parents know and they would talk it over and ––. [1:6]

So, while a child's parents were directly responsible for controlling and disciplining them, they received support, both moral and real, from the community.

It was the parents. And the grandparents. And the grandparents. The grandparents had a lot to do with it too, eh? When my Dad, um, when they were having us children, um, like, I, I can't remember, we always ate around the table – big family and my grandmother would even scold my Dad at that time, you know, she would say, "Never scold your children at the dinner table. Never scold them. If you have to scold them do it some other time, not when they are eating because they are going to get all, um, ... angry or they'll push their plate away, they won't eat – they'll get upset," and things like – that – she had a strict rule about that. And with other things too, she still scolded my Dad. [1:6,7]

In them days, they were, well, like I said, they were sort of strict you know. If you ever heard anything, you know, any scandal or anything, you know, it would go around and, and um, another thing, when something happened with children or something they had old Chiefs and Councillors and you would have to go, like a judge or whatever, they'd have to go and sit in front of them and they would get a preaching to or whatever, you know – they done something wrong. I don't know if that um, involved marriages, like, if a couple were not getting along or something – maybe – I think even that, they would have to go and sit in front of the old Chiefs, the Councillors, and they would talk to them. Like as a counsellor would, you know? Marriage counsellor – whatever. And they done that to children when they, like one of the kids – the big church we had it was beautiful but one of the kids went and broke a window and still at that time, 1940s going on to 1950s, they were still doing that. "Oh, umm, so and so went and broke a window," rather than the parents discipline them, "Okay, you're going to go in front of the Chief and Councillors. And you're going to get talked to," you know. [1:12]

To be called up in front of the Chiefs was a terrible punishment in itself.

They would be afraid to go, you know. I don't know if they ever gave them any sort of punishment – just a warning, I guess, you know, so they would know. And I think that went on until the late forties maybe – yeah, late forties. [1:12]

Theoretically both parents were equally responsible for the discipline of both male and female children, but because children spent a lot of time with the parent and/or grandparent of the same sex, learning traditional or simply useful skills, then in practise the parent of the same sex did the largest amount of disciplining.

I, um, there was a lot of – I think mainly with the women and the grandmothers had a lot to do with it. And of course, if it was something more serious then the fathers or whatever. I think, well, well I should say that with the boys the fathers and the grandfathers, you know, when it came to work, you know, they would um, my father would talk, and my grandfather would talk to the boys. You know? [1:7]

The gathering and preserving of food was a vital part of everyday life for the Sechelt people. Everyone took part and skills were learned by being a part of the group and helping as one was able.

Like we'd – in my younger days, like, I shouldn't leave that out, they did a lot of hunting and fishing in them days. They, um, we ate a lot of deer meat, you know. And we do everything with it, roast it, fry it and stew it up. And dry it also. Um, but I never really learned how to, they done that, you know, my grandmother that was, um, I never really learned how to do that, but I learned how to, I watched her how she done the berries. Dried the berries also and stored them away. You know there's a lot of things. ... Smoking fish. Oh yeah, we learned that at an early age 'cause we helped, eh? Clean, course, um, my mother would say we'd mess up the first few fish, you know, but we all took part in – if we weren't cleaning fish we'd be helping with the sticks, put the sticks on and hanging it up and whatever. ... Yeah, it's just a natural thing, you know, you just er, – they don't say "Come here you are going to learn." No you just go automatically there and you're going to do it, you know, because if you don't they are going to call you and teach you anyway. And um, I enjoyed doing it, mind you, with my grandmother. Like when she used to do the berries ...... and um, what else. Oh, another thing they did with the fish was the open fire ..... around the ...... well, they did it mostly at the beach where there is rock, and they had a fire and they put your fish on a stick, you know, and put it around the fire and that's where the people – the people used to like working together too – not only our family, other families would be close by and then we'd sit around the fire and tell stories. That was fun. I enjoyed that you, know. [1:9]

You know, you wanted to be involved in everything, you know. Um, like I said, in berry picking with my grandmother. Maybe there was the odd time when all the children were swimming and she'd pick me out you know. "Come on, we're going picking berries," it was a hot, hot day you know. But I never – we never said "No." Never fussed and said I didn't want to go. And she'd go out trolling you know in the boat. I had to row the boat and you know I enjoyed that too. A lot – a lot of things. But, um, when I was talking about the – this supposed to be involved with the men and I would be wanting to go too you know. But my Dad always said "Yeah, okay come on," you know. Or my grandfather or my uncle. And whatever they were doing. ... A lot of things that I learned. Even when we used to go out fishing on the seine boat then. I never went out with my Dad when they were gill-netting but on the seine boat, bigger boats, you know.[3] Even let me steer the boat. I loved doing that. My – one of my uncles even got me to dock the boat one time. Quite a large boat, eh. Course they had the power, I think the other boat – my Dad's boat was a little more difficult because it was a wheel that you had to turn. It was a cat motor – a great big cat motor and was a little more difficult for me to handle you know, 'cause you had to turn these wheels. But the other boat, my grandfather's, and now I was so proud of myself for doing this, you know. "Okay you want to dock the boat?" I said, "Sure, I want to dock the boat," so I went down you know, coming in, and a perfect landing. You know things like that. ... I think – I think a lot of um, people in my days, like my friends, my cousins, we were always together. Um, yeah, yeah, they were, we were always together. Like I said um, in the sawing the logs, all the kids were down at the beach, you know? Maybe some were just playing but we – we liked to get involved. Even with the sawing, it's hard you know, with the old saws, and we'd say, "I want to do that," you know. So I had to try, you know. Things like that. You just enjoyed doing it. ...... So the only thing I didn't get into is basket weaving. Now I'm just kicking myself. Why didn't I do that instead of being involved in –– [laughs]. ... I loved watching them. Maybe I just figured I wouldn't be able to do it – I don't know. They done such perfect work you know. ...... But they never really did sit me down and say, "Here, try it," you know. Um, my grandmothers on both sides were good at basket weaving. ... They were always making baskets. Um, later on in years – yes, they were selling them. Like, mostly tourists –– we had this steamship that used to come in every week. Maybe twice, three times a week. There was always a lot of tourists on them. Lots from the States and they would come around the Reserve and the women were always sitting on their porches and maybe you've seen some of the pictures here. They were always sitting on their porches and doing their um, their basket weaving. And people would be taking their pictures or asking them, "When will that one be done? I'd like to buy

---

3 Gill-netting involves setting a straight net in which fish are entangled by the gills. A seine net is set in a circle with floats at the top and weights at the bottom and then the net is drawn in, trapping the fish inside.

that one." Or some would make orders, but they sure didn't get very much in them days. Today they are worth a lot of money you know. But a lot of them made baskets too for picking – like, they called them spiht'-yoos I think. ...... You know that's when they first started. I don't know. But, they made um, for picking berries too, and um I know in my time my grandmother, I think I mentioned, made a little suitcase at one time. Course the nuns took it away from me and gave me just a shoe box in return. Because she wanted to send it to France to one of the nuns there in France. And um, today I feel sorry – I get mad that they gave it to her. I would have still had it today. And she would make me little baskets for my bobby pins or my –– lipstick or whatever. Things like that. Sometimes she's put a cover. But I don't know what I've done with them two. ...... But, they would make different things, you know. My grandmother on my mother's side made a great big basket for a dog. That one person ordered from the States and even wrote the name "Champ" on there. I don't know if you've seen the picture? ... I think it's in the –– museum here. They used to have it out. It's a beautiful, oh – about this big I guess round [holds arms out approx 0.75m diameter]. About so high (0.5m). "Champ" written on it. Beautiful. I don't know how much – I think like two hundred dollars for it. Today it would be worth two thousand dollars. Worth a lot of money today. You know, when they didn't get very much for them in them days. So –– . [3:12-14]

In fact, Bernie's memories of her childhood are largely happy ones.

Oh, my childhood was as happy, happy days. I remember a lot of happy – . Even in the school, like we talk, a lot of people talk about the school. Where there was a lot of um, ... in the residential, there was a lot of things happened there. But we found – I was quite happy there, but in my younger days, like I said, I was with my grandparents quite a bit. I didn't um, feel that my parents were pushing me away or anything, I didn't feel that way. Like, we were always just one big family and we were always together. Very seldom I was away from them. Once in a while they would take me up, up the Inlet. That part was dying off then, when I was getting older. But they took me up, my parents stayed down here. But I, –– didn't miss them too much because I was with my grandparents, they were just like my mother and father. They raised me and we did a lot of things together. [2:21]

Like, I was well taken care of, like I said, by my grandparents. Only one, one side, my Dad's parents. Not too much of my mother's. I didn't learn too much from my mother's side and that. But um, I – all through my childhood days were happy days as far as I can remember. Like, I say this all the time, especially up the Inlet, I spent a lot of my younger days up there. Fishing and picking berries, doing this and that with my grandmother. And of course I helped my mother a lot too. I never complained, you know, like it was just a daily thing you know. 'Cause we had a lot of time um, swimming and things like that. But we, we did a lot of hard work too. As a child I did a lot of um, heavy work, like packing water. Chopping wood even. Things like that, but I didn't find it difficult. It was fun. We even, up here [points to mountains], I used to even go up with my grandfather, and my Dad. Course there was a lot of wood up there in them days. And we all had wood stoves and they would go up the woods there and –– "Can I go, Can I go?" They'd have these old – no powersaws – these old saws you know. Axe, and um, knock down a tree. Um, cut it up you know. And then they would roll it down – there was just trails. This highway wasn't busy then – there was just a road. It wasn't a highway then. Trails going up here and would come down – they would put two sticks on this block and roll it down. I mean I wasn't asked to go and do this, but I wanted to go and do it. You know things like that. ... It was fun going out with them. And once in a while they would say, you know, "Keep out of the way now." Especially if a tree is coming down or –– I did a lot of that even when my Dad was hand-logging up there. Um, we'd go up and – course we had to keep our distance you know. Things like that. I enjoyed doing. Out fishing. My Dad went out in a boat. Set the net – I would want to go. Not that I was a tomboy or anything. We just wanted to be involved in everything they did, you know. And um, down at – the waterfront there, when we didn't have the wood, we'd go down to the beach and pick up the – we had a lot of driftwood coming in – bark or whatever. Pick that up too. Put them in boxes and ...... um, I didn't find it hard. Kids today: I find them lazy. You know. In our days it was fun. Fun for us doing that you know. Like I said a lot of things they didn't ask us to do we just – . [3:11,12]

Storytelling was an important part of family life. It served as a pleasurable social experience, but it was also a time for learning.

Well, there's another thing, in the evening like, when we've all had our supper or whatever you know, um, the people would go around visiting each other. And then their story-telling would start again you know, in the house there, they would serve you tea and they would have home-made preserves you know like berries, blue berries, black berries and whatever they preserved. They'd open a jar and they would have that to eat and their Indian bread, you know, whether it be fried bread or the baked bread, you know, there's a few ways you can do the Indian bread you know, and um, then they would have the story – and children, mind you, too, they would make them stand up and sing or something on a little awful box, you'd have to stand up and sing and entertain the guests [laughs], it was fun, you know? ... I heard lots of stories but I said to Valerie, "Oh, I'm just kicking myself for not remembering them." I said, "I wished in them days they had one of these recorders or um, you know, be writing down the – ." Even as I grew older after I got married my grandfather was still alive –– and um, we were living with him – this was down here at Sechelt, um, he, he liked cooking too and he would call us, you know, "Dinner is ready," you know. Course it would be fish, or you know, he liked doing his fish – you know, bake it in the oven, throw potatoes, onions – . As soon as we'd get to the table he would start. Not only the story-telling of um, like, animals or the hunting or whatever or [indistinct] or something, but he would tell us about our relatives, who we were related to. We even have relatives in North Van(couver), up Powell River, and like, even around here, er, "You know so and so, they're," and he would use his hand, "you're related to this one, you're related to that one," and he would tell us how we are related to them, you know. It was very important. Because as children growing up they don't want, um, inter-marriages I guess, you know. "You don't look at that boy, you're related to him," you know. So it was, you know, they always told you who your – and respect them, you know and ––. [1:10,11]

The adult world of work, paid or otherwise, was entered early by many Sechelt men and women, or perhaps one should say boys and girls, for they started work early in those days. The necessary skills were frequently taught by parents or other family members, and often they began to be acquired from early in childhood. The two main jobs open to the men were fishing and logging, both of which their ancestors had been doing for centuries.

Like, my older brother now, like Valerie's Dad, he started working when he was fourteen, thirteen or fourteen years old. He started logging. With fishing it's different. You can go out with your Dad even as a young boy, you know, you don't have to do too much, but you're on the, boat, like, learning, you know. But logging is a little different, you have to work. And he started quite young. And, um, I must say too, my Dad, he got his first boat, this is a seiner, when he was seventeen years old. He was a skipper of his own boat. He had a seven-man crew under him. He was only seventeen. ... These were company boats you know. They all worked for B.C. Packers. There was other people that worked for different companies. They went out. This was, you know, I guess – in that year, like I said he was seventeen and um, he talked about it to like, my brother, you know. "I started working when I was fourteen, and I started logging when I was a young boy too." You know, he would tell his boys, you know. So they would know and learn, you know. And sure enough my brothers they, the three older brothers, they all were fishing and logging. [1:7]

Some women worked right with their men.

So actually I went out cooking for my Dad. It was all like a family group, you know. My brothers and I went out with him a few summers. ... I was, I guess, sixteen – seventeen. And I also, um, went out cooking for him when they, they – him and his Dad, my grandfather they had a little what did they call it – hand logging they called it. You know they had their own logging – little camps here and there on the Band lands, eh, and um, once in a while I'd go up and cook for them. ... you know, mind you, my Dad used to scold me – I didn't know how to cook – he taught me how to cook. ... My Dad was a good cook, not my mother so much. My grandmother was a good cook, very good, and my Dad, not my mother so much. I mean she'd cook but, you know. He would scold me, like when you're doing, stew, you know, it's – of course simmer it for a long time. Even cutting vegetables he would come and scold me "No, you don't chop it up with that cabbage – you do it this way," you know. And that's how I learned. ... My Dad? Where did he learn how to cook? From my grandmother I guess, like I said she was a good cook. And um, they, I think they all knew how to cook in them days you know they all had to learn. ... Um, um, but I mean some people would just cook, fry an egg or whatever, like that, but he – he, my Dad was a good cook. Like for instance, I don't eat clams, eh. But he would do everything with the clams just so I would um, you know, um, want to eat it. He'd curry it, he'd stew it up or whatever, but I still wouldn't eat it. [1:7,8]

But, um, on the way up North too, going up travelling, they use to hunt on the way. You know, we'd go along the shoreline there, you know, and they'd hunt – deer meat. Catch a deer and, you know, they'd skin it – and they had big hatches on them seine boats. And they'd hang it for like, two, a couple of, two, three days to hang it in the hatch, you know. And er, we'd have fresh deer meat. You know, ate a lot of deer meat and fish. And um, ... anyway after – oh, I enjoyed that. I really enjoyed that. Going up North and I – . [2:3]

The major source of paid work for the women was sorting and cleaning in the fish canneries.

And my Dad, one year too had all the girls – a bunch of girls from here – um, – um, more or less hired and they – he knew the – the company, the guy that um, the B.C. Packers. He um, fished for the B.C. Packers and he asked my Dad and my grandfather if he would pick up a bunch of girls here to go and work at the cannery up there. So which they did. We all travelled together at that time, they had two fish boats and they got girls on both – we travelled together. You know. That was fun, they enjoyed that, and they worked in the camp. I guess about maybe eight of them. My sister was one of them. Almost a family. Anne Quinn was another one. And um, I only worked in the cannery there once – part of the summer I think. Then I was back on the boat, again. [2:3]

But in between working there was still time for play.

Even after I left school we had an old hall there, they had basketball hoops there. And we'd go – that's where we'd spend recreation time. Course that's after we'd done our duties at home you know. Our chores. We weren't allowed to leave unless we had done our work at home first. And then we'd go and gather at the hall and play basketball. If not, we were outside. ... Boys and girls, yeah. Some, some were a bit older than me and we'd choose sides and play, you know. That's all the activities we had in those days, that I remember. I know later on in years they had er, what do they call them, horseshoes thing, you know, yeah.[4] But it was strictly baseball and in, in my time basketball. And that's the – all I can remember in sports. [3:2,3]

---

4 Horseshoes is played by tossing a series of horseshoes at a short stake in the ground with the aim of getting as many as possible actually hooked around the stake.

Church going was also a pleasurable social, as well as religious, experience for many people in Bernie's young days. The presence of the Catholic Church in Sechelt since the last quarter of the nineteenth century had a profound effect on the people, as had the banning of the potlatch which had once been so central to their culture. Many of their traditional beliefs had been cast aside and replaced, outwardly at least, by Catholic teachings.

... the big church that we lost. That was a beautiful church. And, er, people were going to church still in them days. Not today, we're losing it, you know. And we had nice priests here. And, er – . ... Well, even when I was out of school, my Dad still got us up on Sunday mornings to go to church, whether we wanted to or not. But we, we didn't fuss. I mean, I always wanted to go, I didn't er, like, maybe a few mornings, sometimes I didn't want to go. And all the different days – Easter, and we had different things too like May –– in May they had some sort of procession out here, you know. That was nice in them days. Everybody got together, you know, and people were close, you know. ... and after church the men would all sit, I don't know if you've seen any pictures we have. One right there [points to picture on wall of Cultural Centre]. They all sat in front of the church after Mass and would talk, you know, tell stories and talk and, and, er, I used to hang around for a bit, you know, and then go and play. [2;8]

... And when we used to go into Vancouver, too, and when I was talking about my parents, they used to like to go. You know, I guess it was to get away from here and like a holiday for them. And Sundays still my, my parents used to go to this big church. They have a big church in Vancouver there, and they used to go there. Real beautiful church. and er, my grandmother had, like we had relatives all over too. Like North Van(couver) and Nanaimo, and grandmother used to take me to North Van(couver) to visit a relative there. I was quite young then, of course they had a big, their church is still there. They've got a big church and she would take me to church. [2;9]

Community celebrations were important when Bernie was young. These were usually connected with Catholic religious festivals, but often had facets far removed from the religious.

Um, we had a lot of celebrations at Easter. Of course this was connected with the school, I think at that time – this was when I was younger. And it had to do with their religion too and we used to have people coming from, up from Powell River coming to celebrate Easter with us, you know. Spend, like, a whole week here. And um, they had sports days for all the children, for all the people, sports for children and then it went on to adults. Baseball – they had lots of things happening at Easter, during Easter. Course the religion came first, a Mass. Then they had the procession of the Virgin Mary, things like that eh? And then the sports and whatnot after. Baseball after the sports. ... Oh, sometimes yeah, the priests were involved in arranging the baseball. Not the – well I think they were even involved in sports. This was done on um, the Reserve there, not on the school grounds. On the Reserve there – they've had that park there for um, oh years. 'Cause it's in my Dad's time, I guess, they played baseball. They had baseball games going on there. And um, they had a lot of things happening in Easter. And the children would get together. I remember going to, when the two Bands would get together we would go to this – there was a few kids that were involved in um, music, um, accordion, guitars, whatnot, you know. And um, we'd go to a certain house and they'd play the guitar and the accordion. You know all this happening during the Easter week. So I – I used to find it fun. We don't have that today. Even – the – they had that going for years, the Easter – . Well it came down to just um our People and then they – I don't know why, maybe – I don't know why – what year the people from up there stopped coming from Powell River. The Sliamon people. They stopped coming. But our celebrations still continued and our sports day until – oh I can't remember when. They'd have a sports day every Easter Monday. And had that going for – in my days, I guess, after ...... I think um – maybe until as far as to when I got married. Oh, and then the soccer took over. When our boys really got involved in soccer then they start leaving – going to Victoria on Easter week. And then, there was a lot of people that used to go there. So that sort of um, slowed down the activities here for the Easter week, eh. Um, a lot of people you know, that the soccer, maybe two – three soccer teams plus the fans you know, that was like a getaway for them. That's – that's sort of slowed down the sports days then, which we don't have any more. [3:1,2]

Christmas, too, was a mix of religion and the older traditions of Sechelt family gathering and gift giving.

At home, like um, we all gathered at my Dad's like – we were a big family except my brothers, well they were starting to have their own families. But we still gathered at my Dad's place to have it. A big dinner, like a family dinner. And um, of course me being the oldest I was always there to help prepare the food, you know. My Dad was, like I said, my Dad was a good cook you know. And um, we'd start early in the morning cutting up vegetables and um, he'd have me baking pies. I'd bake about twenty pies maybe and um, like, my brother William, he'd take one or two pies home to his family. And Gilbert would take some home for his. You know distributed amongst the family. My Dad had me doing this you know. Lemon pie, apple pie, cherry pie and what do you call it, mince meat pie. Different types of pies and I, I wasn't good at baking cakes but I was good at doing pies, eh? And we all – like I said, oh, and then of course midnight Mass. Um, in them days there wasn't too much um, um, um, alcohol in them days. There was you know, we had our little bit of liquor, but not like later on in years when the liquor started really getting bad on the Reserve. We'd go to church, midnight Mass. We'd all gather at my Dad's place again and we'd have coffee and, like, a piece of pie or whatever. Then everybody would head home. You know, after Mass – like two or three in the morning. And like I said, then the next day then it was Christmas dinner. Which went on for years. I mean with our family. I don't know what other families, I think the same thing. It was real traditional, um, I think in them days for families to, to always get together. Today it's not like that eh? We all drifted apart when my Mom and Dad passed away. We all – we don't get together any more. We have barbecues once in a while. That's another thing we used to have. Barbecues, family barbecues. Then of course my mother went first, then my Dad, then even that died. After my Dad passed away then that sort of stopped too, eh. But um, years ago like people, even not family – not families they, other people, we always liked to get together and visit each other and like we were always close, a close Reserve. You know. Like I said even up Jervis (Inlet), when we were up there, people from further up – um up there, there was some up from Xunichen like I said and there was some Reserve and then a whole bunch would come down and visit. That was um real traditional in them days. So – anything else about Christmas. I think, well, the main thing about Christmas and Easter was always the religion first. The midnight Mass and our Dad always made us go to church too, Christmas morning or something like that. It's not Christmas unless you went to church you know. [3:4,5]

*But, like many of the Sechelt people, Bernie only attends church occa-
sionally now.*

I only go now, on just special occasions. Um, like, you know, weddings and funerals or whatnot, you know. Ahh, people don't go to
church any more, eh. Our church has been closed off too, for a
while. They want to fix it up and –– they tell us we can go to the
other church, the white church, but, er, I don't feel right, going
there, you know. But mind you, over here we get a lot of white people coming, especially for midnight Mass at Christmas, you know.
You look out, like a mouse in the choir. I've been in the choir since
my school days, I guess. ... Well Christmas is not Christmas without a midnight Mass, you know. [2:8,9]

Like, a lot of people say today, I think it's because we had so much
of it when we were in school and we were like, forced to go to
church. Not that I didn't like it. I liked going to church. I didn't
mind. Mind you, I didn't mention towards the end of my school
years, maybe a year or two before the school ended they were now
starting to slow down, um this, like they, we were supposed to go
like, every day not just Sunday. We were going every morning, um,
to Mass and they had a little chapel. Mass first and then breakfast.
We were always on our knees – you know. Right from when you got
up in the morning you were on your knees, you know. But the last
year or two I think it was, they gave us an option. If you wanted to
go or ––. But we had to go like two or three times a week, not miss
every morning, you know what I mean? Um, so after school, and
my – my Dad, um, pretty well everybody – they were all religious,
you know? Um, after school my Dad still got me up Sunday morning to go to church. And as I got older he sort of just left it up to
me. And I would go most of the time you know. And um, course
holidays, and there was a lot of holidays. Like Catholic holidays too,
where you had to go – Palm Sunday, Easter Sunday for the Mass,
um, Good Friday, Holy Saturday. All them different – . You had to go
to them you know. I guess it was after. Course I was married in the
church. Our old church. After that then I start slowing down. I think
a lot of people did you know. When they grew older they slowed
down. Mind you, I still went every now and then you, know. I liked
that old church, like I missed it. You know it had three big altars. I
even liked the little chapel in the school. But I guess the thing was
I didn't like being forced to go to church. Maybe that was the prob-

lem. Where everybody slowed down and like, one friend of mine said too um, "I quit – the reason I quit going to church is when the priest said" um, this is from a different reserve, "When the priest told me that I had to put more than two dollars in the collection plate." She said, "That's why I quit going to church." But um, I really didn't mind. I wasn't religious. But I didn't mind. But like I said, I just had too much of it I guess, as a child. And growing up, and you know? I think, in fact, for years after we had bruises on our knees 'cause we were on our knees all the time. ... Even at home. Um, when we had deaths – we had the wakes – at night. They carried that on in people's homes – they'd have a wake, we'd be on our knees to say the rosary or something, for some person who had passed away. Even carried on in their homes. So, yeah, that was – like I said, too much of that in the younger days. But today, I was just telling my daughter, I said "If I had my car." I always had a car after I got married – but it's a bit of a walk for me now to go to church. I don't think we have a priest now anyway. My friend Stella she goes still every Sunday. I wouldn't mind. ...... But when it was forced upon us as kids it was sort of, you know. [3:8,9]

Consequently Bernie did not make a big thing of her children attending church.

So – and um the thing is too with my children – mind you the school was still in – you know, the nuns and the priests were still here, and as our children were growing up, of age, they would call them or come and give us notices and they had to go. Course all the children were baptised. All my children were. We all made sure of that. And um, when they became of age then they would send us notices for um, they had to go to catechism to learn the religion. Used to go through the other, like um, um first communion, and this and that you know. My oldest son there, the one I raised, even served Mass. When it came to the other ones, they went and done all that but I never really sent them to church or brought them to church, maybe. Just when they were little, like I said, my grandfather would bring them to church. And I had another uncle, Benny, he was a great one for going and he would bring my little girls to church too. But when it came to my younger boy, he doesn't even know religion at all I don't think. But he was baptised – and confirmation you know. As long as they had all that I think we didn't mind, you know. It's all up to them after that. And they're, in this day, in their age group –– . [3:10]

By the time Bernie was old enough to marry the traditional practice of arranging marriages had all but died.

Mind you, um, they, they had this um, what they called the fixed marriages I think, before. They tried that with me. Um, when I was what, twenty, I was like going up North with my Dad then and I told myself I would never marry anyone from this reserve. You know. ... I'm going to marry someone outside. Because, because like maybe I was always told we were related or you know, um, I ...... a few of us got together, you know, we'd talk about marriage, you know, when you are growing up, teenagers, whatever. I said "I'm not going to marry anybody from here, I'll --. Whether it's somebody from another reserve or whatever." And I also said, "I'm not marrying young." You know. I think in my mother's day, or even before that they married quite young – I think my mother was seventeen. My Dad was nineteen when they got married. So you know when you're learning these things you tell yourself. "No I'm not going to get married that young." You know. And um, this um, my grandmother on my mother's side, her sister-in-law tried to arrange for me to marry one of the – uh, I wasn't related to him, he was a Paul, and um, I come back from up North. Mind you this boy was um, um, ... working for my Dad on the boat, he was one of the crew members on the boat. And he was a nice person, shy, he was very backwards. And maybe because he was, like, say when they're earning money, you know, they thought. "Oh, this man is a good provider, he is a good worker, you should –," you know, talking to my mother – trying to set me up with this, um. And this boy even bought me a ring which I didn't even um, and he was a friend of my brother's, you know – they were real close buddies, you know. And we took it like er, I would talk to my sister-in-law and we would laugh about – like as a joke you know. But um, of course I was seeing other boys and that. I gave it to him back, you know. I don't know whether he was, you know, seriously looking at me or whatever. Like I said he was shy, a shy person and um, so I gave it to him back. I said, "No." I never, whatever her name was, Ellen he, that was his um, he was related to her, not that close but like an Aunt or something. He had no parents. His parents died when they were – there were three brothers, their parents um, died when they were quite young. So I think they were raised by this old lady who was related to Ellen, the one I was talking about. Trying to arrange, I think she was a great one for that, this lady [laughs]. [1:11,12]

In the previous generation, however, it had still been quite common.

Um, when they talk about, like my parents, for instance. I think, and um ...... on her mother's part, see 'cause my Dad was ...... was working and a provider, you know he was out and he was young and he was fishing and logging, and see, my mother's mother, I guess, was looking at that and try to, you know. My Dad talks about it, you know, and he laughs you know, "I seen your mother looking at me," you know, and I think my mother was kind of shy too, but I think she was sort of pushed to, you know. They never had a chance to, more or less you know, see other boys and my Dad, I don't think he had a –– they were just like more or less put together you know. [1:12]

Bernie stuck to her vow not to marry a local boy and not to marry as young as many of her parents' generation had.

I was twenty-two, twenty-two. ... I married a guy from, he's from Alberta. Um, Slave Lake? That's near Slave Lake, and I got four children – one, two –– I get confused 'cause I raised one, we raised one – my sister's boy – she passed away and um, we raised him. I didn't think I was going to have any children. We were married seven years before I got my oldest daughter. So I married a Cree [laughs]. And um, he worked over here and he fished with my Dad and he taught him how to log. And things like that. [1:13]

At that time too, um, like I said, I think we were only – there was no clinic here. The Hospital was in Pender Harbour there. At that time I didn't know I was having miscarriages. Like, I think I mentioned before, my Dad thought I was a very delicate person, you know. Guess when I was, when I got pregnant – in them days too we were still carrying our water I think from outside. Well my parents had the house, we lived in a little, little house next door and we had no plumbing in there so we used to have to go next door to get the water. And to the washroom there. It was quite close together there. And then, um, we had a wood stove. I used to pack wood, you know. And like, when my husband was working away, you know. And I guess when I got pregnant I – lifting too much heavy stuff maybe. And then finally anyway – my grandmother of course, no, I think she was gone – yeah, that's right too. Otherwise, she probably would have noticed and helped me out, you know, because my grandmother, at times she could tell by just, like a woman sitting there, that she was pregnant. [2:4]

And she probably would have helped me. I think maybe I had two miscarriages. Well I know I had one, I know of one I had before my daughter was born. They brought me up to the hospital. The doctor came over to the house and it was too late. The roads were rough at that time. And it wasn't paved. I had my first daughter in nineteen um what, sixty. ...... Sixty – I think. ...... And from there I was stuck at home after, I couldn't travel anymore. [2:5]

Bernie's children were all born in hospital, the first two at Pender Harbour and the last in Sechelt when the local hospital was finally built.

They were all born here, yeah. At um, Pender Harbour. One was born here when they moved the hospital. Yeah. ...... So -- . [1:13]

Three yeah. From my first husband, yeah, I married again, second husband, then I had another girl which is a Downs syndrome. She's living in Vancouver. But my second husband passed away years, years ago. When she was three, I was .... Yeah, I had two, two girls and one boy from my first marriage. [2:10]

Her child-raising skills, like other necessary knowledge, Bernie had learned by observation and helping throughout her own childhood and adolescence. But the strong family ties, as well as the physical closeness of everyday life, meant that child care was shared around.

...... and um, I – of course my mother, they, they, they were very helpful – to look after, and tell you what to do. Of course I knew from growing up too because I had so many brothers and sisters you know. And um, but they always wanted to keep her, you know. "Oh we'll keep her if you want to go out," or whatever. "We'll keep her." They, they, that was um, well they already had their first grandchildren from my brother, you know, but my first, you know. Your first child, and they always look to the first, your first child you know. [2:5]

These offers of care extended to periods of several weeks if necessary.

But anyway, from there I um, and then, oh in them days too we used to go up berry picking in the States. Like the men would go up North fishing and the women or older people that stayed home, we'd um, those that um, those Japanese people. They used to come over and hire people from different parts. We'd go there. We enjoyed that, it was like a holiday for us. [2:5]

Ah, we went to um, different places in the States, but the main one was a place called Fall City, in the States there. ... There's another

little place called ah, Carnation, right close to, to, a ways, I don't
know, up from Seattle. On the weekends I know we used to go into
Seattle for the weekend. [2:5]

They picked a variety of berries.

Ah, strawberries. And from there we um, when that was over if we
wanted to stay a bit longer we'd go into raspberry picking. And they
had, like, cabins or whatever, you know, where we stayed. We really
enjoyed it. We had a lot of fun. You know with all the children, you
know. ... Yeah, and like older people, my grandfather and my grandmother, no not my grandmother, she was already gone. But my
grandfather used to, to come up there, go with us. My Dad would
be up North fishing. My mother didn't come too much, I don't think
she – but we used to all go there. You know, different families.
[2:5,6]

*These trips helped to extend Bernie's special relationship with Valerie,
her elder brother's oldest child.*

But I'll tell you one story, [laughs] about, um, Valerie, my niece
Valerie. She was, I can't remember how old she was then ––. I
think, um ...... I don't know. Her mother decided to go up fishing
with my brother that year. She went once or something. She wanted somebody to watch – Valerie, or, and the other children – I can't
remember. But anyway, I already had my daughter, I left my daughter with my mother, at home. You know, you go there to work. ......
So we went, and um, my friend Stella came along with us. Her husband was up North fishing too. And we didn't go too far, just across
the border here. Custer, I think they call that place, near Lyndon.
And ...... we went there, berry picking, ah. It was raspberries this
time. And we took Valerie along .... And we didn't have too much
money. We, we, but we had, like fun, you know. We'd pick berries,
make enough money for our meal and, and whatnot, you know, and
um, and the girls just enjoyed it, you know. And of course, they
never lasted that long. It gets real, real hot during the day, especially in the afternoon. They'd take off, and go where there's a river or
something, close by. And um, and then in the evening we'd sit
around and, and tell stories, or, or they met friends. And they'd get
together and go, go to different parts of [unclear] and that's the first
time I think I took Valerie away with me, you know. As she was
growing up. ... I think she must have been, like about ten, something like that. ...... Ten, twelve, something like that, anyway. And

Stella had her daughters there too, so they, they chummed around together, and they met different people. ...... And um, we used to go shopping in this store there and we'd, er, like Stella stayed right next to me in this, er, cabins, or whatever we were in. And we'd get together and cook our dinner, you know, and we'd make our own bread and, er, you know, instead of cooking separately we'd get together and cook our supper, you know. And, er, once in a while Stella and I, we'd go to the store, and the kids would come home and "Oh, let's go to the tavern, you know." We'll go and have a, I'm not a beer drinker, you know, but the beer over there is milder. Light. So we went there. We travelled, our boss there took us in by truck, or little bus or something. I said, "Well how are we going to get home?" You know. We were like, five miles away, you know, from – . I said, "How are we going to get home now?" This was the fun part of it. We used to have fun over there. So, and she laughed, Stella was, she didn't care about anything, you know. But I was always afraid. She's, she's a mischief type. So anyway, "Oh, we'll find a way," you know. So she looked around and we seen these two Native people, they were on their, they were, lived in the States there at a place called um, Chehalis, just a little place called Chehalis, there. And there's also one over here and that's where their mother came from and they were coming to visit her. And she boldly went up and asked them, "Can you — ?" And they didn't know which way, there's two borders, like, Blaine here and the other one was further up and they were asking where the border was, you know. "Okay, you take us home, we'll tell you where the border is." [laughs] So we went and got them lost [laughs], they were quite peeved with us. So, and we finally found were we lived, and we just told them to go back to the border there, you know, it was getting rather dark. At that time it got foggy too, you know, after midnight, or something, a little foggy. But I don't think they were very pleased with us [laughs]. But Stella, she just laughed about it, eh. Like I said, we used to have a lot of fun down there. ... And Valerie, I think, really enjoyed it. We talk about it quite often. We did a lot of crazy things down there. Another time we hitch-hiked and I was afraid, you know, 'cause I had thongs on, you know, and she'd be laughing, you know. But we were, and today we wouldn't dare do that, you know, not today. But at that time we were lucky to get some nice people to pick us up and bring us home. But um, Valerie was quite close to me, you know, she would — we always looked up to somebody. In my time I looked up to one of my aunts. I, er, I always when I was young I liked the way she dressed, she had a lot of beautiful clothes, they always kept their clothes in a trunk, you know. You always looked up to somebody, you know, and I guess Valerie did that to me, you know, some older person. [2:6,7]

I'll tell you another story about Valerie, er, like after I was married, um I had, like for my wedding dress I wore a pale, pale green chiffon, like, dress, you know, with white, sort of velvety pumps, you know. And um, couldn't get a veil to go with it so I got a white, a short little veil, or whatever. I can't remember. And then for evening, you know you have, in our old hall, had an old hall for the evening after, you know, if you want to change, and I had another beautiful dress, a chiffon, I can't remember the colours, they were beautiful. It had like layers, you know. Beautiful dresses. So I hung them up, but at that time we moved in with um, my brother. Like I said we didn't have a home yet, still and my parents' place, you couldn't call it, so we moved in with them. From there we went up fishing again, with my husband there, and that's before I had children. I'm going back again. And like I said Valerie was growing up then, I think this was before our berry picking days. And they were quite mischief, you know, they were at the waterfront there, there was a wharf, they had a wharf down there and they lived kinda close to the water there. Anyway, um, I came back, I had all my clothes in a closet there, you know, in the bags. And it was saved, the top layer of my cake. Had a three.–. You know how you save things like that, you know. Came back ...... looked at my dresses, they were all full of tar. "Oh, my God, what happened?" Now, and nobody, you know owned up to it, for, for, I don't know, years. I think it was just, not too long ago that we were talking about it, yeah. And she's (Valerie) talking about it, see she was quite young, she didn't remember. I said, "That's what happened to my dresses. That was you." Her and another, um friend of hers. This girl is now living with my son there, they chummed, she was older, and they chummed around. "Oh, let's go down the beach and play –– dresses, shoes, they're ideal, shoes. And, er, they went, they didn't go on the wharf but they went like, under the wharf there, and there's this tar on them, er, ... the pilings, you know. And my dresses, they were ruined. You know I felt so bad, for them. You know, it wasn't for years later I found out it was her and her friend. [laughs] But, like, when I got home I asked my sister-in-law, Melanie, the one we were talking about, what happened. And she says, "I don't know." I don't know whether she knew or not, she probably had a hunch that it was them that took it out, but er, but I was quite angry about it. But, you know — [laughs]. [2:7,8]

By the time Bernie's children reached school age the old residential school was gone and her children all attended public school.

So with my girls, um, they were, they were going to the white school by that time .... I think ...... I'm just trying to think now, some of them went to Gibsons, but none of my children went to Gibsons, to the high school there. ... I can't remember when they built that high school (in Sechelt). It was just the elementary school there. So when she was still in elementary I think, I think they were building that high school .... So, so they all went to this high school after they – . [2:11]

Bernie's children all received more formal schooling than she did, but none completed high school.

They all dropped out. They had still, in their time, they were having other problems up there you know. Fighting with the – and I, I remember I used to have to go up there. Oh, and I, oh, and they got into trouble – talk to the, um principal, and um, it's still a little bit difficult today, you know. Little problems that we have up there. Like I had a grandson, was going up there. But I'd go up and have a meeting, a session with the um, principal —— . I'd have someone with me, you know, someone come up, and uh, talk about their problems. This was always fighting with the white, the white girls, you know. And, er, of course, it was always, like, one-sided, you know, they were always quick to say "Well your daughter started it first," you know. We had a lot of trouble with that. And um, I said at one time to one of them, I don't know which daughter, I had to go – . I said, "The trouble with our children coming to school nowadays, they can't learn. When they come to school they always have to be on the defensive, you know. How do you expect them to learn? As soon as they get up there, they're into fighting," or what ever ...... So, it, it's still going on today, you know, and – oh, my grandson I went up with. This was still the same thing. Met with the, of course it's a different principal, he was the vice principal. And we'd go through, by this time I'm getting angry, you know, and I'm coming out and I said, "I'm not going to listen to this any more, you know. You look into the boy that he had a fight with, you know. Right away." Oh, at one time she had, my daughter, had a fight with this girl. So they had her waiting outside the office there, and the principal's phoning the other girl's mother, er, a white girl, and my daughter overheard him say, "Oh, it was the little Indian girl's fault." My daughter overheard him say this. So when I went and had a speech – I can't remember who was the school co-ordinator then. I went up and I think this is when I said that, you know, I was getting quite angry then and I had mentioned what my daughter overheard. But still, they were always on the defensive themselves, you know, with the teachers. So you can't get anywhere, you know, unless we have someone stronger, or go as a group I guess. Well they are now starting to come and have, I came in here I think, at one session. Oh, down the hall I think, they're now starting to, there's a couple of teachers there that are getting quite ...... look into this in more, you know, they're caring more for the Native people, you know. [2:11]

But few parents were as assertive or determined as Bernie. Most did not go to the school to confront the staff.

Ah, very, very few. I think, ah ...... for the reason that er, they weren't, they knew they weren't going to get anywhere anyway, you know. You would say, "What's the use of going up there, when, when they're just going to defend the little white girl, anyway. Or the white boy, or – ." [2:12]

Bernie feels that much of her attitude and the strength to act on her beliefs was learned from her father. He provided her with an unusually strong and positive model as he worked for the welfare of his people.

Yeah, yes, oh yes, yes. Ah, he did a lot of that. Up to the school. And up to the, when the children started, were integrated into the white school. He's the one that started this, and, er, he was up there quite often and had meetings with the principals and whatever. And bring them, right when this office (the Band Office) opened up, um, when I walk into this room I always picture them still here, all the Chiefs. And not only that, when our people had problems on the reserve, with the police, he would be right there too. He acted as a lawyer, you know, ... [2:12]

OK, um, like I said, er, he had, er, a lot of influence over the school. Ah, things that were happening at the school. Different problems that they had, and, er, when he heard of any problems he'd be right there, you know, to defend these people ...... or whatever, you know.

And then another thing was with the police when, the, ah, the younger people had problems with – boys, you know, boys will be boys eh, break and entry and this and that, you know, little ...... not real heavy, um, things, you know, but um ...... like steal a chocolate bar or whatever, you know what I mean? And they would get into trouble, the police were quick to go and, you know, but he was always there to defend – . And it wasn't only his family, everybody, you know. And ...... um, he would always have, um, close contact with the police. There was one that he knew very well, a constable. He was really, he was a nice guy, this one. He started coming in and sitting with my Dad and started working on problems with him, you know. ...... With, er, like, er, concerning, concerning the Band, eh, the reserve. ... There, there was people too that moved into Vancouver. There was, there was quite a few people that were living in Vancouver. And were –– getting into er, you know, drugs and things like that, too and they even used to get my Dad to go and er, to sort of help the, the lawyer out. He had, he, he knew a couple of lawyers real well. One is still alive today. Um, that Doug, he's a real big lawyer, that he's fighting the real big cases for the land claim business. And my Dad knew him from years –– before he got into be a great big lawyer, you know. He worked with him and another lawyer – investigating, um, these drugs and things that were happening to our people in Vancouver. And people that were getting into trouble in Vancouver too. In one case where he went to – . I won't mention any names, or. He went and defended one girl there, and he's – . Like my Dad used to blame the government and whatnot for a lot of things that were happening in them years. Like I mentioned before, they were quick, to, to blame you, blame us, you know, for, for different things. My Dad mentioned, er, one case –– he was into a lot of court cases, like, I mean, right along with the lawyer. And er, he said, "What's happening today?" At that time, it was years ago, ... um, there was no work for our people, like for the younger people. And they were starting to drift into Vancouver, and starting to drink, get into drugs, whatnot, and no money, er, not, I can't remember all the words he used but, er, and this is the reason why they were drifting into Vancouver, and there's nothing there for them. Things were changing in them days, like, er, years ago, in my time as a young girl, I mentioned that we used to travel up the inlet, hunting, fishing, and that was starting to ...... um, die away at that time, you know. Like, er, we were close to our family, and, but as, er, years went by, you know, like in my daughter's age, I guess when she was born in the fifties, in the fifties, ... and going on sixties. Then things were changing, you know, and we weren't travelling up, up the inlet any more and kids, they weren't in the, in the school any more in the, er, residential school any more, like. Like we weren't protected, you know what I mean. Um, ... and they were starting to drift into Vancouver and getting into trouble. My Dad was, er, there ...... quite often. And mind you, he wasn't getting paid for it. Like today, everyone's getting paid for it, no matter what you do now today. He did a lot, a lot of work for the Band, you know, and, er, he was, he was er, he wasn't a Chief. They had a Chief, they had Councillors. He was, um, oh, what do you call it now? He was a spokesman for them, anyway. And, er, they didn't have the s.... , oh, the Band Office then. He used to have this office down at his house there. It was quite a big house, you know, like living room and dining room part, kitchen, and you know he would have his little office there and people would be phoning him there, people that were in need of help, this and that. And he, he was one of the first ones that had a telephone, you know, and he would phone. And, um, ... and get them help, whatever. ...... And people who were getting into trouble. Even, even people, a few of the men that er, were in the army, you know, were in the army. They came back and they didn't know anything about, um, where they could have got a pension, some kind of a pension. He even looked into that and got some of them, you know, they didn't know how to go about it. Looked into it and got ...... army pensions for them. Things like that, you know. [2:12-14]

Clarence Joe, Bernie's father, was influential within the Band, but he was also well respected within the wider community.

Like I said, ... I don't know if I mentioned, they called him um, "The Ambassador." ... there was a write-up about him, I put that, I think I have it at home. 'Cause he was the one, one of them that he, that spearheaded the school up the Inlet too. I think I talked about that in the last session. Where they sent um, some of the children, up to the Inlet there. They started a school up there. ... halfway up, it's at Vancouver Bay [pause]. Anyway, they had that school up there. And that's where I, they, they left a lot of things up there after it closed down. They um, turned it into a ...... a logging company used it for a while. And I went up there cooking, you know, my sister and my sister-in-law, two of them. Actually Valerie's Mum was one of them and another one. We took turns cooking up there. And we run into a lot of um, stuff that the school left there, books and things like that and clippings of different things like, was up on the wall, you know. Things that were happening on the reserve and the Band and that's where I found this clipping of my Dad where they called him "The Ambassador." ... Um, in the sixties, yeah. About that time. I guess he was getting quite powerful then, about the sixties, I guess. He was a powerful man, he was quite –– known up and down the coast here. And he was er, they had a er, a thing called the Native Brotherhood too, he was into. And there was seven men, I think seven, and he was one of them that were powerful in, in, working together from different, with different Bands from way up North, The Island (Vancouver Island), Campbell River, here, um, Powell River, there was seven of them. They called them the big seven, they called them. They did a lot of work for the people, the Native people. And they got this er, there was no such thing as family allowance then, you know, where they – the mother's allowance, or whatever they called family allowance. And what was the other one? Oh, something to do with the, um, the health or ...... but those two things they did, they got for the Native people anyway. So he was quite a powerful man, my Dad was in, in, in, er, –. Years after he started he was even going right over to Ottawa to these, when he couldn't get through to the um, Indian Affairs in Vancouver. Like he would say, "Well, I'm not going to get anywhere with you people, I'm going to go above your head and go right to Ottawa and talk to them." Over what he wanted, something – you know, he would demand it, you know. He would, he would get it too. He always got what he asked for, different things. So he was quite powerful, well known and well liked. Like, he dealt with a lot of people. He didn't um, like, fight with people, you know. Like today I think about the way things go sometimes, he would say, "No, that's not the way to go about it, you know." I can't remember, there was one thing – "No, that's not the way." ... And at times, when he was going to travel he had suits, different suits, you know and um, course he put them in the cleaners – if not, you know, "Could you press up my ....?" and my mother was getting kind of a little bit um, peeved at this time, you know, so he would ask me to do it, you know. I'd get his white shirt – he was always well dressed, with a suit and tie and everything. Even at home, you know, he dressed up. He was always, and this is another thing, he

taught us, er, like um, ... er, young people that were going to
court, like, say when a relative, nephews, my nephews, I had a lot
of nephews. You're, when you're in trouble, and he's going to go
...... "And I want your hair cut and I want you dressed in ...... you
know, dressed up, clean clothes," this and that, you know. When
you go and appear in court. You know, things like that, and er, -- .
He would sit at home and er, you know, they would always come
and say, "Hi, grandpa," you know, come – and er, even at times
when they were getting older, the nephews and whatnot, they
would come in, "Hi, grandpa," you know. They had, they had been
drinking, you know. My Dad loved to cook and he would say, "Sit
down, I'm going to cook for you, cook you a big breakfast," you
know. "No grandpa, we don't want any." "Sit down! I'm going to
cook for you." And then they knew what was coming -- he was
going to start preaching to them! [laughs]. And they did, they
always listened to him, you know. This respect among family. And
they sat, they knew what they were in for too [laughs]. So er, things
like that, he taught us a lot. I didn't, I, like I say, I think I mentioned
the other session we had, I learned a lot from my Dad and also my
grandmother. It was his mother, not too much from my mother. Or,
on my mother's side, you know. I was closer to my grandmother on
my Dad's side, not my mother's – she was kind of um, er, how
would I put it? ...... She had a temper, you know. She was, she would
come down and visit us and she was always um, um, talking to my
mother and made sure that we, we did this and did that, before we
went out er, like I said they were all strict, you know. But she
would, but my grandmother, my Dad's eh, she was a kind person.
She never talked rough to us or anything where the other one, did,
you know, and was always scolding us for things that we didn't do.
But my, my Dad always said, er, "Just sit and listen. Don't ever
answer back, don't say anything even if she's wrong you sit there
and listen to her." ... Respect. Very important. [2:15-17]

*Bernie and her family did little to actively teach and pass on the cul-
ture to their children. The old ways were perceived as being gone
already. English language and white culture were seen as the way of
the future, so Bernie did not speak the language to her own children,
although they did have the chance to hear it spoken by some Elders who
still used it regularly for their own private conversations.*

Um, I think that by the time I, my daughter was born that the language was already dying off. And her Dad, well, being a Cree, didn't

speak Cree either. Um, we all talked about it, "Wouldn't it be nice if you knew Cree and taught her Cree and then me also teaching her." You know, er, the language, our language. I had an Uncle that was very good with, with my – with another Uncle, that's on my mother's side now this time. I shouldn't have cut them, my mother's side, too much. But I had an Uncle, he was a very happy – person, you know. Real humorous, he was always ...... and he loved children and he would – when we got together, um, he would um, nick my children and talk to them in, in our language all the time. And of course, he would tell them what he was saying. And then he even started making them count in our language, you know. Of course, they forgot it I guess. But he would always talk to them in our language. [2:17,18]

And then I have a sister from Powell River she taught him (my son) how to (count) and I had it taped you know and then I don't know what happened somebody destroyed that tape. I felt really sorry for him. But um, that's, that was lost a long time ago. [1:20]

Bernie and others who have some understanding of the language are now attending classes to relearn their language.

Well, we come to the language, it's called Corrections really. And um, they've got it written down now where we have to learn how to read it ... . Listening to it now it's coming back, you know what I mean, but we still don't talk it. Like Stella and I and a few others we talk to each other, like with words that we know we try to – but it's pretty hard to get back, but –– not that we don't know it, or we know the language, if somebody was to speak to me in, in, I would understand, you know, but to answer them, I would have um, difficulty into, you know, putting it into like a sentence or whatever, you know. [1:21]

The Sechelt people as a Nation are making an effort to regain their culture and to pass it on to the younger generation. They see language as central to this process and are working to incorporate language classes into the schools.

... I went and I took one lady's place here and, um in the nursery year to teach for a while until she came back. It's just the, like the um, counting, the numbers, from maybe one to twenty, that's the little ones, and um, maybe some animal names and um, things like that. That's the little ones, that's easy. But now we have two women that are up at the school where I'm – I think maybe at the end of this month, I might be going up there to take her place because she's going up to the camp. So it's coming back, you know. [1:21]

By the time I spoke with her a second time, Bernie had begun to help with the language classes at the school.

Oh, I enjoy, enjoy it. Um, like I say, we're teaching but we're not like, getting into sentences. They're doing mostly, er, putting it into little songs, little rhymes, you know, this and that, eh. Well, as you can't take a child and talk with a sentence, um, you know. You know what I mean? "Just come here and sit down." There's this lady that came from, um, New Zealand, I think it was, or –. And she said, "This is the way you should be teaching the children. As soon as they walk in through the door, don't speak English to them." Soon as they walk into the door, "Mi-la t'ek'ish – Come in and sit down," you know, and, and try not to speak English at all. Of course you're going to tell them what it means, but not –– you, you don't even have to tell them, you make signs and they'll know, you know. And sit down. "This is the way you teach them," she said, and this is the way we were taught anyway, as young kids, you know. [2:18]

However, some traditional activities did remain for Bernie's children, even if they were hidden under a white veneer.

No, um. Like when my children were born, like everything here had already been changing you know. And um, like, I, when I mention it when the Elders get together, you know what I should have been doing with my children. I guess in my time, like I'm sixty-two now and I sort of blame myself, maybe I should have started doing that too to my children when they –– but like I said, by that time my children were being born, everything was pretty well lost. By that time. We still had our smoked fish you know. I think that's about the only thing we had left. Even by that time our men, there was no hunters any more, things –– everything was gone, you know ––. [1:22]

But they still picked berries.

Oh yeah, we still picked berries, yeah. We still picked berries and um, I never really sat them down either to talk about my days and how we worked hard and how we did this how we did that – not really. [1:22,23]

And they still went up the Inlet in summer.

We still did. Yeah, yeah. We still did. Um we, we, like my Dad, there was a few people, my grandfather and Stella's family – her husband

and her father and mother, there was still a few people, like in the fifties, sixties, still have a boat out here and we'd all pile on the boat and go around – go up the Inlet. There was nobody living up there then, but we'd just make a trip up there and go pick berries. And um, pick buckets of berries and come home and can it, or preserve it. And, today we don't even do that now today. That was like fifties, and sixties I guess. Um, maybe when my mother was still alive. I can't remember what day she passed away. But um, even preserving now, we, I don't know just lazy or whatever, they go buy or freeze it, that's it, that's it. Since we got the freezer now, no more. Maybe do a little bit. My mother used to do a lot of her, like peaches, pears and that. I used to have to go down and help her. Go to her house, strawberries, you know when the strawberries would come out she'd go and buy flats of strawberries. Peaches and that – she did a lot of that. And fish, ... and even the smoked fish, we started preserving in jars. No more you know, drying it up and even in the freezer you can only leave it for three months, after that it's not tasty. And we started like um, the smoked fish now, where they start to really dry, to keep it. Now we, we just put in a day or two, I like it when it's just a day or two and get it fresh like that, you know. And they can preserve it like that too. Just put a little water to seal it you know. A lot of women do that today I think. And freeze it. They are getting more spoilt now we, we even have, our Band here they get it done over here at Wilson Creek somewhere they have it smoked and sealed in the what do you call it -- ?[5] [1:23]

Bernie still smokes her own fish and one daughter, at least, is interested in learning traditional food preparation from her.

I still have my smoke house. I prefer doing my own. I don't like the way they do it. A lot of people say it's not very tasty, you know. I don't think they leave it, just the skin part gets smoked and – I don't know – not like the way we do it anyway. ... My one daughter is pretty helpful, but the other one, she doesn't even eat fish. She doesn't like fish. Even the fresh salmon, she's not very fussy. [1:23]

And like I'm getting older, they should be doing it themselves now, eh. Like I'm starting to tell them now, "I'm not going to be here that long, you guys have to start learning how to do your own. What

---

5 The Band now sends fish in large quantities to be commercially smoked and sealed in cryovac packs before being distributed to Band members.

are you going to do when I'm gone?" You know. "There'll be no more." Like our age group I don't know. ... Um, they said "Oh yeah." Like my older daughter, "I know how to do it," you know. It's just that they depend on me to, you know, but she comes and helps. But not so much in the, it's kind of a trick to cutting up the fish. No – she's not very good at that. But she'll put it on the sticks for me and hang it up. Oh she does the salting and, um. [1:24]

And then we also do it around the fire too, we do some around the fire, like an open fire. Build a fire and we put them on, on bigger sticks and the little sticks across to hold it. You leave that like the tail on, to put the wire to hold the fish up and then you sharpen the other end to put in the sand, soften up the ground and ...... she's learning all that, er, like I say, I'm not going to be around –– she likes her fish but the other daughter doesn't. She's not a fish eater, or she doesn't care for seafood. So she's not too interested in, in learning. And er, and also canning. Um, she comes and helps me to cut up the fish and can, you know. We do, we do the sockeye in cans like that. She'll help me out with that. But, like I said, the other daughter doesn't. And my son's not interested at all, the younger one. Not interested at all. He likes fish, but he, he's just, I don't, not into learning how to do it. But I think my daughter will ...... she'll, you know, she'll be the one after I leave. She'll, you know, she'll know how to do it. She's quite helpful. You know, she comes to me and she'll learn. Even like cooking, like I said I learned from my Dad, and she learned from me how to do different things. Just the bread, she hasn't quite ...... it's pretty hard for people, our, our Indian bread we call it. White people call it bannock, you know. Um, then we do the bannock, but there's different ways of doing it. My daughter loves it. They all loved it, the bread. But they could never learn. There's a, like I say, a trick to it, you know. It's like doing, if you're going to do pastry for a pie you don't overknead it, you know, you just –. So there's a trick to the Indian bread too, you know. You, it's just basic, you know, flour, salt, baking powder, butter. But if you're going to knead it too much, and you bake it, it'll come out hard as a rock, you know. So they can never learn how do you do it, eh. I said "Well watch," you know. And then the other one would do is the fried bread too. Same thing only you just deep fry it like donuts, eh. And they all loved that. But they just could never learn. [2:19,20]

Even though she values the language and the culture and would like to see what still remains preserved and used by future generations, Bernie has doubts about how much can really be regained and retained.

Oh God, that's a tough question. I really think, I shouldn't say this but I don't think it (the language) will really ever come back you know. A lot of people are interested in learning, like the older, like say my, daughter's age group, like in twenty or thirties, like children that are thirty or whatever –– they start taking classes but they dropped out, they quit, you know, the two ladies that were teaching them, you know. I don't know why. But I don't know if it will ever come back. I don't think so. It's lost, you know. They are trying, you know, but it's pretty hard. See, when you learn the language, we have to learn it at a very young age. You know, like I say, I used to listen to my grandmother. They spoke to you all in our Native language not in English. My grandfather – he spoke English, but not –– very, you know – used broken English. My grandmother used to have a hard time with him, she spoke English too but um, like they just talked to us, you know, so you had to learn, you know. So you had to learn from that very young age, you know. But teaching them now. Mind you the little ones are very quick to learn, you know. But some of them are not interested, you know. So I really – I hate to say it but I don't think so, I don't think it will ever come back. ...Today it's so –– I don't know...... they're losing it, you know what I mean, the culture, everything, you know. [1:21]

But despite this pessimism, Bernie believes that an effort should be made.

Well, like I say it's um, ... when I come to think of it, you know, they're really trying, at least they think it's important. I really don't know. I really don't know. Like I said, I don't think it will ever come back, but if they really, really, were determined to learn to keep up, 'cause once they leave school too it's going to be forgotten. Just like a lot of our kids took French and then when that was over it's forgotten. I have one grandson who is fifteen now and I said "Well, you are taking French in school. Say something to me in French." You know. He wouldn't. You know. Out of school now, he took French but it's forgotten now, you know. So I think it will be the same with our language. Once they are moved to the high school whatever, it will be forgotten. I don't know. I shouldn't say that. But maybe – you never know. It will never be fluent any more like um, like um, maybe they'll just learn a few words you know. And that will be it. You won't have any people, like two people talking in our language to each other – I don't think so. You know, but they will maybe have a few words, or a couple of sentences or something like that, but not fluent like our parents and grandparents. [1:22]

The revival of other spiritual practices like the sweat lodge and traditional singing and dancing is also on the agenda.

They – I don't know what they had before they, the Catholic religion came. But after – I don't think they had much at that. I mean it's coming back now but, um –– I don't remember anything. ... It's all them years when they – well they took all that away from them, I guess years ago in my – or even before my grandfather's time, I guess. They became strictly Catholic and – just became good Christians then. So now that the religion has died off, now it's coming back. They are trying to bring it back. ... They seem to be pretty well going for it. So even the younger children are getting involved. Because um, I don't know. They, you can't seem to get them to go to church or anything like that. So I think that's good for them, to get into something like that. That's what they had years ago. Like I said, before my grandfather's time. They had their own spiritual things or whatever they did – I don't know. Their ceremonies, of course all that was stopped by the government and by the Catholic religion. It was taken away from them. ... I never did see any of that. I don't even know if they had any Indian dancing there or drumming. Nothing that I can remember now. They are getting all that back. They said we had this years ago. There's a few people that remember. Even that – that there [points to carving of double headed eagle], that came back from another – . ... That was ours from years ago, way back. Another Band said, "That belongs to Sechelt." Things like that. I don't remember anything of that. Like I said, when we had the Catholic religion they just – there was nothing of that – around. [3:10,11]

VALERIE BOURNE

Valerie was born in her great-grandparents' house on the waterfront in Sechelt, the oldest of the nine children of William Joe of Sechelt and Melanie (nee Paul) of Stoney Creek.

Ah, I was born December 26, 1949 in um, my great-grandfather's house. I was one of the last chil.... ah, children that my great-grandmother – midwifed —– at birth. [1:1]

Ah, after me they were all born in Pender Harbour Hospital. That was the closest hospital, and my last brother, was the very last one in the family, was born in the Sechelt Hospital which opened in 1963. [2:1]

Her great-grandmother died shortly after she born so she wasn't available to help Valerie's mother with subsequent births, though Melanie would have preferred this to going into the hospital.

No, um, my mother never like the hospital. She, she always, she would have preferred to have all her children at home and um ...... I don't know, I just don't think she had as much choice as we – as we

191

do now. Um, ... it's really hard to say. I know that my Mom didn't like the hospital. She would have rather have had them at home in a familiar surrounding. [2:1]

Of her surviving siblings all but the two sisters still live in Sechelt.

In order? Okay. Um, I'm the oldest, Audrey is next, Randy, Willard, Janice, Bradley, Rena who is now passed away, Wayne and Clark. Nine of us.

By the time Valerie went to school the old residential school had ceased to be a boarding school for Sechelt students, although those who came from further away still lived there during term.

I attended the residential school here in Sechelt, with ah, there was children who boarded here from other, other Reserves and other Bands. But ah, I attended as what they called a day, — day scholar which meant I, I could go home every day. The other children who were boarders were taken from their families and put here for their education. [1:2]

I know the Sliamon people, they knew their language fluently as children. Some of them, even at my age they didn't know English when they came in. Ah, they only knew, they only knew their own, their own language and — they had to start speaking English – and they were punished, physically for speaking their language. It must have been so traumatic for them, ah, they would get hit or have to kneel in the corner all day, if they said even one word in their language. And they were being taught French! At the same time. So it was quite confusing, really confusing for everybody. [1:9]

And I attended um, from kindergarten to grade eight here. And then I went to public school which was really scary for me because I hadn't been in a lot of contact with a lot of white people until I got into public school. And, um, it was quite frightening for a while and this was in Gibsons, Elphinstone (secondary school). And I attended there for two years and then moved to — North Van(couver) and did the rest of the years to grade twelve in North Van(couver). There was more um, things for young people to do down there. [1:2]

Living in North Vancouver also saved the daily travel to Gibsons.

Every day, yeah. We'd leave at, ummm, very early in the morning, like 7 o'clock and have to wait around and we'd be the last bus back too. So it was, it was a very tiresome day for .... especially when

you're a teenager, you're growing and all you want to do is sleep. ...
I think there was ....uhhhh.... roughly about twenty of us from the
Band going every day. [1:2]

*White children from Sechelt bussed down to Gibsons too, but usually
on a separate vehicle.*

No, no, we all had the same route, like, um, um, you could catch an
earlier bus if you wanted. But um, our bus was the last bus and
there were some white kids that came on with us but I'm sure they
got a rough time too. So, – yeah, it was kind of difficult for white
kids to be with the Native kids. 'Cause there was – I think, really
when I remember back, I know that there was still of lot of ah, prejudice. You know, and I could feel it when I walked into the school,
you'd actually hear some remarks, you know, "Indians are here,"
and we put up with stuff like that. ... Yeah, we were, a very small
minority. It was, it was strange. You know, ahhh, although there was
the, the, the Chinese kids, a few of them. There wasn't a lot of different races here. [1:3]

*Native Indian children were a very small minority at the school—
about twenty out of some four hundred students.*

Mostly white people, yeah. And, ah, ... just, they had a biased
opinion about the Indian, the Native people here at the time. It was
difficult, it, it was it was difficult because first being a teenager, –
and your hormones jump all over the place, but when you have to
go into a situation like that where you feel really uncomfortable
every day —— our learning wasn't – there, because you carried a lot
of ah, fears around. [1:3]

*In the early 1960s very few Sechelt children went on to high school;
very few Native Indian children anywhere did, but the situation for
those living in small rural communities was particularly difficult. It
was something of a circular situation—because there were so few who
even made the attempt to gain a secondary education there was frequently no local school, so students had the extra difficulty of travelling
to the nearest one.*

Yeah, that's true. Yeah, oh definitely. That's true. It's hard enough
to make changes and —— and when you're all of a sudden just, when
you've come from a residential school where it's all Native children
and then all of a sudden you're in with, um, other, with er, minori-
ties, white people, you just .... the changes are so incredible for you
and you're so scared that ..... . [1:4]

... The youngest one Clark – graduated. Yeah. I think um, my parents really took interest, 'cause he was the baby. Took interest in him and really um, babied him and um you know did everything for him and, but um – I think when we all look back on it the ones that had the best chances were from Bradley on. Brad – that would be Bradley, Wayne – mostly because my Dad and Mom were working and they had more – they had more money. We were very poor when I was growing up. We barely had food so um, after half of the children were born, I think the latter half had the best chance. And my Mom and Dad really paid attention to their schooling and went everywhere when – like if Rena had an award given to her my Dad would make sure to be there. To be with her to support her so I can see them all having the better education. And mostly because my Mom and Dad were always in the school um, with Clark. Every time something happened they would be at the school. A social function – they would be at the school. Um – me being the oldest I had to get my wings right away and – 'cause they – they were raising all these other kids and they really didn't have the time. ... I think their whole attitude – well, my Dad's attitude towards education was always when – he would always say, "I'm not educated and I want you to be." But for –– for the oldest it was more or less you were on you're own and you'd better, you just better get it done. But um, it changed. He got – they got more involved with the younger kids. [4:4,5]

Valerie remembers lots of games during her childhood, even though there were also lots of chores to do.

Yeah, we played lots of games. Um, you know I used to remember my Uncle Ashwah. ... His name was Uncle Arthur, we called him Ashwah. ... He was nice, he's my grandmother's brother. He was the baby of her family. But um, he used to play a lahal game, bone game. And he would try to trick us and if we couldn't guess the hand he had his, his coin or whatever he was holding, a bone, or rock in then, um, we would have to sing or we'd have to show a trick or whatever. But he did, he played that game with us quite often. And apparently, you know years later I – it's a game where they gambled, our people gambled and um, I never did really – I'll have to find out how the whole game is played so um, but we, I grew up with no TV –– and sometimes a radio. My great-grandfather always had a radio. So we really had to entertain ourselves and one of my favourite things I remember in grade one, I was thinking to myself – I was watching this teacher read and it amazed me. She was reading from this book and I couldn't believe it. And I would look at these words and they would mean nothing to me and I thought I'm going to learn how to read and I'm going to learn how to read really well. And she would have this storytelling every day and nobody ever told me a story from a book. I heard stories just around, like, a fire, you know, and bedtime stories, but I would watch every movement she made when she was reading and she would act out some parts and I thought, "That's so cool." I would think to myself. So I learned how to read and I, I loved reading after that. It was my favourite pastime thing to do in the evening was to read. Read anything. I loved the stories. ... I would borrow books from the teacher and I would promise to bring them back when I finished them. She always loved, you know, giving me the books 'cause um, well I mean it was good for her I was reading so – but it just amazed me when people used to read. You know I just –– it was a whole new world for me that opened up, but um – . The other things I used to do as I got older was um, oh, storytelling was our other favourite thing at night. I had an Aunt Gladys who is Bernie's sister. She was um, always in charge of the kids. Like every – remember I told you everybody had their duty.[1] One was cooking, one was for – she was the one that watched us and she did a lot of baking too. 'Course they all baked. But um, her favourite thing was to get us about – just when it got dark and tell us a ghost story. And she would just, she would just go on and on and she made all these things up as she went along –– and I used to just love her stories. And then, when she was um, finished, we'd all feel so good we'd go to bed and so she was the storyteller and that was another way we passed our time. Outside, was mostly for things like hide-and-go-seek which was our – 'cause we had the whole Reserve to hide in and it was um, I, you know – for me I guess white people only have this certain backyard – we had this whole Reserve and we could go anywhere and it would take them, whoever the – was – hiding their eyes – it would take them a long time to find us. ... the whole Reserve would play. Like, if one kid would go to the post where we

---

1 This was a system instituted by Valerie's grandmother at the time when twenty-five of the family were living together. Each of the adult women and older girls was given major responsibility for a certain task, e.g., cooking, laundry, child care, etc.

usually hide, other kids would see him and sure enough the whole um, Reserve would get into the game. And um we'd play kick the can which was another favourite. Our favourite. And um, run over, run over? is it?

Red Rover, all over?

Yeah, that one. Gosh it's been so long. We would skip. Um ...... a lot of swimming. Just tons of swimming. I remember being in that water from ten o'clock in the morning one day, I couldn't wait to get out of bed to go swimming and ten o'clock in the morning I went in the water and I didn't get out until 8 o'clock that night. Not once did I come out of the water. I stayed in all day. And I remember going, oh, it was so funny. My Mom said, "By the time you get home you're like a seal. You never get out of that water." And I remember playing – just swimming by myself all day, just doing different things in the water. Pretending I was a mermaid or pretending I was a seal or something. Whatever I did. But, I went home that day and my Mom said, "Are you hungry?" and I said, "Yeah." She made me a peanut butter sandwich and I was flaked out on the couch. I was sleeping. I can still remember how my body felt. It was so relaxed from swimming. Every muscle was just –– and I just dropped and slept. I had such a good sleep that time. But um, yeah, we were all swimmers in those days. Um, what else did we – ? We used to have a wharf just um ...... right beside the Reserve now. Um, there was a – we all used to go in there and have diving contests. And um, we'd have jumping contests, diving contests, whatever, we would figure something out. ... We were like one big, big family. And if one kid got there, again every – it was like the Pied Piper. Everybody would get there and we would play together all day, all day and it's amazing, with not a lot of fights either. We were very cooperative with one another and um, whoever – the oldest one was usually the leader and they would, they would be the judge or whatever, whatever had to be done, but – the things that we thought up, nowadays my, you know, my kids go, "I'm bored, I'm bored. If I don't have a Sega game on or a video game on I'm bored." And it just blows me away. [laughs] So –– no we never had – or else we would just build forts in the bush or on the beach 'cause there was so much wood on the beach. We would build forts and um, Donna Joe who is the teacher now, she's – a few years older than me – her and I played house every day and we never got tired of it. She would build her house up and then she would help me build my house. We would have our dolls. And my mother and her mother would save tin, little tin cans for us and um, cartons, you know, old cereal boxes and we'd have them all stacked up like we were the mother of the house. It was so funny. [4:7-9]

As a young child Valerie was not particularly aware that she was Native, or indeed that there was any difference between white people and her people.

I never thought of – you know, I never even knew about white people when I was – at that age – I would hear little, little bits and pieces about white people. 'Cause there was hardly any white people in those days. When I was a young girl. But I'd never met one and so I didn't know. And I'd never, ever been in a white person's house until I got, like in my teens. So it was like, I had no idea of how they did their house. ... Um, I – I guess it was hard for me to imagine that. Um, 'cause I remember hearing about white people. I think this idea struck me when I was about nine or maybe even ten years old and I – I kept hearing about this white people thing. And I went to my Mom and I said, I said, "Are they different from us Mom." And she said, "Yeah –– a little bit." And I said, "But do they go to the bathroom like we do?" You know because I was worried about when I would go to their house if I had to go to the bathroom then what was I going to do. You know little kid things that – so it just, and she said, "Yeah they do." And I said, "Oh," 'cause I thought they didn't. I thought maybe they were different. Really different you know. So um, yeah that was the first thing that really .... that really struck me I guess. And then when I actually started meeting –– um, um, white people it – they were the same as me. I thought, "What's the big thing, the big deal here?" You know? I mean once in a while my, my um parents would bring some people home .... and I used to think, "They are no different from my parents – they are the same. So what's the big deal?" But that's amazing how – how we thought, 'cause we hadn't been, seen a lot of white people when I was a child. So it's really amazing now um, thinking to myself, "Boy I must have been really backwards thinking stuff like that." But this is probably what we all thought when – as Native children. That we were really different, different in other ways. And er, now you look at it and you think to yourself, "That's so ridiculous, isn't it?" Um, um, –– it's so, how, how this fear gets implanted in children's minds, eh? And they have this fear, and if nobody – if they don't express that fear it gets bigger and bigger right? So – and that's exactly what racism is, it's big fear. Just blown out of proportion in somebody's mind. So um, I was glad I was always very open-minded and not really um, um .... one to get into a corner, get cornered by something. But I was –– and yet my teachers were white, so – I'd never even thought of them as being white. But when my mother mentioned that they were white that's, I think it was then that I thought, "Do they go to the bathroom like we do?" 'Cause I never seen them leaving the classroom, like we do. [4:10]

Because the community was still strongly Catholic, church festivals were an important part of life.

Christmas and Easter were a real celebration for our people. Um, the Catholic celebrations came up – everybody prepared their bodies and their souls for, for midnight Mass and it was a real time of cleansing your, your soul – in the Catholic way. And our church was decorated and the whole community got together 'cause it was a beautiful, huge church and when the trees went in the kids were so excited and –– and um, I would go and watch my Dad decorate it and then we'd, we'd, we would be practising in the choir about two months before that. Doing our Latin hymns and our Christmas songs and preparing for the high Mass. It was called a high Mass and we would prepare for that months before and on the, on the night it would come, everybody would go – kids, right from the eldest to the youngest would be in church. And um, um, it was just an incredible time for us. Wasn't really focused around the gifts like they are now. Christmas is about who's got the biggest presents. It was more focused around the church and um, going to confession and receiving God into your heart. And it's, that was the time for us. And then Easter was the same. We would, we would go through fasting in the spring, of course it's spring too in Native culture – we would fast in the spring – in the beginning of spring but um, religiously, Catholic religionwise, we would fast and yeah, because it was the time Christ was going to come back and that, we would, we would cleanse ourselves to receive Him into our heart again so – and we would have these big productions you know, doing the um, Stations of the Cross and different things and then again the choir. But in the home um, um, I guess, mm, Christmas meant –– well there was a lot of baking done to prepare – baking? I remember my family – you know I was just thinking about this yesterday. Somebody said, "What does your house smell like?" And my husband was cleaning out the cupboards with Pinesol and I said, "Oh my God, it smells like Pinesol." And they said, "Do you remember what your house as a child smelled like?" It smelled like raisin pies and apple pies and with a lot of spice, and blackberry cakes and um, yeast breads in the oven. And all these wonderful, wonderful – clams on the stove, wonderful, wonderful smells and I can remember them and when I think about them I can actually smell them cooking in the ovens and it was so wonderful, it was – and that's what Christmas is about. This real food, eating, and when you're a kid that hardly had any food all year and then all of a sudden everything is out and you're, you're – I think it just amazed me when I would wake up and see all these cakes and pies and – my family, my aunts and my mother had made for this big dinner. We would always get together and have big family dinners. That would mean my Dad's whole – all his brothers and sisters, um right back to his great-grandfather, or his grandfather – it would be my great-grandfather – would be there. So –– it was just a time for all of us to be together and then, of course, the Elders would, the older people would have their punch and –– and um, my age – we would dance for them. Like show them the new dance of the day or whatever. So we were all – we were really entertaining people. ... And then there was other, you know, Easter things like we would have a sports day. The whole community. We'd have a sports day. And we'd have races set up for twenty-five cents, you know. And um, um they'd show off their best racers and, but everybody would be encouraged, right from small, to married couples, to Elders, would have a race. Everybody would. It would be such a fun time for everyone and those are the times that people um, really want back. A sense of community – real community. [4:11,12]

Gathering and preserving traditional food is the one aspect of culture that Valerie sees as having been kept, though certainly not intact. Salmon remains an important part of Sechelt life, both as a part of the diet and in terms of maintaining traditional social activity.

I think the last thing we – one thing that we never gave up was, was preserving our food, our own food. We never let that part go. It was –– smoking the salmon – in the fall and that was a real family, traditional family gathering for a lot of people. That kept us –– together as families. And uhh, I know that it was such a fun time for everybody too. We're filled with happiness because we've got all this, this fish to do, but we're getting together again as, as family.

And staying – and doing something that's our culture, our tradition and, uhhh, we've never let that go. ... Yeah, just people who were living here anyway –– ahh, but –– I know that when we smoke fish we do extra because other people will come and ask us for some. Like my mother's from the Carrier Band, she's Carrier and Native and they love how we do our fish because we do it different from them.[2] They sun dry theirs and we smoke ours, so we – we know – we used to trade it off. She'd take some of theirs and send them some of ours. Yeah. It's different – still different ways of people doing it. [1:10]

But other foods were also important.

Berries, berries, that we um, that we pick, pick all summer and, and now we freeze them. Before we used to preserve them and um, and we still do the fruit. The other thing was we, we dig for cockles. And we can dry them and preserve them. Which some people still do, yeah. But I still keep my kids into that one, and, ummm .... the whole family takes part. I mean, I had done it all my life. We would go round picking food in different seasons and I always liked doing that, being out and, and getting food. But, uhh, it's a real, like I say, a real family, ahhh, time for everybody, even berry-picking, the whole family would go. ... You never talked about it, never. It wasn't, ahhh, no one said to us, "This, this is important, it's part of the culture." We just thought, "Hey we're getting food, this is it," you know, and if we don't pick it now it's going to be gone and we won't have a chance till next year again. So, yeah, and we were always on time. I mean, I, I think when I was a little girl I used to tell the seasons from when we used to pick different things. 'Cause when you're a kid you don't know the seasons, so, I, I could tell if we were picking briar, briar roots to eat that, it was spring, that the berries would come next. And that we'd always have to be right on time to pick them. [1:10,11]

Briar roots were a snack or a treat rather than a food, but in Valerie's childhood every little bit of food counted.

Just ate, just ate them, picked them, brought them home, peeled them and then we'd eat them. ... Raw, yeah, it was like a treat for

2 The lands of the Carrier people lie several hundred kilometers north of Sechelt and in from the coast. Salmon returning up the rivers to spawn were an important part of their diet even though their lands were far in from the coast.

us. It was, ahhh –– very rarely did we, we have, get candy in those days. It was like a real treat for us. ... They're not really sweet, no, I don't know, they're crunchy. They, they're like, hmmmmm, ... Celery, they're like celery. [laughs] And, and mostly, in those days we were very poor, and uhhh ...... we didn't bring a lot of, we didn't use a lot of milk and a lot of good food. We, we, what we had was what we had. Sometimes it was just potatoes and rice. And so, you supplemented it by going out in the bush and picking all these different things, and like you know, we were, even as little kids, we never –– if we went on a hike we never brought a lunch because we knew there was berries and we knew where to get them, and what to eat and what not to, what not to bother with, yeah, so we .... [1:11]

Mostly the food-gathering and preserving skills were learned from Valerie's grandparents.

From my grandparents. Mostly the grandparents, and, yeah, I mean my grandmother was a great one for, for ummm, teaching us how to preserve food and pick the food and – because after a while we had to go and do it ourselves. We –– it was like a natural thing for us. ... Yeah. Yeah. So we never, never gave up the food part. I mean, we had to supplement a lot of our food. [1:11]

Her grandparents played a significant role in Valerie's life. This was partly a traditional practice, but was also necessary when both parents were as busy as Valerie's, either within the home or at paid work.

I think because my parents, ummm, did a lot of – well, my Dad was working all the time, he was earning an income and my mother would work hard at home so my grandparents who had – my grandmother who had more time, although I don't believe that [laughs] 'cause she had thirteen children. My mother had nine children, ummm, ummm .... at least she was more patient, she can go out with us in the bush and say, umm, "Let's pick for the morning." My mother used to pick but she was always in a rush, "I have to get home to do the laundry, I have to –– start cooking, I have .... ," so my grandmother was a little bit more relaxed about going out with us all day. And it was them too that used to take us out on all their trips. They could get in the boat every weekend, and go digging clams, or, or picking berries up the Inlet, blueberries. And they were always on time with the, the tides and the seasons, the different, you know, natural kinds of things. And the other thing that they really taught me was, ummm, visiting .... your relatives was very important, and no matter where they were we would take them ... and it was usually done on a Sunday, you would take that Sunday and bring a lunch and go visit whoever. And we were always travelling. We were going back and forth to Powell River to see the relatives up there or down to Hainey where my grandfather had a half-brother there, and we were always visiting. Every Sunday we would know like clockwork, get up, get ready and go and get, get in the car and .... granny and grandpa would be out pretty soon. We knew that. So, I, and I think my grandmother and grandfather, because I was the oldest grandchild too –– took me a lot, took me everywhere with them. They took me round, when, actually I think I was practically raised by them. Grandparents did that in those days. ... like my Dad was, had lived mostly with his grandparents. I lived mostly with my grandparents. My children actually live a lot with their grandparents. Uhhh, because grandparents can teach you a lot more with more patience and, umm, nowadays, most, most parents have to work and, so – . ... when you're a grandparent, of course, you're getting older and you've got more patience 'cause you've raised your children, and umm, you, you've got a lot more time to offer young, young children. So, yeah, that's, that's, and parents being, you have to go out and work, make the money and work the house and keep everything going. So, it worked out really nicely for, for uhhh, traditional families, close families. The, the, uhh, grandparent was the important, the important people in there, because they did the raising of the children. And I still see it happening nowadays –– the grandparents take the role of raising their, their, young grandchildren, because the mother's out working and there's a lot of single parents these days. There wasn't as many – so it works out quite, that's why I think for a long time we never got used to that daycare system. But I see that changing a lot more now. I always think that's one of the things that I'd like to hang on to, is the, when I have, when I'm a grandparent ... is to take that role of teaching grandchildren. [1:12,13]

In the course of the interviews, Valerie clarified for herself her thoughts on the role her grandparents played in teaching her about her culture.

Not, until I spoke to you in the last interview, did I realise that what I was talking about was their way of life. It was the way they lived. It was, it wasn't anything that they took and it wasn't like they were going to say, "Hey we're going to have some fish head soup – come on and I'll teach you some culture." They would just cook it and we would eat it. And we would all sit down and really enjoy it. And it – it was a very subtle teaching, it wasn't something that – once in a while my grandmother would say "Come sit down and I'll teach you how to crochet – I'll teaching you a new stitch," and –– but the rest of it was very subtle. It was um, um, we were kids and we would get up in the morning and they'd say "We're going to go visit" –– I mean even visiting was a traditional value. Um, my grandfather always used to say um – "Every Sunday you make sure you visit someone 'cause they are your people and they mean a lot to you. And you show them that – you show them the respect." So every Sunday that's what we did. He – he didn't only say it – he did it. And, nowadays you have parents saying it and not doing it, you know? And that's not teaching their kids very much. I mean, even I'm guilty of that. So –– um, my grandfather was very traditional. Clarence, Clarence Joe was his name. Very traditional man. We were always um, doing something like clam digging, or fishing or going up to the different Reserves that we – that belonged to the Sechelts and spending some time there, and he would um, we would berry pick, we would visit, we would have um, nice times together as a family. I think one of the best times that I had with them was, every night just before we went to bed it was – they would open a jar of preserves and the whole family would sit around the table and we would talk about what we did that day. And my grandfather, he was such a nice special man. He used to sit there and listen to all of us. And really listen. He wasn't like – he didn't have time – he would laugh if you had something funny to say, or if you had a problem he would tell you a story and not try to handle your problems for you. So all his life he was trying to teach us something. ... He'd try to help us with the problem we had and um, he always had a story. He always had a story. Every time, all of my life I've been listening to my grandfather's –– stories. My grandmother was more quiet. She was the person in the background that um, would ...... make the baskets, she was always crocheting and she had some really nice work. And, she hardly said a word, but she was a real listener. Like she would – their listening skills back then were so .... so, so good. Now days I think I don't have the patience to listen to my kids' stories. But I think that allowed us to be creative. Telling a story about what happened that day because I know my Auntie Shelly and they would talk about dreams and, and she would just have, like, a two-hour dream. We'd all have to sit there and listen to her stories, it got really humorous sometimes. Yeah, and they just allowed us to sit there and we couldn't get enough of that. When you are a child I think you want someone to listen to you. And they did – they really fulfilled that for me. And – whereas my own parents were always working hard. My Dad would be logging all day or fishing all day – whatever he was doing. And my mother had nine kids so .... when it got dark she was in bed. So it was nice when my grandparents used to listen to us. And hear us and help us with our daily joys or sorrows or whatever it was. ... Um, I would go stay – I lived with them a lot of times and I would go to their house and that was their routine. We knew their routine too. They had a routine too so it made it easy to figure out what we're going to do next. And in my house, in my Mom and Dad's house there was a routine but it was – it could be put off by anything. Like having nine little kids, had um, and having to be quiet when my Dad went to bed we – there was not enough play time with my parents. And my Dad before he died he actually apologised for that. For not having spent a lot of time with us when we were growing up but he also said that he had to work a lot and now I understand that. And, I think that's one of the things I really like to do with my kids is have that special time together with them, where they can talk to me and feel good and just um, I think, I think um, under my grandparents I flourished as a child. And that's what I want – I'd like my kids to have that. My kids don't have any grandparents from either side so – grandparents are so important. That's what I really think about now. So important. So –– I hope to be here a long time for my grandchildren. [2:9,10]

Learning took place in two very different ways. Much was learned simply by being with people, as in the case above, but specific skills were sometimes consciously and directly taught, or at least an attempt was made to teach them, as with basketry and crochet.

I think – she (grandmother) tried to teach um, us a few times, me and Audrey and Shelly and Lucy – we're all –– . ... Um, Audrey is my sister, Lucy is my cousin, Shelly is our aunt, but we're all in the same age group and she'd try to teach us sometimes, and she –– we were so active, like very, really active. She used to get frustrated with us and send us away. But um, I think you get a –– now I have just learned about teachable moments. When is a good time to teach kids and um, I used to think – Granny used to get us just at the wrong time. [laughs] Oh, yeah she always tried to teach us her different skills that she had. And sometimes – I think after a while she just more or less just let us watch when we wanted to. And she was always digging – you know getting roots for her baskets, before her arthritis came along. And then after she got arthritis real bad, she just stuck to um, crocheting. But she had some really fine crochet. She used to make dolls, just beautiful dolls. Now I look back and I think "Oh, I should have saved one of those dolls," you know. All the things that you think about that she made – I could have saved one of them – just for a keepsake. I think a lot of us do that now. Um, and again that was a time when we were changing. When we were .... um .... culture was a sort of taboo thing, and you had to – you just didn't practise it a lot. [2:10]

Traditional society was very much divided by gender. Men and women had their separate, complementary roles. While Valerie does not remember specifically being taught or confined to the female role by her grandmother, she could see this separation in the older generations.

I know the hunting was, uhh, ... was very different. I remember hearing my grandfather –– used to tell my Dad, "We're going to go hunting tomorrow." And one of the rituals was they would have a river bath. 'Cause the, the deer smells the scent of every man. The other ritual was my Dad wasn't allowed to sleep with my mother –– on the hunt, when he was hunting. My grandfather was very strict about that and uhhh .... Just, just because the deer picks up the scent, yeah. So, it was more like a cleansing, fasting thing. They made –– a lot out of that. Cleansing .... and the river bath was important and he, my grandfather really tried to stick to traditional ways. Even though he knew in his mind that we, eventually we have to assimilate with white – education, he always tried to maintain that, that cultural part without being so blatant about it, without being so open about it. 'Cause, one of the things that we never lost was, was the food. Uhhh, gathering the food, we never lost that. The language was more blatant, see we weren't taught the language, it was, sort of, "OK, I know I have to .... learn English to, to make it in this society," so ummm, my grandfather, without ...... being conscious of that, knew that he was going to keep some traditional values there. And, my grandmother, she was a very, very traditional woman, she was .... ummm, very quiet, only spoke when ahhh, she was spoken to, didn't have much to say, but was very, the strong force behind the marriage. Ahhh, my grandfather and grandmother's marriage was traditional, they were picked for one another. They were the last –– from this Band to be –– traditional, and umm – . ... My Dad was born in 1930 .... three, or was it 1930? So they must have been married in 19...... ten, twelve. ... And they were picked .... for each other .... and my grandmother knew her role as a woman, and accepted it, but was the strong force behind it –– all the same. She was so cool now when I think of her. I, I think, I could never put up some of the things she did. You know, uhhh .... and quiet about it, very like .... ahhh, not saying much, but my grandfather, ummm .... knew always that he was keeping ... knew he was instilling some traditional values in us, all the time, he knew that. But, ahhh, yeah, when my grandmother said, "Let's go do this," he would drop everything and he would say, "Let's go do it." ... that was, that was the way it – . They were, ahhh, the society ran, the society ran on, on women having the power. [1:13,14]

... that was the – even when I look back at my grandmother and the .... child bearing was such a – it was magnificent you know – it was this highly thought of task, it was like my grandmother had thirteen kids. That, that made my grandfather rich, you know. That's how they used it. "I'm a very rich man, I'm a wealthy man I have all these children." And he always said that, "I'm a very rich man." Nowadays if you have more than four they think you're crazy. [laughs] More than two! So, even that, when I thought about it, I thought, "Boy these women knew their roles and they knew who they were." Nowadays we struggle with who we are and who we are as women. And I have to think about my grandmother a lot. I always have to ask, sort of ask her spirit to come and help me when I have problems. 'Cause she knew how to handle everything. And just in her quiet way, like she was very quiet and I really admire her quiet now. 'Cause when my husband is doing something now I cannot be quiet. [laughs] So –– just things like that. Just being quiet was an admirable thing. You know, when you think about it. 'Cause um .... it must have took a lot of strength for her not to say things to her kids and to her grandchildren. But to you know, to want to – to want to correct them, but it was more of a learning, a learning consequence. You learn on your own, and you'll know. She didn't try to help us out of a lot of things. [2:11]

Valerie has many happy memories of her childhood, but there are also many that are not so positive. Her overall feeling is a sense of confusion.

The best word that comes up for my childhood was confused. Um, actually Howard Ringer asked us that same question. And the first thing that came to my mind was confused. And a lot of people had said that – confusing time, 'cause um, um, nothing was, um, consistent. Nothing in your life was consistent. Um, nowadays you can say, you can give your children consistency and you can allow them to be really open-minded about changes and what's going to happen and where we are headed as a Nation. We weren't, in my time, we weren't as a Nation – people were fighting amongst each other and um, the Catholic Church was overruling everything, um, being a Native person was not good. Um, um, we had no traditions left. They were almost all gone. Um, just the housing that we lived in was very poor and um, because our parents weren't educated, only could go to grade six – that was it. So they never got the good jobs. They had to fight for everything they – they wanted to do and living on Reserves and having an Indian Affairs person come in to – to oversee you too, as well. It was just a really confusing time for me. Just um, nothing made sense. It was um, you grew up accepting what it was – what your home was. And then to top it all off twenty-five people living in one house. That was awful. It was an awful time. But we made it work. It was um, so I – I always knew I was loved by – because I was the oldest of my – my, the oldest grandchild – I'm the oldest child – I always knew I was loved, but I wonder about my brothers and sisters that they always knew that – if they always felt it and how confusing it must have been for them to not have the same as what I had. I always felt I was very lucky, so – but, um, yeah just going back, it's all sorting out in my mind now. [4:15]

I think I grew up very confused. And .... I had to, I think in the last ten years, really, identify who I was. And I really had to say "Yeah, I am a Native person. But what do I know? I don't know anything about my culture." I had, I had to go to other, see other people learning their culture and say that, that belongs to me too. I can understand that children have an identity – problems, because we had no identity, I just had no identity. I just, I .... I grew up thinking I was white but knowing I was Native. And it was very difficult . So, really, like I say, confusing and .... when you look at our young people nowadays, and most of our children are halfbreeds ...... I don't know what they're thinking. It must be difficult, difficult for them because um, I remember how difficult it was for me to grow up like that. Yeah, nothing was done Native. [1:9]

As soon as she left high school, Valerie began working. Over the years she has had a wide range of jobs, most of them in people-oriented areas. Her first job, however, was in one of the canneries doing work that had become associated with Native women over the previous few generations and which has close connections to Sechelt women's traditional work.

Yeah. I've been working most of my life. And actually my first job was in a cannery and I didn't like that at all. [laughs] ... My Mom and them talk about their best time of their life was working in the cannery – not me. [laughs] ... Just sorted fish, you know. Handled fish all day and it was um, it was back-breaking hard work. You know and we weren't making much money, it was a very low wage, so –– but it was still work. [2:4]

Valerie seems to find most satisfaction in jobs that involve people. For the past while she has been working for the Band as Cultural Officer, which has involved a wide range of activities including occasional teaching and curriculum development. At the time of interview her job had just been changed to Educational Officer and was to involve permanent part-time teaching in the elementary school language program as well as curriculum development for other levels. Valerie was looking forward to her new role.

I worked (in daycare) for .... three years. I did two years of um, as um a daycare worker and then the last year I was, I was the supervisor so – . It was –– it was you know, I really like kids so it was good for me. [2:4]

... [laughs] I've done a lot of jobs. Um, I was a teacher's aide, and um, a preventative worker for the Band. I had an after-school program, um, I ran a summer camp up in Deserted Bay; um, ... did some receptionist work; I took, lately I've just been taking a lot of courses to keep up with the times, like computer courses. I was deathly afraid of the computer when I first got on; I wouldn't even touch it for, like, a week and once I got the hang of it I, I just love it now. So I've been doing a lot of upgrading in the last few years to get myself up to the standard that I could get employment .... you know anywhere. Got a lot of experience now. [2:4]

I've even picked leaves which I, you know when you get to winter and everything the, the forestry has shut down and it's – nothing else is happening – so my husband and I tried picking leaves once and that was .... I didn't know how to pick them so – . ... They use them for florists. For floral arrangements? ... Actually, there's a, there's a small industry here for that. But I tried that. I think all of us – most of our Band members have tried that. ... We didn't know how to bunch them. I'm sure if I would have stuck with it I would have eventually learned, but, but again it wasn't my, my bag you know. I liked to – I think what I really like to do and have enjoyed is working with kids. I find um, working with children is so rewarding and um –– you can just be yourself with kids. You don't have to be this different person you know, like you are with adults. So I really enjoyed the kids so I'm happy I'm going back to the school next year to be an instructor. But I guess I'll take on the challenge. It's a challenge. [2:4,5]

Despite the strong Catholic influence within the family and the community, Valerie and her husband Ken were not married in the Church. There was a further factor, that of retaining her Native status, that was important too.

No. I, um I didn't get married in the Church. I was going to and Ken actually – he did take some Catholic lessons, but never agreed with them. [laughs] So I thought – I mean I can't force this guy to um, to you know get married in the Catholic – but it wasn't about the Catholic Church. My marriage was more about me losing status as a Native woman and marrying a white man. Had I married Ken years ago – like I had planned – I would have lost status and my grandfather was really worried about that. He came to me and he said, "I want you to hold your wedding off until all this is done. It's not fair to our women what the government is saying about you. If you marry Ken you'll, you'll not be known as a Sechelt woman any more." And that was very important to him. I couldn't see it then, but I listened to him – I, I listened to him. But now I see what he meant. And I never did lose – my sister married her husband a few years after I had decided to get married and she lost status and had a hard time regaining it. But it was – it was a political thing. ... I waited a long, long time. I got married after all my children were born. [laughs] They were all there. ... It was um, they were all there to witness it. I was going to get married a year after I met Ken. That would be twenty years ago now. But instead I got married fifteen years after, we had lived together. So – yeah, it was kind of like you know – here I was – again, here was a thing. I was Catholic. Been brought up in all the Catholic ways, to live with someone with

sin. So to me I thought in my mind "Here I am every day commit-
ting this mortal sin." And then politically I would be, I would not
have been known as a Sechelt woman. That would have been taken
away from me. And so I had to give one up to retain the other. And I
thought it was so unfair and so I had to really um, go to my Grandpa
and say to him. "Am I sinning because I'm living with Ken and I
want to marry him but um, I'll lose status and I really need to know
from you that it is okay. Or I need to know from someone that it's
OK." So he said that it's OK, "We'll recognise in our eyes that you
are married to this man." And so it was heart-breaking for me at
that time – because I had the whole thing planned and it would be a
nice church wedding and whatever. ... Being Catholic on the one
hand, and being a Native woman and marrying a white person on
the other hand. There was really no justice. So, uh, I don't know –
whatever one was most important became your priority and mine
was always to listen to my grandfather and know what he said was,
was right and to really put my faith in what he said, and to this day I
never regretted it. [4:13,14]

*Valerie has four children, a largish family by today's standards, but
much smaller than Sechelt families in past generations. All four were
born in the Sechelt Hospital.*

Um .... I never experienced having any of my children at home, but
um, I'm sure I would have liked to have had them at home. Hospi-
tals were so .... sterile, they were not familiar and um, ... I found
that doctors and nurses probed at you too much and it made me
uncomfortable. ...Um, when I had my first son Aaron, it was
because it was my first child my Mom wanted me to be with a doctor. And then when I had my second child, who is Brandi, she was
born very, very sick and nearly died. It was, it was – she was dying
as soon as she was born and after that they just didn't want to take
any chances because I was um .... high-risk. And my third child Josh
was also born very sick and nearly died and they ended up shipping
both him and Brandi to Vancouver Children's Hospital. So with my
last one there was just – I was put in the hospital a month before I
delivered. So, there –– like I guess the good part is that when they
are sick they can, they can find out right away –– start treating
them for whatever it is. Both of them had blood disorders and had
to be transfused. Um, with their own blood though, not with donated
blood, so that was one thing I – Ken and I both really worried about,
not to transfuse anybody else's blood into them. So they did it

somehow in a machine that put their own blood – that took it out and put it back into themselves. So no, I guess I really didn't have a choice. Um .... after that I just felt like I should have been in the hospital 'cause, um, I don't know, I guess different complications come up with people now. Then – I'm, I'm not sure. Ah, my mother was pretty healthy and, and I mean strong and delivered her babies with no problems. And my grandmother too. She had all her children – I'm sure – at home. [2:2]

By the time Valerie was adult much of the religious celebration had been abandoned, but the family gatherings remained important.

We still get together as a family. We still go to my Mom and Dad's house and have a big dinner and whoever shows up is welcome. Nobody is ever turned away. Um, we still get together and give gifts out at the house and –– . ... But the only thing that has changed is the religious part of it – which I really loved when I was a kid – was the religious part. The spiritual part. I really loved that, celebrating. Even if it's not the Catholic way – and you know we can all say the Catholic nuns and priests did us wrong. But we still loved that spiritual part of it – when I was a kid. And that's a real loss for me. It's like it died with my parents and then my grandparents and my great-grandparents – it's all gone. And it will – it's sad because for me I have to reconcile with that. I have to say, "Okay I'm going to let that go." And then traditionally we have to start doing, thinking up some traditional ways to celebrate these holidays. So it means something spiritual to our children, because I think a lot of our children grew up in that transition where no spirituality was taught to them at all. And so they've lost that.

You said that when we were up at the cemetery that, um, that you thought it might be possible to sort of reconcile at least some aspects of the traditional belief with some aspects of Christianity?

Yeah, I really, you know, we are being, we know that, everybody leads – in my idea, everybody – there is a God and how you celebrate that God is, is your own right. And how you choose to walk the paths with your –– with God is your right, and um, I think once we've got over all of this, this .... hurt and heartbreak from what residential schools did to us, we're going to say, "Okay, let's be spiritual again." 'Cause that's what we need, that's what we lack. And um, that somehow the Elders were right. They were right to make a big production out of, out of honouring their gods and that –

that has, you know we shouldn't have hard feelings about it. That we do need that and I think my best memories are of being in church on Christmas day; of being in church on, on Easter day and the, the comfort it gave me. And um, looking back I think my Aaron and Brandi haven't had that comfort so they don't know what their spirituality is all about. But I've decided that Josh and Kahn are going to grow up with some spirituality and that's the sweat lodges and the traditional ways that we have of honouring our Creator and every day is just an honour to get up and thank the Creator and allow them to know that they have the freedom to do that in any way they want. And at any time of the day that they want, not just when we go to church. That we honour our God, our Creator, but it's all the time. So we start looking at this world very spirituality and honouring it a lot more that um, I did, um, just on Sunday. ... I stopped – I was pregnant with Josh. Josh is ten now and I would go to church every Sunday – faithfully. And I remember there was a lot of back-biting in those days. People talking about others – saying they are hypocrites and they, they go to church every Sunday and yet they hate all week. And then go to church on Sunday and pretend that there is love in their hearts. And I sat down, and I thought about it and I said, "Gee Ken," I said to my husband, "I think I'm a hypocrite 'cause I go through that, and maybe I shouldn't even be going to church." So I quit. And, it's been ten years now, since I haven't gone to church. But um ––. [4:12,13]

Valerie remembers her mother with great affection and also with great admiration for the way she lived her life.

Well, my mother was um, she was born up in Stoney Creek. She's not from Sechelt – she is a Carrier Indian from up north. She married my, my Dad when she was eighteen. Both of them got married when they were eighteen. And .... when I, when I think back about my childhood, and now that we're talking about traditional ways, my mother was a very traditional woman. She –– I have this memory of her always making different things with .... with nothing really. She used to, I – I, we used to pluck ducks. My Dad was a duck hunter and um, he used to bring ducks home for us to eat. And my mother was one of those that would save everything –– everything. And we used to pluck ducks and she knew how to do that. She knew how to do everything. And –– we were plucking – I used to watch her – I used to help her and then she'd have these duck feathers all stored in bags that she had saved from other sources. And she used to put them up in the attic and I used to think to myself, "Gee, why does she save everything. I can't believe when she saves everything, you know." .... And then one day I got home and she says, "Oh, I made you a mattress." She said, "Go try it," and I went and it was the softest duck-down mattress. I couldn't believe that that's what she was doing it for. And she was always this woman that was — she didn't say much. She never like, sat down with me and we would talk. My mother was always working. That's one thing that I remember about her, a very, very hard worker. Not like today where you got laundromats and dishwashers and you've got everything. My mother did everything. Um, from nothing. She would carry in water for her laundry. Boil it. Do the laundry. And all this would be done before nine o'clock in the morning. And my Mom had nine children — and all by herself too. Like she went to the hospital alone and had them by herself. No one was there to support her. And then, I don't think I ever thought of .... any of this until after my mother was gone. About how strong, how strong she was and how much I appreciate her now. 'Cause when I think I have it tough, I always remember my Mom having to do it and it was so much harder for her, but she still did it. And without, without a complaint. Nowadays, we complain about "Oh, I worked hard all day, or I did this." And she would actually have jobs outside the home to bring in extra income. ... She would um, work in the fish plants, or she'd house clean, or you know what we would consider menial jobs, babysit. My mother — raised a lot of uh, my cousins. Their mothers used to leave them behind and she would end up raising a lot of them so it meant for her a lot more children in the house and she always had to provide for them somehow. And I used to – I remember this one story, my — two younger brothers, they were small then about four and five. She thought, "Well they need new jeans, their jeans are getting all torn and everything." And she would save all these work pants that my Dad used to have. If he got too big for them, he'd say, "I can't fit this any more," and she'd save it. And she'd say, "Oh," and she'd measure my little brothers' legs and in one hour they'd have new jeans. She had this old treadle machine that – and she had it all her life, like she never, never traded it in for a new one. So um, or they would have a new shirt made out of somebody's old dresses or whatever. And she was — she was quite an amazing woman to me. Um, she'd never sit there and say um, "Oh they need new clothes um, where can I get some money to go and buy it." She would just make it. Make it up and – and make it. Or she would know how to make a .... meal go much further. There was twenty-five of us living in our house at one time. And you know how as a young girl grow-ing up you want your Mom to spend some time with you? Well she never could. And I remember I used to get really upset with her – almost angry with her to come and sit with me and talk with me. And that's when the twenty-five of us were all living together. She would, she would be washing clothes from probably about four or five in the morning um, then she'd be cooking, then she would be hanging curtains or washing floors or cleaning up the little ones. Or doing the dishes. And she would do this till about –– till my Dad got home and he was a logger at the time. He would go out logging all day. And then we'd all have dinner. She would clean up. And then she would go to bed. And I used to – I remember thinking, "Why can't she just sit up and talk with me?", you know, so um –– I didn't realise that hey, she must have been tired or – she never said a word. And sometimes she would read, she would go to bed and read and I would go and sit with her on the bed and we'd talk a little bit and I guess I wanted her more for myself. I didn't want to share her with all these people. And I felt it was um ...... there was a time I think I just wanted all these people to go away. "Go away, this is my Mom, and I want more of her." But she, never, ever said anything she just – like she knew what she had to do and she did it and, and that was what I guess being a woman was all about in her days. It was um, just get up and do it, don't complain. Get it done. And if you have no free time for yourself, well that's too bad. And even – I think –– I forget which child was being born – probably her eighth child and I remember my Dad saying to me, in front of me, not say-ing to me but saying it in front of me to my Mom. "Did you tell her yet?" And my Mom said, "No." And I said, "Tell me what? What are you going to tell me?" And Dad said, "Tell her now." And she said, "Oh. I'm having another baby." And I, I think that was the, the –– only time I got really upset with her. And I said something like, "Another baby? We hardly have any food, we hardly have anything and you're going to have another baby? And, and I think that's how I put it to her. "Don't you believe in birth control?" I said to her. And she said, "No I don't, I don't believe in birth control, and I won't take it and if God – if God wishes for me to have a lot of chil-dren then that's what I'll do." And there was, there was no two ways about it that's what she wanted to do. And she – so to me now when I think of it, that was very spiritual. That was a spiritual way of thinking. But for me, I just thought it was a bigger burden, I guess. [3:1,2]

But if Melanie's own life was difficult, she had dreams for her children's futures.

I think she wanted – She always kept saying, "Oh, I wish you'd be a stewardess, a stewardess so you could go and travel. You're tall, you're nice and tall," she'd say. And she'd always say, "You're beautiful." She'd tell everybody they were beautiful. She had this um, she always had these dreams for any young person that was .... or a teacher, "I wish you'd be a teacher," or um, she'd have dreams for all of us. She'd ask what we wanted to do in our quiet times, when we used to lay with her. I remember laying with my Mom until I was very old ..... [3:8]

These quiet times in bed at the end of the day were particularly important to Valerie.

I think we talked mostly about what I did that day. Or who said what or, and if – if I had a fight with another kid I would say it to her and she would sort of help me out and say, "Well, the next time just walk away." But even when, times when we didn't talk, she would just hold me and she would um, sing to me. My Mom was always singing. She loved to sing. She sang while she worked or she was whistling or –– whatever. But sometimes she would just sing to me or she would um, have I – I guess I always knew my mother was thinking about me 'cause she would always have something prepared in her mind of what to say to me and it – I – I knew that. I could feel that. I knew that she – even though it looked like she never was, um, noticing me she was in those quiet times and I would know. So um, um, yeah it – even if the hug only lasted for about, about five minutes and, and sometimes, I wish that you know .... would have lasted longer in my life, but – . .... I think I got more because, um, I think my mother –– thought being the oldest I had a lot more pressures than the, than the next kids. And she knew that she depended on me a lot more and it was um, like really being supportive to me and, and building me up so I would have enough um, um –– strength to – to carry some of her load. So I don't think it was – it was – mostly me. Yeah. But even now when I think about it, my Mom and Dad – my mother was always saying special things to me and she would say, "Don't tell the other kids that I said this." And I never would. I – she would always say, "This is between me and you. And if you tell them they'll feel like I don't love them." And so I would never say that to them. I would hold it in my, in my heart. And I think she was just saying, "Just so you make it through this time," 'cause I – I remember being a kid, um, when I was a kid I was always very sick with pneumonia and I think she was always really worried about that. 'Cause the house was always cold or there was never enough food so it was um, her way of saying, "It's okay, I still love you, and you'll be fine," you know. So it's at times when I think of my Mom and think she was – she was giving me the strength to one day um, when she was gone, to keep moving on. And doing all that. [4:5,6]

Melanie and the children were regular churchgoers in those days.

Yeah, we all did. All of us went. Every Sunday and special holidays, we – that was –– one thing Native people did was go to church every Sunday and special holidays. Yeah, we would all dress up and go. My Dad would never go though, my Dad was neat. Never into going to church and –– and praying. Said he had enough of it when he was in residential school. [laughs] ... He said all they did was pray, pray, pray. But my mother still went, even though she grew up in Lejac[3] from the time she was five years old to um, probably fifteen, and then from fifteen on she worked. Um, went out on her own and worked in a cannery up in Naimu. And I think, I think I only asked, spoke to my Mom once about that. My Mom didn't talk about herself too much either. But, 'cause it was very hurtful for her to talk about losing her Mom and her Dad and being orphaned at five years old.[4] I know she used to – well once in a while – cry for her Dad, but she never liked us to see her cry because, ah, she thought it would hurt us to see her cry. So she was always very careful about her, her emotion in front of us. ... Um, her mother died in childbirth, and her father .... I think –– he drank something and it was – it had some – it was old or whatever, stale or something and he got sick and died. You know very quickly, like the same night that he drank the stuff. And so at five she was –– she had no

3 Lejac Residential School at Burns Lake, BC.
4 Melanie's early life is dealt with in some detail in the biography of her sister Mary. See Bridget Moran, *Stoney Creek Woman Sai'k'uz Ts'eke: The Story of Mary John* (Vancouver: Tillacum Library, 1988).

parents and her older sister who is um, Mary John – she wrote
Stoney Creek Woman. Um, she was, she tried to raise my Mom
after and once she started having her own children it became very
hard on her so she put my Mom into residential school. It was time
for her to go to school anyhow. I don't think there was much say
about – about – about it –– the whole idea. So, I think when my
Mom was about ten or eleven she got tuberculosis and they
shipped her down to the hospital at Coqualeetza in Chilliwack for a
few years too. So –– . ... and now when I think about it I think, you
know losing your parents at five, getting tuberculosis at ten and
then having you shipped all the way down here and no – no family.
It must have been incredibly lonely for her. But she never said a
word. Never said a word and –– I think, I think .... that was one of
the reasons my mother said to me, "That's why I had nine kids. So
I would never be lonely again. I would always have all of you here
with me." So, and so protective of all of us kids you know. Making
sure we had everything and she even said, "I like to spoil all of you
because I never was." And –– I bring it back in little bits and pieces
you now. Everything that she said to me over the years as I was
growing up and I put it all together and I –– you know she knew her
purpose in –– she knew her purpose and she had her vision. And
her children and her husband were the most important. Her family
was the most important thing in her life. Right till the day she died.
Her family was number one with her that she would never, never
um –– let them go. And um, she –– I think .... all the time we were
growing up she gave up a lot of things to –– so we could have
something. Or she would make, my mother um, was um, one of
these women who knew how to work with leather. She knew how
to tan hides and um ...... she used to make us buckskin dresses for
um, –– for parades or dances that we would have when we were
children. My sister was an Indian princess and my mother made all
her costume for her. And she would bead, bead work on it. She
would put all her bead – and cut the fringe. And it felt so wonderful.
I remember sitting there while she was working with this smoked
leather. And it smelled like my Mom. She used to make moccasins –
everything. ... my mother made me a jacket too one time. And I
thought, "Ah, I'm ashamed to wear this," I thought to myself 'cause
I – I was with a generation where there was no culture taught or
that we had learned it so well from the residential school that Indian was bad. And so we became ashamed of anything that was

traditional or cultural for us. And I remember saying -- her saying -- being very, very proud of this, of this jacket she had made me. And saying, "Try it on," and I tried it on to please her, but I was sort of sitting there rolling my eyes. She never said anything to me. She never -- she knew -- but she never said a word. And .... she -- she would say things like "I'm very proud of you." And I -- I couldn't understand why she would say that, you know. When I would be sitting there with this awful attitude, I guess. And her heart was so big. She was very kind, very generous. And she -- she always practised what she spoke. It was not saying something and doing the opposite. It was all -- everything she said -- which is what she did herself so -- very honest and truthful. So .... when, I when I think of my Mom I think of her as a very respectful woman. And very strong, and courageous, and but um, also very directed in her life. Not wishy-washy -- never swayed when she made a decision. Always um, stood by her words. And she learned when she came here -- she found my Dad. She fell in love with my Dad. [3:3,4]

Valerie enjoys telling the story of how her mother and father met and married.

... the first time she had seen my Dad, and it took me a long time to figure this out -- my Auntie Bernie told me that. "I was in the TB hospital with your Mom, I think we were about ten or eleven years old." And she said, "And William came to visit me." Um, he went to visit his sister. And that's the first time my Mom laid eyes on him. And they were eleven years old. My Mom decided then that she loved him and that she was going to marry him one day. And she never seen my Dad until they were seventeen again. That must be six or seven years later. And she was working in a cannery in Naimu and my Dad's boat pulled in. And somebody said, "The Sechelt boats are here." To everybody in the cannery. And I guess my Mom ripped off her apron, ran down the dock and she said there was my Dad getting off the boat and she said, "William Joe -- I know who you are." And she put her arms around him and she hugged him. I asked my Dad, "What did you do?" [laughs] He says, "Well, I didn't know this woman. She was telling me she loved me and [laughs] I'm getting off the boat, you know. She's all so happy to see me." He said, "So I went out with her, I went out with her and next day I left," and he says, "I thought I'd never see Mom again, never." And they took off. They went fishing and I guess my Mom was so in love with him she found her way down to Vancouver. And she knew who um, Dad's uncle was – Benny. And she went to Benny. She found Benny in Vancouver. Can you imagine – in Vancouver. And she said I want you to take me to William. So Benny had to get on this – the Union steamship with her – that's how they got here. And she got off, she went to my Granny and Grandpa's house and Benny brought her there. And I, I got all the story from everyone of them. Like I asked my Granny and Grandpa, "What did you do?" "Well, this strange woman walks in our house and says she knows William. William is our oldest – he's our baby. He is out hunting ducks." And um, they told her well his room is there, "Go and lay down – you must be tired," or whatever and they – I guess my Dad walked in the door. My Granny spoke Indian to him. "There's a woman in your room, says she knows you." And my Dad said, "Who?" "Go and see," they said. He walked in and here it was my Mom again. [laughs] ... After that they were married, yeah. 'Cause now my – his great-grandparents, that would be Basil and Mommie, Poppie and Mommie that was my grandfather's parents. They lived next door. And I guess my Dad had been living with my Mom for about three months by then and my – his grandmother went to him and said, um, "You're not bringing shame on the family, you're marrying that woman. And that's it. I'm getting everything ready for you." And um, after that they had to do it, 'cause she was the top. I mean, if you said, "No" to her that would be like a sin today. So she demanded that he do the right thing and bring respect back to the family. So, they got married and a year later I was born. [3:5,6]

... Catholic wedding, church wedding. She had everything. Um, um, when I look at the pictures, they are very beautiful, very beautiful wedding. The cake and everything was all made by my Dad's grandmother and um, everyone was there to celebrate with them so – . She was a very persistent woman, you know. Just from that story you can tell that – "Okay I love this man, that's it. Nothing is going to get in my way." And once she had her children it was the same thing. "I love my children. Nothing is going to get in the way. I know what I have to do." So all of her life she knew what she wanted and went out and got it. And she knew that if ah, she had to make money that was what – she had to go and work and get that money and bring it home. So yeah, very, very strong. Keep coming back to that word. ... I think after her own parents died she searched for that connection to be a part of a family. When I think about it. Once in a while I would hear her, all – you know, during my lifetime with her – very seldom would I hear her say she was lonely. But she would. I mean she would get up and say, "Oh I'm so lonely for my home." But as soon as she said it and it was out she was back doing her – her work and, or I think only once in my life I heard her say she missed her Dad. And um, I think in the last few years she went home more often, because she felt like .... she needed to, to touch base with other people. She was so afraid about losing her language. Soon as she felt like she was losing it, it would scare her and she would say, "I'm going home, I'm going home. I have got to talk my language," and as soon as we went up to her, her home town it was – she did nothing but speak her language. And then as soon as she felt like it was okay we'd come back, home here. But she learned my Dad's language fluently. She could speak our language better than he could. So, she was ah, she was ah – incredible. [3:5,6]

Valerie also had a close relationship with her Aunt Bernie, her father's sister.

... my Auntie Bernie was always very special to me, because um, I think what I liked the most about her was that she wouldn't let anybody put her down. In those days women were very, they always listened to their, to their men and um, if they didn't they would – they would be beaten. And my Auntie Bernie wouldn't put up with that. And I used to remember her. And nobody would ever answer my Dad back 'cause he was this big, big huge man and to answer him back was like a sin almost. You know? And I remember her answering him back and he got up to – to hit her – and this is his sister – and she said, "You try it and I'm going to hit you right back." And that's what happened. And I – I was lying in the room and I was going, "Yeah Bernie, get him," you know. [laughs] But I had never seen that before in my life. Because my mother always did what my Dad – without answering him – she did what he wanted. Always. And she would never answer him back. I've never heard my Mom, until later, later years, ever say anything to my Dad. And I was proud of my Mom the first time she told him to shut up too. Because it was like a big step for my mother. To tell my Dad to shut up. I mean nowadays we throw that word around like crazy. But, but here's Auntie Bernie, just feisty and, and never backed down from anybody. I – I just felt this special connection with her all of my life. But to me when I was growing up too – she was so beautiful. And I just, I always admired her beauty. And um, she still is – she is sixty-two and she still is beautiful. So – it um .... and the only other – I think the real important thing was she seen me as a human being, not as a kid. In those days, when you were a kid it was um, how does that saying go, "All children should be seen and not heard?' And that's how we were treated. And she would look at me and she would ask me how I was and she would hug me and she would take me on little trips with her and treat me like a real human being not like a kid that was annoying her. And that's what I really admire about her. ... she would take me to Vancouver. To a play, a Disney play or something and she would –– take me to the States when we used to go picking. Just her and I used to go. And we'd share a cabin and we'd –– that's how we would live our life – from day to day. ... I was seventeen then. Um, and she, like you know when you are seventeen sometimes you just want to sleep. 'Course she used to get up at five or six to go picking and she'd say, "No, no you just sleep don't worry about it. When you are ready come down. I'll be there." And she would tell me where she was going to be. And I used to think, "Oh that's nice." 'Cause um, I know when we used to – when we used to have to do work with my Dad it was, "Get up and do the work now or else." You know? But here was this adult being so nice to me I couldn't believe it. 'Cause it was different. And children were not treated very well in those days. When I look at now, and all the rights that children have and how well off children are protected, I think to myself, "That's so unreal," because we never had any of that stuff. I never even knew I had rights. I just thought I was a little slave. You know, with no rights. It was unusual. So for a person to come in and treat me like – special, it was so nice. And she always did. She did from that time on. She had a special connection with me too. ... I think from that day on I learned how to treat children as human beings, as special, special people. [4:6,7]

Schooling today for Sechelt children is in some respects vastly different from when Valerie was a student, and yet many of the problems remain much the same. The residential school is gone and children attend the local public schools, both elementary and secondary, right in Sechelt. But they are still a minority.

In the elementary school it's about, let's say ...... out of a 100 per-cent, probably .... a good 40 percent now. 35-40 percent. ... In the high school it's probably still about .... hmmmm, 18-20 percent. Yeah, very low yet. [1:6]

And there is still discrimination.

When I look at our school system nowadays I still see the same thing happening and I ask myself, ah, "What's going on? How can, how can we change it to make our children more comfortable in public schools?" And, and one of the – the big things I, I can see is that parents, yeah, have to go to the school all the time and show that – make their children feel fairly safe, and ah, I attended the high school up here one time and it was so incredible. The kids were so glad to see me there. They were just really happy and they were .... it made them feel safe, and I, I did ask my nephew, Nathan, who's a grade nine student, ... I said "How did you feel when I went up to the school? Did you feel like you didn't want me there?" And he said, "No," he said "It felt really good when you there." He said "It made me feel like it was my school." ... I wanted to see the kids and, and sort of hang around and see what they ..... and it was lunch time and I had nothing else to do so I went and seen my nephew, and um, I just sat around and talked to the kids. Just, just a pop-in day –– nothing really special going on. But I felt so good, I couldn't believe it. So I think if you get a parent up there every day it's going to be, it's going to make an amazing difference for teenagers. [1:3]

Sometimes the discrimination is from other students, but sometimes it is from staff and the system itself. Sometimes it is subtle and sometimes overt.

I still see our children dropping out at –– grade ten, just the same. They pack it in and, and .... one of the .... it seems er, the main reasons for this is – the teachers give up ..... and they have no, er –– I guess, coping skills. I know my, my niece, er, her name is Rita, she, she was a high academic student and I think when she got to grade eleven, and Rita, Rita's halfbreed, her mother's German, and her father's my brother.... but she, she was academically a high student and she was always on the honour roll. For the last two, three years she was on the honour roll and um, one of the teachers said to her "Oh, gee Rita, I thought girls like you dropped out in grade ten." And with a remark like that ..... meaning that Native girls, er, all got, by now you should have been pregnant and have dropped out. Uhhh, meaning that all Native girls get pregnant at a very young age and drop out of high school. And a remark like that one ..... I have discussed it with my sister-in-law and my brother ..... a remark like that could devastate a young person that .... has no self-esteem, no confidence. And they just, they get pushed around and they say "I'm out of here. I can't take stuff like that." But she, she talked to her parents about it and they, they went and demanded an apology for her, and in front of the whole school. So – . ... Uh, yeah. I was very, very proud of them for doing that because a lot of parents just sit back and let their children take abusive remarks like that. Whereas my parents never entered the high –– I won five awards in grade ten and I, I was so pleased with myself and I told my parents and they, they never came to the awards night. You know, so I was just .... I .... they accepted it that way because, mainly because, uh, with residential schools you didn't get involved. Everything was left up to the priests and it was in their hands .... the missionaries. They took control of everything, they controlled everything. So our parents never thought of even entering the school, never thought of questioning the teachers on their skills, so, when I got into high school my parents never got involved. I was a little bit better with my, my own children. At elementary level I was always involved in their education. But at high school, again, I kept –– my idea was "Well, that's the teacher's problem. It's their –– it's their umm ...... they're there to teach my child and if they're not, well, I'm not getting involved." So, yeah, we have this um, really, ummm, cut-and-dried opinion about what teachers should be doing and not doing, you know. Yeah. But I'd like to see a change, uhh, even from my older children to my younger children, there's a ten-year difference in the two little ones' ages, I have really changed my opinions on education. I don't know if it's age, or ... . [1:4,5]

The changes that are taking place are a result of conscious effort on the part of both the schools and the Sechelt people.

I think the teachers are really becoming aware that there is Native people living here. I think a lot, most of the community before that decided that, OK, if we don't recognise them then they're not here, and I grew up with that. That sort of, ummm, how would you say .... that feeling, that I'm not, we're not really here, you know, so, ummm, with the teachers in elementary school now it's, it's amazing, it's just so .... they're so into Native people and they really want to –– this started about ten years ago, they started off, ummm, the Cultural Day, it was supposed to have been a Multicultural Day but it ended up with just us showing our culture for one day, and we'd have dances and we had our, uhhh, we put on all our arts and crafts for a day and someone would do beadwork and carving and basketry and, and uhhh, then we had entertainment in the afternoon and it really opened a lot of people's eyes. And the reason we started that was, ummm, because our kids were going to school and getting bugged about being Indians. And one of the things we said was, "Well if people understood who we were and what our culture was they might appreciate us, uhh, a little bit more." It was like an eye-opener to the community. "Yeah, we do have something to offer." We, we do have a culture even though it is broken, the language barrier was broken many years ago, we still do have something here, and we were proud of it. And so our children should be proud of it too, and, a lot of our kids grew up thinking they were white. That there was, umm, no such thing as a Native person. And I remember, even a story from my, from my son Aaron. He didn't know what an Indian was. Because we never discussed Native and white. Like, my husband's white and I'm Native and we decided not to give him any of these, uhhh, what we thought was prejudiced ideas. But he came home and he said, "Mom, I've seen a big Indian." And I said, "Where?" And he said, "In the bushes. It's big and hairy and it's brown." He'd seen a bear that day and he called it an Indian. [laughs] But, yeah, getting back to the Cultural Day. It turned out – it went really well. Very well. ... It was held right in the school. ... That was started in 198 --2, 1982. We have, we've taped some of them – and we had storytelling. Stella Johnson was our story, one of our storytellers. She's amazing. Oh, we had all kinds of .... last year, so we're having two days, one in May and one in October because we, last year we went up and we um, open fired some fish for the school. Did a demonstration there all day and actually we did about ...... maybe, fifty fish all day, and everybody, everybody in the school got to taste it. So, we really enjoyed that but we have to go with the seasons, you know, there's only a certain time you can take the, uhhh, the dogfish, dog salmon or, or, uhhh, preserve it. Yeah. And the other one is in May, but that's going to be mainly Arts and Crafts Day where we bring all the, the beadworkers and the, yeah, basket makers in and have a demonstration – for the children to go and look at. That'll be happening this May. [1:5,6]

Now that they have self-government, the Band Council is becoming more and more involved in education. They are working at preparing curricula and mounting courses at all levels from kindergarten through to postsecondary.

The Band is starting to implement more courses for um, our own people. They are starting to take education into, into their own hands which is nice. Eventually, we'll have our own school from kindergarten to grade twelve and that's where we need to head. Um, but with the adult courses we're, we are in full control of that and that – . ... But again, getting back to having our, our own school, um, I thought to myself well, at one point I thought to myself, "Well, why should we have our own school? Um ...... that would be –– racist, wouldn't it?" That's what I thought to myself. And then I thought, "Well, we're not different from other people." But we are. It's, it's my thinking has come down to we are different. We have a different culture. We lived by different values in the past. We are different people than everybody else. Um, the whole school curriculum is based around um, white people and how they live. And who their great people were. And their language. We had to do everything their way. Our way is different. We have our own language, we have our own people that we consider heroes and we want to talk about them. Because we want to put them, instil some self-esteem into our children. And unless these people are talked about and our history is talked about our kids will never have that –– that same self-esteem. 'Cause there is nothing mentioned in these schools here for them to really admire someone of their own race. So I think to myself, "Yes we do need our own school. We need to take control now of our own education." And um, being a self-government Band it's going to be a lot – a lot easier for us to accomplish that. ... Um, we, we're talking about it more and more, they're actually um, um, the Chief and Council take it very seriously at this point. And um, we are doing modules now for a program so we're, we're starting on our way. ... We'll have a curriculum ––– . ... And I suppose the next step is to start training our own teachers and then bringing, bringing them back to our Band. Teaching our children. ... Donna Joe. She's the teacher, grade two teacher in the elementary school. And she's um, she's our only one. ... Brandi and Rita, yeah Brandi and Rita are going to take NITEP[5] and then there's a

---

5 The Native Indian Teacher Education Program run by the University of British Columbia. It enables First Nations students to do a large portion of their training for teacher certification on campuses that are close to their homes, in small, supportive groups, before spending their final year at the main campus in Vancouver.

couple of more this year that will be um, headed in that direction too. [4:1-3]

The Sechelt language is perhaps the major focus in the double push to retain the culture and to make schooling a more positive experience for Sechelt children.

In the language, we just started a language program, ahh, the last couple of years. And it's been really slow, but this year, ummm, our teachers have, gosh, about 100 and .... twenty kids being taught the language from grade .... uh kindergarten to grade three. [1:6]

The language classes are open to all children in these grades. They are not compulsory; parents, both white and Native, have the right to have their children exempted, but very few do. As the majority of students at the elementary school are non-Native this means that they are also in a majority in the language classes. This fact caused a problem for some Sechelt Elders who questioned whether the language should be taught to strangers when it was not known by so many of their own people. The positive response of the community generally to the language classes seems to have resolved the difficulty.

Oh mostly, mostly white kids and, uhh, they just love it. I've gone there a few times to help the teachers and it's, it's so well accepted. There's just the odd few that, that can't go. Their parents won't let them go. Not very much, most parents are right into it. But that was the other big question that –– our Elders were asking themselves, "Should we be teaching the white kids our language?" It's very, you know, when you ...... I never, I never answer that one myself .... I, I, I don't know. 'Cause I'm just learning so I, I, this is the first year I've really taken the language seriously and started to learn it. And it's mainly because my, uhhh, six year old was coming home and singing to me in my language and I'd ask him, "What are you singing, what are you saying," and he'd tell me in English. And I'd be so proud of him so I thought, I decided, I'd better go and learn some of this stuff that he knows. So, and the way they were being taught is through singing. [1:7]

Teaching of the classes is done by Sechelt Elders working closely with one of the teachers.

Yeah, Elders. Stella Johnson and Dee Joe, yeah, and, uhh, they're really, they're, they're fun. It's really fun and I think the kids look forward to coming there because they do a lot of singing and counting and ...... and uh, colours. ... Yeah, each class is twenty minutes and I think they have two twenty-minute classes a week. [1:7]

This is a heavy load for the Elders, who are volunteers. Valerie began attending the classes occasionally from interest, but during the course of these interviews her job was changed by the Band Council from Cultural to Education Officer and now includes, along with curriculum development in a variety of areas, assisting with the language classes every day.

They have to go through ah, four lessons and it, it's, when I was with Stella and Dee it was really hard because their day's about repetition, so they're constantly repeating what they say. And so it was good for me though because I was with them all the time and from listening to their, listening to them repeat it over, it sunk in like, yeah. But it sure made – from the time I didn't know –– language was used as a barrier with our Elders. With my grandfather, I, I remember my great-grandfather, he died when I was thirteen, Basil Joe was his name, he spoke broken English but he hardly spoke at all. He was a very quiet man and he would only speak to you if something was really important to him ...... and so I didn't hear him speak very often .... in, in our language. And then my grandfather spoke only our language to my grandmother. They spoke it fluently together – and when they would talk about us [laughs]. ... So it was used mainly to talk about us and we didn't understand what they were saying. But we would know. Like we would look at them and then we'd say, "I know you're talking about me." We all knew that. [1:7,8]

The loss of the language seems to have been most pronounced over the last two generations as the effects of the residential schooling became more evident.

Like, well, naturally, when my Dad, who, who was, ummm ..... going to residential school all of his life, never spoke the language, but he knew it. He knew the language, fluently but he would never teach us. 'Cause there was um ...... but, but I often wonder what my parents went through in residential school because they seemed ashamed of their language after. So we were never taught –– to speak from them, and the only time my Mom and Dad spoke –– the language was when an Elder came in and would ask them – start talking in our language then they'd answer, answer them back. And then for me, I totally didn't know anything. It was, ummm, so foreign to me when I first started hearing it being spoken all the time. And I would look at the Elders like –– they were ...... aliens, you know. It was, it was, umm, I was very ashamed that I didn't know my language. And now that I'm starting to learn it, and becoming more confident in who I am, it's my, it's like my identity has been given to me. And it was so important for, for me, umm, to really want to know the language. Just as clear -- and, you know, well it's never too late. It makes a difference. And I'm so glad my baby knew that. And hopefully my other kids will want to learn. [1:8]

I remember hearing um, my grandparents speak the language and all of them older people talking in the morning or in the evening -- our language. But when it was around us it was English that was used. I don't think they meant to do that. I think it was because they were so afraid that um, okay we were in the culture where it says English was where the jobs were, where the education was, that's -- we had to know English. So they (didn't want) to confuse us with -- with two languages. But then again they were teaching us French in grade one. So I don't know. ... And I remember my Mom speaking her language when her people came here to visit her and other people making fun of her. And -- but she didn't -- she didn't, you know -- it didn't bother her. It didn't get in her way. So when -- when I look at the negativity that was put on -- on anybody that spoke their language I thought to myself oh, "I don't want that -- I'll just speak English." But now -- I mean -- now it's different. I really want to speak our language. And I want to take ownership of our language. Before, I don't think I did. It was very confusing for our generation. ... Yeah, trying to get it back. Yeah, that um .... that if -- I think if our generation loses it -- it is going to be lost. It's um, not going to be pronounced properly and that's what the older generation is so afraid of. [3:7]

Not only Valerie but other parents too have been motivated to learn because their children have been learning at school and this is spreading more generally into the Sechelt community. During the course of these interviews, Brandi, Valerie's daughter, began sitting in on the classes at the elementary school so that she too could begin to learn.

There's a whole class they started here because the parents wanted to learn the language. ... An effect on everybody, yeah. And it's snowballing and it's getting ah, better. The College (Capilano) is using it for the adult education program and it's going well there too. They also have an open one for Monday nights and actually a lot of people, white people, who have read our Sechelt book, have been phoning me and asking me if we can have classes someday. So that they could learn the language. [1:8]

No one is quite sure yet what the outcome will be in the long term and there is still the problem, for some of the Elders at least, of allowing non-Natives to learn the language. Some are also very concerned that the pronunciation be kept pure and they see opening the doors to language lessons as a threat to this.

I don't know yet. You know, even with the, like I said, they're teaching it in the elementary school, we're not sure. We sort of sway back and forth, you know. But I like, I like to be open-minded myself. I think, you know, and say "Whoever wants to learn it is welcome." 'Cause that's the only way you're going to break down racism. I think when, when someone understands me and um, isn't afraid that I'm Native, then, and then they understand my language and my culture. Um, then I think racism will, will start fading away. But, umm, I think if we held it back ..... well, we'd be racist, wouldn't we? [laughs] [1:8,9]

There is also, quite simply, a logistics problem with not only schoolchildren needing language teachers, but also with adult Sechelt and non-Sechelt wanting to learn. There are a limited number of people who are willing and able to be teachers. There is also the problem of learning enough of the language and then using it sufficiently to retain it.

Yeah. I guess whoever wants to learn. I mean, if, if I wanted ... you know, when you teach French, and I was taught French from a very young age, 'cause my, uh, the nuns were French. So we spoke French. And, um, yeah, they weren't afraid to share that with us. Most of the Native kids were, were taught French. From a very young age. Also a lot of our kids were taught Latin. So we have a lot of people that can, that can say Latin. I don't know if they can understand it [laughs]. I think it's mostly praying. ... Not – I can remember it. If, If, I'm sure if somebody spoke to me, but, you know, I haven't um, I took it up to grade eight. And you know, from not using it every day you sort of lose it. And, umm, I, I had no reason to be speaking French after, I think I took, yeah, grade eight or grade nine. I finished. And then I stopped French. But that was only to get into the university. I really didn't take it too seriously, you know. [laughs] Which I never used. But um, yeah. It was kind of amazing for our people to be all speaking French and not our own, weren't allowed to speak their own language. [1:9]

Her role as Education Officer for the Band makes it doubly important to Valerie that she learn her language.

So, definitely the language is the important thing. If I'm going to be teaching, passing on to them .... [1:13]

This is an incentive to her to become fluent.

Hopefully, yeah. Although I, I, see our Elders speaking the language with each other pretty fluently, they still use English – words – in between, yeah. So I don't know how fluent I'll be, I'll, but I'll know some things. Yeah. Enough to make a difference, I guess. [1:13]

The education of her own children has been of great concern to Valerie. She was well aware of the poor track record of Native children and was therefore very keen that they should have whatever advantages she could give them. She was not alone in this. In the early 1970s, the Band began to run a nursery school as a form of early intervention.

Um, it was because they were having a lot of problems with our Native children and their reading. And they decided that – they – actually the school did this test that um, any Native children that went to nursery school before they entered elementary school were better readers. So, I decided that Brandi should go to nursery school because of the – well there's still a lot of dropouts um, in high school because, um, our kids can't read. ... Aaron went to – um, no Aaron is a good example of reading. He did go to nursery school, um, and he did really well in elementary school. And then when he got to grade eight they found – they tested him and in grade nine um, he started getting all these really low marks in school. And when they tested him – his reading level was a grade three and that was in grade nine. So um, I had to, I still, when I look at Josh and Khan and I have to put them in extra reading classes to keep them up and, and I guess when we talk as Native people we think well, English is our second language it's not our first language. So of course we're not going to be very good at English language and not very good at reading. But a lot of our kids have that difficulty still today. I mean it's hard to –– we looked at everything, every possible aspect of what's happening here and um, we still haven't come up with any solutions. That's a really tough one for our education. [2:3]

The nursery school was run by Laurie Paul, a Sechelt woman, and it still continues today, though the enrolment is now mixed.

... the Band decided to put it up and um, Laurie ran it for about twenty-five years now .... It's still very popular. Yeah, it's um, it's um, a mix now, everybody gets to go. Yeah, which is nice for um, the kids in the community 'cause they can, they grow up being familiar with each other. And um, you know, anything that cuts out racism in our town is, is good. But again there's, was a daycare system put in place which I worked in. Um, let's see about .... must be about fifteen years ago now. And the Elders had a hard time with that. Because they felt like it was taking the parenting away from the parents and that parents weren't being responsible for their own children's well-being. But again you had some, you had single parents that needed to use the facility. My grandfather had a hard time with that one. He used to really hate to see kids being ––and I would have to sit down and talk to him about it and say, "Some of these kids need a routine. That's what they lack is routine." And um, this gave them that routine. And the social system that they needed too, was happening in the daycare for them. But um, he never did, never did agree with it. ... the daycare just started up again. It hasn't been running for ten years and then it started up again. But it was quite, again it was quite popular with everybody. Everybody on the Coast heard about it and really liked it. They would come and see 'cause we were always doing, ah, fun things there. A lot of activities, and kids were very, very safe in that daycare, so – . [2:3,4]

Valerie is convinced that one of the major factors in education is the involvement of parents. This conviction has grown over the years as her own children have been through the system,

Um, yeah, I guess when – when you look at children's education and who is responsible for it, it all comes back to the parents. The role of the parents and as much as I felt when Aaron was going to school that oh, this, this – now he is in the teacher's hands it's their duty to –– they are getting paid for it – so, and I would just drop them off and never get involved, but these last few years, I've um, been listening .... at, at every meeting I go to, who is responsible and I have to say to myself, "I am." If I have children in school then I'm totally responsible and before now –– when you've been to school in a residential school .... there isn't um .... you don't make any of the decisions. And so you don't become responsible for any of the decisions that are made; they are all made for you. And the other thing was um, "Always be quiet until you are spoken to," and

I think when I, when my children first started school, I was very naive and very ignorant. Not, not stupid, but very ignorant, but I didn't realise that I could have an opinion in the school system. That um, what I said actually was important. I didn't consider myself important enough to go and say, "Hey, I don't like this," or "Hey, this is working good for my child can we stay – keep using this?" Now I realise that, I've matured and I realise that yeah, I can control some of my children's education. And I have a say, and I can go to any of these meetings and say what I feel is appropriate for my child. Before, I think, Native people just sat back and didn't realise that and didn't enforce it or exercise their, their own um, powers that they had. There was nothing like that. [2:5,6]

So her own attitude has changed since Aaron first started school. On the other hand, so has the attitude of the school towards Native children.

Oh yes the, the – the schools' attitudes have definitely changed along with ours. They're saying, "What would you like – we would like you to come to all these meetings, and we would like you to have an opinion on your child's education." And um, I think more parents from the Band's attitude is changing too. It's a two-way street. We've both had to compromise and really quit blaming one another. I found that um, ah, one of the things is, yes, we've been treated badly by the governments and by the Catholic Oblates but we've got to get over this blame of all white society doing a number on us and start working with the system. Because I thought to myself, I think to myself, the only people that are going to lose out is our children and I really hate to see the kids carrying a chip on their shoulder in school because of what happened many, many years ago. And um, I, one of the other things that we're doing with the school is, is um .... educating them as well about our history and we've got more programs happening in the school from the Band. From our Band's history and our language, so it's just, it's just done a tremendous um, 190 degree turnabout here from, I mean from when I was going to school to now it's just been amazing. So um, I – I really think that it was all the attitudes. It was – both of us had to change and I .... and I .... think now our kids can feel like they are equals. You know, if I don't feel like I'm an equal my child will never feel like he's an equal, because I'll be sending out messages to him. So I have to feel like an equal and my children will all feel the same. And I have to, I have to stand up and say what I think and now I do.

I'm very opinionated now – I say anything. If I – if my children have a fight in school I'll go and try to get to the bottom of it right away. I won't leave it for anybody else to handle – I will handle it, so –. I'm always at school every day. I go up – I go up there every time – every time something is happening I'm up there. But I, I sort of feel sorry for these kids that don't, that parents don't do that for them. That they sort of are –– I remember telling you that when I first went to high school – a public high school – and how I felt. I was so afraid, I was so scared to go. It was like all of a sudden they whipped me out of the Reserve and threw me into this white population and these people didn't like me because I was Native and it was so scary for me. And nobody was there to back me up and I was like um – um …. a little – a scared little girl. And I really feel sorry for those kids that have to put up with that without their support system. So I really want to support my kids in every way that I can. Every which way. 'Cause um, I think in the last few years too, I've taken my parenting role a lot more seriously than I ever did. One of the things, um, that I did with my elder children was always leave them with the grandparents 'cause that's the way I thought it was. Um, after my parents passed away I realised slowly that I had to be the responsible one and in the last few years I've just – I've taken that role so very seriously now. And um, I really want to see my kids be successful in whichever they choose. You know? Doesn't have to be a doctor – a lawyer. It can be anything they want. As long as they –– like what they are doing. But I'm going to be there to support them. [2:6,7]

As Valerie begins her new job as Band Education Officer she sees herself as being in a position of great influence as far as the younger generation is concerned. She sees her position as one in which she can actively work for the things that she wants for herself, for her children and for her people more generally.

Well, I think my main, the main objective from the Band's point of view is to, is to um, allow our children to see our identity which we've – if you, if you went down in front of our hall, they have three totem poles there with no faces. That meant that Sechelts had no identity. And –– I, I can see this whole new job description, from the Band's point of view, is giving our children some identity to say, "Hey I'm proud to be this Sechelt person." And from where I'm standing it's, it's to share what we have with other people. So they lose that fear and there's no racism, that eventually our children will teach us something – how to get along. And I think um, I can see myself being in there somewhere with these kids. Um, that you don't look at colour anymore, you just see a human being and um, a human being with a culture is a lot nicer. But, um, I just .... I don't know maybe that's way off, but I think that um, it would be so nice to see some of these kids really get along and not to have any um, prejudices in their lives. And I think that's one of the things, as human beings, we all strive for. Is peace. Peace for our children. And ah, I remember someone asked me once, "What do you want most in life?" And I said "Peace." And she said "What are you doing to get it?" And I said "Well, I mean I can't go out in the world and help countries that need to be helped." And she said, "No, what are YOU doing about it?" and I said "Me?" and she said "Are you being peaceful at home?" and I had to really look at myself. People give you questions that make you look inside. And I've had to look inside and say "Hey yeah, I'd better start at home. That's the first place. And I'd better start with my own people." And – and start – . So it just rolls. Pretty soon you start at home and then it goes out to the people and then it goes out to the, to the whites and Natives and I mean – there have been times that I've been very angry that my children have had racism thrown in their face, but I had to learn how to talk to them and handle it. And not retaliate any more. 'Cause um, it's, it wasn't in my goal of achieving peace. [2:8]

It's um, the medicine wheel.[6] I never really thought about it until last week. I've heard about it before and I've done – I've gone to medicine wheel teachings, but I thought, "Wouldn't it be nice to apply it to our little guys?" So then they can remember and grow up and say, "Yeah, I learned about that." And that they'll use it in their daily lives and .... there's, there's nothing more beautiful than seeing a well-balanced –– person. You just – to me – I just enjoy looking at people who are so in balance with life and in harmony. So .... I – I'd liked to see that for a lot of people. I'd like to see that for all of my people and it's – it's a long way but, we've done a lot of things that people said we would never do and one of them is survive. We've survived it. We've survived – when I talk to the Elders

---

6 The medicine wheel is not a traditional part of Sechelt culture but comes from the culture of the Plains Indians. It has become a part of the Pan-Indian, or, perhaps more correctly, the urban Indian cultural revival in recent years as an aspect of alcohol and drug abuse healing models.

I can't believe the things we've survived. The diseases – so hey, maybe I'm not reaching far off – I'm probably on the right track–– to helping ––. I think we can always – one of the main things that came up this year was the topic of racism. And that's a very scary and heavy –– racism is a scary word anyhow. And I, and I, again I had to look inside and say – say to myself how am I going to – how am I going to make a difference, but a good difference .... for people. I mean I can't go to an adult and say "You change your mind because I have something that maybe will open you up." But I know that I can reach kids. I can reach kids and kids are so – they're so they're so .... open-minded and innocent and, and ...... they're ...... just themselves. And if you can teach a kid about peace right from the beginning .... you're going to have – you're going to have a fantastic world one day. So that's, I really have to look at my kids and, and teach them about peace and loving their brothers and sisters. And I've been teaching the two little ones about that and it's, it's .... fantastic to see them hug one another and just to tell one another they love each other. It just makes me as a mother feel hey, I've done a good job and that's all I'm – that's what makes me feel –– special. [2:8]

Valerie's consciousness is tinged with sadness about what has happened in the past, but despite this she has great optimism that the route the Band is taking will be positive for the Sechelt people.

I had this really special dream after Basil Joe – who's my great-grandfather – died. And he was in this dream and he had this apple tree behind his house and when it was in bloom it was beautiful. And I loved that apple tree when it was in bloom. And I remember in my dream I was walking by his house and Clarence – that's my grandpa – that's his son, was calling from the window. And he was saying, "Come here. Mana." Calling me. And I looked at him and I said, "What?" I think I was about fifteen at that time. And he pulled – he took me into the house and my grandmother was sitting there and they were both crying. And I – they looked really, really sad and I said to them, "What's the matter?" And he said, "The old man is crying in the back." And I said, "Grandpa the old man is dead." And he says, "I know. But he is crying, he is sitting under the tree – go look. He wants you." I said, "Me?" And I didn't understand. And I went to the back and I started going down his steps and he was going like this. And he had tears coming down, and I had never seen my great-grandfather cry. And I started to go close, but I got frightened because I knew in my mind he was dead. And so I stood still, and I was saying, "What's the matter with you?" And I got scared so I walked away from him. And I said, "I don't know what's wrong grandpa." I said to him, "I can't figure it out. I'm not going to stay here." I said, "I'm going to go to the store," wherever I was going. And my granny and grandpa were crying too. And you know, that dream never leaves me. And all these years, in my mind, I kept saying, "Why is my old grandpa crying?" And one day I was with this um, um spiritual man. A Native spiritual man, and he was talking, and he said, "The grandfathers are crying," and I looked at him right away. He said, "They are crying because you are losing your culture and your traditions. Your language is being lost. That's why they are crying." He says, "Listen to them – they have something to say to you. And they are going to come to you in your dreams and in your daily life and they are going to remind you to get back to your culture. Get back to your traditions. Start speaking your language." And it clicked. That's what my great-grandfather was crying about. I knew it then and there when that man connected me. He connected me to that dream. And I said, "That's what I have to do and Grandpa will stop crying." So – and now I'm learning to write the language, speak some of it and it, and it makes me feel happy because I know – spiritually – in the next world, my, my ancestors are getting happy again. That's where we need to head as a Sechelt Nation. [4:15,16]

BRANDI MCLEOD

Brandi was born at the hospital in Sechelt on October 23, 1974.

Um, my Dad is Ken Bourne and my mother's name is Valerie Bourne. I am their second child, and their daughter. I have one older brother and two younger brothers. [1:1]

Her mother, as we have seen previously, is a Sechelt woman. Her father is a Canadian of British extraction. His grandparents migrated from England and settled near Sechelt early this century.

He grew up here. Right in Salmon Park. Yeah. ... Just right um, not too far from Sechelt, about a five-minute drive out of Sechelt. Yeah. [2:13]

Brandi knows far less about and has had less contact with his family than with her mother's.

My Dad doesn't talk about that. Um, he doesn't – I don't know my great-grandparents and I don't know –– I know not too much about my grandmother and my grandfather on my Dad's side ... . He just always says I look like my grandmother. A lot like her, and I'm a lot like her. ... Um, my Grandma died in December so –– November/December – I was only two months old when she died. (Her grandfather) died four months after, I was born. So I didn't know them. ... Um he's got twin sisters. Yeah, I know them. ...... They're so different from my Dad. It's not like a close-knit family like we have around here – they're not close. They don't really – they get along, but don't get along. So yeah. They, they're totally different from my Mum's family. ... One lives, one lives in Vancouver, and one lives in Dawson Creek. Yeah, and I have an Uncle but um he's mentally handicapped so I don't –– I've only met him once. So my Dad's side of the family they aren't too close. I've met his aunt once – we went and had lunch with her. And I met his cousins just once. ...... So, my dad just usually sticks with my Mum's family. ... Um. ...... I just think he didn't want to remember like how his family was and I – even if he was close with his family it wouldn't have bothered him the way we are with my Mum's family. Either way we'd still all be really close. Yeah. [2:13,14]

Unlike Valerie's and Bernie's experience with the religious education of the residential school, Brandi's schooling has all been done in the public education system.

I went to school at Sechelt Elementary School right here, and then to – , we moved to North Van(couver) and I went to school there for a year, and then we moved up to Powell River for a year, and then I came back to here and I went to Chatelech Secondary. ... I graduated in '93. [1:1]

Since she finished high school, Brandi has tried several jobs.

Umm, I moved away from home after I graduated, for half a year, then I moved back here just two months ago and – I'm taking computer courses and I worked for a while as a teacher's aide, and here (in the Cultural Centre) doing some clerical work too. [1:1]

She enjoyed working with children at the school and plans to take the NITEP course at UBC to qualify as an elementary teacher.

Well, I help kids ...... um, that ...... I guess, need a lot of help. Extra reading. I just do sheets that the teacher gives me. ... I worked with a Native kid and a white kid, with their reading, with the teacher. [1:2]

Schooling is not something that Brandi remembers with unmixed pleasure and looking back over her life was not easy for her. The interviews were fairly unstructured because I did not want to ask too many direct questions, but rather to let her choose what she felt had been important and significant in her life. She was rather shy and reticent at first, but in the second interview she was much more relaxed and had thought over what she had previously said and was often able to elaborate further. She also told me quite a lot in informal discussions in the weeks following the interviews and this material is often included in these interspersed remarks.

In my elementary years, yeah, I liked school. When I got up to high school ...... I just ...... I sort of fell, I think. In my grade eleven year I just sort of stopped going. And then I finally realised that I needed an education, that I could do better for myself, so I went back. But with my school years I had very ...... tough high school years. ... I gave my parents a real tough time in my teenage years. Personally, I don't like thinking much about them. [1:4]

Her earliest schooling, however, she remembers with pleasure.

When I started at nursery? ... Nursery? Ummm, ... (I was) three. ... Ohhh ...... my teacher. Miss Laurie. Oh yeah. I remember I had a good time there. I enjoyed going to preschool. ... Hmmm, I remember this .... ohh .... I remember having a dunce hat. [laughs] ... Oh yeah! [laughs] I would sit in a corner with a dunce hat on. [laughs] ... I can't remember why it is. I remember the dunce hat because we used to sit there and she'd have a chair in the corner and I had to go down and sit in the corner. ... Ahhh ..... It was embarrassing. Yeah ..... facing against the wall. ... But she was, she was nice, I guess it's that we were bad. [1:8]

Elementary school was fun too. She did not find being Native or being one of a minority group stressful at that stage, possibly because there were a far greater proportion of Native children in the elementary schools. She remembers—

Oh, enjoying myself there ..... and my teachers. [1:8]

I went to Queen Mary Elementary School in North Vancouver. ... And then we, then after – that was in grade six. Then we moved back here to Sechelt and then I went to Sechelt Elementary. And then in my um, eighth, in my grade eight year we moved up to Powell River and I went to Brooks Secondary. ... Um we moved to North Vancouver because my Mum was living there, and we had been living with my Grandma, so I moved down there to North Van(couver) with my Mum and stayed there for a year. And then we moved back to Sechelt. My Mum, I guess my Mum just wanted to get away from Sechelt for a year. Then we moved back here. And then my Dad's business was up in Powell River when he had that going, so that's why we had to move up there. ... [2:11]

Brandi noticed a difference in the schools, based mainly on the fact that she felt less comfortable amongst people she did not know well than amongst the familiar Sechelt people.

I liked North Van(couver). ... There was more to do. Go to the movies, and go bowling and more activities for me to do. Yeah. ... (but) I felt more comfortable in elementary, Sechelt Elementary 'cause I knew more people. I didn't really know a lot of people going to the North Van(couver) school. ... there was a lot of Natives in Queen Mary. ... Yeah, and I hung out with most of them, yeah. I don't know. It was a different type of friendship than I had with the people at – my friends at the Sechelt Elementary. 'Cause it took me a while to get to know how they were and they were just different people. [2:11,12]

At Sechelt Elementary at that time there was not much taught about First Nations history or culture, but on Heritage Day the Sechelt people had a chance to display their culture, if only briefly.

OK, ummm, in elementary school, like when I was in grade five, we did this play and it was about the Sechelt, the Sechelt Nation. It was the Beaver and um, it was a Native story and it was, it was about this, this Beaver man who takes away the, the lady in an oyster and she doesn't get back up or anything. It was —– I did that play when I was in grade five with um, Roger Joe and it was really neat 'cause it was Heritage Day at the Sechelt Elementary and we had Native dancers there and ...... so I did that play. [2:1]

Uhh, I don't, I forget who got this play together. It was for our Heritage Day, because every year at the school they have Heritage Day where you can, where the Elders are there and they have their bannock and they do the um, ice creams, berries with ice cream. Like mix up all the berries into ice cream.[1] And they have everything up there, dried fish, smoked fish, and the non-Natives can go around and try all of this. So it's a pretty big event in this school. Yeah. ... I was, I was the umm, the Beaver's – the Beaver was trying to capture me – because he loved me. So that – I played a pretty big part. ... It was funny. Stella and my Mum were just talking about it not too long ago. And me and Roger we're together, um we graduated together actually and so everybody looks at us and laughs because of that play. [laughs] So yeah. [2:4]

At the time Brandi remembers feeling good about having a leading part in a play from her own culture, although she is a little embarrassed about it now.

Yeah, yeah. I did then, but now I look back at it and I just get so embarrassed about it. Yeah. So yeah. It was fun. I liked doing that. [2:4]

At Powell River she had to make new friends again, this time in the much larger and less personal atmosphere of the secondary school.

Um no, I didn't know – no, I did not know anybody. I knew two girls, I think, from soccer tournaments that I've gone to, so I got to know them and then they introduced me to other people and that. I also hung out with Natives up there, up there in Powell River. [2:12]

The situation at high school was not bad in all respects. Brandi enjoyed being with friends outside of class.

Oh yeah, I enjoyed the social life. Being at school. Just the work part I didn't like. [Laughter] [1:5]

Lack of motivation to apply herself to serious study was the main problem.

---

1 Foam berries can be whipped up into a consistency similar to cream. This was a traditional way of eating the berries and is known today as Native ice cream.

I just ..... changed my mind? You know, I guess I just ...... when I was seventeen I almost dropped school. I would go, like, every once in a while. But then I thought ...... my Dad always, always stressed I needed my education. And I finally started realising that. And I just started working and I did good. And in my grade twelve year I did really well. Before that I had a really tough time of it 'cause I was going through all sorts of problems. But then I would go. I enjoyed my grade twelve year, I enjoyed it, 'cause I was more motivated. When I was in grade nine and ten I wasn't motivated at all. [1:5]

My dad was really, really, my Dad is so intelligent. But he, I found his expectations were too high. 'cause he got As and Bs and [laughs] and, I, you know, I tried and I tried but it was like, never good enough when I brought my report card home. It was just like, it was always criticism and um, just, it wasn't fun bringing my report card home if it wasn't good enough. ... my Mum, my Mum was easy on us. Just, you know, "You can do it, just keep trying, keep trying." Yeah. ... Oh yeah it was very important to both my Mum and my Dad. Really important to them. [2:15]

Even so there were some subjects she enjoyed.

Ummm, computers. I really enjoyed the computer class. And ...... sewing. I enjoyed sewing. [1:5]

She no longer sews.

No, not any more. My Mum and Dad gave me a sewing machine but I haven't used it for a long time. [1:5]

But she still has an interest in computers, has taken further courses since leaving school and has used them in clerical work that she has done. Her long-term goal is to be a teacher, as mentioned above.

I want to be a teacher. A grade one teacher. Yeah. ... Because I love kids. They're so innocent and so beautiful and ...... I don't know. I just ...... really like kids. I think they're so funny and you can learn so much from them. [1:5,6]

Hmm, I wouldn't really mind Mexico to teach .... . Hm, 'cause my Mum and Dad took me there on vacation once. I loved it. [1:6]

That vacation stands out strongly in her memory.

Oh, I enjoyed –– I swam, I met people down there. I went out to the markets, shopping – . ... We did it as a family, yeah. Just went looking around at the things on the streets and went and had – ate out together as a family, yeah. And then me and my brother we'd go to the clubs after – like, Aaron he'd take me out. So yeah, I enjoyed that. It was so fun – just meeting different people. ... we were in Mazatland, we were out in the beach, we were right in the city – right in the Golden Zone they call it. That's where all the tourists usually stay. Yeah we stayed where all the tourists stayed – right along the beach. Yeah, And I met a lot of people down there. I just enjoyed myself, it was so much fun and learning how their – , learning how their how their culture is – that's what I did, you know, and I met some ...... some people and they told me about how they have fiestas and stuff down there and I went to a fiesta, did dancing and it was really neat. I enjoyed myself. ... I'll go back there for a holiday. If I can't teach down there I'll go down for a holiday. Yeah, ... the people down there, they are so polite they're really, they're just so polite to you. And I enjoyed that. ... And like more polite than Canadians, yeah. When you are going into a restaurant – like, some restaurants in Canada, some waiters and waitresses can be rude. Down there they are always polite to you. ... I found all of them – I mean all the Mexicans and that, were really, really nice. [2:16,17]

She has no particular plans to teach in Sechelt or to work exclusively with Native children, but she has no objection to the idea either.

I would come back here and teach. ... Oh no, it doesn't matter if they're white or Native. [1:6]

While she was working as a teacher's aide at the school, Brandi started to develop an interest in learning more of the Sechelt language. Her generation is the first that has grown up hearing very little of the language spoken around them and often, as in Brandi's case, hearing none spoken at home. When she was in the middle years of elementary school, she had a couple of years of language when the program was first being started, but that is all. Her youngest brother Kahn is now having regular classes in the new language program at the school that his mother Valerie and her Great-Aunt Bernie are involved with. This too has been a spur to Brandi to learn more.

Actually when I was helping at the school I went to some classes .... that was, like, the first time. I know words, a few words. but not that much. ... I just used to love them (the songs that Kahn started singing at home) 'cause he was just so funny singing them. ... they taught us when I was in elementary, but I forgot because it was just a couple of years, yeah. ... See, uh, like my, my friends April and Shari they know. They, they talk Native, like, all the time. I go, "What are you guys saying?" And I feel really funny 'cause I don't know. Like, I just know a few words. [1:6]

And since the last interview I've been starting to do our language with my Mum at the elementary school. Which is really neat. [2:1]

Brandi was very excited about starting to attend these classes.

Yeah, yeah. I think it's neat. Yeah. I'm so surprised, like, I'm starting to pick up on the words so well now, like, I know a song and I know a prayer, so yeah. I'm enjoying myself. ... I just sit there like one of the kids and just listen, yeah. Yeah, 'cause I thought about it – I thought, "God, I should start learning my language now," and so, yeah, it's fun. I'm starting to pick up on things. ... Khan he still, he still knows a lot more than me. But I'm picking up now so – – . [2:5]

Brandi's boyfriend Steve is Sechelt too, and like her does not speak the language.

Um, no. No. I'm trying – like see – I was just talking to my boyfriend last week. "Steve, when I learn the language real well, do you want to learn it?" And I sang him a song and I felt funny, 'cause he doesn't know it. So I just sang it for him. – but I'll pick up more. ... He laughed at me. After I sang him that song he just said, "Sing it again," and he laughed at me. He said yeah, he'd like to learn it when I get to know it better. Yeah – so I thought that was kind of neat. I'm going to teach him how – the language – yeah. [2:5,6]

Yeah. I try to – – I talk to myself in our language. Like, just so I can get better at it. Yeah, I think I sang that song all night last night. Walking around my house. ... It's um, it's a welcome song. Yeah. They sing, the kids sing it. We sing it when we first get into the class and then we sing a prayer and then we, um, we do skipping and they say it in our language. Yeah. So I haven't, I haven't really picked up on how they say the skipping little thing – song, but I will, yeah. [2:9]

At that point Brandi was looking forward to other options for learning and practising the language.

They have um, actually they have um, language nights for adults just up at the college here. Yeah, so after I've learned all I can now I'll probably start going to that. That one. But right now see I'm just learning the basics – right now. So it's good for me to be up at the elementary school with the kids. Yeah. [2:6]

The children with whom she is learning include those she taught when she was a teacher's aide, as well as her brother Kahn.

Oh, they (the children) think it's so neat. They think it's neat, yeah. ... Yeah. I'm like so excited about learning our language now too. It's, it's, I just, I can't believe I'm picking up so much. Yeah. But all those kids, like even the non-Natives, they know our language so well. I was just so shocked – I was just like "Holy ...." Oh yeah. ... I want to know our language. For when I have kids, I can teach them. And I can teach other people too. So like everybody is getting to know our language now and I thought, "Well why aren't I up – why aren't I trying to do something to learn it?" And after my last session with you, I just kind of thought about it so now I'm really going up to the school every day with Mum. ... I stay there all afternoon with Mum yeah. Um, um. ... Yeah, she's got promoted to being a teacher with the language. ... Yeah, yeah. Mum knows the language well too and I thought if Mum can do it, I can do it, yeah. And those kids –– So yeah, it's neat. [2:6.7]

The fact that she is learning with her mother is also important to Brandi. Traditionally, the mother/daughter tie was strong, both emotionally and in terms of working together. Brandi sees the language lessons as reinforcing this tie.

Yeah, yeah. She, she knows a lot about it and I didn't realise how much she knew in our language. Yeah. Every afternoon, yeah, for a couple of hours. So I'll be going with her, doing that. I'm so excited about it too. I just, see before I never even thought about learning our language because I thought "Well, who can I talk to?" And, but Mum knows it well too. And then I listen to the Elders too and they're having their conversations and I think it's neat. Yeah. ... Oh, like, when they are up here having their meetings – Elders' meetings and then they come out and sit around there and then they talk it. And I sit there wondering what are they saying. Yeah, I'm just so interested in it now. [2:10]

But she is also conscious of one of the difficulties in learning a language that is not in constant use in the wider community, namely, the lack of opportunity to hear it spoken frequently and to practise speaking it without self-consciousness. She sees this as the main reason that she benefited so little from the language classes she did when she was in elementary school.

See I get embarrassed talking about it in front of – saying it, talking our language in front of people? And that's why I had a hard time when I was up at the elementary school trying to say it. 'Cause I'm not, I'm not used to talking it yet, out loud. [2:10]

Her father and her older brother, Aaron, are not involved in learning the language.

Josh and Aaron and my Dad, I don't know. Khan tried to teach Josh the language. He tried to teach me before, you know, singing me songs and –– I don't know about my Dad. My Dad knows a few, a few words in the Sechelt language – But, not a lot. Yeah. But Aaron, I don't know what Aaron thinks. But I thought I wanted to know it. [2:7]

Josh, the middle brother, is in an awkward position. When he was younger, the language classes were for upper elementary students. Now that the program has been changed he is too old.

Yeah – he's grade four. I think they only teach up to grade three. ... And then in grade four they don't –– See, before it use to be just –– they used to teach just the older classes, but now it's the younger ones. Yeah. ... Yeah, I think they should have it for all the kids. Yeah. [2:7]

Her involvement in the language program has made Brandi aware of the different points of view amongst the Elders as to who should learn the language.

Actually, I just heard yesterday, um, when we were going up to the elementary school, for our language classes, some of our Elders didn't like um, that –– the non-Natives knowing our language. 'Cause they are scared that they are going to hold it against us. But I think it's good that non-Natives are learning and they are so excited about it, when I'm up there, they just, they, they know a lot already. And I think it's good – yeah. ... Yeah, and I think that will help with the, so that there won't be as much racism. They'll know where we are coming from. Not like some of the non-Natives around here who don't know where we are coming from. [2:8]

Some of her friends have learned the language from their parents, even though English is the language that is most commonly used in their homes. Brandi perceives this as something that must be positive for them.

Oh it must feel good. ... Oh, I just say, "Hey you .... guys know a lot. Huh! That must make you feel good." [1:7]

Unlike the feelings of shame that Valerie and Bernie grew up feeling about their language, Brandi and some of the younger ones obviously believe that the language offers them some sense of identity and even perhaps some exclusivity.

Yeah, they use it a lot like, yeah, they, yeah. ... I think ...... no ...... they ...... I don't know. They use it a lot, like, when we're in bars. They say ...... They use it a lot in there. And I'm sitting there, sitting there and "My dear God what are they saying?" [1:7]

Yeah. So I just – yeah I want to learn it like, really fluently. Like last time we talked I was talking about how these other girls know it so well and were talking to me and that got me into thinking too like –– "What's wrong with me – why don't I learn it?" ... Oh they, they talk to me in it. Like, one girl was saying, "What time is it?" in our language. And I'm going – and I just looked at her and I was like, well, I don't know – what do you say. I know one word, "chalim." That means "why" so I just looked at her and said "Chalim?" and then they looked at me and laughed at me. But no, I haven't really talked to them. But I pick up words from them. [2:9]

One of Brandi's strongest childhood memories is of spending time with her grandmother, Valerie's mother.

Umm ...... a lot of time with my Granny, my Mum's Mum. My grandparents coming over to our home. [1:3]

There was a lot of comfort and safety in just being with her.

Mmmm, 'cause my Granny, she was such a beautiful person. She was so nice. She always laughed. Hmmm, her house was always open. She was just so nice. I could just sit there and watch TV. [1:2]

Brandi remembers mostly just being nearby in company with the other grandchildren.

Hmmm, I just used to stay around the house with her. [1:3]

On special occasions it would be the whole family and not just the children who gathered.

We all, we always used to go there for dinner on Sunday, Christmas dinner and everyone would be there. [1:3]

She also remembers the very clear gender roles of her grandparents.

Ummm, my grandparents ummmm ...... I noticed that, I noticed my Granny she listened to my grandfather. She, she never ever said anything. He would say, "Oh, give me this, give me that," and she would just do it. [1:16]

This carried over to the teaching of traditional tasks. They were very much gender separated, as the tasks themselves had been in former times.

I just always remember my Granny teaching me. My Grandpa use to stick by the boys, and Granny by the girls. Yeah. ... Yeah, Aaron learned a lot from my Grandpa, yeah. No, I just learned things from my Grandma. Yeah. [2:13]

Her grandparents and her great-aunt often told her stories, but the only actual story she remembers is about Mayuk the grizzly bear.[2]

And Auntie Dee, she tells us stories. ... This is my Mum's Aunty. ... Yeah, she, she tells us stories and they're just so neat. ... Just the way she tells them, and the stories themselves are just real good. ... Yeah, she, I, I really like the story about the dogs.[3] That one just sticks right in my head because she'd have my full attention, 'cause it was such a good story. And then the way she told it too. ... I can't remember how it goes. I just remember that it's a nice story. [1:16.17]

When I asked Brandi what she felt that she had learned from her Grandmother, her immediate response was —

Hmmm, yeah, she taught me ...... she always, always stressed respect for the Elders. [1:3]

But thinking of other things, practical skills or knowledge, she learned was not easy. Unlike the older generations, Brandi and her peers were not required to help constantly with everyday chores, so they did not learn in the way that previous generations had done.

No, Granny usually got up and cooked for us, like she would get up and make a really good meal. [1:3]

However, when the fish came in everyone was there to help as needed.

When they used to smoke fish we used to help set the fire up, and get the sticks for them to stick through the, through the fish and um throw the guts on the beach for the seagulls. And then we use to sit around and watch them bake the fish around an open fire. And then we would help hang it in the smoke house to be smoked. And um, we'd wash the jars out for canning and ...... then we'd just sit

---

2 See Sechelt Nation, *Mayuk the Grizzly Bear: A Legend of the Sechelt People*, illustrated by Charlie Craigan (Gibsons, BC: Nightwood Editions, 1993).
3 This is the story that tells how the people of the Dog clan came to be.

around and watch them. And then after the fish would be done we'd all sit around and eat some of the fish that was done in the open fire. ... Our whole family would go together to do that. Yeah, 'cause every year they got quite a bit of fish, 'cause my Granny use to can it and give it out to her own daughters and sons. Yeah. ... That was a lot of fun, yeah. It was, it was like, really close. Everybody worked closely together doing things, and like, the kids and the adults, yeah, it was fun. [2:12]

Other families would also be busy at the same task.

Um, yeah. Yeah. A lot. 'Cause the fish came for everybody at the same time, so yeah, people would be doing it at the same time. ... It would be done right in the back yard. Yeah, they'd just do a fire right in the back yard ..... and just smoke it there. [2:12]

Although she mostly watched these activities as a child, Brandi thinks she could probably do them if she wanted or needed to.

Yeah, I think I could, yeah. [1:3]

Brandi also remembers her grandparents, and to a lesser extent her parents, frequently telling her how much easier life was for her than it had been for them.

Um it sounds, "Oh, when I was a kid growing up we didn't have this and we didn't have that." 'Cause when we wanted something they would say that. Like, "Oh yeah, we had to live on bread and, and just, we wouldn't have been able to get away with what you guys get away with now-a-days. And, "We had to do without shoes and –– ." It was stuff like that, that they use to say. ... I used to sit there and listen. Yeah. I – I heard that a lot from my Granny and Grandpa. Not really from my Mum. But a lot from my Dad – a lot. His life, his life was different from what my Mum – my Mum's was. 'Cause his Mum was white. [2:13]

She remembers going berry picking with her parents and her Granny and then learning to cook with her parents. The ingredients, such as blackberries and fish, were traditional Sechelt foods, but the ways she learned to cook them were mostly not traditional at all.

Oh yeah, me and my Mum and Dad went picking. And oh, I learned to bake blackberry cakes. ... I haven't baked a blackberry cake for a long time. I used .... I used to cook a lot really .... I'd bake with my Mum and Dad. Cakes and cookies and .... . Mum taught me how to do chocolate chip cookies and after that I used to bake chocolate chip cookies all the time. ... Oh, yeah, my Dad cooked. He used to cook. He taught me, like, how to cook things. [1:3,4]

Her mother and her father cooked quite differently.

Mum's (specialty) is Chinese food and Dad's is fish, doing different things with fish. Like putting different sauces on them, and .... yeah. [1:4]

The fish that her father cooked was fish supplied by the Band rather than fish that he had caught himself. He did not fish at all, so this was not a skill that he could pass on to Brandi or her older brother, Aaron. Aaron was not interested in cooking, but was "off with his friends" when Brandi and her parents cooked. She also remembers watching her mother can berries, but doubts that she could do this herself. However it is a skill that she would like to be able to pass on to the children she will one day have.

I want to be able to show my kids how to do stuff like that. [1:14]

Valerie and the children also used to go to Jervis Inlet in the summer, to camps run by the Band.

We used to go up there every summer for two weeks and go um, clam digging and fishing and oyster – getting oysters and mussels. It was like a family getaway for my Mum and my brothers and myself. ... Yeah. And then my cousins – there would be about twenty of us that went up there. And we'd stay up there for two weeks. It was really nice, it was peaceful. ... they had a camp up there. ... Yeah. dorms, and um we used to go up there when I was young and my Mum used to work for the Band. We used to go up there for a week. 'Cause it was a camp. Summer camp for kids. So I went up – we went up there a lot and they taught us, they brought us up to the falls, and we did a lot of hiking ...... and, and paintings. We did Native paintings when we were up there – crafts. [2:1]

We'd swim and go canoeing and see, we'd go canoeing to different parts up there. And um, go bathe in the river. And um pick berries and we would um, ... there was a lot of things to do up there. It's such a nice place up there. We'd have campfires at night and put the oysters into the fire so that they can open up. ... Yeah, sit around and tell stories. ... Just like, hmmm, about our families and just talk about each other and have a good time and laugh. Yeah. ... Oh and then we'd go boating to Xunechin. That's one of the Sechelts' lands. And then we'd go to Malibu – it's a resort. And we'd go boating around up there. It's so beautiful up there. And what else did we do up there? We did so much up there, it's a nice getaway, to get away from Sechelt and just be with your family. ... Um, people use to come in from like, um, from like, who were boating around up there, like, I met people up there from the States that came up and stayed up there with us for a couple of days. Yeah. Yeah, people were welcome to come up and stay up there. Yeah. So yeah, a lot of people like that. Malibu, that's a resort place. And like, a lot of tourists would like to come up to where we were staying and look around up there. ... They would talk to my Mum about it – yeah. [2:2,3]

Apart from being a happy family time, it also gave the children some exposure to aspects of their culture.

... when my Mum used to work for the Band she used to send us up on almost every one of the summer camp outings – yeah. So that was neat. ... Um, I liked the hiking. Hiking up to the falls. Yeah that was neat. And, um, they were like, teaching us how to be responsible up there, like having, we had our own chores to do and yeah, there was about five or six workers who worked with us. [2:1]

The camp workers were Sechelt teenagers who were taking part in another Band-run program.

They were about, about grade twelve when they did that. So they weren't that old, they were just a few years older than us. Yeah. They used to go to that NES up there. Native (Educational) Studies. They had a school up there. ... They used to go up there and they used to do paintings, they used to like, learning about Sechelt. They used to go to school up there and they use to do drawings. A lot of them did paintings and they are in our Band office. And they went up there just to learn life skills and stuff in June. ... two weeks at a time. You know and then they'd come out. ... And some teachers would go up there too from the high school. Yeah. So yeah, that's where they got, like that's where they picked out the people who watched us up there when we used to go up for those summer camps. [2:2]

Brandi remembers all kinds of games and activities from her childhood.

Ummm, we used to play at all the kids' places, tag, hide-and-go-seek, ummm, my friend Mercy? I stayed the weekend with her all the time and her, her family took us out to Ruby Lake, you know, canoeing. [1:9]

Brandi liked active outdoor pursuits.

Yeah, I used ... yeah. I never liked being there when Mum and Dad used to make me come home. [laughs] I used to .... I liked having my freedom. Yeah. [1:9]

Hide and seek, uhhh, tag, red rover, ummm, oh. A whole bunch of games we used to play. Skip rope, umm, marbles, baseball, ... Uhhh, I think about grade six I started playing on a team. ... I played until ...... maybe thirteen or fourteen and then ...... Yeah, yeah, I enjoyed doing, playing baseball. [1:12]

Some of the enjoyment has gone now, overtaken by the need to perform to a certain standard.

Now I tried playing baseball with the adult team they have and I just, I just couldn't ...... I just had like, no self-confidence, so I don't, I don't play sport as a rule. [1:12]

She tried a number of other activities, as many young girls do. Her parents encouraged her in the hope that she would find something in which she could develop a lasting interest.

Mmmmm, when I was younger I was into figure skating .... I did ballet but not for that long. I had no patience and it was ...... I'm just not the ballet type of girl. ... (but) all my cousins were doing it and I wanted to be there doing it too. [1:13]

Discrimination is something that has not been a great problem for Brandi. As a young child in elementary school she was not aware of it at all, although at high school she did feel it from some other students and in the content of the curriculum, but not from teachers.

Ummmm ...... Not really, I had this one incident with this cop and he was really racist and, umm, he, me and my friends were walking. It was a Saturday and we were .... and we were just walking and he went by, about doing seventy, and we thought "Holy shit," we said something like that and he pulled his car over and got out and started yelling at us and then.... I didn't tell anyone about it because I didn't think it was a big deal. Until a week or two ...... yeah, he was really racist. But I've.... there was racism but I didn't find it till I got to high school. ... It was.... Yeah, it was worse in the high school. [1:12]

Brandi has some definite feelings about what she wants for her own children in the future.

I don't ... what I don't want to do is raise my kids with alcohol. 'Cause when I was growing up there was lots of drinking ... . But the love that I got from my parents I want to give to my kids ...... there was lots .... and I want to be able to give that to my kids ...... and just, hmmm ...... the respect that I was taught ... like that you must respect your parents. I want to teach that to my kids. [1:15]

She also feels that active encouragement from her in all things they attempt will be important for them. She hopes it might encourage them to enter postsecondary education.

It's something that when I have kids, is always encourage, not – always encourage a child to do the best they can and don't, and not to ridicule them or call them names when they don't meet your expectations. And education I think is something that I'll encourage them, to go to college and stuff like that, yeah. [2:18]

The content of the school curriculum and the nature of teaching is also something she sees as important.

I'd like them, ... their culture. their language .... hmmm. [1:15]

Yeah, yeah. Oh yeah, it wouldn't – I think when me and Steve do get married he'll be happy for our kids to know the language, yeah. Yeah. ... Even if I did marry a non-Native um, I wouldn't really care what he said. 'Cause it's our language. This is where I come from so –– And I'm proud like, and if he didn't like it he would have to deal with that. Yeah. See my Dad, my Dad is non-Native and he doesn't say anything about us learning the language. He's happy for us. Yeah. [2:8,9]

Her feelings are based on the fact that she and her peers had very little First Nations content generally, or Sechelt content more specifically, in their own schooling. The latter is something Brandi feels should be rectified.

Yeah. They do have, they teach our language up there, in grade one and two and I noticed when I was up there helping as a teacher's aide, um they, they were just learning about the Haida and the Inuit, stuff about their culture.[4] And I remember doing that, uh, the

---

4 The Haida, a West Coast Band from further north, and the Inuit, from the Arctic, have been included in the BC social studies curriculum for a number of years. For instance, see Heather Siska, *People of the Ice: How the Inuit Live* (Vancouver: Douglas & McIntyre, 1983), and Heather Siska, *The Haida and the Inuit: People of the Seasons* (Vancouver: Douglas & McIntyre, 1984), for early texts.

Inuit and the Haida. ... No, not the Sechelt, nuh uh. [laughs] ... Yeah, I think that would be a good idea for.... See that's the good thing about it, we are, we're getting our language taught to us and when I was in elementary school it was just for Native kids but now it's for Natives and non-Natives, and I think that's good. ... Because, so the non-Native kids can learn about the Sechelt people and ..... [1:15]

Brandi sees Valerie as also being an important teacher of her grandchildren in the future: not just in terms of Sechelt language and culture, but more generally as well. She also sees this teaching relationship between grandparent and grandchild as an important part of her cultural heritage.

Oh yeah. I see her as being a teacher for my kids, when I have kids. ... My Mum, oh yeah, my Mum can, she'll be able to teach them a lot 'cause my Mum knows a lot of things and she'll be able to teach them the language – not just the language like, she'll be able to teach them like morals and values and ...... just love. Yeah, my Mum will be able to do that as a grandmother. [2:18]

Looking back over her nineteen years, Brandi is fairly optimistic about her future, even though she feels that her teenage years have not been easy. The important factor for her, both in getting through the hard times and in planning for the future, is the strength to be found in and from her family.

Um, I've had a good childhood. A good childhood up until I think I got to adolescence. I had a really good childhood, but in adolescence I didn't really like.... But my childhood, um, my Mum and Dad provided for us everything that we needed, and everything that we wanted so I've had just a great childhood with my Mum and Dad. Yeah. [2:19]

TALKING TOGETHER

A significant part of the whole project, both for myself and the six women, arose from a two-hour videoconference between Pearl, Pauline and Charlene in Adelaide and Bernie and Valerie in Vancouver. Brandi was unable to attend this conference, but her seventeen-year-old cousin Samantha Joe came in her place. The text of the videoconference is different in nature and quality to the texts of the individual interviews, and represents a step further on in these women's consideration of the significance of their lives and their places within their respective cultures.

Videoconferencing was not a method of data collection or analysis that had been considered at the start of the interviews, and so its role and development require some explanation. As Elders of their respective groups, both Pearl and Bernie were early participants in the wider project from which this one grew. Valerie and Pauline were also involved, as was Charlene. As the process of interviewing proceeded, it seemed that discussion *between* members of the several indigenous groups who were participating would be advantageous. Videoconferencing was chosen because it offered the opportunity for participants to both see each other and to show each other artworks, artefacts, historic photographs and even video clips of their homes and communities. It also promised a major advantage over non-visual forms of communication in that it allowed participants to observe, albeit unconsciously, the multitude of non-verbal communication signals, including facial expressions

and gestures, that we all use constantly. Videoconferencing, therefore, was chosen because it permitted a far greater degree of communication and facilitated a far more rapid development of friendly
relationships than any other form of communication other than live
face-to-face discussion.[1]

The technology of videoconferencing, though, provided some
problems to begin with. It is a somewhat daunting procedure. The
participants must travel to a studio—in the case of the Adnyamathanha women, this meant a five-hour drive to Adelaide; for the
Sechelt women it was a two-hour trip by road and ferry to Vancouver. The time difference between the two countries meant that conferences had to take place in the morning at the Australian end and
mid-afternoon in Canada, which usually meant that both groups
needed to stay away overnight, and finding times that suited all participants as well as researchers and technical crew at both ends was
no easy task.

Then the apparatus required is intrusive. While the bright lights
and large cameras of a regular television studio were not in evidence, it was perfectly clear that we were being filmed. Participants
could see themselves and the people to whom they were speaking
on television monitors, and no matter how hard we pretended it
was not the same as a direct, informal, personal discussion. There
were often a number of non-participating observers, usually friends
and family, sitting close by. This gave considerable emotional support to participants, but often raised stress levels for technical staff
and researchers in terms of positioning and use of cameras, micro-
phones and other equipment. There were always technical problems of one sort or another. In the earliest videoconferences, movement was a problem. Even normal mouth movements while speaking appeared jerky and odd. Lips and voice appeared unsynchro-

---

1 A videoconferencing network for the Aboriginal people of the Northern Territory is currently proving very successful. Unlike the telephone, which has been
   available to them for a considerable time, videoconferencing, using a single
   microphone and camera in conjunction with ordinary domestic television sets,
   enables group rather than individual communication. While only a few of the
   participants may actually speak, the fact that others are present and are seen to
   be there appears to add something extra to the interaction (*Hot Chips*, ABC TV,
   August 2, 1995; see also Eleanor Bourke, "Images and Realities," in Colin
   Bourke, Eleanor Bourke and Bill Edwards, eds., *Aboriginal Australia* [St Lucia,
   Qld: University of Queensland Press, 1994], 11-12).

nised. If somebody moved rapidly, for instance, laughing or gesticulating with hands, the picture would break up into a meaningless jumble. This improved markedly over the two years of the project, to the point that people walking in front of the screen, though blurred, were usually recognisable, and stationary people could move limbs and torso without affecting picture quality.

Added to this there were sometimes sound delays similar to the ones that may be experienced on telephone connections. In fact they were identical to the ones on telephone connections for the videoconferencing connection is made via telephone. Unexpected technical problems sometimes meant connections were difficult to make and participants at both ends would sit around nervously wondering if the conference would proceed at all. Or a conference would be underway when suddenly sound or picture or the whole connection would be lost and everyone would have to wait for reconnection before trying to pick up the threads of the discussion. Given these circumstances, one might question the value of the communication that could be achieved but all parties, researchers and participants at both ends, were always enthusiastic and felt that the conferences were valuable and that each was an improvement on those that had gone before.

Some of the improvement was, without doubt, due to the improved technology as the series of conferences progressed. But a further and very important factor was that participants got to know each other and to know something about each others' lives and cultures as they participated and/or observed. Thus, by the time Pearl, Pauline and Charlene, and Bernie and Valerie came to confer about their lives, they had already participated in several previous conferences, though not necessarily with each other and/or had observed each other in one or more conferences. Their videoconference was unique in two ways, however, and both these circumstances, I believe, helped to make it particularly successful and productive. First, these two families of women knew more about each other than did most other participants because in the course of interviewing I had spoken to all of them about each other, noting differences and similarities in their cultures or experience, asking questions of one based on the response or insights of another. And, of course, each of them knew me well as a result of all our interviews. The second unique feature was the way in which the conference was structured. Previous sessions had been convened by one of the researchers at either end, though Valerie had on one or two occasions played a key role. Usually there were half a dozen or so participants at each end, and the convenors' job was mostly to make sure they all had reasonable turns at speaking and that orders of precedence in speaking were adhered to when a number of Elders were participating. The result was that while discussions were useful, they were quite formal in structure with a tendency for participants to talk *at* rather than *to* one another. They did achieve the aim of allowing the participants to control the topics and direction of the conference, but it was not possible under these circumstances to encourage the give and take of informal conversation.

A more spontaneous and natural approach was what I felt would be of most value and interest in terms of assisting the women to summarise the data that they had given me. At the start of our conference I suggested this and all six agreed, nodding wordlessly. At that point we were all nervous and they probably would have agreed to anything. I pushed ahead, therefore, and took initial control of the discussion. They had control of the topics, but I would step in quite strongly as one person finished speaking with comments like "Well, what do you think of that Bernie?" or, less aggressively, "Who is going to respond to that?" or "Why do you think that was so?" in the same way as I would with a new group of students at university. Because they already knew or knew about each other and because of their interest in and enthusiasm for what they were discussing, they soon began to take over control from me; within half an hour they needed little further assistance. They were responding directly to each other, interrupting, cutting in with questions. Fortunately there was a flexible period of time available because stopping them once they were into their stride would have been difficult. Their own comments as they said "goodbye" at the end of the session indicate their feelings about the value of the process.

Bernie Sound: Well, Gillian, I just want to say first of all that I'm really pleased to be here and excited, and I think this is something wonderful. I hope this will teach a lot of our younger generation as to what is going on –– happening. But anyway I was just so excited to be here, and um ..... nervous. Anyway I just hope we have another session. Maybe I'll be, maybe I'll do better [laughter].

Valerie Bourne: Gill, for me all of these interviews, and the ones we started with Rita and are carrying on with you and Tony, have been really beneficial to me because .... it gave an awareness of the role I'm playing in this life and the role I'm going .... the teachings I'll have to be able to pass on to my own children. So rather than being general now, I'm asking questions. So I want to thank all of you for that. It's been very .... an eye-opener for me.

Pauline Coulthard: Well, I'd just like to say it's been a pleasure for us too, I guess, to have been talking to people like yourselves on the other side of the world, and I guess to thank Tony and Gill and Rita over there for actually making this possible again. But hopefully if we be very nice to them, maybe we will actually be able to see you guys in person rather than over the video [laughter].

Charlene Tree: Yes, I'd just like to say it's been nice talking to you all and I've really enjoyed this session today. Maybe if Sam or anyone else around her age group – like our generation – wants to write or whatever, and we can compare our differences of our culture and the similarities between our cultures, I'd like that.

Samantha Joe: Well, I had fun to be talking to you guys. Like I haven't really been meeting you, but ––. I'd like to write to you and compare our lifestyles. It was just really neat talking to you at the other side of the world.

Bernie Sound: Technology.

Samantha Joe: Yeah, technology. [27-28]

Prior to the conference I had given all the women a list of possible topics for discussion. It was very general and covered most of the major points that had arisen during the interviews. It was not meant to be prescriptive. Indeed, I purposely made it as general as possible so that any topic could be touched on. The list was meant to serve more as a security prop, for very few people would feel comfortable going into such a situation with no idea at all of what was to be discussed. As it turned out, the discussion centred on only a handful of topics: education in both mainstream and traditional cultures; the role of women and the experience of being a woman, again with reference to both cultures; discrimination; and the problems of finding and nurturing a unity of purpose amongst their peoples. The women themselves chose these topics and chose the manner in which they would pursue them. They did so in the same way that happens in spontaneous conversation, that is, the discussion went backwards, forwards, sideways and in circles. Some points got lost along the way, others were explored more fully. Had there been more time, and had they the energy to continue beyond the two hours or so that the conference took, they would have found plenty more to discuss. However, what they did choose to discuss seems to me in retrospect to include pretty well all the areas that all six women had identified in the course of the interviews as being important to them in terms of past, present and future considerations. Apart from using the closing comments first, I have made little change in the text except to omit a few passages that were repetitive and to group some other passages together for clarity and emphasis. What is different is the insertion of considerably more of my comment amongst this text than in the interview text. This is justifiable on two grounds, I believe. First, the situation was different from that of the interviews, where each woman was speaking one on one with me and recounting her individual thoughts and experience. In some of the interviews there were attempts at explanation and analysis, but the focus was mostly narrow and personal. In the videoconference, however, it was much more a situation of family talking to family, one group of indigenous people to another. Much more of a conscious attempt was made to summarise a collective experience, to make comparisons, to identify similar experiences or outcomes. Second, after two years of ongoing discussions with me and contact with the other group through the previous videoconferences, each family had some knowledge of the other and the other's experience. Their discussion could begin from a basis of common knowledge that might not always be clear to the reader. My comments, therefore, fill in some of the gaps of shared knowledge and understandings, while at the same time extending further some of the women's own summary and analysis.

Early in the conference Valerie raised the subject of their experience as women living within their cultures with aspirations for themselves and their children. She raised the subject of the double burden of being a woman and being Aboriginal. But she also mentioned the power, both potential and realised, that stemmed from that positioning. She attributes a large proportion of the power to having survived the double burden of womanhood. She sees a particularly strong and positive role for women in determining her people's future. None of the other women picked up her comments at first, though later they returned to a fuller discussion of various aspects of their experience as women.

Valerie Bourne: ... being a woman, I encountered many more difficulties, not only with racism but prejudice from our own men. If we married — and a lot of us – I married in an integrated marriage, my husband is white and we have four children. Ah .... if I had married him before 1986 I would have become a non-status person, meaning I would have become white in the eyes of our people. But if an Indian man married a white woman, she would become a status Indian in the eyes of our people. So it was really a, a prejudice, a law that governed us in those days. So as women we had to be more tolerant of ah, um, what happened to us in our lifetime, and I think that um, um, it's only made me stronger because we come from a matriarchal society where three sisters made all of, most of the Sechelt. I don't really know how that story goes and that's one of the things I want to get at. But um, when I look at our lineage I think to myself, "That's why women are strong in our Band and that's why women are the ones that speak out, and that's why women are — ." I think women are going to be the best leaders in this world. From looking at yourselves, you guys look like very strong, powerful women too. [7]

Gillian Weiss: You said earlier on that women were important in Sechelt culture. Women are also important in Adnyamathanha culture. The line goes down through the mother. So what sort of significance do you maybe feel that has for you as women in Sechelt society, and as women in families? It seems to me that the family is very important. You both come from families that value your culture and are working hard to get it back. I'm not trying to downplay the role of men in their families, but women are important too. So what thoughts might you have on that?

Bernie Sound: I think in my time Gill, er, the women were really important. Er, I don't know why men shouldn't — like my grandmother —— I was talking to Valerie earlier on before we came here about things we might touch upon. My grandmother was a very tiny woman but a very powerful woman. Ah, like I said, I was er .... um, out of twelve children and er, at that time she was still —— my father had already had four children and she was still controlling him, ah, scolding him and giving him advice and things like that as to how to raise us and um, how to be, you know, a man and things like that. She had a lot of powerful ways of raising us children —— her children and grandchildren. [15]

In interview, both Bernie and Valerie had mentioned the power of female forebears in terms of their control of and influence over family life. In one sense, perhaps, these women had an advantage over their menfolk in surviving the changes brought by European culture, which included the nineteenth-century Western notion of the inferiority and subservience of women to men. While the traditional Sechelt male roles in the ceremonial lives of their people, as hunters and protectors and as builders of boats and longhouses, were either extinguished by European settlement or superseded by Western technologies, the role of women in what Europeans considered the "private" sphere of the home was less rapidly affected. They were able to retain their traditional roles and sphere of influence longer than their men; no matter what the situation, they still had responsibility for the home, for the care of husband and children. The situation was similar for the Adnyamathanha. It was the "public" male ceremonial and hunting roles that were most rapidly undermined while the female nurturing role was encouraged.

In both the Sechelt and the Adnyamathanha traditions there was evidently equality between the sexes, though none of the women has much detailed knowledge of just how the relationships worked. Pearl, and to a lesser extent Bernie, have both had the opportunity to observe their parents' and grandparents' generations interacting in more or less traditional ways, but these observations were largely made when they were children. However, all the women strongly believe, whether correctly or not, that male and female roles were different but complementary and both were of equal importance for survival. This is a concept that Western feminism has rejected as generating inherent inequalities, but the rejection arises largely, I believe, from the Western emphasis on the individual. In these traditional cultures the individual was of less importance. Survival depended on the whole group and every aspect of life was tied to the group. Some individuals or subgroups might have had more power than others, but this does not appear to have been gender related. Pearl pointed out two of many gender-role differences in her culture. At first glance the man might appear to Western eyes to have the better deal—he was the one who disciplined (but his sisters' children, not his own), he was "the boss," he was the one with "more to say," but this must be offset against the power that came through the female line and extended backwards, forwards, sideways, through all living generations. Each individual was enmeshed in a web of reciprocal powers and responsibilities which can in no way be compared to the linear power structures of the Western, nuclear, patriarchal family. The importance of the female line lay in passing on not only a sense of belonging but the individual's actual place in society.

Pearl Mackenzie: Well, in our culture (it's) really men's job to discipline. In our culture a man have to be older than a woman to marry because he's the boss. He's got to ...... what shall I say? .... Yeah, more to say I suppose, but generation really start from the mother, the woman, you know, and goes right down. Like, moiety we calls it. That leads on, like, I'm the eldest out of my family and all my sisters and their children, well they got to respect me. They all my related. My sisters' childrens got to still call me mother as well, as well as my own three. And um, like Charlene and Kerri when they get children, well that follows on right down, and their children still come under my .... what shall I say? Moiety group, yeah. That really goes on and on.

Pauline Coulthard: Maybe if I just explain a little bit about what Mum is – about moiety system. I don't know whether you might have the same system over there. It's two different sorts of moiety groups that are like -- . They used them mainly for marrying reasons. You weren't allowed to marry anyone on the same moiety line as .... what you are. Um, we have two – they're Arraru and Matheri and my er, Mum is a Arraru person, so therefore I'm one and my kids are, and it sort of follows down the mother's line.

Valerie Bourne: I was going to say to Pauline that we have the similar, except ours is called Clans and I think Gilbert touched on it a bit yesterday. Bear Clan can't marry Bear Clan. So, that would mean you're too closely related.

[Noises of agreement at Adelaide end.]

Pauline Coulthard: And I guess that's one of the things that still is er, very strong. Whether somebody from our group actually marries a non-Aboriginal person, whatever ..... um, like for instance, you know, if my daughter was to marry someone who was non-Aboriginal, because she's Arraru, well he'd automatically be (put) on the opposite side, and that's how we've sort of been working it.

Valerie Bourne: So if Charlene married a white person, she would be, her children would be her lineage?

Pauline Coulthard: Yes.

Valerie Bourne: OK, now yeah, I understand. So your women are really, really important in that role, in the marrying.

Pauline Coulthard: Yeah. [15-16]

The role of female lineage is clearly very important to these women. In itself it gives them a sense of power, for it gives them a direct connection backwards with countless past generations of women of their respective peoples and it gives them an important role to play in placing the next generation within the broader Sechelt or Adnyamathanha communities. While much of their culture may have been lost, this is one aspect of their heritage that they feel they literally possess within their own bodies and they value it accordingly.

Some modern Western ideas of feminism and women's roles, though very different to traditional ideas, are also a part of the women's identities, particularly those of the youngest generation. While all of the six women are independent and determined in terms of pursuing goals they desire, for the older ones this has sometimes been within certain parameters. For instance, Bernie was determined that she would not marry in her teens as was the custom of the times, but she certainly saw her future as wife and mother. When Pearl's husband was alive she allowed him to speak for her publicly, but that is not to say that she had no influence over him in private. In fact, I think she was the stronger of the two in many ways and certainly took the lead in determining the nature and quality of her children's education. She walked a fine line between doing what she wanted or thought was best and what was correct, conventional behaviour (sometimes she followed traditional expectations and sometimes mainstream social standards, depending on the situation) for a "good" wife, mother, woman. Charlene and Samantha, however, are unequivocal about who will control their lives.

Samantha Joe: Well, I if I ever get a husband I guess I'm going to call the shots [laughter]. All of us, uh, me and my girlfriends, aren't types to get pushed around by guys. We just .... we're not .... I don't know, we'll call the shots I guess.

Charlene Tree: Yeah, I guess in the past like, women were sort of kept on a back bench, I guess. They weren't really allowed to have too much say, they didn't really get involved in a lot of decision making. But, but now there's no way I'd let my boyfriend, or whatever, make decisions for me. I mean, I've got a mind of my own so, you know, I'll use it. And um, but .... yeah, Nanna's saying that's not right.

Valerie Bourne: You've got to be careful Charlene. Your Mum and your Grandma are with you.

Charlene Tree: Yeah, I think I should move away from them a bit. Um, yeah, I guess like, traditionally they were sort of –– they weren't allowed to say too much. The men always had the say, whereas um, in .... in my day, like now, there's no way I'd let my boyfriend or husband or whatever, if I ever get married, speak on behalf of me. I mean, I've got a mouth and I've got a brain and if I've got anything to say I'll say it on my own. I don't need people saying stuff for me. Whereas Nanna, I guess things would have been different for her. I mean if my grandfather spoke, I mean, she didn't, whereas it's different for me. I mean I've always spoken my own mind whereas she never did – until now.

Pearl Mackenzie: Yeah, I've got to speak up because I've got no one to speak for me. My husband's gone.

Pauline Coulthard: Because I found too, when I was growing up .... like in Mum's generation women sort of stayed home and did a lot of the women things, I guess, you know, and er, but when

I was growing up I was very determined. Because I grew up with all brothers and I just had to be one of the boys, you know. I mean there was no way I was going to sit home and let them go out and have all the fun, and so I was really determined that –– you know, I spent a lot of time with my father and I think he saw me as one of the, one, one of the sons actually, and the way Mum used to dress me, I mean, they wouldn't have known that they had a daughter anyway. But I remember I had to compete with my brothers. There was times when we went out er, –– because I grew up on a station, which I think you call them ranches over there, um, I had to –– . Like whenever we went out mustering sheep or whatever it was –– er, my brothers didn't want me to ride the motorbikes. They used to actually drain the petrol (gas) tank and take all the petrol out because they thought, because I was a girl, I had to stay home. Er, but I finally got my way. And I guess that's where my daughter gets a lot of determination from, is –– because I said, "Just because you're a girl it doesn't mean that you can't do things." I mean, I believe in ...

Charlene Tree: Yeah, I guess um, we had it pretty different from um, a lot of the girls I went to school with. Like um, a lot of them were like, um, raised to be ladies, I guess. I'm not saying that I'm not a lady – I mean, I am to a certain extent. [laughter] Don't laugh. They all think that's pretty funny. But um, when, when I was growing up, I mean, if I, if I enjoyed doing things that were traditionally boys' things, I guess, I mean, we were encouraged to do it. Like, I mean if I enjoyed going out shooting or riding motorbikes or playing with trucks and cars instead of playing dolls, we were encouraged to do that, whereas a lot of the girls that I went to school with um, did play with dolls and all that type of stuff and we didn't. .... So we were always encouraged to do the things that we enjoyed doing, or that we were interested in, regardless of whether they weren't traditionally girls' things or not.

Pearl Mackenzie: Yeah, well I'd like to comment on that. As I told Gill last night .... Charlene mentioned that going out er, playing with the boys, well I used to play with my brother. You know, do whatever he wanted to do. You know, play balls and er, marbles or ..... I never used to like playing with dolls, although a lot of doll was given to me. But I didn't sit back with my other two sisters and play dolls. I liked to play round and throwing stones and climbing [laughter].

Pauline Coulthard: Now we know where we get it from [laughter].

Pearl Mackenzie: I only told Gill that last night.

Pauline Coulthard: Well, this is the first time I've heard that, so now I can't really get into trouble for the stuff that I used to do.

Charlene Tree: She's always said to us, "You don't do those things." She says "Girls don't do those things. You don't hang around all the boys because girls don't hang around all the boys. You can't have male friends." So you just wait! [laughter].

Pearl Mackenzie: Well, I was only with my brother. My two brothers I suppose ..... I really enjoyed this talk [laughter]. [17-19]

This was a fascinating admission from Pearl. In many ways she was very conservative particularly in regard to cultural traditions. She always appeared to fill perfectly the role of Adnyamathanha woman and wife, at the same time maintaining her determination. The existence of this early tomboy streak helps to explain the existence of similar characteristics in Pauline and Charlene, and also why Pearl was not more strict in demanding that Pauline adhere to "female" activities and behaviour as she was growing up.

Valerie had the last word on the topic.

Valerie Bourne: I think that a lot of the things we try to teach our younger generation is they have the right to choose. They have a choice they can make, and I think that's what ah, we all become educated for. And when uh .... they have the right to be married or not to be married, they have a right to have children or not to have children –– that's their choice. That's why we give them all, pass them, pass on all these stories to them, ah, the older generation, and ah, I think for Bernie, she had very little choice as opposed to me, and then my choices were limited. But Sam is different. I think Sam can, can do anything she wants to do – call the shots if that's what she wants to do, and that's what she's going to do. [19]

They began to discuss what was good and what was bad about being an Aboriginal woman. Almost immediately discrimination was mentioned. All three generations have experienced it in some way, but for each generation the experience has been different. It seems to be a problem that peaked as Pauline and Valerie were growing up. While it has not disappeared, it seems that the youngest generation has the confidence and ability to deflect at least some of its sting. Of course, what has changed is not only Aboriginal perceptions of and reactions to discrimination, but the perceptions and reactions of other sections of society to indigenous cultures and peoples. This is not to say that all sectors of society have rid themselves of fear or prejudice, but as Aboriginal groups on both continents gain a higher profile, their "otherness" becomes less strange, less threatening to many sections of the community. Governments in both countries have embraced policies of social justice and equal opportunity which have gone some way towards breaking down barriers. As Valerie said in interview, discrimination stems from fear: fear of difference, fear of the unknown and fear that the "others" may have or acquire more than their share of land, wealth, power or any other desirable attribute or commodity. The increased education of the two younger generations as well as their growing pride in their heritage and culture have allowed them to stand with greater equality vis-à-vis the white community.

Valerie Bourne: I guess that the best thing about being a Native woman is that I have culture – I have a culture I can pass on to my children and their children and their children. And that culture has made me very proud today. And I guess the worst thing was all these years there've been ignorant people I've run into – ignorant teachers, ignorant ah, friends – that didn't understand who I was and made me feel bad about that. So that, that had to do with the colour of my skin. Or that I was, it was, you know, things that I would not want my children to know. I, I was ah, from all the interviews and all the teaching that we had, I hope that my children will never be racist in this group against anybody. So this is trying to pass on all the time a knowledge of who we are.

Pauline Coulthard: I guess I feel the same way as you, Valerie, um, because you know, I'm proud to be here now and to be able to pass on -- um, not so much to pass on, I'm still learning as well. But, but, yeah, I know my kids are more aware now that er .... about what's happening than I was when I was their age. Now I just feel that I'm really proud that we've got somebody like Mum who's sort of been very strong in passing on a lot of information. But we do still face, not quite a lot, but there is still racism amongst other people, as well as our own. That's what we're starting to find, a lot of our own people are just as racist as what the non-Aboriginal people are. So you know....

Charlene Tree: Yeah, I guess um, I found it particularly hard when I was um, a lot younger. Um, being a lot lighter skinned than my Mum and my sisters, I found that whenever we went and visited, like, other family members, other relations or whatever you want to call them, they were racist against me because my skin was so light. But then again when I was at school I used to get it from them as well. Like all my white friends at school that knew that I was Aboriginal .... gave me hassles because of that, because of my Aboriginality. But that's nothing I'm ashamed of. I'm not ashamed of being an Aboriginal. I'm proud of who I am and where I come from because I can tell my kids about –– Um, even though I'm still learning, I mean I know a fair bit about my culture and um, and my people and all the Dreaming stories that connect us with our land, and I'm proud of that. Yeah, I haven't got anything else to say.

Gillian Weiss: What was it like for you, Sam? Did you have problems of racism amongst your own people as well as your school friends, non-Native people?

Samantha Joe: Oh, it used to be like that and, but now we're trying to turn the tables with our non-Native friends. Not my friends but like my sister's friends. My sister has really white skin and they used to say like –– "Oh, at least you look white, you don't look Native, right." But now we've basically turned the tables. We bug them about being white and that's why they .... they just laugh about it now. It's not like that any more though. Like, nobody bugs us any more because .... I don't know, they know better not to bug us about it.

Bernie Sound: In my time, Gill, I'm just listening to you there – the lady speaking there about the good times and the bad times. In my time I considered myself lucky. Um, when I was little we travelled up the inlet there. Um, um, my Dad used to go up the inlet logging and we travelled with him, fishing and .... and I told my niece one time looking at a picture I said, "When I was little I thought we owned this whole land, this whole inlet," because we were all like .... mostly Native people living there – there were very few white people there. We had very little contact with white people at that time except to go to the grocery store, so I didn't encounter any um, racism so much in my time until maybe .... in the forties, maybe fifties .... then I started to see the racism as more people started to come into our, our .... lands there in Sechelt. So I thought I was lucky. I didn't have to put up with that as a young child. I felt secure.

Pauline Coulthard: I guess Mum er, would have grown up, Bernie, exactly the same as you. Maybe she'd like to comment. Because even now, I mean, when we sort of talk about things, she keeps telling us, "Well back in the good old days, you know, it was ......"

Bernie Sound: Yes, I said that [laughter].

Charlene Tree: Well, maybe she'd like to comment on that.

Pearl Mackenzie: Yeah, well .... yes, that's true, when I was growing up ...... as I said, we was all in a community, you know, Adnyamathanha community. But, um, there was some white peoples around. But we were shy, shy of the white people until the missionaries came and we got used to them. And er, when I got married I went on the eastern side (of the Flinders Ranges) with my husband and very few people that er, sort of, I got used to. And when I was coming to where I am now, coming into Hawker to give Pauline a better education .... because I didn't know much .... and, er everybody sort of welcomed me in Hawker. All the non-Aboriginals, you know, really was good to me and they encouraged me to go to church, although I was a Christian before I left Nepabunna – that's where I grew up. And um, I was sort of going to church at Hawker ... No we were, you know, afraid of white people, you know, what they might call it, but I never ever heard one, you know .... a nasty word was spoken to me about I was black or whatever they could call me. I never had anything like that said to me and when I come into Hawker they sort of more or less welcomed me in open arms. [19-22]

The problems surrounding land claims was an area in which the women found common ground, though the common ground was pain. Much of the pain for both groups seems to arise not out of the battle to reclaim traditional lands but from the divisive effects the long and involved legal processes have on their people. The divisions within their communities cause them pain because, to an increasing extent with each generation, they have come to subscribe to the Western notion of individuality and the right of each individual to pursue his or her own goals, but they still retain a collective consciousness, a feeling that their people as a group are more important than the individuals of whom they are composed. The existence, the nature and the importance of their people as a group, a community, a unique entity, is one of the bases of their pride in their heritage. To this end, the Sechelt with their central Band government have been able to pursue positive methods of healing their communal hurts. The Adnyamathanha, lacking such a structure, have not been so fortunate.

But the divisions are also hurtful to both groups because they work against conciliation and reconciliation between their people and the rest of society in Canada and in Australia. This is one of the most positive aspects, to my mind, of the attitudes and worldview of all these women. Although each sees the situation in a slightly different way, all of them agree that it is the future that is important. They see their own future and the future of their peoples as being one in which their past is cherished and protected, held in trust for generations yet to be born, but in which they can live in harmony with the rest of society and take advantage of the best that mainstream culture has to offer as well. They do not wish to forget the pain and dislocation of the past, but they wish to put it behind them.

The voices in which they speak deserve to be heard, for so often it is only the radical indigenous voice that is heard mouthing a discourse that is full of anger, that will brook no compromise. This discourse is sometimes taken as the indigenous discourse by those who have no chance to hear any other. Frequently it arouses only anger in return and leads only to confrontation. It too has a right to be heard, but not exclusively. There is not one Aboriginal discourse, just as there is not one Aboriginal people. The problem is that speakers of more moderate discourses frequently do not have the means or the motivation to make themselves heard. The discourse of these women represents one alternative, an alternative that offers a multitude of positive possibilities for the future, based as it is on premises of good will, open communication and the idea that both indigenous and mainstream societies can work together in harmony while pursuing sometimes separate goals. It is doubly valuable in that the discourse itself is illustrated in the lives of its proponents.

Valerie Bourne: We're going through the same struggles as the (Australian) Aboriginal people on a daily basis. It was really nice for this conference that we can see our brothers and sisters in different parts of the world and how we're solving all of our problems along the way, but how we're staying united and sharing a lot of our information with one another. This conference has been really important to us because uh, a lot of us don't get to uh, see other places in the world and it's nice to know how you ....

Charlene Tree: Yes, I think there's several different families within our group that are um, sort of involved with all this land claim business. All they're really doing for us really is causing, causing problems between our Aboriginal group and white Australians. Because when they make statements to the press they say they're speaking for the majority of our people, when all they're really doing is speaking for the minority of our group. And er, instead, instead of bridging the gap between um, black Australians and white Australians, they're just making that gap further – dividing us.

Pauline Coulthard: Because I guess we would like to see what happens now. I mean certainly I don't like what happened in the past, but we have to make it a better future for our kids, you know, and live in harmony like the old days too I guess, you know. I mean we're only doing it for our kids' generation and their kids', so I guess all of us together maybe, you know, hopefully in the near future things will get better.

Valerie Bourne: We encountered that, the discontentment like you're talking about – family squabbles and families running our whole Band. What we did was started some healing um, workshops where we could express our anger to what the residential schools did to us, to what the government has done to us, to what white society has brought us. And so that seemed to help our people a lot. We sort of got together after, and so that's why we're at the stage where we can all be united on the land claims – was to get that anger out that we felt, before we could move on to the next stage in our .... destiny in life. I'm sure that ── . I don't know if you guys have healing sessions, or healing centres or whatever, where you can get together and talk about um, what the anger is about.

These healing sessions are a part of the pan-Indian movement, like the medicine wheel that Valerie mentioned earlier. Initial healing workshops were conducted for the Sechelt people by non-Sechelt Indians, but the Sechelt Band has continued some of the practices and incorporated some of their own revived traditions such as the sweat bath and ritual river bathing for purification. While these revived traditions probably differ from the originals, they are a very real constituent of the construction of a contemporary Sechelt culture and Valerie, for one, hopes that they will form the basis of a renewed spirituality amongst her people, especially the younger generations who have rejected Christianity but who, until now, have not had their own cultural alternative. In contrast, attempts to revive some traditional practices amongst the Adnyamathanha have led only to division and bitterness. A group of urban residents of the small cities of Whyalla and Port Augusta has attempted to revive some of the traditional dancing, the forms of which are still remembered even if all their spiritual significance is not. There has also been an attempt to recreate some kind of initiation ceremony to give the young men both a pride in and a sense of belonging to their people and their culture. The latter would have to be a new creation because there are no longer sufficient initiates to conduct a traditional ceremony and the few surviving initiated men are prohibited by their own status as initiates from discussing their knowledge with the uninitiated. The notion of "creating" traditions in this way is unacceptable to many Adnyamathanha, including Pearl and her family. Pearl, as we have seen earlier, had no problems combining both traditional beliefs and Christianity, but this is not an option that appeals to all.

Pauline Coulthard: No, we haven't got anything like that, apart from within our own immediate family. We're able to just sit down – like with my Mum and my kids and my brothers and whatever – and talk about things and see things differently. But no, we haven't got anything where the whole community actually gets together, but maybe that sounds like something that we could be looking into.

Pearl Mackenzie: Yeah, about healing. One suggestion that I can make that we all .... you know, go on Christianity. This is my healing, because I go to church and go to some healing ministries and that. That's one of the ways that people can solve all the problems, is just through God, our maker. "Undakarra" we calls him in our language. So I think if people get together and pray about it, and they really come to grips in Christianity, everything is wipe off and become new to us. That's how I feel now in my Christianity belief. That's all I've got to say I think.

Valerie Bourne: Yes, I'd like to say to Pearl that the Elders that were here yesterday are very um, er, Christian and always go to church, and they were the ones that pulled us together. They were the main catalyst in pulling all of us together. So, um ..... you know, you can make a difference Pearl and what you're saying is true ...... Although I jump and like some –– I think it was Mona – or no Barbara, yesterday, that said her grandmother – jumped from one religion to another. That's how I am. [laughter] But yes, our Elders through prayer, through a lot of prayer ––, have pulled us together. We always remember God in everything we do. Like you said, we're very spiritual people and you saw the little boy singing yesterday? He was thanking the Great Spirit and our kids do this all the time too. So Pearl is very right and we have to get spiritual and give it up to our creators.

Pearl Mackenzie: That's right. Yeah, we are really – Aboriginals are really spiritual people and they pray a lot about things. What's wrong with being ...... you know. It took me a while before I, you know, but I can see it all now, that the only thing that can make things better for us if you take everything to our maker .... God. This is His world, that's what I believe. He made this heaven and earth – we're just living on it. That's how I feel and I was told about it and I read it in the Bible, that .... He's the one that created all the things for us, and everything will be all right if people go to God, take every troubles to Him. I make it sound like I'm preaching. But that's my belief anyhow.

Valerie Bourne: Thank you for reminding us Pearl. We always needed to be reminded. [24-27]

Charlene Tree: Yeah, I mean, there are a lot of people um, in our group that are in positions where they could be doing a lot for our culture, but a lot of them are just in there for themselves and all they seem to be doing is just causing a lot of conflict amongst our people.

Pearl Mackenzie: Yeah, and our fathers used to go out hunting. My Dad was a great hunter and come home with meat and that, you know. Share it around. It gives me a heartache what's going on today, because our very own people, Adnyamathanha people, are doing things for themselves, not sharing with us. Not passing even a message to us what they are intending to do. And it's a really heartbreak —— for me anyway.

Gillian Weiss: Yes, that's something, Valerie, that may be a bit different in Sechelt, given the structure that you have with a Band Chief and a Band Council that really do sort of hold you together as a people. The Adnyamathanha don't have that sort of structure, and right at the moment, with land claims, they're finding that there is a lot of dissension among their people, with several different groups wanting different sorts of things and, as Pauline and Pearl and Charlene have said, going off and sort of doing their own thing. Is that a problem for your people?

Valerie Bourne: The land claims? The land claims started about forty years ago with my grandfather, in his day. And ever since there have been really —— tensions. But the past few years, because we have a, a good Chief and we think he's a fair and just person, we've gotten together on that. But I know that —— because we're only one Band in British Colombia, and in Canada there's many, many Bands and we're all different — we're not the same. We have different dialects, we have different ways and so on. So all of the Bands in Canada are fighting for land claims, and even for self-government, but you have to get together and know what you want before you go and get a land claim, so —— and that takes knowing your heritage, knowing your ancestors, knowing the history, knowing where you live, knowing where you fished, where you hunted. And so we have to gather all that information and put it together on a map, and then that's how we settled our land claims. So we're right in the middle of it right now and we have a seven-step process. That's the one Gilbert wanted to get in with yesterday. We have a seven-step process and right now we're going into step four. But each step is very time consuming and our people get very, very frustrated with the government here. So um, and .... and just before we came here Bernie was making – she was the only one that did her homework today on this conference. She said, "When they had real men," [laughter] I guess there's no real men any more – I don't know [laughter].

Pearl Mackenzie: Not in our group nowadays. I'll say that too.

Pauline Coulthard: I guess we're having the same problem .... .

Charlene Tree: I think a lot of the problems we're having with our land claims are that there are a couple of people in our group who don't really want to claim our land for the Adnyamathanha people as a group, but they want to claim our land for themselves – you know, just for individual families. And um, back .... well, our group, the Adnyamathanha group, there are five different sub-groups which make up that group, but in today's day and age we are collectively known as the Adnyamathanha people. But a lot of the younger generation now –– not my generation and Mum's generation, but the generation in between Mum and um, Nanna, they're trying now to go back to the old ways and divide themselves back into those different groups, and all it seems to be doing is just causing a lot of conflict amongst our people. And um, but I mean I guess if they don't realise soon if we want something like our land back or whatever, I mean we've all got to band together, stand together, because you know, "United we stand, divided we fall." Do you want to add anything to that?

Pearl Mackenzie: I might say something. Yes, that's true what Charlene's saying because er, we were divided into five groups to make up the Adnyamathanha, but now the other younger generation want to go back to one of the old generations ..... what do you call it .... One of the groups, yeah. Different group and –– but I'm satisfied that we was all lived in the Flinders Ranges, and –– you know, claim some of that for themselves. Actually we were free, you know ..... going from place to place. But the others wants it all themselves, but which is not true. And we've got to give white community credit as well because they the ones that sort of came and .... Right back from Ram Paddock Gate. Although we wasn't living in rags or anything like that, we weren't not cared for. We had parents and that. But what I mean, that whites, they provided us with a house and bringing us into the white society. So I can't find any fault because I got lots and lots of friends in white now than ... .

Pauline Coulthard: Udnyus.

Pearl McKenzie: Yes, that might be better. Udnyu's a white person. We've got lots of friends – well I do –– from away back, you know. Now I'm still making new friends and I'm welcome in Adelaide here – anywhere – and with the open arms people come to me, you know.

Charlene Tree: Because you're so cute [laughter].

Pearl Mackenzie: Well, that's what I'm always told. I'm proud of that. So I can't leave the white people out, udnyus, because they the ones that can do a lot for us. People sometimes go about it the wrong way, saying that whites have taken our country away, which they really don't, because we shared the country – we lived on our places. So they're trying to find fault with them. [23-27]

The subject of education, either in terms of formal schooling, or as in the learning of traditional skills or knowledge in the traditional way, or as in the teaching of non-Aboriginal people, was the first topic that was discussed in the videoconference, but so many different themes emerged that seem to be crucial to these women's lives and the ways they have constructed and reconstructed them through the series of interviews that I have left it until last to consider. So let us return to the start of the conference.

Gillian Weiss: ... I guess the best thing to do is to give you a choice of what you would like to start with. Whether you in fact have something that you're bursting to come out and say right now, or whether you would like me to sort of throw in a few leading questions to get you going. I'm happy to do whatever you think would be best.

Valerie Bourne: Hi Gillian. We would like you to throw in some questions to start us off. We haven't got anything we're bursting with yet, but I know by the end of the conference –– [laughter].

Gillian Weiss: OK, well I've got several things that I thought might be useful. You may not think so, in which case just tell me straight up. ... Two things that perhaps might get you started in terms of talking. One of the things that's come through—I think particularly in talking with Pearl and with Valerie, but also with Pauline and with Bernie, not so much with Charlene and Brandi, and I think that's a function of the fact that they're the younger generation—but one of the things that the other four have said is the difficulty in finding time to learn both your own traditional culture and white culture. You both come from families in which white schooling is now very important, and obviously white formal schooling takes up an awful lot of time in childhood, but you also both come from families that value your culture and value passing it on. And trying to find time to, as it were, fit in almost two lifetimes of learning in one childhood is something that you've mentioned as being difficult. Now does that sound like something you'd like to jump in on and follow up?

Valerie Bourne: Yes, that sounds a good place to start. Do you want to start over there or should we start over here?

Gillian Weiss: Well, you're talking—why don't you start Valerie?

Valerie Bourne: OK. Thanks Gillian. Hi again Pearl and Pauline and Charlene I met you all last year. The difficulty we expressed was in learning our culture and going to school full time, or working full time. The fact that -- culture was the way of life -- it was -- we did every day all day -- and what our ancestors would have done all day. And um, a very time-consuming job, especially if uh, our, our, our ancestors, the women, were making baskets which, which they did most of the time -- um, and they had to dig their own roots, and that was an all-day process for them. So when we try to regain some of our culture back, ah, we really have to um, think in terms of buying um, roots now and also, because um, we've been legislated to death here, there've been ah, ever since like, settlement has moved in um, our hunting rights are different – we have to have a licence now – our fishing rights are different. So even when you dig roots you have to be careful whose land you're on. And of course our Elders used to know how to do that without harming a tree, and – to make sure that they would

produce again next year. We don't know that and so um, the
only place I can see us going, and hopefully we're headed in, is
that we'll get a Native – our own First Nation – or Sechelt I
should say, because we are different from other um, Bands
here – that we will get our own school happening where we
can implement some of our um, cultural activities right into
the schooling program, plus getting their academic standard.
But we've ah, now got a language, um, Sechelt language class
happening, and Bernie is one of the teachers and I am in the
process of learning, reading and writing our language, and Sam
here is now just beginning on our language. So it's a start for
us and we've come up to a lot of uh, um, hurdles and maybe
you, Pearl might know that her hurdles are the same as ours,
and Pauline might know that. It gets very frustrating for our
Elders because um, of the lack of respect that, that happens in
the schools.

Gillian Weiss: OK, Pearl, would you like to make any comment on
that, or Pauline?

Pauline Coulthard: Earlier on I told Gill I wasn't really nervous, but
I am at the moment.

Rita Irwin (researcher in Vancouver): We're all nervous too,
Pauline.

Gillian Weiss: Well, Pauline, you've worked in the school up at
Hawker.

Pauline Coulthard: Yes, I guess that we've got the same er, feelings
as what you have. Um, we are now, I mean, I think in the last
twenty-five years or so there's been more documentation on
the things like our language and the foods, and the cultural
stuff as well. But we still find it very hard to um .... get the
respect and stuff of the younger kids, you know. It's still sort
of really hard and I think Mum sort of, because she grew up in
a different generation as I did, when everyone really respected
everyone and everything. I don't know whether Mum wants
to comment on -- ?

Pearl Mackenzie: That's true what Pauline's saying, 'cause I'm the
eldest in our generation and I find it -- . In our culture it was
very -- it was very .... different and that's what I'd like to pass

on to our younger generation, but er, now some of them are interested and some aren't, so it make it difficult because I know the language and I know the culture -- pretty well. [3-4]

Education, in the very broad sense of learning about and how to live within a culture or (in the case of these women who live within their own culture and mainstream culture) two cultures, was a recurring topic in all the interviews. Finding the time, the means and the motivation to learn two cultures was a problem that both families identified, though they did not pursue it further in the videoconference. In one sense it is a problem that each individual must confront on his or her own, balancing different needs and imperatives as they arrive at different stages in the life cycle and deciding which is the most important at any one time.

One attitude to education that the women of both these families have in common is that a formal academic education is crucial for the younger generation. Second, they believe that within this formal educational structure space must be made for the teaching of at least some aspects of their own culture. However, what this should involve and how it should be done is a matter on which the two groups differ somewhat. This is partly a result of their own values, beliefs and perceptions and partly a result of the existing practices and curriculum in the public schools of their respective lands.

Gillian Weiss: Pauline, perhaps you could say something about what exactly happens in the schools in terms of teaching Aboriginal culture generally, because in fact even though you both -- . This is one of the problems. It's easy to say, "Well, we're teaching something in the school." Because I'm the person that's talked to you both, I know that what's happening in the schools in Sechelt is actually quite different to what is happening up in Hawker where Pauline and Pearl live. So maybe you could just explain what sort of teaching the kids get at the Hawker school and then perhaps Valerie or Bernie can talk a little bit about exactly what's happening in Sechelt. I think you'd be interested to know what each other's doing and see the things that are quite different can sometimes both achieve similar ends.

Pauline Coulthard: Well actually my job er -- I'm on leave from my position at the school at the moment until April, and my job role there is er, Aboriginal Education Worker. And we more or less teach Aboriginal Studies to Aboriginal students as well as non-Aboriginal. And er, a lot of it – like we start off with our Dreaming stories .... and the thing is, we find it's very difficult when you teach –– er, Aboriginal Dreaming stories er, within the classroom situation. For kids and teachers to get more of an idea of the feeling of place is actually to be on site. .... I've run out of things to say.

Gillian Weiss: Tell them about some of the teaching you do on site.

Pauline Coulthard: Because the Flinders Ranges, the area that we live in, is full of our Dreaming stories and we actually take students out, not only at Hawker but I have a lot of er, students and kids come up from other schools, like in Adelaide. And also I take part in the –– teacher in-servicing trips over school holidays, and we actually take teachers um, on camping trips for a week and introduce them to the Dreaming and um, they camp out and hear Dreaming stories around the camp fire, look at bush foods, and get them to actually feel what it was like back in the days of old, sort of thing. And then we gradually take them through an Aboriginal settlement where European contact was made and they sort of get into European contact and to what it is like now. It's really tiring work. Sometimes when you spend a week with a group of teachers that don't know nothing, it's really hard and it can be very frustrating. But we enjoy what we do. I'm running out of things to say again. [4-5]

Bernie and Valerie did not follow up with details of learning and schooling for Sechelt children, so the difference between the two situations is not clear. In the Hawker Area School, the majority of students are white and Adnyamathanha children are a very obvious minority. Other Adnyamathanha children attend schools scattered across their traditional lands. Some are small like the Hawker Area School. Others are large urban schools in which there are sizable groups of Aboriginal children from other tribal groups as well, but that still have a majority of white students. Because they are scattered over such a large area and because they have no centralised leadership structure similar to the Band structures of Canadian First Nations peoples, there has been no organised push by the Adnyamathanha people as a group to either develop or implement a specifically Adnyamathanha curriculum. On the other hand, the

Aboriginal Curriculum Unit of the South Australian Department for Education and Children's Services has developed a fairly comprehensive series of Aboriginal Studies units based on a comparison of the cultures, histories and ways of life of three South Australian Aboriginal groups, the Pitjantjatjara who live in the semi-desert lands in the northwest of the State, the Adnyamathanha themselves and the Ngarrindjeri, whose lands extend down the course of the River Murray and along the coast at its mouth. So while this is not a self-generated curriculum, it is quite acceptable to the Adnyamathanha because of its relevance; it is specific to them while at the same time demonstrating that Aboriginal cultures are various rather than universal. Not all teachers who use the units are willing or able to extend their teaching to hands-on experiences in the traditional lands. But for Pauline, and for Pearl and Charlene, this method of teaching is of major importance both for Aboriginal and non-Aboriginal students, children and adults, because this method of learning was important in their lives.

The Sechelt approach is different partly because their people are concentrated into a smaller geographic area and partly because they have a centralised Band structure with the legal right to determine such things as the direction and content of their own education. The British Columbia Ministry of Education Social Studies curriculum has long included units on the Inuit of the Arctic areas and the Haida whose lands lie along the coast to the north of Sechelt lands, but while their inclusion might be a change from a completely white-dominated curriculum, the Sechelt people want their children to learn specifically about their own people and their own history and culture before they consider even other First Nations groups. There is a further factor of importance. Because the residential school experience has been so long-standing and pervasive, the Sechelt as a people are further removed from their cultural roots than many Adnyamathanha. Pearl and the majority of her generation grew up in a situation in which their language and much of their culture were still intact. Bernie and many of her generation experienced up to a decade in residential schools, so that while their grandparents and parents still retained their language and much of their culture they were not permitted to pass it on to Bernie's generation. The violence this has done to Sechelt culture is something that Bernie wants the younger generations to know about.

Bernie Sound: OK. I just want to catch up on a little bit about my back history. Um, like I was born in the thirties and ah .... I often got together with Valerie and tried to educate her on what was happening about that time. And ah .... It was pretty rough in my days when we grew up there because like the um, uumm ...... it was the Depression years. But in our time we didn't have it so rough because our men were hunters at that time, and fishermen, and er, they provided for the whole community. When the men went out they would come home and they would um, um, dish out the fish, or the meat, deer, or whatever they went hunting for, where a lot of people were starving at that time. And um, as I was growing as a very young girl my grandmother, like Valerie mentioned, was making baskets –– the women were always busy –– doing things, um, um, to look after the men – you know, to get them off to work and out hunting, whatever –– and raising the children. Mind you, I'm one of twelve – I'm the second eldest of twelve children. And my brother, being the oldest, which is Valerie's Dad, and er, that would be his granddaughter there, Samantha there. So it was very difficult in that time, when we were growing up in the thirties, for my Dad to look after so many children. And, um at the time – well when I started school, I think maybe about six or seven, it was in the residential school and it was very difficult for us. We're trying to teach our children a little bit about what went on in them years. The children nowadays, they have no idea what we went through in the school – the discipline we had and the, the er, upbringing we had in them years. It's so different nowadays in this day and age, like Pearl says, it's very hard. Our children don't listen to us, there's no respect. I agree with her there and it's very difficult. Mind you there's a big gap between me and the younger generation. Valerie's closer to me. But ah, it's very difficult and I heard her talking yesterday too about the respect and I agreed with her there. But ah, we're getting through to them. If they start learning what we did in my younger days maybe they would start appreciating things more today. I'll pass it on to Valerie for now.

Valerie Bourne: OK Gill. I was, I'm the eldest of nine children and um, my great-grandmother was the midwife who also um, um, brought Bernie into the world. I was the last one that she midwifed and um, she passed on shortly after that, but a very strong, powerful um, woman. I was the last one born in the house .... Sechelt. I did attend residential school from the age of five. And then I went to —— I completed grade eight there and then from there, because we're all Native kids in the residential school, I went to public school because it didn't go beyond grade eight. And in public school the first, it was the first time I encountered racism, which was very difficult because when you're a teenager, ah, it's, it's hard to cope with, so .... that was the first time, eh, and that was the first time I ever got to know ah, white people. I was very uncomfortable for most of my high school years, so I really didn't enjoy being in high school at all. Um, when I was about the age of (indistinct), my great-grandfather – whose name was Basil Joe – took me out in front of his house one day and he said —— he spoke very little English, or broken English, and he said to me, "Do you see that rock over there, and that rock over there?" And I looked at him and I said, "Yeah." Then he said, "You remember that all that land belongs to the Sechelt people and one day you're going to have to say that. You're going to have to get up and say that and fight for your land back." And so, right now, we're into land claims and all these things that our grandfathers, our great-grandfathers told us, we have to start remembering and it has to be documented, so um, our land claim becomes a stronger claim for the Sechelt people. But my, his son, who was Clarence Joe, um, helped close down residential schools, in the, I think the late sixties, and we started integrating with the white children. So um, he seen that, he always told me that education was very important and that was how we were going to win a lot of our battles that we were going to encounter. So that both these men had a real clear perception of what the future was going to bring for us and always talked to us —— they were always passing on the legends, the history of the Sechelt people – always telling us, "Tape it, write it down, remember it. Keep it in there because one day you're going to need it." So when I think back to all those years, I feel both of —— . How would you say that word, looking in to the future? Foreseer of the future? It was like when my grandfather would tell me something, Clarence, and he'd say, "You're going to have to get educated. That's how you're going to fight, through education." And I used to think to myself, "What is he talking about?" you know. Of course, you know – lack of respect and growing up ah, differently from them. It was difficult for him, but he didn't know that all this time I had been listening – I had learnt some things. So when our Elders talk and they say, "The kids aren't listening," I say, "But they are. They can hear everything you say and they're putting it in there somewhere, and they're putting it right in the back of their minds and one day they're going to come out and use it." So this is how I talk to the Elders and tell them not to be discouraged because I can remember things way back that my grandfathers told me and that I will probably pass on to my children and then their children, and make it important for them. [5-7]

For both groups of women the issue of retaining and teaching their language is one of the most crucial issues. Their identity as members of their respective groups seems tied to the language more than to any other aspect of their culture. They are very aware how close both languages are to extinction as well as of the attitudes both of their own people and those of the majority that almost extinguished them.

Gillian Weiss: ... maybe we can go back ... to what we were talking about before in terms of passing the knowledge down from generation to generation, and maybe give Charlene and Sam a chance to respond and maybe try and explain how they feel about that in terms of being sort of the upcoming generation that is going to have to do a lot of the passing on in the future. I know Sam has not spoken about this yet. She may feel a bit wary or a bit shy of coming in. What do you think, Sam?

Samantha Joe: My name's Samantha Joe and (Bernie and Valerie are) my aunt and my great-auntie and I'm in grade eleven and I'm seventeen. And .... yeah, I've been ah, like, a little while ago they got ah —— we have language class up at the high school so I got it for a grade twelve credit 'cause it was prescribed this year. I might – I don't know yet. So I'll be getting a credit for language because they've got a .... I don't know.

Valerie Bourne: So now it's recognised.

Samantha Joe: Yeah, because before they said we had to do it on a voluntary basis. Everybody, all the Natives take it —— a couple of non-Natives take it too.

Gillian Weiss: ... Sam, how do you feel—can I ask you a direct question, seeing as I haven't interviewed you and I haven't asked you these questions before. How do you feel in terms of the children that you will probably have one day and passing on the language that you will have learned and any other information and knowledge that you have about your culture? ... Is that something you've thought about yet? I realise that's probably a horrible question to ask someone who's seventeen. You may not have thought about it at all yet.

Samantha Joe: Well, I think right now I have, I have to learn it all because the Elders aren't going to be around forever. Then I want to pass it on to my children because before I thought it was nothing, I thought like, I didn't want to learn the language, but now I think it's really important to learn it and have –– I'm doing good at it now and we're learning sentences and everything. This is our culture. I think it's really important. I'm going to pass it on to my kids when I learn it. 'Cause I don't want it to get lost.

Gillian Weiss: Let's see if Charlene can add something to that. She's sitting here pretending that she doesn't exist right now, but I know very well that she has lots of things to say because she's said them to me before.

Charlene Tree: I don't know what to say.

Gillian Weiss: Well, how do you feel about your culture and the importance of it for your children and that generation?

Charlene Tree: I guess when the time does come for me to have kids, I would pass on what I know about my culture to them because um, I mean ever since I was little – I mean what I know about my culture wasn't passed down to me from my Mum, um, it was from my grandparents. I spent a lot of time with my grandparents when I was growing up. Most of my childhood was with them, even though Mum was still around. But what I, what I do know, um, was passed down to me from them and –– I guess when I have my kids I'd want them to know just as much about my culture, or their culture, as what I do because it's, it's um, it's a part of my life. I mean, it's where I come from so I'd want them to know just as much.

Gillian Weiss: Well, Valerie just said that when she was growing up
she heard and she learnt a lot that didn't really come to be
important to her till later on. Do you think perhaps that you
have maybe even more knowledge than you know at the back
of your mind that you came across as a child that will be
important as you get older?

Pauline Coulthard: I'd like to just say something, comment on that
um, because when I was growing up it was different to what
my kids are going through now, now that our culture is more
openly spoken about. But I guess when I was growing up it
was different for a child my age, because you didn't, you
weren't allowed to ask too many questions. I mean we had to
sort of sit and talk and listen to the Elders or, you know. But
now our kids are asking a lot more questions, you know. And
also I guess when I was younger I just felt that like, whenever
I heard my parents talking or my grandparents telling me stories, I didn't really listen. I mean I was thinking about other
things, like whether it would be books or comics or whatever.
But now I'm really sorry that, you know, the times they were
telling me stuff, whether it was Dreaming stories or um, bush
food stuff .... I'm still learning and I just feel at the moment I
still, still don't know enough to actually be confident enough
to say when, like, Mum's generation passes on –– at the
moment I still feel that I won't be able to pass on to my kids,
or to my grandkids, so that's why we feel it's very important
that, you know, to do a lot of documentation. And I know there
is some stuff that we probably won't know because a lot of our
older generation have passed on, and I guess Mum's generation is, I mean because they've lived in that generation,
they're finding it very difficult to pass it on because they're
starting to lose a lot of their Elders to actually check things,
you know. Uum, but even when I was growing up I was I
guess I was ashamed to be an Aboriginal person because in
the history books we were taught, you know, that Aboriginal
people were savages and I was thinking, "Gee, I don't want to
be like that," you know. We sort of went one way or the other
I guess. But now I just, it's really good with Aboriginal education that, you know, we're allowed, and our kids are really
proud of who they are and I hope it's going to get better when
I have grandkids. Mum might want to say something.

Valerie Bourne: You sound just like me. That's how I grew up, worried about the monetary things that life could bring and not really paying attention, but not really thinking about and being ashamed of being a Native person too. Um, because you tried not to act like one when you were in white society and all these sad things. There was nothing good about who our people were and that was what we were being taught every day of our lives and a lot of this would come from residential school, but just being an Indian was not good. So, um, that was the same ideas and false ideas that you grew up with. But I think what got me interested in my language mainly was ah, one day my boy, who is eight now – he was six – and he came home and he was singing to me in my language, and I looked at him and I asked him, "What are you singing about? Tell, sing the song again for me." So he sang it and I said, "What does it mean?" and he said, "Mum, that's Shahshishalem," he said to me, which is my language, and I got so embarrassed I said, "That's it, I'm going to, I'm going to go and learn." And so in one year I've learnt so much because I'm just always paying attention now. And the other reason is our Elders are – we have about twenty Elders left that know the language and they're panicking now because they saying, "If we can't pass it on to my generation, it's going to be gone – that no one will know it." So um, I've put my mind to absolutely learning it fluently now and being able to pass it on. I have to take that responsibility, and it's a big responsibility and I'm doing my best but at the same time I say to my Elders, "Be patient with me. It's like a foreign language to me." They try to be patient. And we as well do that with Sam. We try to have patience when we're teaching and sometimes you just run out of it because you think, "Oh they're not listening and they don't care," but they are – I think they are. So I think Pauline I can really, really say to you that I grew up feeling the same and it's an awful, awful feeling. And now today I can say I'm very proud of who I am and my children are very proud of who they are.

Gillian Weiss: Bernie and Pearl, you're both fluent in your languages. Do either of you have anything to add to that in terms of what you can pass on and how you might do it?

Bernie Sound: I want to refer to what Valerie said ah, ah when she was talking about our language there. Um, when I was in school, I didn't get to mention that we lost our language in my time. Like my father was fluent and mother and grandparents er, at that time. At that time, in their time, also they were, they were um, forbidden to use our language in the residential school, and also in my time. But they were lucky. They had er, when they left school their parents were fluent and they, they spoke it very well when they left school, or on their visiting time. But by the time I left school I was er, er you keep saying, "I was ashamed of my language," and maybe I was too. When I tried to speak my language my grandparents or my parents would laugh at me if I made a mistake when I said something wrong. So that way I sort of lost the language and I wasn't fluent. I'm still not fluent today. But I know the language, but there's not enough people to talk to in Sechelt. We only get together, like maybe once a week, and everybody's so happy when they get together, like the Elders that is – the ones that can speak to each other in our language, eh. So at home, like, I can't talk to my children or grandchildren, or you know .... so it's very difficult for us to you know –– just a very few of us that know our language .... so hopefully our younger generation will get more fluent. OK?

Gillian Weiss: OK. Pearl, would you like to say something about language?

Pearl Mackenzie: Yeah, well, I'd like to say that er, I think I was a lucky one .... that I had the whole community with me at the time I grew up, although it was in a depression time as well. And er, we –– I had my grandparents and Mum and Dad and all the other .... many groups, you know. We used to share. But um, now everyone, like our tribe, Adnyamathanha people, we talk a lot when we meet, but some of them can't speak really well. But as to me, I really speak, you know .... really well and also my children can talk. I've got um, two sons and a daughter here, and then, so, my two granddaughters, the eldest ones. But the youngest one couldn't even understand a single word that I talk to her. I've got to repeat it in English and I'm not too good at English myself. And you know .... I can speak really well and I can find the mistake that our people say ....

their words. Some says, the younger ones says, not as sound as that I could. And when I was growing up you know, we never used to ask much questions. And er, the stories and that, that I know about Dreaming time, that we ...... was taught. And er, I just listened you know, and learnt by listening. And um, now the younger ones now trying to .... put it over me ...... and that sort of makes me wild. The stories they, you know, tell .... that you .... which I don't agree with at times, but they turn and twist a little, you know, in their stories. But in the back of my head, I've got it written all up here. I haven't got it on diary, a paper or anything. I've got it all up here. And, er that's what it was just passed down by word of mouth .... in our generation .... generation after generation our culture was passed down, not written words. It was just passed down and we had to listen although we had the community to –– you know, each time we'd go to visit different people .... we'd have a different one, you know, saying the same words. And there is only about five older than I am, and one is really good. It's my auntie, lives up at Nepabunna, and er, me and her can sit down and talk the things of way back .... of what we talk. ... I know it really well. So ...... I'd like to, you know, pass this on to my granddaughters because I can speak to them and they answer me back in the language. But er, the youngest .... is a bit useless [laughter]. She couldn't understand a word.

Charlene Tree: Yes, I just wanted to say something about our language. I guess in a way we can be thankful because Nanna and – or my grandmother, my grandfather and my great-grandmother – they worked with a linguist, John McEntee. And they worked with him for um, er, about twenty years. Yeah, they worked with him for about twenty years and Nanna's still working with him now, and in all that time they've recorded um, a large amount of the um, Adnyamathanha language, which is our language and um, I guess we can be grateful for that because um, until, until they started work there was no written record of our language and since –– well, all those years of hard work of um, writing words out and checking and the rechecking, and with other Elders as well, they've published an Adnyamathanha dictionary, so we now have a dictionary on our language. And um, I think, like Nanna was saying before, even though –– like, I don't know how it is with Sam, but when I, when I was growing up um, I spent a lot of time learning about um, white culture, um, all the explorers of Australia and what have you, but while I was at home with my grandparents, I mean even though I was speaking English, I mean they spoke to us in our language so we sort of are luckier in the sense that we can understand our language. I mean, we can speak some um, sentences fluently, but other than that it's just a few words here and there. But we can understand our language fairly well.

Pearl Mackenzie: Speak sounds.

Charlene Tree: Yeah ...... ummmm.

Pearl Mackenzie: I cut you off [they laugh]. I mean she could speak sounds and saying words and that. .... Although she might ask in English and whatever we give her, you know, in our language she repeats it. And er, from now I think she'll keep on learning.

Charlene Tree: Yeah, um, I guess when, when I was um .... in my early childhood I guess I had no choice but to learn my culture, regardless of whether I was interested in it or not, but as I, um, started –– I guess from my early teenage years, say from thirteen onwards, I um, wasn't really interested in my culture. I mean I just couldn't be bothered. I guess it was just too much pressure learning about .... white Australian history as well as my own. And um, it wasn't until I was about fifteen, sixteen, we had to take um, language classes at school and, and they told us we either had to learn French or German. And then I sat down and I thought about it. "Well, you know, I can't even speak my own language properly. Why, why should I, why should I learn French or German?" And so we approached several of the teachers at school and you know, we said, "We want to learn our own language," and they said "No, it can't happen – it can't happen at school. There's not enough people to teach it." And I said, "Well my grandmother speaks it fluently" and I said, "You know, she'd be more than willing to come in and teach us our language." I said, "I don't really want to learn another language while I can't even speak my own." But um, it turned out they wouldn't let us do that but since then I've taken more of an interest in my culture and where I've come from. And um, even though I haven't been doing much, I've been doing some work with Nanna, recording what I can about my family .... history and um, and my people.

Gillian Weiss: Any comment from your end, Valerie?

Samantha Joe: Well, I'm in the exact same situation like Charlene was in with school. Um, in grade four we got to learn our language and then it just stopped. We all got to grade eight and we had to take French and all of us, all the Native kids, we all just dropped out, so mind you we weren't supposed to. But we just did. And we got mad because we didn't want to take French because we all thought it was a dumb language and it was too hard, so we –– [laughter]. We wanted to learn our language. So um, it wasn't until basically now that we got it up there and everybody takes it, you know. Like um, couple of years ago we got, like, a dictionary too in Sechelt. This guy recorded all the Elders talking. And, um we have it in our book now. We all came back to language class and we're doing a whole bunch of assignments and I'm really interested in it now, but I wasn't at all in elementary school. I didn't like it at all but now I want to learn it. So it's just like the exact same thing as Charlene I guess.

Valerie Bourne: Just to touch up a little bit on what Sam's –– . We also have a linguist who's worked with us for the past twenty years and he's from UBC and his name's Ron Beaumont. When he first started we had 2500 words in our dictionary. Now we've got well over 6000 and we're still adding new words to that all the time. So, ah, he's done a lot of work with our Elders over the past, and Elders that have all passed on, he's got all their words and it's all written and taped and our language is a written language now. Um, that was the only way I could learn Sechelt, was um, to see it written, 'cause um, the language was so abstract to me. I couldn't um, relate it to anything. Just sitting there in the classroom I thought I couldn't picture it. So it was like doing maths, you know, you, you have some numbers and you're trying to solve the problem but you can't really see it. And I'm sure with Bernie and the rest of them, they were doing it while they were being taught from their language. And um, if you go out and travel and your par-

ents have said, "There is the tree," and they'd say the name
of the tree -- our kids sit in the classroom and you have to
really -- because we're a visual people, we had to really, really
um, think about it. So now that I see it written I can, I can, I
can learn right from that. Because I grew up with a written
language and that was English, so um, now I've learned in a
different way. But I'm still learning it which uh, and I don't
know how Sam feels about that. Maybe she thinks about it differently even. You know all our generations, the language, see
it differently. We don't see it all in the same way and mine was
very abstract. Our language is very abstract to me, except
when I see it written. ...... You might have similar differences.
I don't know if I made sense Gillian, did I?

Gillian Weiss: Oh, it made sense to me, yes [others agree]. Did you
have something you wanted to say Charlene?

Charlene Tree: Yeah. I guess what made it easier for like myself and
my younger sister Kerri to um, understand our language is
because when we were younger we spent a lot of time with
like my grandparents, and Mum, and they took us out camping
quite a bit so we were able to get a better grasp of our um, language. Because when we'd go out camping and they'd say,
"Well this is a kangaroo," and like, "The Aboriginal word for
this is 'udlu,'" or whatever, and er, so we were lucky in that
sense that we were able to pick up our language a lot easier.
But if we were to read it, we wouldn't be able to understand
the words because we're not too good at reading our language,
even though we can speak it um, well enough and understand
it very well. Yeah, our language was taught to us by going out
camping and showing us whatever, and showing us the Aboriginal word for different things. That's how we learnt our language.

Valerie Bourne: I think that when we're teaching the kids right
now, for our language we try to give it as much meaning as we
possibly can. For instance if we have January, February, we tell
them in our language what it was, and January was the month
the eagles go and feed and skw'etu, the raven, lays its eggs.
We often tell the kids that if you go out into the ocean you'll
see the eagles in the water. They'll be fishing and you can
watch them all through January. And then in February the loon

lays its eggs, and so we have to give it as much meaning or it'll be nothing to them. It's like teaching you my language and it would mean nothing to you. So ah, that's what we try to think about when we're teaching the children. Give it some meaning because it's really important to them. Our language is a very spiritual language and ah, it's got a lot to do with the earth and the world around us and how we care for it, and even how we pray. So ah, these kids learn all these different meanings, they're taught about ah ..... if we give them one new word a day, or .... there's something that connects them to that word. That's what I'm trying to say. So there's always a connection to who they are as children or people, and the responsibility that they have. So these kids when they first started learning the language, our kids used to sit down and never volunteer to get involved with their language. And in one year you could see that they've gained an identity. They know who they are now, and along with that they've also gained a lot of self-esteem and our kids are right in the front and they're going, "I know, I know the answer. I got the .... I know what it means." So it's just a remarkable change in our children and it feels so good to watch them because I don't think they're going to have the same problems I did with self-esteem when they get older. They're going to know who they are and they're going to know their history and their language and they're going to be proud of that. So that's the other big plus. You know, that's the happy ending, that we have to .... learning our own language. [7-14]

AFTERWORD

How can we, or indeed can we at all, structure and theorise the analysis of the stories of these six women? As I argued at the start of this book, I have been at great pains to try not to intrude myself too much into these women's stories and their own understandings of themselves, their lives and their peoples' histories. For this reason I argue that theorisation, except in the very broad sense of attempting to encourage and facilitate the telling and the understanding of these women's lives through an Aboriginal discourse rather than white academic discourse, seems inappropriate.

On the other hand, structuring the analysis is not inappropriate, and as I have said already the women themselves did this spontaneously as I talked to them individually during the interviews and later as we discussed the transcripts and during the videoconference. There were also a number of discussions between two or even all three members of each family and myself. They ranged from quite formal situations in which we systematically checked transcripts to informal chats over coffee or a meal to extended and mostly social interactions as when Pearl, Pauline and Charlene have stayed with my family and me when they have been in Adelaide or as when I and my family have stayed with Valerie and her family while in Sechelt.

Because our lives have become quite closely intertwined during the course of the project, my voice has become even more a part of the analytic enterprise than I originally envisaged. I believe it has a legitimate place in both the Foreword and Afterword of this book both in its own right and also because the women have sanctioned it through the process of our interaction and collaboration. This is not to say that there are two totally separate parts to the work, "theirs" and "mine." Although they could be read alone, both are a part of the whole; each adds to the other. The women's stories legitimate my analysis of the situation. My words help to make accessible the less obvious meanings, to point out the connections in the women's stories, to place them in the context of their own and each other's lives. And just as my voice, however hard I have tried, does come through to some extent in the women's stories, so theirs come through both metaphorically and literally in mine. This is how it should be; we believe it is an indication of the success of our collaboration.

What then is the significance of the stories? What do they tell us of the lives and experience of six individual women over the span of three generations? What can they tell us about the ways that white settlement of two very different countries on opposite sides of the world have impacted upon two groups of indigenous peoples? What can they tell us about the ways these people reacted and are still reacting? There are some commonalities as well as some experiences that are different for each group of women. An obvious statement, perhaps, but an important one because in summarising and comparing such a range of experience, individual and cultural, with such broad chronological and geographic parameters, it is easy to highlight similarities and miss important differences or vice versa.

For both sets of women, although their lives have been in many ways quite different, the importance of the community stands out in their stories. As a child, Bernie "thought the whole inlet belonged to us," "us" being not just her family but the whole of the Sechelt Nation. Despite spending her school years isolated from both family and community within the walls of the residential school, she recalls the closeness and joy of community celebrations as well as the strength and comfort that community ties provided in hard times. For Valerie too, the Sechelt community was important, although as she reached her teen years community ties were ostensibly breaking down under the combined effects of several generations of residential schooling, the increasing expansion of non-Native settlement all around the Reserve lands and the increasing need for her people to come to terms with and take on the trap-

pings of mainstream Canadian culture and lifestyle. She recalls the
advantage of being able to play "over the whole reserve" with
mixed age groups of Sechelt children rather than being confined to
a single backyard.[1] The sense of belonging to such a community is
something she wishes to regain and retain for future generations.
Though many of the physical manifestations of these bonds have
disappeared in the last two generations, even for Brandi they are
still important. When she moved away from Sechelt, even though
she sought the friendship and company of other Native Indian
peers, they did not replace the community she had left behind. She
was always relieved to come back.

The tightly woven interrelationships that support such a sense
of community are not simple to unravel. So many factors are
involved. Some are unique to the Sechelt situation, others are common to other Canadian or North American First Nations. Yet others
are probably to be found in many human communities. The small
size of the Sechelt Band lands is probably important for it concentrated the people together even while it cut them off to some
extent from their traditional movements around and through their
original lands. The fact that the residential school, for all its bad
effects, was in the middle of their village rather than far away probably prevented greater fragmentation. The practice of children
spending large amounts of time with grandparents or other relatives, even to the point of being brought up by them, seems to have
spread the closeness of nuclear family relationships more widely

---

1 This is an experience that is still very real today. It is partly because the Sechelt
  Band lands are physically quite compact and the town of Sechelt itself is still a
  small safe, semi-rural place. It is also because the community spirit of interaction and of care for all individuals in the group, not just immediate family members, is still very strong. When my family and I stayed with Valerie, my children,
  aged seven and a half and ten, were astounded at the freedom they had to roam
  and play with Sechelt children, apparently unsupervised by adults. My husband
  and I were also quite surprised at how comfortable we felt allowing our children
  to do things that we simply could not permit in our own community on the outskirts of the city of Adelaide. Many country children, in both Canada and Australia, do enjoy considerably more freedom than their city counterparts, but the
  truth is we would not have felt happy allowing our children to roam through the
  whole of Sechelt. It was only when they were on the Band lands, where even
  people we had not met knew who our children were, where they were staying
  and were willing to keep an eye out for them, that we were confident that they
  would come to no harm.

through the group. Bernie brought up one of her sisters' sons, Valerie and Brandi spent large amounts of time with their grandparents. Today Valerie has one of her nephews living with her and her family.

A collective sense of identity is also important in the creation of community.[2] Language and culture form an integral part of identity, and traditionally served to set the Sechelt Nation apart from all other neighbouring bands. Along with their traditional lands, their language and culture served to anchor them in a unique place in their universe. Culture and language, as well as lands, have been eroded over the past century, though it has only been in the last thirty or forty years that the effects of this erosion have been most obvious. For many of Valerie's and Brandi's generations, the sense of identity as members of the Sechelt Nation has all but disappeared. Valerie feels that she is only now building a sense of her own identity as a Sechelt woman, and sees it as crucial that the upcoming generations do not have to flounder through their formative years as she did, trying to create a personal identity with no idea of the collective identity and how they fit into it. This is why the language and what remain of the cultural practices are so important to her. They are important to Bernie too. In the year that passed between the initial interviews and my final visit to Sechelt to tie up the final threads of the research, both Bernie and Valerie had been working regularly in the local schools teaching the language and the cultural context into which it fits. Their own knowledge of and fluency in the language had improved as had their commitment to teaching it to all Sechelt children. But most importantly, I heard them use the language spontaneously and unself-consciously in an ordinary social situation. It was only on a single occasion, but it is a start. For language to be part of identity it needs to be more than an academic study. It has to be a part of everyday life, to be

---

2 Sioui (*For an Amerindian Autohistory,* 22) argues that the "essential values" of Native Indian peoples, which are based on respect for the earth and the circular nature of life itself, have persisted despite the changes resulting from European settlement and, in fact, cannot be eradicated. The experience of many Native Indian peoples would seem to indicate that eradication is indeed possible, but for many, and not the least these three Sechelt women, the conscious retaking, reviving or reacknowledgment of these values is a crucial step in the remaking of identity. A similar situation exists for the Adnyamathanha and other Australian Aboriginal groups.

heard by children in the home and on the street as well as in the classroom.

For the Adnyamathanha women community is also important, but in a very different way, for only Pearl has lived in a purely Adnyamathanha community and then only as a child. Once she married, she and her husband moved from living in close community to living in semi-isolation, where even contact with non-Adnyamathanha people was limited. Pauline began her life in isolation from both the Adnyamathanha and white communities; only Charlene has spent all her life in a township. And yet they are undoubtedly a part of the Adnyamathanha community. It exists, but not in physical space. Nepabunna is perhaps its spiritual home, the place that has come to be seen as physically representing the Adnyamathanha people. But few of them live there. Rather, they are scattered across their traditional lands and beyond in a number of small groups who, like the Hawker residents, form parts of larger mixed communities, or who like some in Port Augusta, a small city of approximately 16,000, live uneasily on their metaphorical outskirts.

What makes the Adnyamathanha people a community at least in the minds of Pearl, Pauline and Charlene is not so much physical position or proximity as the shared cultural and linguistic heritage and the land, the physical manifestation of their people's Dreaming. I have spoken about the importance of identity in the Sechelt community; for Bernie's family the recreation of their group and individual identities is something that is growing out of the already-existing physical community. For the Adnyamathanha the opposite is the case. There is little in the way of physical community, but the people are bound by their individual and group identities as Adnyamathanha. For Pearl, Pauline and Charlene this is particularly strong and is bolstered by family ties as well as traditional knowledge and cultural practices. The ties of immediate family are maintained by frequent visiting or, if this is impossible, then through contact by phone. During the course of the project Pauline resigned from her job as Aboriginal Education Worker in Hawker and took a position managing the Aboriginal Hostel in Port Augusta. Charlene moved to Adelaide and then to a small town on the outskirts of the city to work and to be near her new boyfriend. Then she moved to Port Augusta. Her sister Kerri moved to Adelaide and then to Port Augusta to work. All these movements resulted in further travel as all members regularly visited each other. Add to this the fact that

Pauline's older brother lives with his family in Port Augusta, her younger brother moves between Hawker, Port Augusta and Adelaide and other family remain in Hawker and the pattern becomes a kaleidoscope. If I wanted to contact one of the women I would often call several numbers and get no reply, but once I found a single family member I would instantly be told exactly where everyone was. Within the immediate family then, close contact is of great importance even if physical proximity is impossible. Contact with other members of the Adnyamathanha community is important too, and individuals will usually have a good idea of where others are and what they are doing if they are not at home.

What appears to be equally important, at least to Pearl's family, is regular physical contact with their land. Even living in Hawker, which is in the centre of their traditional lands, is not sufficient in itself, though when Kerri and Charlene were living in Adelaide they returned to Hawker whenever they could. Once in Hawker frequent trips to places of significance seem essential to their inner peace and well-being. "Places of significance" include those sites which are linked by Dreaming stories to the timeless past of the Adnyamathanha. These sites do not seem to be visited specifically, indeed, some are so vast they cannot be; for instance, Wilpena Pound, the huge circle of mountains that represents two snakes entwined, or Nananarrina, the two hills near Copley which also represent a snake in the Adnyamathanha Dreaming. But they were always noted by Pearl or Pauline as we passed them and some or all of the Dreaming story was recounted. I am sure that this was mostly a reaction to our presence but, on the other hand, I doubt that any of the family ever passes a spot that is significant to their culture without noting it internally, even if no words are spoken. This sense of connection to the land is integral to the Adnyamathanha women's sense of identity; it has never been broken. With the Sechelt family, it is something that has been lost to a large extent in the last generation and a half but is now being rejuvenated. It is partly a result of the latter's much more settled lifestyle in a semi-urban society, partly a result of the fragmentation of their traditional lifestyle by the imposition of the residential school and Western lifestyle, but also a function of the nature of the land itself.

The Adnyamathanha landscape is harsh and vast and only sparsely populated, but it is accessible. The roads, particularly the minor ones, are frequently no more than rutted tracks, but except in the worst heat of summer or during infrequent rains many are passable in ordinary vehicles for those who know the area. In a four-wheel drive you can get just about anywhere. With Pearl as our guide we have gone to places that some Adnyamathanha and most non-Aboriginal people do not know exist. Her mental map of her country is formidable in its complexity. We would be following two narrow wheel tracks in the middle of nowhere when she would say "Turn right at the cross-road—it's a couple of hundred yards." Sure enough, in a few moments, a set of even less visible tracks would cross our route. She would laugh at our amazement and say, "You don't think I know where I'm going, do you?"

The Sechelt lands, on the other hand, are mostly accessible only by boat; the inlet is the road to their significant traditional sites and now that few of them are fishermen, fewer of them have boats. The traditional sites of T'sunay (Deserted Bay) and Skwakwiyam (Vancouver Bay) are being used once more by the Band and individual members as camps, where members can learn about culture and tradition or where healing sessions and other group activities can be held, but there is not as yet the immediacy or depth of connection that we observed with Pearl's family. Valerie, though, accompanied us on a trip to Skwakwiyam and took obvious pride and pleasure in being able to show us places of traditional importance such as the spot where, in Sechelt mythology, Raven pushed open the mouth of Narrows Inlet. But much of this knowledge she has only recently learned.

Places that are associated with personal experiences are also important to the Adnyamathanha women: the tree under which Pearl and John were married, the graves of various relations, Ram Paddock Gate where Pearl was born, the area around Martin's Well Station where Pearl and John spent their early married life and where Pauline grew up, Erudina Station which lies next to it and where Pauline worked sporadically when her children were young. All these places we have been told about, many we have been taken to, not just so that we could begin to know them but because it was a good excuse for the women themselves to visit again and confirm their ties. Charlene, though she visits them less, still has a strong affinity with the places that Pearl and John took her to when she was younger.

Another set of "places of significance" for the Adnyamathanha women are those in which traditional food or medicine plants can be found, and they return to them frequently. Pearl structured her time around the seasons and the foods they bring. Staying in Adelaide, she would say, "I wonder if those quandongs are ripe yet?" Going out to find bush tucker is always a source of pleasure. Traditional foods, with the exception of kangaroo, are no longer a regular part of the diet, but they seem to provide a unique nourishment for the identity. Early in our relationship, Pearl and Pauline took my family and me out to look for witchetty grubs.[3] We went to a creek bed a kilometre or so outside Hawker, just an ordinary creek bed, not particularly beautiful or significant. Pauline proceeded to show us how to find the telltale bump that indicates that there is a grub inside a tree, how to make a hole through the bark to where it is lying and how to hook it out without tearing the soft body. Then we made a fire and cooked and ate the half dozen or so that we had gathered. Pearl also showed us some "manna" on the leaves of the river gums, which is actually the protective covering of a tiny scale insect.[4] While we tasted the sweet flakes she told us how, when she was a girl, in a good year the trees would be white with manna and she and the other girls would put mats under the trees and beat the branches to knock the manna off. When we returned to Hawker after only an hour or so, both women seemed relaxed and refreshed, far more so than if they had simply been showing the sights to a family of visitors. They had touched the land to which they belong and even a brief touch was comfort.

Over the years, Pearl and Pauline have taken us, singly and together, to many parts of their land, and just as they always mention the Dreaming stories so they always point out the plants that provided food and medicine, and if they are in season stop to taste. There is an intensity in their relationship with the land and what it provides that has been lost to the Sechelt women. Even though the latter may still pick berries and do so with enjoyment, it is not with a sense that this is something unique to their culture. Perhaps this has something to do with the abundance of berries and the fact that so many of them can be easily identified and gathered without any

---

3 Witchetty grubs are the larval stage of the ghost moth (*Xylentes leucomochla*). The grubs are white in colour with purple markings and grow up to about 10 cms in length and the thickness of an adult's thumb. Cooked, they taste somewhere between chicken and peanut butter and are very nutritious.

4 The sugar lerp (*Spondyliaspis eucalypti*). The Adnyamathanha term is "awari." The name "manna" is a biblical reference, presumably introduced by missionaries.

specific expertise. In Australia edible plants are not easily identified and in the semi-desert of the Adnyamathanha lands they are widely scattered and often the fruit is small and not easily seen. You have to know, for instance, where the quandong trees grow as well as when they ripen in order to enjoy the fruit. Perhaps the skill required to identify and gather bush tucker, as well as the fact that it was so different from what European settlers thought of as palatable food and therefore not prized by them, has served to maintain its value in the eyes of families like Pearl's, which are still close to their cultural roots.

Salmon, traditionally one of the staple foods of the Sechelt people, still forms a regular part of their diet. It is eaten with enjoyment but not so far as I observed with the same special feeling of tradition that is so obvious in the Adnyamathanha women. The kangaroo that we have eaten in Hawker has been shot usually early that same morning by one of the group with whom we have been sharing the meal. The preparation of a fire to create a pit of ashes in which to cook the animal whole is a procedure which takes several hours and adds to the significance of the situation as well as providing a time for socialising. The Sechelt salmon is distributed by the Band to the individual members. The fresh fish may be canned or smoked in individual homes, but the direct connection, the knowledge that this is something you have done yourself as your forebears did, is missing. Even Bernie, who much prefers home-smoked fish, eats the commercially smoked, ready-packaged product supplied by the Band. It is hard to feel an attachment to food in a cryovac pack. Delicious though it might be, it is much the same as any other food you might buy at the supermarket.

The Sechelt and the Adnyamathanha women have yet one more thing in common. It has nothing to do with their respective peoples or traditions but is, rather, a personal factor. Both families of women have had a strong male figure, or figures and role models. In the Adnyamathanha case both Pearl's father and her father-in-law were leaders of her people, and her husband John, though he held no specific position of authority within his own community or in the white community, was known and respected by both. At the annual Angepina Race Meeting, when large numbers of his people were present, he would often "call" the horse races in the Adnyamathanha language. His influence was more direct and stronger within the bounds of his own family. As Pearl's husband, obviously he was of great importance in her life. Their values, attitudes and experience of traditional life were the same, and though their world changed markedly from childhood to adulthood, they valued and actively retained these values and attitudes and passed them down to their children and grandchildren. Pauline's stories of her early life are full of her father. To her, he was not only a beloved parent but representative of the practical outdoor life that she loved, a source of knowledge, a teacher of skills. He continued this role with Charlene too, passing on once more his skills and knowledge, the sense of identity and connection to the land. So that even while their lives were moving in terms of physical space and outward trappings further and further from traditional ways, within them was planted and nourished an Adnyamathanha identity that they will always have. The strength that he passed on to them was not an overt public strength. Neither Pauline nor Charlene would, I think, easily or willingly take on a public, adversarial leadership role, though if they decided to do so I think either would be quite successful. Their strength comes rather from an inner knowledge of who they are and what they want, and they will work persistently, though perhaps quietly, towards that end.

Bernie's father, Clarence Joe, was a model of a different kind. He worked quite openly to improve the lives and experience of his people. Bernie was aware at a young age that his public profile had in some way rubbed off on her; she received somewhat preferential treatment at the residential school particularly after her absence with TB because he demanded that she not be made to work too hard. The nuns knew that he was not happy with many aspects of their system and that he would have no hesitation in confronting them if he was displeased. As she grew up to adulthood, Bernie saw him working through and with the white community to raise his people's standard of living, to return to them their sense of self-respect. She saw him working as a respected member of both the Sechelt community and the wider Canadian society. She was proud to iron his shirts for him when he was preparing to go to Ottawa to talk with politicians. She was proud when, as an adult, she came across the newspaper clippings that called him "The Ambassador" of his people.

Valerie, growing up, spent much time with her grandparents. She did not see Clarence in his public role in the same way as Bernie did. To her he was a beloved grandfather, a traditional man, someone who lived and tried to pass on the old ways, particularly in relation to values and behaviour. Much of what he preached and demonstrated she did not heed as a child, or did not understand. But it remained within her and now as an adult it is providing her with her own source of strength and confidence, enabling her to play an increasingly public role in the life of the Band.

Schooling and education were one of the main focuses of the interviews. What is the significance of the educational experience of these six women? What, if anything, can it tell us about the ways that education and/or schooling can affect the lives of individuals and groups, particularly indigenous groups? Or alternatively, what can it tell us about the ways in which Aboriginal individuals and groups can use education/schooling to mould or direct their lives or their children's lives?

We might draw parallels between improvements in the educational experience for Sechelt and Adnyamathanha Peoples and the growth in the amount, type and structure of education in white society since the development of mass public schooling in the second half of the nineteenth century. The temptation to generalise the similarities between Aboriginal and at least some aspects of working-class experience is strong: social control, resistance, cultural hegemony and bio-politics are just some of the Western academic concepts that spring to mind as possible theoretic structures for analysis and interpretation.

But there are at least two major differences that make this sort of comparison with disadvantaged or oppressed sections of white society problematic. First, the speed of growth in the educational experience is extremely rapid; only three or four generations from what was still basically a traditional oral culture, even though it had already been irrevocably altered by white contact, to postsecondary education. Many white, working-class children do not yet complete secondary education, let alone aspire beyond it. But then neither do most indigenous children, for, as I said earlier, Pearl, Pauline and Charlene and Bernie, Valerie and Brandi are *not* representative examples of their generations despite the fact that some extrapolations can be made from them as individuals to their people as a whole. Second, while one may argue that a working-class culture (or cultures) existed beside the dominant middle-class culture (or cultures), both (or all) of the cultures grew from basically the same roots. This is not the case with indigenous and mainstream

Australian or Canadian cultures. They are about as different as they could be in terms of conceptualisations, attitudes to life and everyday practices.

The experiences of migrant (voluntary or otherwise) groups, particularly those from non-European cultures, may make for a better comparison. For instance, studies of the African-American experience can offer insights into the two-way process of assimilation and the ways in which a subjected culture may take what it wants or needs from a dominant culture while still maintaining some of its own traditions and culture.[5] But further comparisons are not really tenable because of vast differences in the situations and time frames. Even studies of ethnic groups such as the Chinese of British Columbia, who might be said to have at least some similarities with the Sechelt people in terms at least of time frames, geographic proximity and determination to use white education systems, will still not serve.[6] For Aboriginal peoples are not immigrants; it is they who were invaded or, less confrontationally, intruded upon. There can be no comparison between their experience and that of people who have chosen to migrate, no matter how superficially similar some of the situations may appear. And besides, to look at Aboriginal experience through white theoretic constructs is not a valid approach, as I have already argued.

A crucial factor in regard to education in these six personal life stories is the increase with each generation of the influence and importance of formal Western schooling, and the perception of each woman that the acquisition of such schooling is both necessary and desirable, either for her own satisfaction and ability to achieve desired goals or for the future benefit and well-being of her children or for both. The process of this increasing desire for education and the resultant effects are relatively easy to trace. What is more difficult to ascertain is the motivation. Brock has claimed that the Adnyamathanha as a people simply saw the advantages of the white lifestyle and white education and went ahead unproblematically to

---

5 For instance, Eugene Genovase, *Roll Jordan Roll: The World the Slaves Made* (New York: Pantheon Books, 1974), and Thomas L. Weber, *Deep Like the Rivers: Education in the Slave Community 1831-1865* (New York: W. W. Norton, 1978).

6 Tim Stanley, "White Supremacy, Chinese Schooling and School Segregation in Victoria: The Case of the Chinese Students Strike, 1922-23," *Historical Studies in Education/Revue d'Histoire de l'Education* 2, 2 (Fall 1990): 287-306.

incorporate them into their own lives.[7] This is far too simplistic both for the Adnyamathanha as a people or for the McKenzie/ Coulthard family. To a large extent, though indirectly, white education and lifestyle were forced upon them. The first missionaries at Nepabunna appear to have been relatively sensitive to traditional culture and practices. Apart from their obvious aim of conversion to Christianity, they do not appear to have attempted to suppress the language, discontinue ceremonial life or impose formal schooling. In fact they offered only sporadic schooling sessions when other tasks permitted. But increasing white settlement meant that to survive Adnyamathanha people had more and more to supplement traditional methods of subsistence by taking up employment within the mainstream economy. Thus when Pearl and her husband John left Nepabunna soon after their marriage, they lived in European ways rather than tribal ways. Their lives were dictated by the demands of work and they were physically removed from the large traditional extended family groupings. Schooling became more and more an imperative. They recognised this and utilised it as much as was possible. They nevertheless managed to pass on to Pauline and her brothers a large body of traditional skills, knowledge and culture, not sufficient to preserve the culture wholly, but certainly enough to give Pauline both the desire and ability to continue the process with her own daughters.

The Sechelt people did not have this choice. Christianity and European values and attitudes were forced upon them through the residential school experience. While Clarence Joe fought to abolish the residential school, he very much accepted the fact that his people, if they were to have a future, must accommodate to mainstream society. Nevertheless, he clearly saw a place for traditional values and ways within this accommodation. It is noteworthy that for both peoples, one with a benign, non-coercive experience and the other with the reverse, there is a remarkably similar outcome in the present day. This seems to indicate that the success of conversion and assimilation policies in both countries has in some ways been much greater than early missionaries or governments then and even now could have imagined.

Perhaps one of the more important characteristics over the generations in both families is the ability to identify and pursue a

---

7 Brock, *Yura and Udnyu*, 45, 60-64.

course of action that fits with existing values and desires and/or to adapt to some extent those values, desires and practices to fit with what is attainable. They want to have, or at least attempt to have, some control over their lives. This ability is no doubt a personal and inherent characteristic to some extent, but it is a learned ability too. It is an example of learning or education in the broadest sense of the words.

Pearl's father, Henry Wilton, and her husband John's father, Fred McKenzie, were the last two traditional leaders of the Adnyamath-anha, the men who made a conscious decision in the late 1940s to terminate the initiation ceremonies because the physical and cultural environments had altered to the extent that they could no longer be carried out in fully correct ways. John carried on this traditional role in one sense. He was not a formal leader of his people; there were no leaders any more. But he was highly respected by both white society and by his own people. He lived and worked in a white community while retaining his traditional knowledge and values. This desire and ability to preserve tradition where possible, but to accept change where necessary or desirable, seems to have been learned and incorporated by each generation of the family since. McKenzies are not ones to bang their heads against brick walls, demanding the impossible. They are practical people who look for workable solutions and, when it seems desirable, they are willing to compromise.

Bernie's father Clarence Joe, although very different from John McKenzie, was an example to both Bernie and Valerie of compromise, of taking the longer, less confrontational path and using mainstream ways, values and institutions to gain his own ends. Some may see this as a victory for assimilationist policy in both countries, proof of how traditional culture was first eroded and then discarded. Others may see it as an admirable attempt to get the best out of a situation not of their own making. Yet others will have views in between. Each generation has had to cope with life as they have inherited it and have done what seemed best at the time. We in the present may have regrets about actions taken in the past, but we cannot change them. Assessing their significance can be helpful, passing judgment is not.

Another vital factor in the transgenerational experience is the value placed on traditional knowledge and methods of learning. This has not always necessarily been a conscious valuing. Pearl wanted the best she could obtain in all respects for her children, both white education and traditional knowledge, and she simply went about obtaining them as best she could without any attempt to analyse the situation. Pauline has even stronger views arising from her own more extensive formal education and her teaching experiences. Not only does she value both traditional and white knowledge and ways of learning, but increasingly she sees the advantage and necessity of using both together so that both groups can learn effectively together and share each other's knowledges. Charlene too, although she has no experience of teaching either her own children or other people's, favours the combination of both cultures' knowledges and approaches to learning for this is what she has found effective in her own life.

The experience of the Sechelt people suggests similarities, but there is a major difference in both the timing and the impact of mainstream culture and formal schooling revolving around the missionary presence and the residential schooling they introduced. By the time that Bernie was born, residential schooling was well established and while her grandparents, and to a lesser extent her parents, still retained their language and many of their traditional skills and practices, the spiritual basis of their culture had been effectively exterminated.

Bernie's generation was not the first to experience major cultural disruption or loss nor, indeed, the first to receive substantial schooling, but the effects of cultural loss and increased schooling away from family and community seem to have peaked with her generation. Moreover, the nature of the formal schooling was such that it did not offer many options for their future lives. It was segregated schooling, "Indian" schooling, designed to separate students both from their Sechelt community as well as from mainstream Canadian society. Many Sechelt children of this generation finished their school days more literate and numerate than previous generations of their people, but it was virtually impossible for them to obtain any secondary education even if this possibility had occurred to them. Residential schooling taught Native Indian students that at best they were different to whites, at worst inferior. And so they came out of school as a lost generation with little knowledge or understanding of their own culture, but also without the educational standard and skills to compete in mainstream society. The power of the church-run residential school was already under attack, however, with men like Bernie's father Clarence beginning to challenge the situation and to work towards obtaining the goals that they desired in schooling as well as in other areas. He proved to be a strong role model for his daughter when she became a parent. She followed his lead in making her opinions known at the school and constantly defending her children when they ran into problems or trouble, although she was never involved in any formal activities for reform.

The action, though slow and piecemeal, did have an effect, and as a result Valerie's generation did not have to board at the school and had the option of attending a public secondary school. But this brought its own problems as Sechelt students mixed for the first time with white students and encountered the reality of prejudice. Despite the demands of work and family care that were necessary to support their large family and that still only allowed them to exist on the brink of poverty, Valerie's parents acknowledged the importance for their children of obtaining a better education than they themselves had received. Once the older ones were independent they were able to give more than just moral support, and their presence too was felt in the schools, if in a gentle way. Valerie herself has followed the example and her school presence is very strong because it is a mix of three personae—member of the Sechelt community, parent and teacher.

As with the Adnyamathanha women, there has been a passing on of what traditional knowledge and skills still exist. This has not included language for Bernie, Valerie and Brandi nor the traditional women's skills of basket weaving. But some collection and preparation of traditional foods, particularly salmon, which has always been so crucial to the Sechelt, and berries, are still part of their lives. In addition they have passed down an understanding of the importance of family, the significance of relationships and the crucial role of respect, for Elders, for themselves as a people and for their lands. Their emphasis on the importance of the school in retaining and revitalising their culture is much stronger than that of Pearl, Pauline and Charlene, but the reason for it is understandable. The latter learned all of their traditional knowledge within the family for the family still retained this knowledge. Bernie, Valerie and Brandi's family no longer had a wealth of cultural heritage to pass on; neither did most other Sechelt families. A school with a curriculum based on the pooled cultural resources of the Sechelt people, teaching all of the children their language and heritage, is the only way they can see for their culture to continue.

The Adnyamathanha women see cultural continuity as requiring a much less formal structure. Ideally it should happen through the family as was the case with themselves. If this is not possible (and they accept that for the majority of Adnyamathanha children it is not), then it can be done through the schools, but in a way that makes it real and meaningful to students. This requires much teaching to be done on site outside of the classroom. It calls for practical and more traditional methods of learning. This takes a long time, but they believe that children must experience their culture—it cannot be taught simply as another subject in school. They also place a greater emphasis than the Sechelt people on educating mainstream society in regard to their own culture and point of view.

Over the course of three generations these women and their families have been successful in the ways they have approached, appropriated and incorporated two very different cultures and two very different ways of learning. Each group has done it differently because each has experienced white intrusion somewhat differently, but their intentions and goals have been remarkably similar. If nothing else, both mainstream and indigenous societies can learn and benefit from their experience. There is of course a major difficulty. Both Canadian and Australian mainstream cultures and these two indigenous cultures have developed ways of perpetuating themselves which, because they are deep and rich cultures, take whole lifetimes. Learning about mainstream culture and how to live within it does not end just because formal schooling is completed, just as learning about Adnyamathanha or Sechelt culture and how to live within them did not end with initiation as a man or recognition as a woman. Like many other indigenous groups, Sechelt and Adnyamathanha people today have a double cultural heritage. If they are to be successful, and by this I mean having some control over the direction of their lives, being able to access those aspects of both their own and mainstream culture that they wish to utilise, they must know both cultures, have control in both, see the relevance of both. Learning to live well in any one culture takes a lifetime. Finding time for two, as Pearl said with wonderful understatement, is difficult. But the combination of aspects of both is possible as the lives of these six women demonstrate. Over three generations these families have incorporated those aspects of mainstream culture that have seemed to them most desirable and necessary and have retained, or are working to take back, aspects of the traditional that they value and that are still available to them. Their identity as Sechelt and Adnyamathanha women is not identical to that of their great-great-grandmothers, but perhaps in some ways it is stronger, for they have had to fight for it, to remake it for themselves.

For when Valerie and the other women talk about "trying to get it back" they are not simply expressing a desire to resurrect traditional culture, though this is part of the agenda. There is more to it than that. Some aspects of both Sechelt and Adnyamathanha cultures are gone and can never be retrieved. The worlds in which these peoples live is different from that of their forebears. These six women live within the mainstream culture of their respective countries as well as in their own cultures. They have no desire to give up either. What they want is to forge an identity and a way of life that incorporates what they can regain and retain of their traditional cultures as well as what they value and find useful in mainstream culture. And there is a third aspect, I think, that consists of a blend of the old and the new that they and their people are constructing now in the present. It is through a process of combining the three into living cultures that their goals will be achieved in the future.

Appendix 1

Interviews

Interviews taped on the following dates have been used.

Pearl McKenzie
1. February 21, 1993, with Tony Rogers and Gillian Weiss
2. February 8, 1993, Tony Rogers
3. May 21, 1993, with Gillian Weiss
4. December 9, 1994, with Gillian Weiss

Pauline Coulthard
1. February 7, 1993, with Tony Rogers
2. May 21, 1993, with Gillian Weiss
3. December 10, 1994, with Gillian Weiss

Charlene Tree
1. February 6, 1993, with Gillian Weiss
2. May 20, 1993, with Gillian Weiss

Bernie Sound
1. April 20, 1994, with Gillian Weiss
2. May 18, 1994, with Gillian Weiss
3. June 9, 1994, with Gillian Weiss

Valerie Bourne

1. March 14, 1994, with Gillian Weiss
2. April 21, 1994, with Gillian Weiss
3. May 17, 1994, with Gillian Weiss
4. June 9, 1994, with Gillian Weiss

Brandi McLeod

1. April 14, 1994, with Gillian Weiss
2. April 20, 1994, with Gillian Weiss

Les Wilton

1. November 21, 1992, with Tony Rogers

Videoconference, February 8, 1995

1. Bernie Sound, Valerie Bourne and Samantha Joe in Vancouver with Rita Irwin; Pearl McKenzie, Pauline Coulthard and Charlene Tree in Adelaide with Gillian Weiss

BIBLIOGRAPHY

Aboriginal Education: Aboriginal Perspectives across the Curriculum. Adelaide: Department for Employment, Training and Youth Affairs and South Australian Department for Education and Children's Services, Aboriginal Education Unit, 1996.

Adnyamathanha People, The. Aboriginal People of the Flinders Ranges: An Aboriginal Studies Course for Secondary Students. Adelaide: Education Department of South Australia, 1992.

Ahenakew, Freda, and H. C. Wolfart. *Our Grandmothers' Lives: As Told in Their Own Words.* Saskatoon: Fifth House Publishers, 1992.

Aken, Linda. "Pimosatamowin Sikaw Kakeequaywin: Walking and Talking." *Canadian Journal of Native Education* 19, 2 (1992): 191-214.

Alcoff, Linda. "The Problem of Speaking for Others." *Cultural Critique* 20 (Winter 1991): 5-32.

Alpern, Sara, Joyce Antler, Elisabeth Israels Perry and Ingrid Winther Scobie, eds. *The Challenge of Feminist Biography: Writing the Lives of Modern American Women.* Chicago and Urbana: University of Illinois Press, 1992.

Archibald, Jo-ann. "Giving Voice to Our Ancestors." *Canadian Journal of Native Education* 19, 2 (1992): 141-44.

———. "Researching with Mutual Respect." *Canadian Journal of Native Education* 20, 2 (1993): 189-92.

315

Ashworth, Mary. *The Forces which Shaped Them*. Vancouver: New Star Books, 1979.

Attwood, Bain. *The Making of the Aborigines*. Sydney: Allen and Unwin, 1989.

Attwood, Bain, and J. Arnold, eds. *Power, Knowledge and Aborigines*. Special edition of the *Journal of Australian Studies*. Bundoora: LaTrobe University Press in association with the National Centre for Australian Studies, Monash University, 1992.

Austin, Tony. " 'Mainly a Question of Environment': The Kahlin Home for Aboriginal Children of Mixed Descent 1911-1927." *History of Education Review* 21, 2 (1992): 3-18.

———. "A Progressive in Capricornia: Cecil Cook and "Half-Caste" Education." Paper presented at ANZHES Conference, Melbourne, December 9-12, 1993.

Axelrod, Paul. *The Promise of Schooling: Education in Canada, 1800-1914*. Toronto: University of Toronto Press, 1997.

Axtell, James. *After Columbus: Essays in Ethnohistory of Colonial North America*. New York: Oxford University Press, 1988.

———. *Imagining the Other: First Encounters in North America*. Washington, DC: American Historical Association, 1991.

Barman, Jean. "Separate and Unequal: Indian and White Girls at All Hallows School, 1884-1920." In Veronica Strong-Boag and Anita Clair Fellman, eds. *Rethinking Canada: The Promise of Women's History*, 215-33. Toronto: Copp Clark Pitman, 1991.

———. *The West beyond the West: A History of British Columbia*. Toronto: University of Toronto Press, 1991.

———. " 'Oh, No! It Would Not Be Proper to Discuss That with You': Reflections on Gender and the Experience of Childhood." *Curriculum Inquiry* 24, 1 (1994): 53-67.

Barman, Jean, Yvonne Hebert and Don McCaskill. *Indian Education in Canada*. Vol. 1: *The Legacy*. Vancouver: University of British Columbia Press, 1986.

———. *Indian Education in Canada*. Vol. 2: *The Challenge*. Vancouver: University of British Columbia Press, 1987.

Bataille, Gretchen, and Kathleen Mullen Sands. *American Indian Women: Telling Their Lives*. Lincoln: University of Nebraska Press, 1984.

Battiste, Marie, and Jean Barman, eds. *First Nations Education in Canada: The Circle Unfolds*. Vancouver: University of British Columbia Press, 1995.

Beaumont, Ronald C. *She Shasheshahlem: The Sechelt Language*. Penticton, BC: Theytus Books, 1985.

Bell, Diane. *Daughters of the Dreaming*. Sydney: Allen and Unwin, 1983.

_____. *Ngarrindjeri Wurruwarrin: A World That Is, Was and Will Be*. North Melbourne, Victoria: Spinifex Press, 1998.

Bertaux, Daniel, ed. *Biography and Society: The Life History Approach in the Social Sciences*. Beverley Hills, CA: Sage, 1981.

Blackman, Margaret. *During My Time: Florence Edenshaw Davidson, a Haida woman*. Rev. ed. Seattle: University of Washington Press, 1991.

Bolles, Edmund Blair. *Remembering and Forgetting: An Inquiry into the Nature of Memory*. New York: Walker, 1988.

Bourke, Colin, and Bill Edwards. "Family and Kin." In Colin Bourke, Eleanor Bourke and Bill Edwards, eds., *Aboriginal Australians*, 85-101. St Lucia, Qld; University of Queensland Press, 1994.

Bourke, Eleanor. "Images and Realities." In Colin Bourke, Eleanor Bourke and Bill Edwards, eds., *Aboriginal Australians*, 1-16. St Lucia, Qld: University of Queensland Press, 1994.

_____. "Australia's First Peoples: Identity and Population." In Colin Bourke, Eleanor Bourke and Bill Edwards, eds., *Aboriginal Australians*, 35-48. St Lucia, Qld: Queensland University Press, 1994.

Brewster, Anne. *Reading Aboriginal Women's Autobiography*. Melbourne: Sydney University Press in association with Oxford University Press, 1996.

Brock, Peggy. *Yura and Udnyu: A History of the Adnyamathanha of the North Flinders Ranges*. Adelaide: Wakefield Press, 1985.

Brodzka, Bella, and Celeste Schenck, eds. *Life/Lines: Theorising Women's Autobiography*. Ithaca, NY: Cornell University Press, 1988.

Broome, Richard. *Aboriginal Australians: Black Response to White Dominance 1788-1980*. Sydney: Allen and Unwin, 1982.

Bull, Linda. "Indian Residential Schooling: The Native Perspective." *Canadian Journal of Native Education* 18, Supplement (1991): 1-63.

Buss, Helen M. *Mapping Ourselves: Canadian Women's Autobiography in English*. Montreal: McGill-Queen's University Press, 1993.

Casey, Edward S. *Remembering: A Phenomenological Study*. Bloomington: Indiana University Press, 1987.

Cawte, John. *The Universe of the Warramirri: Art, Medicine and Religion in Arnhem Land*. Kensington, NSW: New South Wales University Press, 1993.

Chapman, Valerie, and Peter Read, eds. *Terrible Hard Biscuits: A Reader in Aboriginal History*. St Leonards, New South Wales: Allen and Unwin: Journal of Aboriginal History, 1996.

Coates, Kenneth. "'Betwixt and Between': The Anglican Church and the Children of Carcross (Choutla) Residential School, 1911-1954." *BC Studies* 64 (Winter 1984-85): 27-47.

Coulthard, Clifford, Desmond Coulthard and Christine Wilton, comps. *Mt Chambers: An Aboriginal View*. South Australia: Aboriginal and Historic Relics Unit, 1989.

Christie, Michael. "Educating Bungalene: A Case of Educational Colonialism." *History of Education Review* 23, 2 (1994): 46-54.

Conrad, Margaret, Alvin Finkel and Cornelius Jaenen. *History of the Canadian Peoples*. Vol. 1: *Beginnings to 1876*. Mississauga, ON: Copp Clark Pitman, 1993.

Cruikshank, Julie. *Life Lived Like a Story: Life Stories of Three Yukon Native Elders*. Lincoln: University of Nebraska Press, 1990.

_____. *Reading Voices*. Vancouver: Douglas & McIntyre, 1991.

Cummings, Barbara. *Take this Child... from Kahlin Compound to the Rhetta Dixon Children's Home*. Canberra: Aboriginal Studies Press, 1990.

Davis, Christine, Clifford Coulthard and Desmond Coulthard, comps. *The Flinders Ranges: An Aboriginal View*. Adelaide: Department of Environment and Planning, Aboriginal Heritage Branch, reprinted with amendments 1986.

Davis, Christine, with McKenzie, Pearl. *Adnyamathanha Genealogy*. Adelaide: Aboriginal Heritage Branch, South Australian Department of Environment and Planning, 1985.

Dawe, Helen. *Helen Dawe's Sechelt*. Madeira Park, BC: Harbour Publishing, 1990.

Devi, Mahasweta. *Imaginary Maps*. Translated by Gayatri Spivak. New York: Routledge, 1995.

Dietz, Mary Lorenz, Robert C. Prus and William Shaffir, eds. *Doing Everyday Life*. Mississauga, ON: Copp Clark Longman, 1994.

Down, Barry. "A Different, More Practical Education: Aboriginal Education in Western Australian Secondary Schools after the Second World War." *Education Research and Perspectives* 21, 2 (1994).

Duff, Wilson. *The Indian History of British Columbia* Vol. 1: *The Impact of the White Man*. Victoria: Provincial Museum of Natural History and Anthropology, 1964.

Edwards, Bill. "Living the Dreaming." In Colin Bourke, Eleanor Bourke and Bill Edwards, eds., *Aboriginal Australians*, 65-84. St Lucia, Qld: Queensland University Press, 1994.

Elder, Bruce. *Blood on the Wattle: Massacres and Maltreatment of Australian Aborigines since 1788*. French's Forest, NSW: Child and Associates, 1988.

Fisher, Robin. "Missions to the Indians of British Columbia." In W. Peter Ward and Robert A. J. McDonald, eds., *British Columbia: Historical Readings*, 113-26. Vancouver: Douglas & McIntyre, 1981.

Fiske, Jo-Anne. "Carrier Women and the Politics of Mothering." In Gillian Creese and Veronica Strong-Boag, eds., *British Columbia Reconsidered*, 198-216. Vancouver: Press Gang Publishers, 1992.

———. "Child of the State, Mother of the Nation: Aboriginal Women and the Ideology of Motherhood." Paper presented to the joint meetings of the Atlantic Canada Studies and BC Studies Associations, May 21-24, 1992.

Fletcher, J. J. *Clean, Clad and Courteous: A History of Aboriginal Education in NSW*. Carleton, NSW: J. J. Fletcher, 1989.

Folds, Ralph. *Whitefella School*. Sydney: Allen and Unwin, 1987.

Fonow, Mary M., and Judith A. Cook, eds. *Beyond Methodology: Feminist Scholarship as Lived Research*. Bloomington: Indiana University Press, 1991.

Genovase, Eugene. *Roll Jordan Roll: The World the Slaves Made*. New York: Pantheon Books, 1974.

Gerard, A. E. *History of the United Aborigines Mission.* N.p.: United Aborigines Mission, n.d. (Mortlock Library, Adelaide).

Gluck, Sherna Berger, and Daphne Patai, eds. *Women's Words: The Feminist Practice of Oral History.* New York: Routledge, 1991.

Goldman, Anne E. "Is That What She Said?: The Politics of Collaborative Autobiography." *Cultural Critique* (Fall 1993): 177-204.

Goodall, Heather, and Jackie Huggins. "Aboriginal Women Are Everywhere: Contemporary Struggles." In Kay Saunders and Raymond Evans, eds., *Gender Relations in Australia: Domination and Negotiation*, chap. 19. Sydney: Harcourt Brace Jovanovitch, 1992.

Gresko, Jacqueline. "White 'Rites' and Indian 'Rites': Indian Education and Native Responses in the West, 1870-1910." In David Jones, Robert Stamp and Nancy Sheehan, eds., *Shaping the Schools of the Canadian West.* Calgary: Detselig, 1979.

Grimshaw, Patricia, Marilyn Lake, Ann McGrath and Quartly Marian. *Creating a Nation.* Melbourne: McPhee Gribble, 1994.

Guha, Ranajit, and Gayatri Chakravorty Spivak, eds. *Selected Subaltern Studies.* New York: Oxford University Press, 1988.

Haagen, Claudia. *Bush Toys: Aboriginal Children at Play.* Canberra: Aboriginal Studies Press for the Australian Institute of Aboriginal and Torres Strait Islander Studies, 1994.

Haig-Brown, Celia. *Resistance and Renewal: Surviving the Indian Residential School.* Vancouver: Tillacum Library, 1988.

Haig-Brown, Celia, and Sophie Robert. " 'Sophie Robert': Remembrances of Secwepemc Life." *Canadian Journal of Native Education* 19, 2 (1992): 175-89.

Harris, Stephen. *Culture and Learning: Tradition and Education in North-East Arnhem Land.* Canberra: Australian Institute of Aboriginal Studies, 1984.

Harris, Stephen, and Merridy Malin, eds. *Indigenous Education: Historical, Moral and Practical Tales.* Darwin: Northern Territory University Press, 1997.

Hart, Max. "Traditional Aboriginal Education." In Bill Menary, ed., *Aborigines and Schooling.* Adelaide: Adelaide College of the Arts and Education, 1981.

Hill-Tout, Charles. *The Sechelt and the South-Eastern Tribes of Vancouver Island.* Edited with an Introduction by Ralph Maud. Vancouver: Talonbooks, 1978.

Hunter, Robert, and Robert Calihoo. *Occupied Canada: A Young Man Discovers His Unsuspected Past*. Toronto: McClelland and Stewart, 1991.

Ing, N. Rosalyn. "The Effects of Residential Schools on Native Child-rearing Practices." *Canadian Journal of Native Education* 18, Supplement (1991): 67-117.

Jeffries, Teresa. "Sechelt Women and Self Government." In Gillian Creese and Veronica Strong-Boag, eds., *British Columbia Reconsidered*, 90-95. Vancouver: Press Gang Publishers, 1992.

Jelinek, Estelle C. *Women's Autobiography: Essays in Criticism*. Bloomington: Indiana University Press, 1980.

Jolly, Lesley. *Waving a Tattered Banner: Aboriginal Language Revitalisation*. Brisbane: Aboriginal and Torres Strait Islander Studies Unit, University of Queensland. 1995.

The Kaurna People: Aboriginal People of the Adelaide Plains: An Aboriginal Studies Course for Secondary Students. Adelaide: Education Department of South Australia, 1989.

Kirkness, Verna. "Giving Voice to Our Ancestors." *Canadian Journal of Native Education* 19, 2 (1992): 145-49.

Krupat, Arnold. *For Those Who Come After*. Berkeley: University of California Press, 1985.

———. *I Tell You Now: American Indian lives*. Lincoln: University of Nebraska Press, 1987.

Lester, J. Yami. "Pages from an Aboriginal Book: History and the Land." In Bill Menary, ed., *Aborigines and Schooling*. Adelaide: Adelaide College of the Arts and Education, 1981.

Lightning, Walter C. "Compassionate Mind: Implications of a Text Written by Elder Louis Sunchild." *Canadian Journal of Native Education* 19, 2 (1992): 215-53.

McCalman, Janet. *Journeyings: The Biography of a Middle-Class Generation, 1920-1990*. Melbourne: Melbourne University Press, 1993.

McConaghy, Cathryn. "Fashion and Prescription in Representations of Indigenous Education." *Discourse* 15, 2 (December 1994): 81-84.

McDonald, Connie Nungulla, with Jill Finnane. *When You Grow Up*. Broome, Western Australia: Magabala Books Aboriginal Corporation, 1996.

McKibbin, Eileen. "The Oblates of Mary Immaculate and the Sisters of the Child Jesus Mission and Residential School on the Reserve #2 of the Sechelt Indian Band, Sechelt BC." History 205 Paper, Special Collections, University of British Columbia Library, 1986.

McLoy, Peter. *The Survival Dreaming*. Linfield, NSW: Management Interface Pty., 1995.

Menary, Bill, ed. *Aborigines and Schooling*. Adelaide: Adelaide College of the Arts and Education, 1981.

Moran, Bridget. *Stoney Creek Woman, Sai'k'uz Ts'eke: The Story of Mary John*. Vancouver: Tillacum Library, 1988.

Morgan, Sally. *My Place*. South Fremantle, Western Australia: Fremantle Arts Centre Press, 1987.

Morel, Petronella, ed. *Warlpiri Karnta Karnta-Kurlangu Yimi/ Warlpiri Women's Voices: Aboriginal Women Speak Out about Their Lives and History/Stories*. Alice Springs, Northern Territory: IAD Press, 1995.

Morris, Barry. *Domesticating Resistance: The Dhan-Gadi Aborigines and the Australian state*. Oxford: Berg Publishers, 1989.

Muecke, Stephen. *Textual Spaces: Aboriginality and Cultural Studies*. Kengington, NSW: New South Wales University Press, 1992.

Narogin, Mudrooroo. *Writing from the Fringe: A Study of Modern Aboriginal Literature*. Melbourne: Hyland House Publishing, 1990.

The Ngarrindjeri People: Aboriginal people of the River Murray, Lakes and Coorong: An Aboriginal Studies Course for Secondary Students in Years 8-10. Adelaide: Education Department of South Australia, 1990.

Neiser, Ulric, and Eugene Winograd, eds. *Remembering Reconsidered: Ecological and Traditional Approaches to the Study of Memory*. Cambridge: Cambridge University Press, 1988.

Nyoongah, Mudrooroo. *Aboriginal Mythology*. London: Aquarian, 1994.

Olney, James, ed. *Autobiography: Essays Theoretical and Critical*. Princeton, NJ: Princeton University Press, 1980.

Parry, Suzanne. "Half-caste Children and Their Schooling." Paper presented at ANZHES Conference, Melbourne, December 9-12, 1993.

Personal Narratives Group, eds. *Interpreting Women's Lives: Feminist Theory and Personal Narratives*. Bloomington: Indiana University Press, 1989.

Peters, Margaret. "Children's Culture and the State: South Australia 1890s-1930s." Unpublished Ph.D. dissertation, University of Adelaide, 1993.

Peterson, Lester. *The Story of the Sechelt Nation*. Madeira Park, BC: Harbour Publishing/Sechelt Indian Band, 1990.

Pitjantjatjara in Change, The. Adelaide: Educational Technology Centre, Education Department of South Australia, 1981.

Reynolds, Henry. *The Other Side of the Frontier: Aboriginal Resistance to the European Invasion of Australia*. Ringwood, Victoria: Penguin, 1982.

_____. *Frontier: Aborigines, Settlers and Land*. Sydney: Allen and Unwin, 1987.

_____. *With the White People*. Sydney: Penguin, 1990.

_____. *The Law of the Land*. Sydney: Penguin, 1992.

_____, comp. *Dispossession: Black Australians and White Invaders*. Sydney: Allen and Unwin, 1989.

Riddett, Lyn Anne. "Finish, I Can't Talk Now: Aboriginal and Settler Women Construct Each Other." Paper presented at the University of Saskatchewan, January 26, 1995.

Reimer, D., ed. *Voices: A Guide to Oral History*. Victoria: BCARS, 1988.

Robertson, Beth M. *Oral History Handbook*. 2nd ed. Adelaide: Oral History Association of Australia (South Australian Branch), 1983.

Rogers, Tony. "Art and Aboriginal Cultures." *Australian Journal of Art Education* 17, 2 (Autumn 1994): 12-20.

Rogers, Tony, and Rita Irwin. "Art and Indigenous Cultures—A Comparison with the Canadian Experience." *Australian Journal of Art Education* 21, 2 (Summer 1998): 36-43.

Ross, Betty. *Minerawuta: Ram Paddock Gate: An Historic Adnyamathanha Settlement in the Flinders Ranges, South Australia*. 2nd ed. Adelaide: Aboriginal Heritage Branch, Department of Environment and Planning, 1989.

Rowley, C. D. *The Destruction of Aboriginal Society*. Ringwood, Victoria: Penguin, 1986.

Saunders, Kay, and Raymond Evans, eds. *Gender Relations in Australia: Domination and Negotiation*. Sydney: Harcourt Brace Jovanovitch, 1992.

Savala, Refugio. *The Autobiography of a Yaqui Poet*. Edited with background and interpretations by Kathleen M. Sands. Tucson: University of Arizona Press, 1980.

Sechelt Nation. *Mayuk the Grizzly Bear: A Legend of the Sechelt People*. Illustrated by Charlie Craigan. Gibsons, BC: Nightwood Editions, 1993.

Shapiro, Ann-Louise, ed. *Feminists Revision History*. New Brunswick, NJ: Rutgers State University Press, 1994.

Sherwood, John, ed. *Aboriginal Education: Issues and Innovations*. Perth: Creative Research, 1982.

Simon, Judith, ed. *Nga Kura Maori: The Native Schools System, 1867-1969*. Auckland: Auckland University Press, 1998.

Sioui, Georges. *For an Amerindian Autohistory: An Essay on the Foundations of a Social Ethic*. Translated from the French by Sheila Fischman. Montreal: McGill-Queen's University Press, 1992.

Siska, Heather. *People of the Ice: How the Inuit Live*. Vancouver: Douglas & McIntyre, 1983.

————. *The Haida and the Inuit: People of the Seasons*. Vancouver: Douglas & McIntyre, 1984.

Slipperjack, Ruby. *Honour the Sun*. Winnipeg: Pemmican Publications, 1987.

————. *Silent Words*. Saskatoon: Fifth House Publishers, 1992.

Snow, Dianne. "(Re)writing the Collective Self: Aboriginal Autobiography as Cultural History." Paper presented at the Australia/New Zealand and Canadian History of Education Association Conference, University of Melbourne, December 9-12, 1993.

Spivak, Gayatri Chakravorty. *In Other Worlds: Essays in Cultural Politics*. New York: Routledge, 1988.

————. "Who claims Alterity?' In Barbara Kruger and Phil Mari, eds., *Remaking History*, 269-92. Seattle: Bay Press, 1989.

————. *The Post-Colonial Critic: Interviews, Strategies, and Dialogues*. New York: Routledge, 1990.

Stanley, Tim. "White Supremacy, Chinese Schooling and School Segregation in Victoria: The Case of the Chinese Students' Strike, 1922-23." *Historical Studies in Education/Revue d'Histoire de l'Education* 2, 2 (Fall 1990): 287-306.

Sterling, Shirley. "Quaslametko and Yetko: Two Grandmother Models for Contemporary Native Education Pedagogy." *Canadian Journal of Native Education* 19, 2 (1992): 165-90.

Stewart, Hilary. *Cedar: Tree of Life to the Northwest Coast Indians*. Vancouver: Douglas & McIntyre, 1984.

Sutherland, Neil. "When You Listen to the Winds of Childhood, How Much Can You Believe?" *Curriculum Inquiry* 22, 3 (1992): 235-56.

Swain, Tony. *A Place for Strangers: Towards a History of Aboriginal Being*. Cambridge: Cambridge University Press, 1993.

Thompson, Paul. The Voice of the Past: Oral History. Oxford: Oxford University Press, 1978.

_____. "Cultural Transmission between Generations within Families: A Life Story Approach." In *Memory and Multiculturalism*. Proceedings of the VIII International Oral History Conference, Siena-Lucca, February 25-28, 1993, 1143-52.

Titley, Brian. "Duncan Campbell Scott and Indian Education Policy." in J. Donald Wilson, ed., *An Imperfect Past: Education and Society in Canadian History*, 141-53. Vancouver: UBC CSCI, 1984.

Tolcher, Helen. *Drought or Deluge: Man in the Cooper's Creek Region*. Melbourne: Melbourne University Press, 1986.

Tuchman, Barbara. "Biography as a Prism of History." In Marc Pachter, ed., *Telling Lives: The Biographer's Art*, 133-47. Philadelphia: University of Pennsylvania Press, 1981.

Union of BC Indian Chiefs. *The Sechelt Act and What it Means*. Vancouver: Union of BC Indian Chiefs, 1988.

Urion, Carl. "Changing Academic Discourse about Native Education: Using Two Pairs of Eyes." *Canadian Journal of Native Education* 18, 1 (1991): 1-9.

Ward, W. Peter, and Robert A. J. McDonald, eds. *British Columbia, Historical Readings*. Vancouver: Douglas & McIntyre, 1981.

Weber, Thomas L. *Deep Like the Rivers: Education in the Slave Community 1831-1865*. New York: W. W. Norton, 1978.

Weiss, Gillian. "Three Generations of Women: Learning and Schooling amongst the Adnyamathanha." *Historical Studies in Education/Revue d'Histoire de l''Education/History of Education Review* (special issue), 23, 3 (October 1994): 171-99.

_____. "Three Generations, Two Cultures, One Aim: Education, Experience and Aspiration amongst Adnyamathanha and Sechelt Women." In *Aboriginal Studies in the 90s: Visions and Challenges 1*, 1-10. Collected Papers of the 5th Annual ASA Conference, Riverview College, Sydney, October 1995.

_____. "She Shashishahlem: An Overview of the Language and Cultural Curriculum of the Sechelt Indian Band, British Columbia, Canada," In *Aboriginal Studies in the 90s: Visions and Challenges 1*, 107-18. Collected Papers of the 5th Annual ASA Conference, Riverview College, Sydney, October 1995.

Wharton, Herb. *Unbranded*. Brisbane: University of Queensland Press, 1992.

White, Ellen, and Jo-ann Archibald. "Kwulasulwut S Yuth: Ellen White's Teachings." *Canadian Journal of Native Education* 19, 2 (1992): 150-64.

Wilson, J. Donald. " 'No Blanket to Be Worn in School': The Education of Indians in Nineteenth Century Ontario." In Jean Barman, Yvonne Hebert and Don McCaskill, eds., *Indian Education in Canada*, Vol. 1: *The Legacy*, 64-87. Vancouver: University of British Columbia Press, 1986.

Wong, Hertha Dawn. *Sending My Heart Back across the Years: Tradition and Innovation in Native American Autobiography*. New York: Oxford University Press, 1992.

Woodcock, George. *British Columbia, a History of the Province*. Vancouver: Douglas & McIntyre, 1990.

Woolmer, George. *Traditional Ngarinyeri People: Aboriginal People of the Murray Mouth Region*. Adelaide: Aboriginal Education Section, Aboriginal Education Resource Centre, Education Department of South Australia, 1986.

Yates, Lyn. "Feminism and Education: Writing in the 90s." In Lyn Yates, ed., *Feminism and Education*, 1-9. Melbourne Studies in Education 1993. Melbourne: La Trobe University Press, 1993.

INDEX